THE QUEST FOR EQUITY IN HIGHER EDUCATION

SUNY series

FRONTIERS IN EDUCATION

Philip G. Altbach, Editor

The Frontiers in Education Series draws upon a range of disciplines and approaches in the analysis of contemporary educational issues and concerns. Books in the series help to reinterpret established fields of scholarship in education by encouraging the latest synthesis and research. A special focus highlights educational policy issues from a multidisciplinary perspective. The series is published in cooperation with the School of Education, Boston College. A complete listing of books in the series can be found at the end of this volume.

THE QUEST FOR EQUITY
IN HIGHER EDUCATION

TOWARD NEW PARADIGMS IN
AN EVOLVING AFFIRMATIVE ACTION ERA

BEVERLY LINDSAY AND
MANUEL J. JUSTIZ

Editors

STATE UNIVERSITY OF NEW YORK PRESS

Published by
State University of New York Press, Albany

© 2001 State University of New York

For information, address State University of New York Press,
90 State Street, Suite 700, Albany, NY 12207

Production by Cathleen Collins
Marketing by Jennifer Giovani-Giovani

Library of Congress Cataloging-in-Publication Data

The quest for equity in higher education : toward new paradigms in an evolving
affirmative action era / edited by Beverly Lindsay and Manuel J. Justiz.
        p.   cm. — (SUNY series, frontiers in education)
    Includes bibliographical references and index.
    ISBN 0-7914-5061-9 (alk. paper) — ISBN 0-7914-5062-7 (pbk. : alk. paper)
    1. Educational equalization—United States. 2. Education, Higher—United States.
    3. Affirmative action programs—United States. I. Lindsay, Beverly. II. Justiz, Manuel J.
III. Series.

LC213.2.Q84 2001
379.2'6'0973—dc21   00-049233

10 9 8 7 6 5 4 3 2 1

Contents

Preface

> Offering every American a fair chance to achieve success is a central tenet of our constitutional and political system, and is a bedrock value in our culture.
>
> —White House Affirmative Action Review,
> July 19, 1995

The contemporary era of "affirmative action" began in 1961, when President John F. Kennedy used that phrase for the first time in Executive Order 10952, creating the Equal Employment Opportunity Commission. He admonished employers to "take affirmative action to ensure that applicants are employed, and that employees are treated during employment, without regard to their race, creed, color, or national origin." Over the course of an almost forty-year history, the idea of taking affirmative action to help eliminate the effects of past and present discrimination based on race, color, religion, sex, or national origin has taken many forms and generated much debate. As we enter the new millennium, California's Proposition 209, Washington's Initiative 200, the *Hopwood* decision in Texas, and the class-rank plans in Texas, California, and Florida represent the latest milestones in the continuing struggle over how to achieve the equity and fairness inherent in the affirmative action concept.

In his 1996 address "Mend It, Don't End It," President Clinton asserted that "Affirmative action has not always been perfect, and affirmative action should not go on forever. It should be changed now to take care of those things that are wrong, and it should be retired when its job is done." In many ways, this assertion defines the current status of the debate over the efficacy and legitimacy of affirmative action as a public policy initiative in achieving equity and fairness. What have we achieved? What, if anything, should we be doing differently to maximize those achievements? Is affirmative action still a viable and legitimate approach to realizing the "bedrock value" articulated in the White House's 1995 Affirmative Action Review? The beginning of the new millennium is a timely point for reassessing where we are and where we are going in our effort to promote fairness and equity in our society.

Given the volatility of the issue and the dynamic nature of the debate, a need has developed for an updated study of where we are with this critical public policy issue. This volume provides such an update, with the latest thinking about "affirmative action" and proposed alternatives. It is the culmination of collected works initially begun by the key original members invited to a special symposium of senior scholars held at the 1997 annual meeting of the American Educational Research Association (AERA) in Chicago, Illinois. Titled "Affirmative Action in Higher Education: Critical National and Regional Perspectives," the symposium was sponsored by the AERA's higher education division. What began as collegial debate and dialogue has emerged as the chapters that comprise this volume. The presentations in this collection contribute to the case for conceptualizing new paradigms for policy makers in the continuing effort to attain fairness and equity in our institutions of higher learning.

In his decision in the landmark *Bakke* case, Justice Lewis Powell wrote "the attainment of a diverse student body . . . is a constitutionally permissible goal for an institution of higher education." In the language of the courts, this has become a "compelling interest" on the part of our colleges and universities. It is their way not only to promote equity of opportunity for the college-age population, faculty, and administrators, but also to ensure that their students are receiving the highest quality education through exposure to the full diversity of ideas and values that characterize contemporary society. Few question the principle; it is the process that generates the greatest debate. Hopefully, this volume will provide an updated context that will help policy makers arrive at sound decisions in pursuit of the principle.

The production of such a volume is no small task. Three years in the making, *The Quest for Equity in Higher Education: Toward New Paradigms in an Evolving Affirmative Action Era* represents the collective achievement of many busy and dedicated individuals. The individual authors are preeminent authorities in the field, both scholars and administrators, who have invested a great deal of time and effort, despite extremely busy schedules, to ensure that this volume materialized. As editors, we owe a tremendous debt of gratitude to each of the contributors for their painstaking work, their commitment to the project, and their perseverance in staying the course begun at the AERA conference in 1997.

In addition, we acknowledge with sincerest appreciation the indefatigable efforts of those who worked "behind the scenes" to bring this book to fruition. Special appreciation is expressed to Michael Laubscher, former Assistant Dean in the Penn State University Office of International Programs and current Director of Special Projects for Texas A&M University's Office of International Programs, for his skillful editorial assistance; Janet Haner, publications editor for the University Office of International Programs at Penn State University; Chuck Halloran, assistant to the Dean of the College of Education at the University of Texas at Austin; Monica deMello Patterson, former doctoral assistant in the University Office of International Programs at Penn State University; and Maria Poindexter, current doctoral assistant in the University Office of International Programs at Penn State. Without their unflagging assistance, the manuscript simply would never have gone to press.

The work on this publication has witnessed the transition from one century to another. Let us hope that the transition ensures the first self-evident truth cited in the Declaration of Independence, that all human beings are created equal. The collection of articles in this volume will inform public policy debate as to how this nation can most effectively establish this basic tenet as a reality in higher education.

Beverly Lindsay
The Pennsylvania State University, University Park

Manuel J. Justiz
University of Texas at Austin

PART I

Setting the Stage

CHAPTER 1

The Landscape for Conceptual and Policy Issues

BEVERLY LINDSAY AND MANUEL J. JUSTIZ

A situation is not a destination.

—David Carter, March 1998

A great deal of knowledge of late has been delivered to the public by academic literature and research, as well as through newspaper and popular media sources, focusing on the multiple issues that encompass educational equity, particularly affirmative action. California voters captured public attention when they passed Proposition 209 in 1996, which led to the elimination of race-based policies and hiring standards in state agencies. Shortly before the referendum passed, the University of California Board of Regents voted to discontinue admissions and hiring policies that permitted race as a salient variable, effective in the 1997 academic year. In 1999 the state of Michigan faced a similar challenge to dismantle affirmative action in its higher education system.

The trend in recent publications has additionally, and perhaps more forcefully, been fueled by the changing climate in the United States, as evidenced by recent events on Capitol Hill. Congress sparred with President Clinton's administration over the issue from the time of his inauguration in 1997. Clinton's vision to "lift the burden of race and redeem the promise of America" (Clinton, 1996) was reinforced by the summoning of an advisory board, the President's Initiative on Race. The board, chaired by distinguished historian John Hope Franklin, issued its report to the President on September 18, 1998. After more than a year's review of the racial climate in America, the advisory board made salient recommendations, which included the establishment of a permanent council (disbanded immediately with the new Bush administration) to further the dialogue on race and explicate the value of diversity in higher education.

Available literature on affirmative action focuses on several key conceptual and factual areas. These can be categorized as: (a) the historical specificity of today's policies and why affirmative action programs should be in place in the United States and in the academy (Duster, 1996; Justiz & Delco, 1993; Clarke, 1996; Patrick, 1996; Alger, 1997; Bensimon & Soto, 1997); (b) the impact of affirmative action programs in increasing representation of various racial and ethnic groups and women in the workplace, the academy, and the like, as delineated in *The Shape of the River: Long-Term Consequences of Considering Race in College and University Admissions* (Bowen & Bok, 1998) among others (Orfield, 1998; R. Wilson et al., 1993; Montero-Sieburth, 1996; Norton, 1996; and Chliwniak, 1997); and (c) varying critiques of affirmative action programs in their present form (Connerly, 1998; Edley, 1996; Kekes, 1997; Tierney, 1997). Some evaluations focus on ways to maintain existing policies—to continue to "push it along" (Francis, 1993; Norton, 1996; Yates, 1996); while others center on the use of refreshed criteria in admissions procedures as well as hiring practices (Fish, 1994; Carnoy, 1995; Valle, 1996). Various scholars and politicians vie for class-based rather than race-based corrective policy (Canady, 1996; Chavez, 1996; Loury, 1996; Campbell, 1998). Certain authors assess the counter positionality of reverse discrimination, defining that phenomenon and arguing whether the condition is practically or realistically possible (Simon, 1993; Gresson, 1995; J. Wilson, 1996; Giroux, 1997).

Despite increased public discussion about, notable policy changes in reaction to, and legal emphasis on affirmative action, relatively little has been published of late that focuses on the subject, particularly on how it relates to continuing policy issues of equity and diversity in the academy. Jossey-Bass, Inc., Publishers, includes a comprehensive explanation in their 1994 volume, *New Directions for Institutional Research* (edited by Daryl G. Smith, Lisa E. Wolf, and Thomas Levitan): a section entitled "Studying Diversity in Higher Education" makes a strong case for increased academic research that scrutinizes diversity issues. In 1990, Philip Altbach and Kofi Lomotey published *The Racial Crisis in American Higher Education* through SUNY Press, a study that promotes increased support for research on race-related issues as well as enhanced public policy to combat institutional racism. Altbach and Lomotey focus on broad issues in relation to curriculum, admissions, and campus studies in notable American colleges. Mildred Garcia's 1997 volume, *Affirmative Action's Testament of Hope*, marked an examination of affirmative action and higher education. While her edited book delves into historical and sociological contextualization of the affirmative action tension, it, as well as the aforementioned works, does not engage in an extensive critical interrogation of policy issues facing the academy in the coming millennium.

From the preceding review of the literature, it is evident that a need exists for a volume with a broad base that includes the practical administrative implications of affirmative action decisions and issues in higher education. Policy makers have had limited opportunity for informed dialogue in respect to shifting issues, legislative events, and court decisions. In the past few years, similar volumes have investigated various implications within the academy (Cahn, 1993; Sellers, 1994; Browne-Miller, 1996; Garcia, 1997). The authors of this volume seek to build on these analyses: the broader issue is equity in education; the central question is how institutions achieve and maintain equity. There has been much debate on affirmative action in higher education, and there is a need to examine the facets of this policy and phenomenon.

This volume investigates the role of equity (justice and fairness), diversity (various demographic concerns), and affirmative action in colleges and universities in the United States—the policy and programmatic mechanisms offering educational opportunities to those who have not been full participants in American higher education. Background information is offered via a breakdown of relevant demographic characteristics in American higher education, a review of the literature, and an examination of the evolution and current state of equity and affirmative action in the academy (chapters 3 and 5). The information contained herein fills an unexplored void in the literature regarding higher education. The need for a critical examination of the issues occurs in light of public debates, voter referenda, and legislative enactment—all of which interact to influence public policy. Providing information and critical skills to students and scholars, preparing students for the world of work (especially in a rapidly changing technological environment), and generating new research and knowledge bases are missions of higher education that can be enhanced with affirmative action. In addition, research and scholarship needs to address social inequities. *The overarching issues are equity and diversity, but affirmative action is a means to attain the democratic goals of a civil society* (chapter 11).

Given recent legislation, judicial decisions, and public referenda, an urgent need exists to analyze the shifting components of the paradigms associated with educational equity. The recent Presidential Initiative on Race grappled with these issues by building on the reports from the American Council on Education (ACE) and the Education Commission of the States (ECS) (*One Third of a Nation: A Report of the Commission on Minority Participation in Education and American Life,* 1989) and the National Task Force for Minority Achievement in Higher Education (*Achieving Campus Diversity: Policies for Change,* 1990). In addition, education policy groups and state legislators are working to alleviate the problems created by the recent upheaval. The Joint Center for Political and Economic Studies produced *The Inclusive University: A New Environment for Higher Education* in 1993, a report that highlights aspects of college teaching, admissions and hiring policies in relation to Black students and faculty. The 1997 Texas

Higher Education Coordinating Board generated studies and reports focusing on diversity and access to promote the development of guidelines for admissions, financial aid, and other procedures in the wake of the *Hopwood v. Texas* decision.

In this anthology of original pieces, the present volume seeks to move beyond these contexts to gain deeper insight into today's issues in order to assist higher education policy makers in the preparation of new policy and alternative plans to replace current affirmative action procedures. Shifting paradigms are characteristic of the new era. This collection of works is a critical examination of current sociopolitical issues vis-à-vis their relationships with and impact on the higher education academy as it seeks to include various demographic groups within student, faculty, and administration populations. A series of critical questions are raised and probed. The principle of equality that is the basis of democracy dictates the accommodation of diverse groups within the state, region, and nation at colleges and universities. How is this to be accomplished in light of recent legislative and judicial decisions? How may universities develop a sound knowledge base on equity issues that contributes to subsequent higher education and public policy? What is the import of legal issues emerging from particular judicial decisions, even those of the Supreme Court? What are the economic implications for colleges and universities choosing to use affirmative action plans? How has the country's economic situation affected the climate regarding affirmative action and equity? How are the issues presented and played out in various settings, such as Historically Black Colleges and Universities (HBCUs) and diverse geographic areas like California, Hawaii, Pennsylvania, or Texas? How can we address current ills that still exist within the social context of affirmative action policies and programs today? How do we ensure that the current situation of racial and ethnic minorities and women does not remain their disparate destinations? The underlying motif for such probing questions is their relationship to the examination, development, and formation of public and higher education policies in the present evolving era.

The work at hand serves as a guide to conceptualizing internal academic policies. Its updated focus on the issues will aid University presidents, chancellors, and other administrators in disseminating information to university faculty and students, as well as to external constituents. Faculty who teach graduate and upper-division undergraduate courses will find chapters useful for courses exploring critical social and political matters in academe. Critical recurring motifs are examined from various geographical perspectives and disciplines such as higher education administration, public administration and policy studies, sociology of education, political science, urban studies, higher education, education policy studies, law, and American studies. State and federal policy makers, senior staff for state and federal legislators and executives, and similar professionals involved in the preparation of legislation regarding education and equity should find this careful examination of the issues to be helpful.

Why Is Diversity Important in Higher Education?

Certainly higher education is a key social institution in a democratic society. As Thomas Jefferson originally advised in a letter to M. A. Jullien in 1818 (Bottorff, 1979), and as Meyer (1977), Carnoy (1992), Aronowitz and Giroux (1993), and Lindsay (1989, 1997) more recently assert, a critical purpose of the educational institution in a democratic society is to prepare its citizens for their role as participants in that society. Specifically, Lipkin writes that education "must prepare individuals for the full and equal citizenship that is required by the liberal democracy" (1994, p. 77). Others argue that more specifically, the university has a strong moral and ethical responsibility. As Giroux explains, "the institutions of higher education regardless of their academic status represent places that affirm and legitimate existing views of the world, produce new ones, and authorize and shape particular social relations" (1990, p. 114). Consequently, the curtailment of equity policies is viewed by many in academia as threatening to democracy. A related argument is proposed by such scholars as Altbach, Berdahl, and Gumport (1994). They state that universities need to achieve broader representation of racial and ethnic minorities in order to reflect the images of American society. This stance maintains that through broader representation, universities preserve the integrity of democracy by encouraging participation of all citizens.

The American Council on Education states that diversity in higher education is of extreme importance and needs to be recognized as part of the academy's mission. This collective diversity among institutions is one of the great strengths of America's higher education system, which has helped make it the best in the world. Preserving that diversity is essential if we hope to serve the needs of our democratic society (ACE, 1998). The Office of the President of the National Association of State Universities and Land-Grant Colleges (NASULGC) also endorses diversity as an integral part of the role of universities, stating, "We are committed to maximum access and the educational richness that can come from diverse student bodies—and because it is in our society's best interests" (Magrath, 1998). As critically argued by Justiz, Delco, R. Wilson, and Callan (1994), the widening international market economy of the United States needs to create a labor force prepared to work in a diverse global environment. Indeed, to paraphrase William Julius Wilson, it is in the nation's best interest to promote diversity on campus in order to prepare students to function in an increasingly international world, thus promoting the economic vitality of the individual and, by extension, of the country (1998).

ACE outlines the following reasons why many universities have reached the common principle of diversity. It (a) enriches the educational experience; (b) promotes personal growth and a healthy society; (c) strengthens communities and the workplace; and (d) enhances America's economic competitiveness (1998). ACE maintains that diversity on college campuses need not be acquired through the use of quotas or the unnecessary admission of unqualified applicants. As pointed out in "On the Importance of Diversity" (1998):

> Achieving diversity on college campuses does not require quotas. Nor does diversity warrant admission of unqualified applicants. However, the diversity we seek, and the future of the nation, do require that colleges and universities continue to be able to reach out and make a conscious effort to build healthy and diverse learning environments appropriate for their missions. The success of higher education and the strength of our democracy depend on it.

However, in order to achieve the diversity that promotes healthy learning environments, universities need to be able to engage actively in, and not be restricted by, their efforts to promote positive conditions. Accomplishing and maintaining the aforementioned is the challenge.

The Demographic and Contextual Realities of Diversity in American Higher Education

Reports such as *One Third of a Nation* (1989), *The Federal Glass Ceiling Commission Report* (1995), and *Affirmative Action Review: Report to the President* (1995) (called for by President Clinton and authored by George Stephanopoulos and Christopher Edley, Jr.) describe the reality of access to jobs and education by minorities and women in American society. Schement (1998) describes the demographic distributions of minorities in the United States: the largest concentrations are in the Southeast (African-Americans), Southwest (Chicanos), and California (Chicanos and large numbers of recent immigrants). Cities such as Los Angeles, Philadelphia, and New York have substantial concentrations as well. Indeed, in California and in New York, approximately 100 languages are spoken by students in public schools. By the year 2020, Los Angeles will be 40 percent Latino, with whites accounting for only 32 percent of the population; Asian-Americans will comprise 15 percent, African-Americans 7 percent, and Native Americans 5 percent. In the New York City metropolitan area of 2020, whites will represent about 50 percent of the population, Latinos 22 percent, African-Americans 18 percent, and Asian-Americans 9 percent (De Vita, 1996, pp. 24–27; Schement, 1998, p. 13). How to categorize mixed-race students is emerging as a new cultural, political, and economic challenge since historically in the United States mixed ancestry was usually identified with one demographic group.

These demographics suggest that geographical variations for policies and programs may be needed. Specific state or university policies that work effectively in Philadelphia or New York may not be appropriate in Albuquerque, New Mexico, or Charleston, South Carolina. Other demographic databases reflect whether affirmative action programs have made any real changes in terms of admissions and faculty diversity in higher education (Nettles and Perna, 1997; Cohen, 1997).

Scholars report that women and minorities have progressed due to affirmative action programs in higher education (R. Wilson, 1995). In 1981, Blacks comprised 4.1 percent of college faculties. By 1991, they made up 4.7 percent. This increase has been attributed to affirmative action. Yet, as is evident by the statistics, there is still progress to be made if parity is to be achieved. In spite of the steps achieved, the following statistics and realities remain:

- Despite a nationwide increase in enrollment overall, representation of young people of color at Traditionally White Universities has not kept pace with their increasing percentage in the college-age population (ages 18–24). While more than 30 percent of high school graduates are American Indians, Hispanics, and African-Americans, the percentage of those groups at 4-year colleges is much less, at only 16 percent (ACE, 1998).
- The population of racial and ethnic minorities is rising in different parts of the country. In public schools in some geographic areas, a contrast is present in that the racial makeup of the teacher pool is predominantly white (American Federation of Teachers, 1998).
- The *Journal of Blacks in Higher Education* (1994) found that an increasing number of Blacks were awarded PhDs in the natural sciences in 1992 and 1993. However, these graduates are not being recruited to the faculties of America's highest-ranking universities (1995, cited in ACE, 1998).
- Minority applicants pursuing faculty positions found that particular institutions limited their hiring searches once minority hiring goals were met; despite continuing vacancies, advertisements were pulled from minority publications (Finkelstein, 1984, cited in ACE, 1998).
- Minorities, especially women, often fill nontenured faculty positions. "The possibility of their developing a critical mass and thereby becoming a permanent presence can be ensured only with the continuation of some form of affirmative action" (ACE, 1998).
- Less than 6 percent of university presidents are African-American; and more than half of those are chief executives at HBCUs. In the mid-1990s, none of the less than 40 African-American women who were chief executives were in what Carnegie defines as Research I universities, which are commonly regarded as among the top institutions in the nation (Chliwniak, 1997). The portrait was the same in 2000.
- Chliwniak (1997, p. i) reports that just 16 percent of college and university presidents and only 25 percent of chief academic officers are women. Yet

women make up more than 52 percent of the current student body at colleges and universities. She also relates that although there are balanced numbers of male and female instructors and assistant professors, there is a significant imbalance at the full professor, tenured level. Also significant is the fact that at institutions of higher rank, the disproportionate representation of men to women is even greater (Chliwniak, 1997, p. ix).

Discrepancies abound, as observed in the preceding descriptive statistics. Many of the inequities arise from practices within higher education institutions; yet they are equally, or in some instances, more, influenced by factors external to universities.

This volume seeks to delve into multiple dimensions of the continuing role of higher education in contributing to social equity, the role of equity within universities, and external historical, sociopolitical, and economic factors influencing the interplay between the academy and fairness. These factors, found in contemporary and emerging public policy, judicial decisions, legislative resolutions, public referenda, and higher education policies and plans, are salient features of the book. This introduction briefly highlights the historical specificity of recent affirmative action policies in the United States—especially those that pertain to higher education and the academy from a moral/ethical ground of fairness and equity.

By examining how various past controversies have influenced and informed present policy, this work also aims to connect cultural understanding of race and gender relations to how those relations may have been formed. It is important to analyze the historical underpinnings of the present-day policy in order to understand how what Deval Patrick calls "the skillful rhetoric" (1996, p. 142) has become part of the popular culture of most United States residents. In order to appreciate the complexities of the affirmative action debate, the authors present and examine the current arguments. Without that fundamental basis, the inquiry loses objectivity, for as Duster states, "Fairness to the individual must always have a social and historical context" (1996, p. 45). Understanding historical reality should inform today's policy makers, especially when attempting to understand the discourse of today's leaders, both within the academy and without.

Historical and Policy Underpinnings

Programs have been initiated by national, state, and local governments that epitomize the nature of affirmative action, including the 1954 Supreme Court decision *Brown v. Board of Education* in Topeka, Kansas, which found segregation of schools to be illegal. However, the first time the term *affirmative* was used to describe action taken to rectify past institutional racism was by

President Harry Truman's Committee on Governmental Contract Compliance. In 1953 he agreed that the Bureau of Employment should "act positively and affirmatively to implement the policy of nondiscrimination in its functions of placement counseling, occupational analysis and industrial services, labor market information, and community participation in employment services" (AUAA, 1997; Marable, 1996, p. 5).

In 1961, President John F. Kennedy was the first to use the words "affirmative action" to define steps to be taken when he issued Executive Order 10952 (AUAA, 1997). This order created the Equal Employment Opportunity Commission (EEOC) and admonished Americans to implement affirmative action to ensure that applicants were hired, and employees managed, without regard to race, creed, color, or national origin. While JFK's rhetoric encouraged the prohibition of discrimination, cleared the way for a civil rights statute, and increased opportunities for minorities and women in education and employment, in actuality this rudimentary form of affirmative action advanced only apprenticeship and training programs.

In response to repeated protest and violence in the South (including state responses to federal court orders to desegregate the University of Alabama and other universities), Congress passed the Civil Rights Act of 1964. This made discrimination illegal in private establishments with a public constituency, outlawed discrimination in federally funded programs, and prohibited discrimination in both private and public employment. Also included in the Act was the intent to redress the inequality of employment and educational opportunities. During President Lyndon Johnson's incumbency, the passing of the Voting Rights Act gave power to the Department of Justice to take affirmative steps in eliminating exclusionary practices. President Johnson articulated the reasoning behind the new policies in a historic speech to the graduating class at Howard University on June 4, 1965; he stated that although these new statutes ensure freedom, freedom itself does not ensure equality:

> It is not enough to open the gates of opportunity. All our citizens must have the ability to walk through those gates.

> This is the next and the most profound stage of the battle for civil rights. We seek not just freedom but opportunity—not just legal equity but human ability—not just equality as a right and a theory, but equality as a fact and *as a result.* (Johnson, 1965; emphasis added)

John Hope Franklin explains that if one looks at the legislative policy and socioeconomic conditions of previous historical eras, governmental action is needed to guide the country in both private and public sectors toward erasing the color line (1993). He maintains that without legislation, judicial decisions, and executive orders, individuals and groups of individuals are incapable of sustaining actions that would make the country a better place in which to live.

In 1965, the Higher Education Act, along with the Elementary and Secondary Education Act, followed Title VI of the 1964 Civil Rights Act. This resulted in the 1966 guidelines produced by the Department of Health, Education, and Welfare on school desegregation and made discrimination illegal in all federally assisted programs, including federal grants-in-aid. The Equal Employment Opportunity Act of 1972 was passed during the term of President Richard Nixon. It extended the EEOC's jurisdiction, gave more credence to negative effects of institutional racism, and provided the protection of class action lawsuits. Yet it was during the Nixon and Ford eras, from 1969 to 1977, that the "set-aside" affirmative action policies that are often criticized today were implemented (Marable, 1996, p. 7). In addition, by the mid-1970s, affirmative action plans were no longer limited to race-specific goals. These programs had expanded to include women, people from ethnic and racial backgrounds, and the disabled. In fact, these programs (in certain ways) now targeted a majority of the population of the United States.

The Roots of the Contemporary Period of Affirmative Action

In 1978, with only 14 years of practice in affirmative action campaigns, the Supreme Court began hearing cases that raised accusations of reverse discrimination and other critical issues concerning the constitutionality of affirmative action policies. According to some (Howard, 1997), the Court's mood when presiding over these significant cases seemed to be intent on reversing progress achieved in Civil Rights legislation. Others state that these cases tidied up loose ends in order to ease the transition toward lawful, democratic, and equitable policy (Garcia, 1997). Several cases pertaining to higher education and other institutions illustrate the discussion: *Regents of the University of California v. Bakke* (1978), *Steelworkers v. Weber* (1979), and *Adarand Constructors, Inc. v. Peña* (1995). Another example is the Fifth Circuit Court of Appeals decision of *Hopwood v. Texas* (1995), the Fourth Circuit Court of Appeals decision in *Podberesky v. Kirwin* (1994), and the role that the Supreme Court played in future policy by deciding not to hear these cases. Such legal cases are discussed in detail in the section "Legal and Economic Perspectives" in chapters 3, 4, and 5 as they affect students, financial aid, hiring practices, and the like.

The *Bakke* case represents the heart of the issue, but several cases highlight the differences in interpretation of the legal view. In 1978, *The Regents of the University of California v. Bakke*, and *United Steelworkers v. Weber* heard 1 year later, became the first Supreme Court cases to weaken previously enacted executive orders, amendments, policies and programs focusing on equity and the alleviation of discrimination via affirmative action. *Bakke* maintained that a race preferential program where spaces are set aside for individuals of a preferred category was unconstitutional—yet race could lawfully be considered as one of the criteria for academic admissions (Jones, 1996, p. 150).

In 1995, a University of Maryland scholarship targeting Black students was found to be racially discriminatory by the Fourth Circuit Court of Appeals. The Supreme Court refused to hear *Podberesky v. Kirwin*. As a result it has become more difficult to administer race-exclusive financial aid scholarships. The Department of Education states that the original decision holds that colleges and universities may establish race-targeted scholarships to remedy the present effects of prior discrimination, provided that they are narrowly tailored (Winston, 1995).

Also in 1995, the Supreme Court decided to hear *Adarand Constructors, Inc. v. Peña* (1995). This case has attracted much attention due to its restrictive ruling. However, many believe that it was a logical progression after several other cases skirted the issues highlighted in this case. Again, the Court held that racial classifications need to be scrutinized and narrowly tailored in order be effective. While the limits may not directly affect race-based admissions and hiring practices in colleges and universities, they may aggravate those receiving federal monies, including financial aid packages.

The Fifth Circuit Court of Appeals in 1996 found in *Hopwood v. State of Texas* that certain admissions procedures at the University of Texas School of Law disregarded the Equal Protection Clause of the Fourteenth Amendment. The judges found that the use of race or ethnicity in admissions to promote the diversity of a student body was illegal. Although an appeals court cannot reverse a Supreme Court decision, *Hopwood* maintains that the University of Texas program did not use race and ethnicity in a proper manner to promote diversity in its law school (Atwell, 1996). Since the Supreme Court refused to hear this case, other schools considered it a sign to reexamine their own race-based programs, admissions procedures, and financial aid. Two years after the ruling, admissions officers in Texas institutions are feeling the effect. "The *Hopwood* ruling appears to conflict with previous Supreme Court rulings that endorsed, albeit narrowly, affirmative action, forcing the higher education bureaucracy to scramble for ways to (a) encourage diversity while (b) not mentioning race" (Taylor, 1996, p. 14).

Since *Hopwood*, the University of Texas at Austin has experienced a decline in minority applicants. When compared to the previous year, white applicants dropped by 14 percent while African-American applications declined 21 percent, a proportionately greater impact because the original pool of applicants was smaller (Richardson, 1997, p. 18). Texas leaders both in the academy and in state government engaged in serious legal and rhetorical battles concerning the scope of the *Hopwood* decision. The State Attorney General, Dan Morales, and others state that *Hopwood* is binding to the entire Fifth Circuit Court District, while others assert it applies only to the University of Texas. With the decline in admission of minority students, Texas academic administrators are worried about the turn in higher education. Richardson (1997, p. 19) reports that the state's top minority students are expected to seek higher education elsewhere. The resulting social and economic issues present a rising dilemma, since shortly after the turn of the century, African-Americans and Hispanics are expected to constitute the majority of the Texan population. In 1997 the Texas Higher Education Coordinating Board reported that Blacks and Hispanics were represented in significantly higher numbers in community and junior colleges. African-Americans comprise 12 percent of all Texans, 9.14 percent of enrolled students at public universities, 10.23 percent of students enrolled at community and technical colleges, and 4.3 percent of those at health-related institutions (Richardson, 1997, p. 21).

In 1996, California voters passed Proposition 209, which created a state constitutional amendment making it illegal to use race-based criteria in state hiring practices. In 1997 the Ninth Circuit Court of Appeals upheld the referendum's constitutionality. Yet as of this writing, a stay on the enforcement of 209 is in effect while critics vie for its appearance at the Supreme Court level (Americans United for Affirmative Action, 1997). While the legal status of this referendum is pending, the California Regents decision to end affirmative action policies in admissions, hiring, and awarding of contracts (American Association of University Professors, 1996) brought many issues to the forefront of the affirmative action debate. Many in the academic community believe that the Regents' actions will lead to a national trend that could result in fundamental changes in admissions and employment policy, scholarship programs, and the diversity of student populations and faculties (Levin, 1995).

It is interesting to note that only 30 years have elapsed in the ordering, passing, and implementation of affirmative action policies. Within that time, the resulting educational and social changes have occurred very slowly. Why is it that this relatively short history of laws and policies has led so many to seek reversals? A discussion of counterpoints to affirmative action contributes to an understanding of the phenomenon.

Counterpoints to Affirmative Action

Some of the basic works on the subject of diversity and affirmative action include those by Kahlenberg (1996), Orfield and Miller (1998), Hacker (1992), and Carnevale and Stone (1995). *The Shape of the River: Long-Term Consequences of Considering Race in College and University Admissions* by Bowen and Bok appeared in 1998, attempting to support affirmative action admissions with hard quantitative research data. Thernstrom and Thernstrom offer an alternative view in their 704-page volume *America in Black and White: One Nation Indivisible* (1997), complete with 70 charts and graphs and six chapters of historical context.

Divergent economic policies, characterized by decreased domestic spending, deregulation, and program cuts during the last two decades have resulted in considerable job loss and economic insecurity, fueling the debate between proponents and opponents of affirmative action. In the years 1990–1992, California alone lost 1.5 million jobs (Duster, 1996, p. 50). Affirmative action programs, immigration laws, and welfare programs were targeted as a result of recent economic trends. Social reform strategies were used as a scapegoat to explain the economic downturn of the 1980s and early 1990s. Coupled with the economic decline, broader political currents shaped the issues surrounding affirmative action. Household income polarization opened and then widened the gap between the top and bottom economic sectors. Williams (1996) and William Julius Wilson (1996) discuss an additional societal phenomenon in the alterations that occurred during these years. Increasing technological advances rendered certain jobs obsolete, reduced wages of others, and ultimately changed work and school environments irreversibly. Williams concludes that "Working and middle-class Americans were encouraged to divert their attention away from the global economic and technological roots of their problems and instead to affirmative action, other anti-discrimination policies, social programs for the poor, and immigration" (p. 249). Further elaboration of economic and fiscal realities occurs in chapters 5, 7, and 8.

Some see the 1980s as an example of what would happen if affirmative action were to be totally dismantled. In general, a number of affirmative action cases heard by the Supreme Court at this time reduced legal sanctions and lightened the financial liability of employers found guilty of affirmative action violations (Williams, 1996, p. 251). Congress passed a civil rights bill in 1991 that counteracted earlier Supreme Court decisions, ensuring for the first time that women could collect punitive damages for sex discrimination and allowing minorities and women to sue in discrimination cases. Affirmative action was further defined in cases heard during this era, and the Supreme Court narrowed the grounds on which individual intent to discriminate is based. Individual motivation, intentionality, and personal culpability must now be proven before race-based programming can be used to redress past inequities.

Rush (1994) and Connerly (1998) discuss the main points regarding opposition to affirmative action. An underlying theme is that affirmative action policies and programs are fundamentally unfair. They argue that affirmative action places an unfair burden on innocent victims, does not take into consideration the hardships of whites and men who might also benefit from preferential treatment, lowers standards for admissions and employment, and casts a stigma on minorities and women as they enter the labor force and seek promotions. On closer scrutiny, opposition arguments are supported by two main contentions. The first is the argument for reverse discrimination. Here, some posit that affirmative action policies displace traditional beneficiaries with women and people of color. Important components of this belief require attention: the belief in the concept of "white innocent victim" and the related concept of unfairness to the individual versus the group.

With regard to the concept of innocent victim, according to Rush (1994) the effect of the language used in the *Bakke* case has deeply altered the justification of arguments against affirmative action policy. She explains that if there is to be an innocent victim, logically, someone needs to be found guilty. If Allan Bakke were found to be the innocent victim of unfair treatment, then who is the guilty perpetrator? Rush concludes that it is the woman or person of color to whom the race- or gender-preferred slot was given who becomes the perpetrator of the unfair treatment and not society or past historical events. Included in this logic is the position that if someone were innocent, they need not be held accountable for redressing historically placed wrongs. She continues, "It is quite telling and significant that this phrase is used only to describe whites, so that the language in more recent Supreme Court cases is directed at innocent white victims. Ironically, the phrases innocent Black victim, and innocent female victim are never heard" (Rush, 1994, p. 216). In spite of arguments focusing on the individual, larger social issues remain.

Duster further explains that the "seemingly flawless" argument of those who attack affirmative action disembody the individual from any social, economic, or historical context (1996, p. 42). Once done, this decontextualization easily compels an individual of goodwill to see the unfairness in set-aside programs and race-gender-based scholarships. He elucidates, "Indeed, since there are only individuals, and individual responsibility and individual entitlement are the only currency in the contemporary discourse about race policies and affirmative action policies, not having had a personal hand in the opposition of others makes one innocent. The fact that one's group has accumulated wealth 10 times that of another group is rendered irrelevant by the legerdemain of invoking individual fairness" (Duster, 1996, p. 44). By excluding race, ethnicity, and gender, we fail to identify with the historical and social context of groups; thus we fail to admit that institutional discriminatory structures and practices bear on society.

The economic recession during the 1970s and 1980s bolstered the myth of unfairness—a time of increasing job loss and insecurity, a decline of purchasing power, and an increase in higher education costs. Affirmative action became defined as a rigid system of inflexible quotas that rewarded the incompetent and unqualified at the expense of hardworking taxpayers (Marable, 1996). Merit was then viewed as a way to solidify privilege, while the language was turned around so that the true victims of discriminatory practice would appear to be the perpetrators of the abuse. In the end, the discourse of fairness became so distorted that it became a source of distrust and betrayal.

Despite the accusations of reverse discrimination, the demographics remain. J. Wilson maintains, "Every available indicator demonstrates that white males *still* do dramatically better than any other group in higher education" (1996, p. 88; emphasis added). And, he asks, "If women and minorities are gaining tremendous advantages from affirmative action, why do they hold the less desirable part-time and non-tenure-track positions?" (p. 89). In 1992, faculty breakdown at research universities was white males 66.5 percent, white women 21.0 percent, African-Americans (men and women) 3.2 percent, and Hispanics (men and women) 1.9 percent. He contrasts these data with faculty composition at lower-paying 2-year colleges: 6.1 percent Black, 4.1 percent Hispanic, and 37.7 percent white women. The disparities between groups in higher education begin in undergraduate or graduate school, where the disproportionality between whites and other groups sets up the future relationship. For example, Black and Hispanic students were more likely to need loans. In 1992, over 45 percent of whites finished college without incurring debt, compared to about one-third of African-Americans and Hispanics. Students with heavy debts are not eager to assume more loans to pursue graduate study. Other reports conclude that without affirmative action programs, fewer Blacks would be admitted to institutions such as graduate and medical school (Cross, 1994).

Once a degree has been attained, the picture remains the same with regard to salary differential and senior positions. In a recent *Chronicle of Higher Education* report, Moses (1997, p. 60) relates that female faculty members (depending on their rank) earn between 85 and 96 cents for every dollar earned by their male equivalents. Further, female administrators, depending on their job and type of institution, earned from 1 cent to 39 cents less per dollar earned by male administrators—areas further analyzed in chapters 7, 8, and 11.

How Can We Achieve Equity in Institutions of Higher Learning?

Marable argues that, although legal segregation was outlawed over 40 years ago, we have not yet reached the point where we have a color-blind society. While institutional racism remains a fact of our society, affirmative action must continue to focus on discrimination and racial inequality (Marable, 1996, p. 12). How can society move out of the current legal and rhetorical morass in order to achieve equity? Some suggestions for higher-education admissions policies embrace a rethinking of the admissions process. This would entail the incorporation of multiple measures of competency that will allow for diversity, while reevaluating tenets used previously that curtailed the admissions of certain groups due to culturally biased standards. An example of the latter type of college admissions measure is the Scholastic Aptitude Test (SAT) score that is historically normed for white high school students. In reevaluating the appropriateness of SAT scores, the use of statistics by admissions personnel should be taken into account, as well as accuracy and the standard of error.

Other possible admissions policies and strategies include outreach to public high schools by flagship universities in order to prepare and then recruit their top students (Young, 1995). Universities often develop "pipelines," pools of potential students in grades K–12, nurtured through a series of institutional initiatives. Academic responsibility to these pipelines will help to generate qualified diverse student populations in the future. In addition, multiple criteria in the admissions process could be utilized. These might include new models for merit, diversity, family income, locale of high school, or budget of high school (Shea, 1995; Valle, 1996). Devon (1998) refers to measuring "the distance traveled" by each student in order to arrive at the door of the admissions office. A critical element of this approach is to determine how the aforementioned criteria are defined. Other kinds of preferential treatment in the admissions process are also under scrutiny, like special admissions for athletes, musicians, artists, applicants from rural areas, children of faculty, children of alumni, and female science majors (Lederman, 1995; Bergmann, 1997; Wolf-Devine, 1997). Empirical support for various race-sensitive admissions policies can be found in Bowen and Bok's *The Shape of the River: Long-Term Consequences of Considering Race in College and University Admissions*. The authors recast the debate over affirmative action since longer-range positive outcomes are documented.

The authors in this volume seek to address the following illustrative questions in light of the evolving models that emerge as responses are formulated. What criteria should determine admissions for underrepresented groups into colleges and universities? How do we weigh arguments for open admissions against specific affirmative action criteria? What kinds of scholarly credentials are needed for senior professors versus those for associate professors? How should the credentials and criteria vary by disciplinary areas? How should court decisions be viewed in light of changing demographics throughout the country? What are the practical administrative policy implications for a judicial decision such as *Hopwood*? How do presidents and provosts effectively disseminate new policies and plans to students, parents, legislators, civic leaders, and other audiences who have varying levels of knowledge about such matters? Chapters 2, 3, 6, 9, 10, and 12 seek to analyze and explicate responses to these illustrative queries.

Origins and Organization of the Volume

An introduction to the collected chapters and the issues addressed in the volume is provided in Part I. Following this introductory chapter, the second section of this volume deals with legal and economic perspectives. Chapter 2,

"Judicial and Legal Perspectives on Student Affirmative Action in Higher Education" by Ida Elizabeth Wilson, provides a careful examination of judicial decisions on student financial aid as a form of equity and admissions policies. Illustrations from public and private universities are analyzed. The likelihood of future policies concerning admissions and financial aid is elucidated vis-à-vis current judicial and public debates.

Chapter 3, "Affirmative Action Retrenchment and Labor Market Outcomes for African-American Faculty" by Samuel L. Myers, Jr., and Caroline S. Turner, examines the interplay between economic realities, the pool of minority student and faculty applicants, and higher-education equity. The chapter seeks to explore questions such as how new policy paradigms might be developed or modified to link economic realities and equity in higher education.

In chapter 4, "The Effects of Public Policy Conflicts and Resource Allocation Decisions on Higher-Education Desegregation Outcomes in Pennsylvania," James B. Stewart discusses the current status of efforts to assess the efficacy of Pennsylvania's efforts to comply with Title VI desegregation mandates. Pennsylvania is one of the original Adams states for which no final determination has been made regarding compliance status with dual systems of higher education for Blacks and whites. In November 1995, the Commonwealth of Pennsylvania was notified of the intent of the Department of Education Office for Civil Rights (OCR) to resume its scrutiny of the state's desegregation efforts. OCR proposed that the review proceed via a "partnership" approach similar to the one instituted in Florida. Various aspects of the partnership process are described and discussed, including stakeholders represented, development of a framework to assess desegregation outcomes, and critical issues that remain to be addressed, particularly in light of economic and employment realities in the Commonwealth.

Chapter 5 is "The Threatened Future of Affirmative Action and the Search for Alternatives." Here, Reginald Wilson elucidates components of select university programs on various diversity initiatives and what impact such initiatives have had over the years on enrollment, retention, and the academic achievement of various racial and ethnic groups. He discusses the effects of court decisions on the course of affirmative action. Cases such as *Hopwood* (1995), *Podberesky* (1994), and *Fordice* (1992) impact the future of these initiatives and propel alternative policy strategies employed to offset them.

Part III contains chapters devoted to the interrogation of public and education policies. Manuel J. Justiz and Marilyn C. Kameen discuss how the Hopwood decision forced Texas universities to reexamine their admissions processes in chapter 6, "The Real Question After *Hopwood*: Why Equity in the K–12 Pipeline Will Change Our University Campuses for the Better and Help Preserve a Citizen Democracy." In the exponential growth of its minority population, Texas is at the leading edge of a nationwide demographic trend that presents enormous challenges for colleges and universities. Within the framework of the *Hopwood* decision, policies must be designed to ensure that educational diversity is achieved. Increasing access to education and improving educational attainment among emerging demographic populations in the kindergarten through secondary education, and indeed, 2-year colleges, is critical. The K–12 population flow to universities would help equip tomorrow's citizens with the necessary skills and knowledge for rewarding and productive lives, and further, to provide society with a resource pool of advanced skills, talent, and leadership. Justiz and Kameen articulate specific policy matters that universities can address to increase cooperative endeavors between colleges and schools.

Chapter 7, "Forces Eroding Affirmative Action in Higher Education: The California-Hawai'i Distinction" by Joanne Cooper, Kathleen Kane, and Joanne Gisselquist, examines the status of women in higher education, the events surrounding affirmative action in California, and the situation for women and minorities in another highly diverse state with a different history, the state of Hawai'i. Considering the divergent histories, it is unlikely that the political environment around affirmative action in California can be used to predict future changes in Hawaii. This chapter presents a closer examination of the situation in Hawaii, illuminating a particular cultural history and an accompanying commitment to community. It then examines the impact of fiscal constraints on that commitment, providing additional information about the complex forces that come to bear on affirmative action policies and procedures as we enter the millennium.

Chapter 8, "The Continuing and Expanding Roles of Historically Black Colleges and Universities in an Era of Affirmative Action and Diversity in Higher Education," is written by Antoine M. Garibaldi, Horace G. Dawson, Jr., and Richard A. English. It is critically observed that at an HBCU, the population group that is the minority in larger society is the majority on Black campuses. A question that arises is: Do the original issues still exist that surfaced during the *Adams* case, which decreed that dual segregated systems of public education were disadvantageous to Blacks in several fiscal, curricular, and physical areas? If so, how might they be addressed? HBCUs, while set up originally for African-Americans, have always had open-door policies in terms of other demographic groups. For example, at a prominent private HBCU, 85 percent of the undergraduate student population is Black, 50 percent of the graduate students are white, and 80 percent of continuing education students are white. With these shifting demographics, how does affirmative action play out in this kind of academic venue? What are the roles for HBCUs in the international arena, an area where few minorities have been represented?

Part IV concentrates on senior executive views and initiatives on affirmative action policies. Chapter 9, "Equity in the Contemporary University," is written by Graham B. Spanier and Mary Beth Crowe. The chapter examines salient components of the equity debate as faced by university presidents in light of the multiple missions of comprehensive universities that have expansive athletic programs; a myriad of undergraduate, graduate, and professional degrees; immense research enterprises; and extensive outreach and public service endeavors. Defining equity within the several programs and the use of affirmative action are perplexing challenges. For example, it is often stated that athletes, while meeting the National Collegiate Athletic Association (NCAA) admissions requirements, do not meet the requirements of regular matriculants. Simultaneously, students admitted as a result of affirmative action, depending upon the institution, may not meet regular admission requirements. Why might special treatment be viewed favorable for the former group and not the latter? How does one define equity for admissions in the context of highly competitive programs in fine and performing arts where SAT or Graduate Record Examination (GRE) scores may be unreliable predictors of artistic ability? How might the land-grant mission of addressing the needs of the state citizenry correlate with rigorous admission requirements at the flagship campus? What is the end result of students admitted in light of such illustrative questions? Exploring answers to these policy and programmatic queries and positing innovative solutions are foci of the chapter.

In chapter 10, "Forging New University Initiatives in the Twenty-First Century: Women Executives and Equity," Beverly Lindsay examines institutional policies initiated specifically under university women presidents. Programs embracing diversity and equity in the university have been developed in light of innovative mission statements and strategic plans by women executives to address recent legal and political imperatives. Of particular note will be their executive participation in changing institutional climates in an era of shifting state and federal policies—particularly since they began their careers when equity and affirmative action were gaining prominence in the American higher education scene.

Chapter 11, "Civil Society's Cross-National Response to Affirmative Action," written by Maxine Thomas, provides an overview of several international examples of affirmative action–like programs (United States, South Africa, China, and Sweden) that seek to address interaction between minorities and nonminorities or to redress gender inequality on college and university campuses. Programs that provide support, goals, quotas, preferences, aid and other mechanisms to incorporate the needs of minorities in a society are examined. These programs will be grouped under the general umbrella of affirmative action–like initiatives, although such programs are called by various other names outside of the United States. The common questions and issues that colleges and universities face in these programs and the issues they raise in various nations are considered. The chapter closes with thoughts on the implications these programs have for the future of the nation, higher education, and our global civil society.

The concluding chapter, in Part V, "Toward the Evolution of Dynamic Policies for Equity: Emerging Paradigms for Policy Change," by Beverly Lindsay, Manuel J. Justiz, and Marilyn C. Kameen, highlights the present situation in academia in an effort to envision the future. How will the current debate shape future affirmative action plans? How will academia embrace new goals of diversity and equity in order to address societal ills? These questions will be utilized to explicate a critical summary analysis regarding the development and articulation of dynamic inclusive new policies. Vital to this discussion are three key points: (a) the current struggle in the public policy arena to deal with changes in terms of majority and minority access to equity; (b) the laws that accommodate and influence public policy; and (c) the principles of democracy that facilitate public and educational policy changes.

Toward New Policies

Policy analysis and planning entails the critical examination of salient issues pertaining to higher education with the aim of presenting options, designs, and programs to encompass all demographic groups (Lindsay, 1995, p. 169). The boundaries of affirmative action need to be examined and the intrinsic workings require systematic restructuring of various programs to achieve equity. Stimpson (1993) offers suggestions to renew the undertaking of affirmative action in higher education. She suggests that it be broadly redefined, studied, examined through new scholarship on diversity, and reworked to address the needs of students. In conclusion, Marable clarifies:

> We need a thoughtful and innovative approach in challenging discrimination . . . We must build on the . . . general public's commitment to social fairness with creative measures that actually target the real patterns and processes of discrimination that millions of Latinos and Blacks experience every day. And we must not be pressured into a false debate to choose between race and class in the development and framing of public policies addressing discrimination. (1996, p. 15)

Since a color-blind society does not currently exist and various demographic realities remain, viable policies and programs to ensure equity remain paramount challenges in higher education. We do not wish for the situation to remain the destination.

Note

The authors gratefully acknowledge the assistance of Monica deMello Patterson in writing this chapter.

References

Adarand Contractors v. Peña, 513 U.S. 1012 (1995).

Alger, Jonathan R. (1997). The educational value of diversity. *Academe, 83*(1), 20–23.

Altbach, Philip G., & Lomotey, Kofi (1990). *Racial crisis in American higher education*. New York: State University of New York Press.

Altbach, Philip G., Berdahl, Robert O., & Gumport, Patricia J. (1994). *Higher education in American society*. Amherst, NY: Prometheus Books.

American Association of University Professors ad hoc Commission on Governance and Affirmative Action. (1996). The Board of Regents of the University of California, governance, and affirmative action. *Academe, 82*(4), 61–66.

American Council on Education. (1998). On the importance of diversity. Retrieved May 1998 from the World Wide Web: http://www.acenet.

American Council on Education and Education Commission of the States. (1989). *One third of a nation: A report of the Commission on Minority Participation in Education and American Life, May 1988*. Washington, DC: American Council on Education–Education Commission of the States.

American Federation of Teachers. (1998). Retrieved August 1998 from the World Wide Web: http://www.aft.org.

Americans United for Affirmative Action. (1997). Retrieved November 1997 from the World Wide Web: http://www.auaa.org.

Aronowitz, Stanley, & Giroux, Henry A. (1993). *Education still under siege*. Westport, CT: Bergin and Garvey.

Atwell, Robert H. (1996). Letter to President Clinton. American Council of Education. Retrieved June 1998 from the World Wide Web: http://www.acenet.edu.

Bensimon, Estela M., & Soto, Marta. (1997). Can we rebuild civic life without a multiracial university? *Change, 29*(1), 42–44.

Bergmann, Barbara R. (1997). In defense of affirmative action. *Academe, 83*(1), 29–33.

Bjork, Lars G., Justiz, Manuel J., & Wilson, Reginald. (1994). *Minorities in higher education*. Washington, DC: American Council on Education/ Oryx Press.

Bottorff, William, K. (1979) Thomas Jefferson. Boston: Twayne.

Bowen, William G., & Bok, Derek C. (1998). *The shape of the river: Long-term consequences of considering race in college and university admissions*. Princeton, NJ: Princeton University Press.

Browne-Miller, Angela. (1996). *Shameful admissions: The losing battle to serve everyone in our universities*. San Francisco: Jossey-Bass Inc.

Brown v. Board of Education, 347 U.S. 483 (1954).

Cahn, Steven M. (1993). *Affirmative action and the university: A philosophical inquiry*. Philadelphia: Temple University Press.

Campbell, Tom. (1998). Affirmative action in high education—The price is unacceptable. In *Tom Campbell—U.S. Congress/News articles*. Retrieved September 1998 from the World Wide Web: http://www.campbell.org/news/ article6.htm.

Canady, Charles T. (1996). The meaning of American equality. In George E. Curry (Ed.), *The affirmative action debate*. Reading, MA: Addison-Wesley.

Carnevale, Anthony P., & Stone, Susan C. (1995). *The American Mosaic: An In-depth Report on the Future of Diversity at Work*. New York: McGraw-Hill.

Carnoy, Martin. (1992). Education and the state: From Adam Smith to perestroika. In Robert F. Arnove, Philip Altbach, & Gail P. Kelly (Eds.), *Emergent issues in education: Comparative perspectives*. New York: State University of New York Press.

Carnoy, Martin. (1995). Why aren't more African Americans going to college? *Journal of Blacks in Higher Education, 6*, 66–69.

Carter, David (1998, March 24). Challenging the culture. [Invited keynote presentation], Pennsylvania State University Conference on Workforce Education, University Park, PA.

Chavez, Linda. (1996). Promoting racial harmony. In George E. Curry (Ed.), *The affirmative action debate*. Reading, MA: Addison-Wesley.

Chliwniak, Luba. (1997). Higher education leadership: Analyzing the gender gap. *ASHE-ERIC Higher Education Report, 25*(4). Washington DC: George Washington University, Graduate School of Education and Human Development.

Clarke, C. (1996). Affirmative action in higher education: A case for clarity. *Community Review, 14*, 59–66.

Clinton, William. (1996). Mend it, don't end it. In George E. Curry (Ed.), *The affirmative action debate*. Reading, MA: Addison-Wesley.

Cohen, Jordan J. (1997). Finishing the bridge to diversity. *Academic Medicine, 72*(2), 103–109.

Connerly, Ward. (1998, April). Speech for a series sponsored by Penn State Young Americans for Freedom. University Park, PA.

Cross, Theodore. (1994). What if there was no affirmative action in college admissions? A further refinement of our earlier calculation. *Journal of Blacks in Higher Education*, (5), 52–55.

Curry, George E. (Ed.). (1996). *The affirmative action debate*. Reading, MA: Addison-Wesley.

De Vita, Carol J. (1996). The United States at mid-decade. *Population Bulletin, 50* (4). [Brochure]. Washington, DC: Population Reference Bureau.

Devon, Richard. (1998). [Background for Pennsylvania Space Grant Consortium.] Unpublished document, Pennsylvania State University.

Duster, Troy. (1996). Individual fairness, group preferences, and the California strategy, *Representations, 55*, 41–58.

Edley, Christopher Jr. (1996). *Not all Black and white: Affirmative action, race and American values*. New York: Hill and Wang.

Ethridge, Robert W. (1997). There is much more to do. In Mildred Garcia (Ed.), *Affirmative action's testament of hope: Strategies for a new era in higher education*. Albany, NY: State University of New York Press.

Federal Glass Ceiling Commission. (1995). *Good for business: Making full use of the nation's human capital: The environmental scan: A fact-finding report of the Federal Glass Ceiling Commission*. Washington, DC: United State Department of Labor.

Fish, Stanley. (1994). Affirmative action and the SAT. *Journal of Blacks in Higher Education,* (2), 83.

Francis, Leslie P. (1993). In defense of affirmative action. In Steven M. Cahn (Ed.), *Affirmative action and the university*. Philadelphia: Temple University Press.

Franklin, John H. (1993). *The color line: Legacy for the twenty-first century/ John Hope Franklin*. Columbia: University of Missouri Press.

Garcia, J. L. A. (1994). The aims of the university and the challenge of diversity: Bridging the traditionalist/multiculturalist divide. In Mortimer N. S. Sellers (Ed.), *An ethical education: Community and morality in the multicultural university* (pp. 21–48). Oxford and Providence, RI: Berg Publishers.

Garcia, Mildred. (Ed.). (1997). *Affirmative action's testament of hope: Strategies for a new era in higher education*. Albany, NY: State University of New York Press.

Ginsburg, Mark, & Lindsay, Beverly. (1995). *The political dimension in teacher education comparative perspectives on policy formation, socialization and society*. London and Washington, DC: Falmer Press.

Giroux, Henry A. (1990). Liberal arts education and the struggle for public life: Dreaming about democracy. *The South Atlantic Quarterly, 89*(1), 114. Duke University Press.

Giroux, Henry A. (1997). *Channel surfing: Race talk and the destruction of today's youth*. New York: St. Martin's Press.

Graham, Hugh D. (1990). *The civil rights era: Origins and development of national policy/1960–1972*. New York and Oxford: Oxford University Press.

Gresson, Aaron D. III. (1995). *The recovery of race in America*. Minneapolis and London: University of Minnesota Press.

Hacker, Andrew. (1992). *Two nations: Black and white, separate, hostile, unequal*. New York: Charles Scribner's Sons.

Hilton, Keith O. (1995). Politics, not pragmatism, led University of California vote, say observers. *Black Issues in Higher Education, 12*(12), 7–9.

Hopwood v. State of Texas, 518 U.S. 1016. (1996).

Howard, John R. (1997). Affirmative action in historical perspective. In Mildred Garcia (Ed.), *Affirmative action's testament of hope: Strategies for a new era in higher education.* Albany, NY: State University of New York Press.

Johnson, Lyndon Baines. (1965). To fulfill these rights (Commencement Address at Howard University).

Joint Center for Political and Economic Studies. (1993). *The inclusive university: A new environment for higher education.* Washington, DC: Joint Center for Political and Economic Studies.

Jones, Elaine R. (1996). Race and the Supreme Court's 1994–95 term. In George E. Curry (Ed.), *The affirmative action debate.* Reading, MA: Addison-Wesley.

Journal of Blacks in Higher Education. (1994 Autumn). Good news: The African-American presence in the Ph.D. pipeline grows by 15 percent. *5,* 14–45.

Justiz, Manuel J., Delco, W., Wilson, Reginald, Callan, Patrick, et al. (1994). *Minorities in higher education.* Washington, DC: American Council on Education/Oryx Press.

Justiz, Manuel J. & Delco, W. (1993). Factions, human diversity, and education: What constitutes the public good? *Community College Journal, 63*(3), 18–21.

Kahlenberg, Richard D. (1996). *The remedy: Class, race, and affirmative action.* New York: Basic Books.

Kekes, John. (1997). Against preferential treatment. *Academe, 83*(1), 35–37.

Kull, Andrew. (1992). *The color-blind constitution.* Cambridge, MA: Harvard University Press.

Lederman, Douglas. (1995). The special preferences are not limited to Blacks. *Chronicle of Higher Education, 41*(33), A16–19.

Levin, Daniel J. (1995). A preference for action. *Trusteeship, 3*(3), 8–9, 11–12.

Lindsay, Beverly. (1989). Cross-cultural perspectives on women in higher education. *Sage, 6*(1), 92–96.

Lindsay, Beverly. (1995). Sociopolitical realities and teacher education in a new South Africa. In Mark Ginsburg & Beverly Lindsay (Eds.), *The political dimension in teacher education comparative perspectives on policy formation, socialization and society.* London and Washington, DC: Falmer Press.

Lindsay, Beverly. (1997). Toward conceptual, policy, and programmatic frameworks of affirmative action in South African universities. *Journal of Negro Education, 66*(4).

Lipkin, Robert J. (1994). Pragmatism, cultural criticism and the idea of the postmodern university. In Mortimer N. S. Sellers (Ed.), *An ethical education: Community and morality in the multicultural university* (pp. 49–88). Oxford and Providence, RI: Berg Publishers.

Lively, Kit. (1995). Preferences abolished. *Chronicle of Higher Education, 41*(46), A26–28.

Loury, Glenn C. (1996). Performing without a net. In George E. Curry (Ed.), *The affirmative action debate.* Reading, MA: Addison-Wesley.

Magrath, C. Peter. (1998). Community letter from the office of the president/ NASULGC. Retrieved May 1998 from the World Wide Web: http:// WWW.NASULGC.NCHE.edu.

Marable, Manning. (1996). Staying on the path to racial equality. In George E. Curry (Ed.), *The affirmative action debate.* Reading, MA: Addison-Wesley.

Meyer, John. (1977). The effects of education as an institution. *American Journal of Sociology, 83*(1), 55–77.

Montero-Sieburth, Martha. (1996). Beyond affirmative action: An inquiry into the experiences of Latinas in academia. *New England Journal of Public Policy, 11*(2), 65–97.

Moses, Yolanda. (1997). Salaries in academe: The gender gap persists. *Chronicle of Higher Education, 44*(16), A60.

Mosley, Albert G., & Capaldi, Nicholas. (1996). *Affirmative action: Social justice or unfair prejudice?* New York: Rowman and Littlefield.

National Association of State Universities and Land-Grant Colleges (NASULGC). (1998). On the importance of diversity in higher education, *Newsline: A Monthly Update of News and Analysis from the National Association of State Universities and Land-Grant Colleges, 7*(3), 7.

National Task Force for Minority Achievement in Higher Education. (1990). *Achieving campus diversity: Policies for change.* Education Commission of the States.

Nettles, Michael T., & Perna, Laura W. (1997). *The African American education data book, Volume 1: Higher and adult education, executive summary.* Fairfax, VA: College Fund/UNCF.

Norton, Eleanor H. (1996). Affirmative action in the workplace. In George E. Curry (Ed.), *The affirmative action debate.* Reading, MA: Addison-Wesley.

Orfield, Gary. (1993). Federal policy and college opportunity: Refurbishing a rusted dream. *Change, 25*(2), 10–15.

Orfield, Gary, & Miller, Edward (Eds.). (1998). *Chilling admissions: The affirmative action crisis and the search for alternatives.* Cambridge, MA: Harvard Education Publishing Group.

Patrick, Deval. (1996). Standing in the right place. In George E. Curry (Ed.), *The affirmative action debate.* Reading, MA: Addison-Wesley.

Podberesky v. Kirwin, 38 F. 3rd 147, (4th Cir. 1994).

Regents of the University of California v. Bakke, 438 U.S. 265. (1978).

Richardson, S. (1997). Texas educators seek clarification on *Hopwood* decision: Minority admission to Texas elite public colleges in free-fall. *Black Issues in Higher Education, 14*(5), 18–19, 21.

Rodriguez, R. (1996). Life after Hopwood. *Black Issues in Higher Education,* *13*(12), 8–10.

Rosen, J. (1998, Feb. 23 & Mar. 2). Reconsidering proposition 209. *The New Yorker.*

Rosenfeld, Michael. (1991). *Affirmative action and justice; A philosophical and constitutional inquiry.* New Haven, CT and London: Yale University Press.

Rush, Sharon E. (1994). Understanding affirmative action: One feminist's perspective. In Mortimer N. S. Sellers & Andrew Altman (Eds.), *An ethical education: Community and morality in the multicultural university* (pp. 195–232). Oxford and Providence, RI: Berg.

Schement, Jorge R. (1998). Thorough Americans: Minorities and the new media. In *Investing in diversity: Advancing opportunities for minorities and the media.* Washington, DC: Aspen Institute.

Schement, Jorge R., Greenberg, A. A., & Brody, R. (1998). *Minorities and the new media: Implications for the twenty-first century.* Las Vegas, NV: Broadcast Education Association.

Sellers, Mortimer N. S. (Ed.). (1994). *An ethical education: Community and morality in the multicultural university.* Oxford and Providence, RI: Berg.

Shea, C. (1995). Under UCLA's elaborate system race makes no big difference. *Chronicle of Higher Education, 41*(33), A12–14.

Simon, Robert L. (1993). Affirmative action and the university: Faculty appointment and preferential treatment. In Steven M. Cahn (Ed.), *Affirmative action and the university: A philosophical inquiry.* Philadelphia: Temple University Press.

Smith, Daryl G., Wolf, Lisa E., & Levitan, Thomas. (Eds.). (1994). Studying diversity in higher education. In *New directions for institutional research* (81). San Francisco: Jossey-Bass.

Steelworkers v. Weber, 443 U.S. 193. (1979).

Stephanopoulos, George, & Edley, Christopher Jr. (1995). *Affirmative action review: Report to the president.* Washington DC: The White House.

Stimpson, Catherine R. (1993). Has affirmative action gone astray? *Thought and Action, 8*(2), 5–26.

Taylor, Ronald A. (1996). Fighting back: Affirmative action professionals on the front line. *Black Issues in Higher Education, 13*(7), 12–14.

Texas Higher Education Coordinating Board. (1997). *Second status report: Advisory committee on criteria for diversity.* The Texas Higher Education Coordinating Board.

Thernstrom, Stephan, & Thernstrom, Abigail. (1997). *America in Black and white: One nation, indivisible.* New York: Simon & Schuster.

Tierney, William G. (1997). The parameters of affirmative action: Equity and excellence in the academy. *Review of Educational Research, 67*(2), 165–196.

United States v. Fordice, 112 S. Ct. 2739 (1992).

Valle, Victoria. (1996). Sitting in for diversity. In George E. Curry (Ed.), *The affirmative action debate*. Reading, MA: Addison-Wesley.

Williams, Linda F. (1996). Tracing the politics of affirmative action. In George E. Curry (Ed.), *The affirmative action debate*. Reading, MA: Addison-Wesley.

Wilson, John K. (1996). The myth of reverse discrimination in higher education. *Journal of Blacks in Higher Education*, (10), 88–93.

Wilson, Reginald, Anderson, Martin, Astin, Alexander W., Bell, Derrick A., Jr., Cole, Johnnetta B., Etzioni, Amitai, Gellhorn, Walter, Griffiths, Phillip A., Hacker, Andrew, Hesburgh, Theodore M., & Massey, Walter E. (1993). Why the shortage of Black professors? *Journal of Blacks in Higher Education*, (1), 25–34.

Wilson, Reginald. (1995). Affirmative action policies have helped minorities, women progress. *Higher Education and National Affairs*. American Council on Education.

Wilson, William Julius. (1996). *When work disappears: The world of the new urban poor*. New York: Knopf. Distributed by Random House.

Wilson, William Julius. (1998, April). When work disappears: Implications for citizenship in multicultural societies. [invited keynote address]. AERA Conference, San Diego, CA.

Winston, Judith (1995). Letter from Judith Winston, General Counsel, United States Department of Education, to College and University Counsel regarding the Supreme Court's denial of certiorari in Podberesky v. Kirwin, 38F. 3d 147 (4th Circuit 1994) and its decision in Adarand Constructors v. Peña, 115 S. Ct. 2097.

Winston, Judith (1996, July 1). Letter from Judith Winston, General Counsel, United States Department of Education, to College and University Counsel regarding Hopwood v. Texas, 78 F. 3d 932 (5th Circuit 1996) cert. denied, Texas v. Hopwood, No. 95-1773.

Wolf-Devine, Celia. (1997). Which side are the angels on? *Academe, 83*(1), 24–28.

Yates, A. C. (1996). Affirmative action debate should not hinder university commitment to equal opportunity, *Journal of College Admission* (152–153), 58–61.

Young, C. E. (1995). Maintaining diversity without affirmative action. *Higher education and national affairs*. American Council of Education.

Legal and Economic Perspectives

CHAPTER 2

Judicial and Legal Perspectives on Student Affirmative Action in Higher Education

IDA ELIZABETH WILSON

Affirmative action programs for students in higher education were born in the controversy of the civil rights movement. The decade of the 1990s, however, yielded serious legal and philosophical challenges to those programs, and those challenges are likely to continue well into the twenty-first century. Institutions that believe in the value of affirmative action in achieving racial and ethnic diversity have found themselves on the defensive against virulent attacks. On the other hand, advocates of affirmative action have been agonizingly slow in mounting a counter-offensive and in developing effective strategies to deal with these well-organized and alarmingly successful assaults. The purpose of this chapter is to discuss the judicial and legal perspectives on student affirmative action in higher education. The current state of the law is, overwhelmingly, on the side of promoting diversity. However, in choosing to promote and enhance racial and ethnic diversity in their student bodies, educational policy makers must ensure that their decisions do indeed have a sound legal foundation.

Federal laws and the court interpretations of those laws will obviously constitute a substantial part of the discussion. However, since the premier federal statute used to support affirmative action is permissive rather than mandatory (i.e., prohibits discrimination but does not require affirmative action), states are at liberty to restrict or preclude policies and programs that treat students differently based on their racial and ethnic classification. It is therefore important also to discuss how public and private institutions are dealing with issues of race and ethnicity in areas like admissions and financial aid. This is especially relevant in light of recent court interpretations and state initiatives. Historical evidence suggests that diversity does not happen naturally, but requires the deliberate imposition of specific standards. Institutions committed to racial diversity must therefore find lawful ways to achieve diversity without practicing unlawful discrimination.

This chapter will focus discussion on the current state of the law and on what institutions may do within the seemingly shrinking boundaries of the law to achieve and maintain racial and ethnic diversity within their student bodies. The discussion begins with a review of the current state of the law associated with issues of admissions and financial aid.

Legal Basis for Affirmative Action Programs

Any discussion of the judicial and legal bases for racial equity in educational policy must include a review of Title VI of the Civil Rights Act of 1964. The U.S. Department of Education Office for Civil Rights (OCR) has responsibility for Title VI regulatory compliance in institutions that receive federal financial assistance. Its implementing regulations (34 C. F. R. 100, 1994) and Final Policy Guidance (59 Fed. Reg. 8756, 1994), along with official interpretations of judicial decisions, are instructive in illuminating the current state of Title VI law with respect to admissions and financial aid.

Title VI prohibits discrimination on the basis of race, color, or national origin in programs and activities that receive federal financial assistance. In an era fraught with litigation pitfalls, institutions of higher education that act affirmatively to promote diversity in their student bodies and to remedy the present effects of past discrimination need warning signs that point to potential missteps vis-à-vis Title VI. In its recent pronouncements, OCR has been attempting to do just that, albeit not without challenge. On February 23, 1994, OCR published a Notice of Final Policy Guidance on financial aid (59 Fed. Reg. 8756, 1994). The Department, through OCR, has continued to assert *Bakke* (*Regents of the University of California v. Bakke,* 1978) as the law of the land—at least outside the jurisdiction of the Fifth Circuit, following the confusion of *Hopwood* (1996)—in admissions and financial aid decisions. An understanding of the five basic principles enunciated by OCR in its financial aid Guidance, discussed below in detail, provides a defining rationale for the federal government's position on this issue. Although the Guidance specifically addresses financial aid, it has implications for policy on admissions as well.

Financial Aid Issues

OCR's Final Policy Guidance on financial aid reportedly considered various studies and comments on its proposed policy guidance. It also considered court interpretations issued prior to publication. The Guidance is instructive in both the rules it lays down as well as the rationale it provides for the rules. Those rules provide strong support for affirmative action when properly implemented. Essentially, OCR enunciated five principles for taking race or national origin into account in awarding financial aid.

Principle 1. Financial Aid for Disadvantaged Students

A college may make awards of financial aid to disadvantaged students, without reference to race or national origin, even if that means the awards go disproportionately to minority students. Colleges are allowed to define the circumstances under which students will be considered disadvantaged, so long as their definition is not based on race or national origin. OCR indicated that an applicant's character, motivation, and ability to overcome economic and educational disadvantage are justified considerations in both admissions and financial aid decisions.

The use of disadvantage status is deemed by OCR to be consistent with the U.S. Supreme Court's decision in the 1983 *Guardians Association* case (1983). That case interpreted Title VI to prohibit actions that while not intentionally discriminatory, have the effect of discriminating on the basis of race or national origin. OCR also agreed with the eleventh Circuit's caveat in a case against the State of Georgia (*Georgia State Conference of Branches of NAACP v. State of Georgia*, 1985), in which the court stipulated that actions having a disproportionate effect on students of a particular race or national origin are permissible under Title VI if they bear a manifest demonstrable relationship to the institution's educational mission. Awarding financial aid to disadvantaged students, according to OCR, supports a sufficiently strong educational purpose to justify any racially disproportionate effect the use of this criterion may entail.

Principle 2. Financial Aid Authorized by Congress

Put simply, this principle states that financial aid programs for minority students authorized by a specific federal law cannot be considered in violation of Title VI. OCR considers it a basic canon of statutory construction that the specific provisions of a statute prevail over the general provisions of the same or a different statute (*Singer Sutherland Statutory Construction*, 1992). The Patricia Roberts Harris Fellowship, for example, provides statutory authorization for scholarships for minority students. The specific statutory authorization for those scholarships prevails over the general prohibitions in Title VI. OCR cautioned, however, that the fact that Congress has enacted specific federal programs for race-targeted financial aid does not serve as authorization for states or colleges to create such programs of their own.

Principle 3. Financial Aid to Remedy Past Discrimination

This is a somewhat controversial principle because few institutions, unless discrimination was clearly *de jure*, are willing to admit that they practiced past discrimination. Although policies based on race or national origin are "suspect" and subject to strict scrutiny, they are not absolutely prohibited in fulfilling this principle. However, to survive the strict scrutiny test, they must be based on a compelling governmental interest and must be narrowly tailored to serve that interest (*Richmond v. J. A. Croson Co.,* 1989; *Wygant v. Jackson Board of Education,* 1986). One such compelling governmental interest repeatedly sanctioned by the courts is ensuring the elimination of discrimination on the basis of race and national origin. A series of cases have held that narrowly tailored race-conscious measures to remedy discrimination, will satisfy the strict scrutiny requirement (*United States v. Fordice,* 1992; *United States v. Paradise,*1987; *Swan v. Charlotte-Mecklenberg Board of Education,* 1971; *McDaniel v. Barresi,*1971; *Green v. County School Board of New Kent County,* 1968).

The *Fordice* court further found that states that operated *de jure* systems of higher education have an affirmative obligation under the Fourteenth Amendment to the Constitution and Title VI of the Civil Rights Act of 1964 to dismantle those systems and their vestiges. They must, in other words, act affirmatively to overcome the present effects of past discrimination based on race. The Department published a "Notice of Application of Supreme Court Decision" with an effective date of January 28, 1994, interpreting that decision (U.S. Department of Education, 1994).

According to OCR Guidance, even in the absence of a finding by a court, legislature, or administrative agency, a college, in order to remedy the effects of past discrimination, may implement a remedial race-targeted financial aid program. In *Wygant* (1986), Justice O'Connor noted that a violation of federal statutory requirements does not arise with the making of findings; it arises when the wrong is committed. Thus, making institutions wait for a finding before implementing remedial programs would defeat the purpose of Title VI. Voluntary affirmative action to remedy past discrimination serves its purpose.

In *Richmond* (1989), the court again emphasized that remedial race-conscious action must be based on strong evidence of past discrimination. Evidence of past discrimination may, but need not, include documentation of specific incidents of intentional discrimination. Evidence of a statistically significant disparity between the percentage of minority students in a college student body and the percentage of qualified minorities in the relevant pool of college-bound high school graduates may also be sufficient. This approach is analogous to the one accepted by the courts in employment discrimination cases (*Hazelwood School District v. United States,* 1977).

Principle 4. Financial Aid to Create Diversity

An interest in creating a diverse student body tends to be the rationale that is most often cited by institutions of higher education in support of affirmative action policies. In April 1998 a long list of research universities took out full-page advertisements in several newspapers across the country, such as the *New York Times,* supporting voluntary affirmative action to achieve diversity in their student bodies.

Title VI regulations permit a college to take voluntary affirmative action, even in the absence of past discrimination, in response to conditions that have limited the participation of students of a particular race or national origin (34 CFR 100.5 (i), 1994). *Bakke* (*Regents of the University of California v. Bakke*, 1978) is the case most often cited in relying on diversity as the legal foundation for voluntary affirmative action. Although the court struck down the university's quota system of setting aside a specific number of slots for minority students, it upheld the principle of using race as one of several factors in making admissions decisions. It did so to permit the school to obtain the benefits of a diverse student body. The Court's ruling highlights the fact that within the context of higher education, Title VI is often the source of tension between the notion of academic freedom, a tenet with roots in the U.S. Constitution's First Amendment, and the Fourteenth Amendment's commitment to "strict scrutiny." Justice Powell wrote in *Bakke:*

> This clearly is a constitutionally permissible goal for an institution of higher education. Academic freedom, though not a specifically enumerated constitutional right, long has been viewed as a special concern of the First Amendment. The freedom of a university to make its own judgments as to education includes the selection of its student body. (*Regents of the University of California v. Bakke, 1978*)

The means to fulfill their academic mission through the robust exchange of ideas that accompanies a diverse student body must, however, comport with the requirements of the Fourteenth Amendment. Justice Powell found that the Medical School could advance its diversity interest under the First Amendment in a narrowly tailored manner that passed the Fourteenth Amendment's strict scrutiny test by using race or national origin as one of several factors—a "plus factor"—for applicants in the admissions process. OCR determined that if an institution's voluntary affirmative action program meets the Fourteenth Amendment's strict scrutiny standard, it will also comply with Title VI. OCR stated that it would, in fact, presume that a college's use of race or national origin as a plus factor is narrowly tailored to further the compelling governmental interest in promoting diversity. To benefit from this presumption, the college need only periodically reexamine whether its use of race or national origin continues to be necessary to achieve a diverse student body.

To determine whether a program is narrowly tailored, OCR identified several indicators:

1. The efficacy of less intrusive alternative approaches must be considered.
2. The extent, duration, and flexibility of the racial classification must be addressed. The amount of financial aid awarded based on race or national origin should be no greater than is necessary to achieve diversity.

3. The duration of the targeted classification should be no longer than is necessary to achieve its purpose, with periodic reexamination to ascertain whether it is still necessary.
4. The classification must be sufficiently flexible so that exceptions can be made, as appropriate.
5. Consideration must be given to the burden imposed by the targeted classification on those excluded. Generally, the less severe and more diffuse the impact the better.

Principle 5. Private Gifts Restricted by Race or National Origin

Pursuant to the Civil Rights Restoration Act of 1987, Title VI covers all of the operations of a college if the college receives any federal financial assistance (42 U.S.C. 2000d-4a(2)(A), 1964). Since a college's award of privately donated financial aid is within the operations of the college, the college must comply with the requirements of Title VI in awarding those funds. In other words, Principles 3 and 4 apply to privately donated funds, and institutions may justify awards based on race and national origin in accordance with the wishes of the donor. The privately donated funds can be targeted in order to remedy past discrimination or as a plus factor to achieve a diverse student body. Private donations may also be solicited in accordance with Principles 3 and 4 consistent with Title VI.

In order to give institutions time to comply with the Final Policy Guidance, OCR allowed colleges two years after the effective date to adjust their financial aid programs. Colleges, however, were permitted to continue financial aid to students on the basis of race or national origin who had either applied for or received that assistance prior to the effective date. Aid to those students is allowed to continue for the duration of their academic programs at the college.

Despite the instructive nature of OCR's Guidance and the assurance that affirmative action can be lawfully practiced by institutions of higher education, the climate against affirmative action to achieve diversity has continued to escalate among individual states. Opponents have chosen lawsuits as well as other initiatives through state legislatures and voter referendum drives to achieve their anti–affirmative action purposes. University of California Regent Ward Connerly has been active in organizing anti–affirmative action initiatives at the state level, beginning with his own state of California. The Center for Individual Rights has been quite active in supporting anti–affirmative action lawsuits. Together, such efforts have been devastatingly successful in weakening diversity efforts in several jurisdictions and in chilling the climate throughout the country.

Impact of Anti–Affirmative Action Climate: Cases and State Initiatives

The University of Maryland at College Park established the merit-based Benjamin Banneker Scholarship to be awarded solely to African-American students. Daniel Podberesky, a scholarship applicant born in Costa Rica, sued the university for discrimination in violation of Title VI of the Civil Rights Act of 1964 and 42 U.S.C. §§ 1981 and 1983. Although the district court ruled in favor of the university, the final appeals court decision favored the plaintiff. The appeals court held that the university did not provide sufficient proof of the need to limit the scholarship to only one race. The court reasoned that even if it assumed that every predominantly white institution of higher education practiced past discrimination, that circumstance reflected societal discrimination and societal discrimination is insufficient to support a race-exclusive remedy. To justify a race-exclusive remedy, the court concluded that the present effects of past discrimination must be clearly evident and the remedy must be narrowly tailored. In this case, the court found inadequate and unreliable evidence of the present effects of past discrimination, and also found the program not narrowly tailored—a finding difficult to overcome, since the university had not considered a race-neutral alternative. Consequently, the court found the program to be in violation of the Equal Protection Clause of the Fourteenth Amendment to the U.S. Constitution. Because the U.S. Supreme Court declined to consider further appeal of the decision, the decision of the Fourth Circuit Court of Appeals was allowed to stand.

Following the Fourth Circuit's position in the case of *Podberesky v. Kirwan* (1995), OCR issued a letter from Judith A. Winston, General Counsel, dated September 7, 1995, to college and university attorneys. In the letter, OCR reaffirmed its commitment to its Policy Guidance on race-targeted financial aid and noted that the Fourth Circuit decision did not signal a need for revision. The Counsel explained that the U.S. Supreme Court's decision not to hear the University's appeal on the case should not be misinterpreted. By denying the University's request for an appeal, the Supreme Court neither ruled against race-targeted scholarships generally, nor affirmed the circuit court's decision that the University had not submitted sufficient evidence to justify providing such aid.

The *Podberesky* decision (1995) followed Principle 3 of the Guidance, that race-targeted financial aid is permissible to remedy the present effects of past discrimination, provided the remedy is narrowly tailored to meet that objective. The university's evidence, however, was found factually insufficient to justify its race-exclusive remedy and not narrowly enough tailored. Because of its particular facts, it is reasonable to assert that the case left the integrity of OCR's Guidance intact.

In summary, OCR's legal counsel concluded that under governing legal standards, race-targeted financial aid is permissible in appropriate circumstances as a remedy for the present effects of past discrimination and as a tool to achieve a diverse student body. OCR stated it would continue to implement its financial aid policy under Title VI and to support race-targeted financial aid programs consistent with its policy.

OCR had occasion to visit its Guidance again in addressing a scholarship program at a university in Florida. On February 21, 1997, OCR issued a report of its findings on a complaint alleging that Florida Atlantic University discriminated against white students in restricting participation in the University's Martin Luther King Scholarship (MLK Scholarship) (Shannon, 1997). OCR found the program in compliance with Title VI, although certain modifications to strengthen its legal foundation were suggested and subsequently implemented. OCR cited Title VI, its implementing regulations on financial aid, and its Final Policy Guidance on Race-Targeted Financial Aid as applicable legal standards for its position.

The MLK Scholarship program was initiated in 1984 as a race-exclusive scholarship program designed to recruit qualified Black students to the University. It was restricted to Black applicants. In 1995, the MLK Scholarship was converted into two scholarship programs. One was based on financial need (MLK Scholarship) and one was based on academic achievement (MLK Scholars Award). Both continued to be restricted to Black applicants. The University identified Principle 4, an interest in achieving a diverse student body, as the justification for its MLK scholarship programs.

As evidence of its interest in fostering a diverse student body and of the need for the MLK scholarship programs to help achieve it, the University offered the following:

1. The University cited its published commitment to achieving and maintaining a diverse student body, such as statements in its catalogs.
2. The University presented evidence that, while the undergraduate enrollment of other racial and ethnic groups increased over the past several years, the enrollment of Black students did not.
3. The University conducted interviews with students that disclosed many could not have attended the University but for the MLK scholarships and other scholarship programs in which race was a consideration.
4. The University monitored the results of its many recruitment programs that did not include race as a consideration. It demonstrated that while they were effective in recruiting white, Hispanic, and Asian/Pacific Islander students, they were not effective in recruiting Black students. This assessment was designed to address the obligation to narrowly tailor programs to meet diversity goals, in accordance with Title VI and Fourteenth Amendment mandates.
5. In proving that the program did not unduly burden nonbeneficiaries of the program, the University provided evidence that it allocates only 7–8 percent of its scholarship financial aid to race-targeted programs. Monies not allocated to these programs go into funds to recruit and retain other groups that help the University achieve its diversity interest.
6. In addition to the MLK scholarship programs, the University also funds three other race-targeted scholarship programs: the Southeastern Consortium for Minorities in Engineering (SECME), the Minority Education

Achievement Award (MEAA), and the South African Scholarship. The evidence disclosed that the SECME and MEAA scholarships were restricted to minority students: Black, Hispanic, Asian, and American Indian. The South African Scholarship was restricted to Black South Africans.

In order to strengthen its legal position following the OCR investigation, the University agreed to the following modifications in its race-targeted scholarship programs:

- SECME scholarships will be revised to include race as only one factor for consideration, consistent with Principle 4 of the Guidance dealing with financial aid to achieve diversity (59 Fed. Reg. 8756, 1994).
- The MEAA program was changed to the Transfer Educational Award, and its criteria revised to comport with Principle 1 of the Guidance dealing with financial aid to disadvantaged students without regard to race (59 Fed. Reg. 8756, 1994).
- The South African scholarship program was opened to all South African students without regard to race.
- The University agreed to periodically reexamine the programs to assess their effectiveness in meeting diversity interests. The review will determine whether to continue the race plus approach, return to the race exclusive approach, or discontinue them if diversity needs have been met.

The above terms were placed in a Resolution Agreement to be signed by the University President or designee and monitored for implementation compliance by OCR. Data to be provided to OCR for monitoring purposes included:

1. Data on the number of students by race who applied for, received, and were denied any financial aid offered by the University, including the above-referenced programs;
2. The total amount of non-race-targeted institutional aid awarded to students by race; and,
3. The total of race-targeted institutional aid awarded to students by race. The University agreed to provide OCR with the criteria used to process financial aid applications and to maintain files of rejected applicants for OCR review on request.

It seems clear from this case study that OCR intends to base its review of voluntary affirmative action programs for student financial aid on the principles enumerated in its Guidance. Institutions of higher education would be well advised to review their financial aid programs that consider race as a criterion in light of the Guidance, and to make modifications for conformity, as appropriate.

While the findings in the Maryland and Florida cases can be reconciled with OCR's policy Guidance and *Bakke*, the Fifth Circuit's ruling in *Hopwood* is not so easily explained. Although the court could have ruled more narrowly that the University of Texas Law School admissions policy did not meet the *Bakke* "narrowly tailored" test for achieving diversity or remedying the present effects of past discrimination, it chose to rule on much broader grounds. It effectively declared *Bakke* no longer binding in holding that the state's interest in achieving a diverse student body is not a compelling enough reason to meet the difficult constitutional standard of strict scrutiny for racial classifications.

The *Hopwood* court took the position that the University of Texas Law School could not take race into account in admissions, either to promote diversity or to remedy the effects of the state's formerly *de jure* system of segregation in public education. The court stated the Law School could only seek to remedy its own proven history of discrimination. The U.S. Supreme Court's denial of certiorari to review the lower court's decision left the Fifth Circuit's position as the apparent law of the land in the states of Texas, Louisiana, and Mississippi, which comprise the Fifth Circuit. Its denial of certiorari does not mean that the Supreme Court departed from Justice Powell's opinion in *Bakke* that a college has a compelling interest in taking race into account in a properly devised admissions program to achieve a diverse study body. Nor does it mean that the Supreme Court accepted the Fifth Circuit's narrow view of the permissible remedial predicate justifying the consideration of race by an institution of higher education in making admissions decisions. The Supreme Court neither affirmed nor reversed the Fifth Circuit's decision. It simply declined to review it. Justice Ginsburg explained that since the 1992 admissions policies at issue had long since been abandoned and would never be reinstated, there was no longer a live case or controversy on which the Court could judge the important constitutional issues raised in the petition.

OCR continues to assert that, outside of the Fifth Circuit, an institution of higher education can take race into account in a narrowly tailored procedure to remedy the present effects of prior discrimination or to achieve a diverse student body. The law within the Fifth Circuit is unclear but will, no doubt, be clarified through subsequent litigation.

In her letter to Senator Ellis (1997), Assistant Secretary Cantu made four points:

1. OCR will conduct a review of the Texas system of higher education to determine whether vestiges of its formerly segregated system remain. Its standard for review will be those established by the U.S. Supreme Court in *Fordice* (*United States v. Fordice*, 1992).
2. If the review finds there are current effects of past discrimination in violation of Title VI, and if it is determined that the violation cannot be

corrected by race-neutral means, Texas will be required to take narrowly tailored affirmative action measures to eliminate the vestiges of its discrimination. OCR deemed this consistent with *Hopwood*, which recognized that an institution may take affirmative action to remedy the vestiges of its own discriminatory system. OCR expressed its expectation that if the findings warrant, Texas will undertake such remedial action voluntarily.

3. Outside of the Fifth Circuit, OCR will continue to adhere to Justice Powell's opinion in *Bakke*, which permitted appropriately tailored affirmative action to remedy the present effects of past discrimination or to achieve a diverse student body.

4. Pending further developments within the Fifth Circuit or the U.S. Supreme Court, OCR noted that it will not require or encourage any institution within the Fifth Circuit to engage in race-conscious affirmative action that is inconsistent with the prohibitions of *Hopwood*.

Assistant Secretary Cantu stated that it is the belief of the United States that the *Hopwood* panel was wrong in rejecting *Bakke* and in imposing its narrow interpretation of the permissible remedial predicates for affirmative action. She urged that in appropriate subsequent litigation the *Hopwood* decision be overturned. It is very clear that OCR strongly supports Justice Powell's opinion in the *Bakke* decision and that his opinion will continue to form the basis for OCR's Policy Guidance and enforcement under Title VI.

Whatever OCR's position and influence may be outside the Fifth Circuit, the impact of *Hopwood* on admissions to the University of Texas was immediate and dramatic. The University reported that undergraduate applications from Black students to the University's Austin campus fell 26 percent and Hispanic applications fell 23 percent (American Association of State Colleges and Universities, 1998). The University of Texas Law School had a stunning 42 percent decrease in applications from Black students. In the wake of such devastating fallout, the Texas Legislature enacted legislation in 1997 requiring the state's premier public universities to admit the top 10 percent of seniors from every public high school in Texas (Bowen & Bok, 1998).

Authors Bowen and Bok in their book *The Shape of the River* (1998) discuss the use of grades and class rankings, instead of standardized test scores, in contributing to the diversity of the student bodies at premier institutions in the state of Texas. They acknowledge that it is too soon to gauge the impact of the legislature's policy, but note that Blacks are only half as likely as whites to finish in the top 10 percent of their high school class and less than 40 percent as likely to earn an A average. On the other hand, they note that such a policy could give many minority students who attend high schools that are de facto segregated a much better chance of gaining admission to a premier public university than they had before. The effect of such a policy, they speculated, tends to shift decision-making responsibility from directors of admission at institutions of higher education to high school guidance counselors and to the prospective students themselves.

Bowen and Bok expressed concern that in the rush for class rankings, students may avoid the more difficult courses or even seek transfer to less demanding schools. They expressed doubt that basing admissions to academically selective institutions on any simple criterion, such as being in the top 10 percent of one's high school class, is likely to be an effective substitute for race-sensitive admissions policies. The authors conclude that only through the use of race-sensitive admissions policies can great colleges and universities adequately address the clearly race-based problems such policies seek to overcome.

The long-term results of the Texas legislature's policy, intended to promote diversity at its most selective institutions of higher education, remains to be seen. Advocates of diversity will, in any event, surely applaud the legislature's imperfect efforts to overcome the harsh results of *Hopwood* and to promote diversity in the student bodies of its premier institutions of higher education.

Admissions Policies: Lawful and Unlawful Affirmative Action Programs

The Final Policy Guidance on financial aid also addressed admissions issues and is an instructive reference. In light of various administrative challenges, court decisions and state anti–affirmative action initiatives, OCR directed a number of letters to University Legal Counsel and issued various statements on the issue of race conscious admissions programs. Discussed below are two programs: the first at the University of California at Los Angeles (UCLA) and the second at Boalt Hall on the campus of the University of California at Berkeley. One describes a well-intentioned but unlawful attempt at voluntary affirmative action to achieve diversity. The other describes a model of lawful affirmative action to achieve diversity.

OCR conducted an investigation of the UCLA undergraduate admissions program following a complaint that it discriminated against Asian American applicants to its College of Letters and Science (L&S) and the School of Engineering and Applied Science (SEAS). During the course of its investigation, OCR examined the student affirmative action plans for L&S and SEAS to determine their compliance with Title VI. It published a lengthy report of its findings (Palomino, 1995). OCR found that UCLA did not discriminate against Asian-American student applicants for admission, and it also found its student affirmative action programs in L&S and SEAS in compliance with Title VI and *Bakke* (Palomino, 1995). Highlights of the UCLA system in place in 1990 that OCR found to comply with Title VI are as follows:

- It was the express policy of the Regents to seek to enroll, on each of its campuses, a student body that not only demonstrates high academic achievement or exceptional talent but also encompasses the broad diversity of cultural, racial, geographic, and socioeconomic backgrounds characteristic of California.
- The Regents required each of its campuses to admit 60 percent of its students on academic factors only.
- The remainder were reviewed and given a supplemental ranking. At least seventeen factors were considered in developing the supplemental ranking. Race and national origin were "plus" factors among the many others.
- All UC eligible applicants had an opportunity to compete.
- A matrix was developed to rank UC eligible students using a combination of academic and supplemental evaluations.
- Over 50 evaluators were assigned to review the applicants, and each application was reviewed at least twice.
- The University developed the matrix approach after conducting studies that established that a race-neutral admission process would be ineffective in establishing a diverse student body.
- UCLA reviewed the impact of race in its admissions decisions and noted that the contribution of race declined from 1988 to 1989 then leveled off in 1990.
- Academics ranked first in importance and the supplemental ranking was second.

Thus, OCR concluded that although there were race-conscious elements in the admissions process, they were narrowly tailored to the University's stated policy of achieving a student body that reflected the diversity of its state. The program chosen was rationally based on research, and it was not unduly burdensome to those who did not benefit from the plus factor. All UC eligible students had an opportunity to compete for admission to UCLA. A review process was established to ascertain the impact of the factor, and the University implemented modifications to its program in accordance with the findings of its periodic review.

Although OCR found UCLA's program to be an example of a lawful race-plus admissions program to achieve student diversity, it outlawed the more restrictive program at a different California institution of higher education. On September 25, 1992, OCR issued a report to Dr. Chin-Lin Tien, Chancellor of the University of California at Berkeley, concerning its findings pursuant to a Title VI compliance review of the affirmative action program for admission to the School of Law, Boalt Hall (Jackson, 1992). The case is instructive in disclosing how a well-intended program, implemented for the right reasons, can violate Title VI in the way it is designed. OCR reviewed the procedures used in 1988, 1989, and 1990 and found that some of Boalt Hall's admissions procedures were inconsistent with Title VI regulation.

The features of Boalt Hall's affirmative action admissions program are as follows:

- In 1978, it established an overall annual goal of admitting from 23 to 27 percent of each class from certain racial/ethnic groups through special consideration. More specific goals were established for each special consideration group: 8–10 percent for Blacks, 8–10 percent for Hispanics, 5–7 percent for Asians, and 1 percent for Native Americans. Since 1978, Boalt Hall consistently met or exceeded the 23–27 percent annual goal.
- In establishing the percentage goals, Boalt Hall took into account the general information on discrimination against racial and ethnic minority groups, the representation of such groups in the school and in the legal profession, and their representation generally in the U.S. population.
- The goals were established to achieve diversity, not to remedy past discrimination.
- Among the factors considered by admissions evaluators were: test scores, grades, state residency, difficulty of course work, employment obligations while in school, graduate studies, extraordinary extracurricular or personal contributions, work experience, and minority race or ethnicity. Of the factors, only race and ethnicity were closely monitored in relation to the percentage goals. There were no benchmarks established for the other factors. Specifically excluded from consideration were age, gender, geographic origin, or intended use of legal education.
- Special consideration files were separated by race or national origin for each targeted group.
- Evaluators were told how many from each file, including the special consideration groups, to admit or put on the wait list. They were told to deny the remainder.
- Candidates within each file group were compared only with candidates in that group. They were not compared to candidates in any other group or other batches of files. Special consideration candidates were rank-ordered separately. All other candidates were rank-ordered for placement on either a resident or a nonresident list.
- In 1990, more than 34 percent of the incoming class was made up of applicants from minority groups receiving special consideration, exceeding Boalt Hall's stated annual goal. It met or exceeded goals for each of the separate racial and ethnic subgroups as well.

OCR found that the manner in which race and ethnicity were considered had the effect of circumscribing competition and effectively excluding applicants from consideration for available positions based on their race or ethnicity. This approach, they concluded, was inconsistent with Title VI. The University entered into a conciliation agreement with OCR designed to remedy the defects in the Boalt Hall affirmative action admissions program. The most significant changes included agreements that:

1. Applicants will not be considered separately for admission or admitted separately based on their race, color, or national origin.
2. Applicants will not be excluded from consideration for available spaces in the program based on race, color, or national origin. Spaces in the law school will not be set aside based on race, color, or national origin.
3. If achieving a diverse student population is determined to be an educational objective that will affect admissions decisions, diversity considerations will not be limited to race, color, or national origin. They will include a variety of factors deemed important to establishing a diverse educational environment.
4. If the school adopts numerical or percentage equal opportunity participation goals that reference race, color, or national origin, the goals will not be applied in the admissions process in a way designed to ensure the result for the targeted group of students.

Language in the conciliation agreement made it clear that the agreement did not prohibit affirmative consideration of race, color, or national origin for remedial purposes, should such a consideration be in response to a finding of discrimination by an authority empowered to make such a finding. Also, special recruiting efforts to encourage a pool of minority applicants were not prohibited by the agreement.

Although the student affirmative action admissions programs at both UCLA and the initial one at UC Berkeley were both established to achieve a diverse student body, a review of the program design and methodology of each provides a clear contrast in approaches. The approach implemented by UCLA appears to be consistent with OCR regulatory Guidance and with court interpretations of what is Constitutionally permissible under *Bakke*, which is still good law in every jurisdiction except, arguably, the Fifth Circuit. The modified program at UC Berkeley appears to have been brought into Title VI compliance following OCR review and consequent modification.

The subsequent course of political events in California, however, brought chaos and uncertainty to carefully established student affirmative action programs designed to achieve and maintain diversity. Even before the passage of Proposition 209 in California, the Board of Regents of the University of California system took action that prohibited the use of racial and gender preferences as a criterion for admissions decisions at the system's nine campuses. After the passage of Proposition 209 by California voters, also known as the California Civil Rights Initiative, the use of those preferences in admissions procedures was banned at all state colleges. In reaction, minority enrollments plummeted and institutions scrambled to repair the damage.

The damage was substantial. Following the ban on race-based admissions by the University of California Regents and the passage of Proposition 209, the number of minority students enrolled at the University of California's business and professional schools during the 1996–1997 application cycle fell dramatically. New Black applicants to the system's three law schools decreased 63 percent over the previous year. Hispanic enrollment at the University of California's five business schools fell 54 percent. Students who applied in the 1996–1997 academic year were the first to be impacted by the new rules (American Association of State Colleges and Universities, 1998).

In 1997, 14 African-American students were admitted to the University of California Berkeley's Boalt Hall School of Law. All 14 opted not to attend the school. The one Black student that did begin first-year classes at Boalt Hall had been admitted in 1996 and deferred his enrollment until 1997 (Johnson, 1999). As he began the fall semester, the lone African-American student was greeted by a barrage of reporters and television cameras and forced to hold a press conference. Before the ban, 8 percent of Boalt Hall's first-year class was composed of African-Americans, 14 percent were Asian, 11 percent were Hispanic, and 2 percent were Native American. After the ban, the minority enrollment dropped to 20 percent—14 percent Asian, 5 percent Hispanic, the single, deferred African-American, and no Native Americans.

Frank Bruni interviewed a number of students who were offered admission to the University of California's most selective campus at Berkeley (Bruni, 1998). After the ban on affirmative action, only 191 Black students were offered admission among the 8,034 students admitted for the class of 2002. One senior Black student, previously relied on to help recruit new minority students through the Black Recruitment and Retention Center, indicated that she and her fellow students could not, in good conscience, advise students with a viable alternative to choose Berkeley. They advised Black high school seniors who visited the campus that the University did not want them and they should not enroll. Although Berkeley officials asserted that the University was as receptive to minority students as ever and that the decline in Black student admissions was an unavoidable consequence of Proposition 209, minority students nevertheless felt betrayed and insulted. Even the most intense recruitment efforts could not make up the drop of African-American students from 7.3 percent of the entering freshman class to less than 2 percent. Some members of the Black faculty, although not all, indicated that they ignored the University's request to make contact with prospective Black students. Even the Director of Black Student Development at Berkeley advised students to go to Stanford University instead. The freshman class of Hispanic students also suffered a significant decline. Chancellor Berdahl indicated that he spent hours exhorting students not to give up on Berkeley, noting there is no place where the issue is being confronted more viscerally (Bruni, 1998).

To counter the effects of the ban on affirmative action and increase minority student enrollment at the University of California's Boalt Hall School of Law, officials made a number of changes. Among them was increasing the length of the personal essay statement, visiting more Historically Black Colleges, and enlisting minority alumni to host parties for prospective students. The University also launched an all-out campaign to convince those accepted to attend, including a day-long orientation at the school and dinner with Berkeley's first Black mayor, Warren Widener, an alumnus of the law school. These extra efforts helped boost the fall 1998 first-year enrollment of minority group members to 18 percent Asian, 3 percent African-American, 23 percent Hispanic, and 2 percent Native American (Johnson, 1999).

In light of the controversy surrounding the passage of the California Civil Rights Initiative, Proposition 209, a discussion of OCR's position on its impact appears appropriate. OCR took the opportunity to address this in a March 19, 1997, letter from Secretary Richard Riley, U.S. Department of Education to "Dear Colleagues" (Riley, 1997). In that letter Secretary Riley confirmed that the passage of Proposition 209

- Did not change the obligation of school districts and colleges to abide by federal civil rights statutes in order to remain eligible to receive Department funding; and
- Did not change the obligations of schools participating in the small number of federal programs administered by the Department to consider race, as appropriate, under the terms of those programs.

The Secretary expressed continuing support for appropriately tailored affirmative action measures as important tools in their efforts to ensure that all students achieve high standards. It is clear that from OCR's perspective, the use of race as a factor for participation in sponsored federal programs is not only appropriate, but also required. Secretary Riley enumerated a number of programs sponsored by the Department that enjoy the Department's continued support. He reminded educational institutions of Title VI protections for students and employees and of their affirmative duty to eliminate the effects of prior discrimination. The Secretary made it very clear that Proposition 209 did not change the mandates and rights provided by federal statutes like Title VI. He stressed that those federal rights remain as effective in California after Proposition 209 as they do elsewhere in the United States to remedy the effects of prior discrimination and to achieve a diverse student body.

Perhaps bolstered by success in California, organizers of that drive joined forces with affirmative action opponents in the state of Washington to launch a similar campaign. It, too, was successful. Voters in the state of Washington passed Initiative 200 in 1998, a Proposition 209–like initiative that banned the use of race in state hiring, contracting, and college admissions. Already, the University of Washington Law School reports a decline in minority enrollment. According to an associate dean of the law school, the school made 22 fewer minority admissions because of Initiative 200 ("Minority numbers down at Washington law school," 1999).

Private Schools and the Impact of Anti-Affirmative Action Laws and Court Decisions

To date, litigation and other anti-affirmative action initiatives have been directed at public institutions of higher education. Although private institutions are not under identical legal constraints, it is clear that they have not been unaffected by the issues faced by their public counterparts. The immediate impact on private schools, however, appears to depend on the unique characteristics extant in each state. Those in California appear prepared to stay the course in considering race as a factor in admissions. Those in Texas, however, seem resigned to reexamine and revise their student admissions policies out of concern over repercussions from the state.

Proposition 209 in California was directed at public institutions of higher education. Private schools in California, therefore, may continue to voluntarily use race as a plus factor in admissions and financial aid decisions, consistent with Title VI, OCR Policy Guidance, and *Bakke*. Stanford University, an elite private institution of higher education, still practices affirmative action. It admitted 238 Black students to a freshman class half the size of Berkeley's. Private institutions appear to have benefited somewhat, at least in the immediate aftermath of Proposition 209, with minority students preferring them to the most selective public institutions of higher education, like Berkeley (Bruni, 1998). Minority students may view private institutions in California, at least those that choose to retain their student diversity programs, as providing a more welcoming academic and social environment.

Court cases, like voter initiatives, have also been directed at public institutions of higher education. Although the *Hopwood* decision specifically prohibited race-based admissions policies in a public institution of higher education, Texas State Attorney General Dan Morales expanded its reach beyond admissions by declaring that financial aid decisions based on race were also to be prohibited as a means to achieving diversity. Because private institutions award financial aid that includes federal funds, the Attorney General's declaration acted to bring even private institutions in Texas within the *Hopwood* prohibitions.

Rice University in Texas, in a quandary over how to handle scholarship monies specifically designated for minority students, held onto the money while the university decided what to do (Stephens, 1999). A task force reviewed the university's admissions and financial aid guidelines. The result was a revised procedure directing the admissions committee to consider students' life experiences and community service activities in addition to quantitative measures of success. Rice asked its donors to conform their criteria to the university's revisions. Rice also initiated the Barbara Jordan scholarship, named after the prominent Black Congresswoman from Texas who died in 1996. The first group of recipients of the $30,000 scholarship included three Black, three Latino, and three white students. The idea of the scholarship is, in part, to counter the negative perceptions that may be associated with the educational climate in Texas caused by *Hopwood*. Rice also redirected a scholarship established for Latino students to one for students with Spanish language ability to make the criteria linguistic rather than ethnic or race-based.

Texas Christian University (TCU) also revised its financial aid policies in compliance with *Hopwood*. TCU hoped to attract more minority applicants by offering scholarships to first-generation college-bound students. That strategic policy was ineffective, however, because there were so many white students who also qualified under that policy.

The policy changes made by Rice and TCU clearly illustrate the devastating reach of *Hopwood*, reflecting an extension of public school prohibitions into private education based on the fact that their financial aid programs include federal funds. In apparent acknowledgment that the state's interpretation of *Hopwood* reached too far, however, Morales's interpretation of *Hopwood* was rescinded. Texas Attorney General John Cornyn, Morales's successor, withdrew the Morales opinion that *Hopwood* applies to student financial aid programs as well as to admissions (University of Texas system news and public information, 1999). University of Texas System Chancellor William H. Cunningham expressed deep appreciation for the attorney general's efforts on behalf of the University of Texas and all of Texas higher education. The impact of the Attorney General's policy reversal, however, is yet to be determined.

Like institutions in California following Proposition 209 and in the Fifth Circuit following *Hopwood*, private institutions of higher education in the state of Washington were also anxious. The dean of Seattle University, a private Jesuit school, expressed concern about the impact of Initiative 200 generally on higher education for minority students. Acting on such concern, a coalition of independent Jesuit universities issued a statement endorsing affirmative action policy at the annual conference of the National Association for College Admissions Counselors (NACAC).

The concern of private institutions in jurisdictions with anti–affirmative action laws and court decisions is understandable, but it must be emphasized that such concern is not based on expressed provisions in any current federal or state law. Private institutions have not been targeted for private litigation or for state initiatives. Those in jurisdictions without anti-affirmative action laws and regulations appear to be in the best position to exercise leadership in promoting racial and ethnic diversity in their admissions and financial aid programs. It is reasonable to speculate that elite private institutions in states where there have been no anti-affirmative action laws enacted or court decisions rendered would see an increase in applications from the best and brightest minority student applicants. Those applicants who generally have several options, it seems logical to conclude, would choose to go where they are made to feel most welcome. And in light of the high cost of most elite private institutions, the availability of financial aid as an incentive would seem to be one indication of just how welcome they are at those institutions. A very small sampling of such institutions tends to support this notion. According to Duke University's director of undergraduate admissions, they are comfortable with what they are doing and are achieving a more diverse student body. They claim a record number of African-American and Latino students in last year's freshman class, with 10 percent and 5 percent of the class enrollment, respectively (University of Texas system news and public information, 1999).

Because the minority student population in Maine is so small, Bates University expends a great deal effort recruiting out of state to achieve a diverse student body. The Dean of Admissions indicated the university works hard to fulfill its ambitions for a diverse class, undeterred by all the debate about affirmative action elsewhere (University of Texas, 1999). The Director of Admissions at Oberlin College in Ohio says her staff considers such factors as whether the student's primary language at home is other than English (University of Texas system news and public information, 1999). Columbia University in New York and other Ivy League institutions continue to administer student financial aid programs established for the benefit of minority group members. Listings appear on their web sites or through communication with their financial aid officers. Such highly selective institutions seem determined to preserve as much autonomy as possible and to define for themselves who will be admitted to their institutions consistent with their established mission and purpose.

In their book, Bowen and Bok identified four general areas of consideration that the most selective institutions consider after identifying those individuals who seem capable of completing the course of study successfully. Since there are far more applicants capable of successful completion than there are seats available, other factors are used in the selection process to aid in deciding among the remaining candidates:

- The first consideration is to admit an ample number of students who show particular promise of excelling in their studies. By and large, such students have the greatest likelihood of taking full advantage of the academic strengths of the institution and contributing to the education of their peers. They play an important role in setting the academic tenor of the institution.

- The second consideration is the need to assemble a class of students with a wide diversity of backgrounds, experiences, and talents. Graduating students and alumni—of both undergraduate colleges and professional schools—regularly stress that much of what they gained from their educational experience came from what they learned from their fellow students. The recruitment of minority students is one part of the search for diversity, but so is the admission of students who can participate actively in a broad array of athletic, artistic, and other extracurricular activities that will enrich undergraduate life and expose students to new experiences.

- The third principal consideration is to attract students who seem especially likely to utilize their education to make valuable or distinctive contributions to their professions and to the welfare of society. Colleges and universities receive an exemption from taxation because they serve a social purpose. Educational institutions have long made deliberate efforts to attract and educate students capable of making a difference and contributing something special to society. Before the turn of the century, Jane Stanford declared that the "chief object" of the new university she had helped to found was "the instruction of students with a view to producing leaders in every field of science and industry." Today, almost every selective college and professional school makes a similar claim.

- The fourth consideration is to respect the importance of long-term institutional loyalties and traditions. Almost all selective institutions give some advantage in the admissions process to applicants whose parents or other family members attended the institution (often called "legacies") and many also pay special attention to applications from children of faculty and staff. At least one highly selective institution that seeks to retain strong roots in its community is said to give greater preference to applicants from local public high schools than to any other special group (Bowen & Bok, 1998, pp. 23–24).

Private institutions have a very real and very significant interest in protecting their current right to determine who is admitted to and who receives financial assistance from their institutions. Theodore Cross, editor of *The Journal of Blacks in Higher Education*, puts forth a persuasive rationale for the absence of litigation against selective private institutions' use of race-sensitive admissions policies. In his article "Why the Opponents of Racial Preferences Haven't Taken America's Private Universities to Court" (1999), he offers the following reasons:

- It would be the mother of all lawsuits. To take on one Ivy League institution is to take on all of them. Cross predicts that the huge financial resources at the disposal of such selective institutions will cause most conservative private litigators, and those with limited budgets, to pause.

The reputations of such institutions as icons in their communities are also deterrents to litigation. Their track records are such that when you pick a fight with them, you lose.

- The law treats private institutions differently than public institutions. The Fourteenth Amendment prohibits states from denying persons equal protection of the laws. On its face, at least, it appears that affirmative action at private institutions would have to be challenged on the basis of some statute, government regulation, or judicial precedent. Cross argues that under Title VI of the Civil Rights Act of 1964, there is no clear judicial authority applying the Equal Protection Clause to admissions at private universities. He insists this is true despite the fact that virtually all private institutions receive substantial amounts of federal assistance through tuition support and other aid. There is no clear precedent that would make such institutions "state actors" and treat them as state agencies for purposes of applying the Fourteenth Amendment because they receive federal financial assistance. When dealing with statutory construction, moreover, courts have tended to support programs intended to increase minority representation in areas of underrepresentation. Cross cites the Supreme Court's decision in *United Steelworkers v. Weber* (1979) as a classic example of construing a federal statute (Title VII in this case). The statute was construed as permitting the use of race in employment decisions in order to forbid the very evil that Congress was intending to prevent—to wit, the denial of employment opportunity to African-Americans. State schools are easier targets because arguments about race can rest on clearer constitutional language.

- The courts have a passion for private decision-making. The author points out that the Rehnquist court has shown a propensity toward protecting the freedom and autonomy of private individuals and institutions. Private institutions may, under such a philosophy, retain their freedom to adopt admissions policies they deem best suited for their educational needs. The court's protection of private choice could quite logically result in an interpretation that private institutions are free to use race-sensitive admissions policies.

- There is a gap based on race in standardized test scores and grades of students admitted to private institutions. The gap at private institutions such as Harvard, notes the author, tends to be smaller than the gap at public institutions. In such cases, the court could easily affirm the 1978 *Bakke* ruling, permitting race as a consideration in admissions decisions when other qualifications are more or less equal. Opponents of affirmative action are much more likely to choose a case that presents a factual record that more starkly affirms their argument that such programs are unfair to large numbers of better-qualified white students.

- Counting the likely votes on the Supreme Court is not a sure thing. Based on their past voting records, the author predicts that Justices

Rehnquist, Kennedy, Scalia, and Thomas would vote against race-based admissions programs. He predicts Justices Breyer, Ginsburg, Souter, and Stevens would support race-based admissions programs. O'Connor, he asserts, would likely break the tie in favor of race-based admissions programs, given her positive comments regarding the use of race to promote diversity.

In summary, Bowen and Bok found that contrary to perception, the use of race in the admissions processes of selective institutions of higher education have, over the last 20 years, been highly successful. The data overwhelmingly demonstrate that minority students admitted to selective schools had strong academic credentials, graduated in large numbers and did very well after leaving college. By every measure of success (graduation, attainment of professional degrees, employment, earnings, civic participation, and overall satisfaction), the more selective the school, the more Blacks achieved (holding constant their initial test scores and grades). This evidence dispels the notion that the consideration of race in admission to selective institutions has done a disservice to minority students by placing them in schools in which they are unable to compete. While it is true that there remains a gap in the graduation rates of minority and majority students, such a gap is not explained by minority students' inability to complete the curriculum at selective schools. In fact, the graduation rates of Black students are substantially *higher* at selective institutions—75 percent of Black students graduated within 6 years from the school they first entered, as compared with the 40 percent of Blacks and 59 percent of whites who graduated from the 305 schools across the country tracked by the National Collegiate Athletic Association.

There is also no evidence (again contrary to prevalent misperceptions) that the consideration of race in the admissions process stigmatizes minority students. Black graduates of the most selective schools are the most satisfied with their college experience. Over 90 percent of both Blacks and whites reported that they were satisfied or very satisfied with their college experience. Moreover, almost 80 percent of white students favored either retaining the current emphasis on a diverse student body or emphasizing it more. Even white students who had been rejected by their first-choice school, and who might therefore be prone to oppose diversity efforts, supported an emphasis on diversity just as strongly as students who were admitted to their first-choice schools (Bowen & Bok, 1998).

The depth, breadth, and quality of the research conducted by Bowen and Bok are likely to be cited far and wide in support of race-sensitive admissions policies. By demonstrating that such policies not only significantly benefit minority students but also enrich the experiences of all students while causing only a slight impact on the opportunities for white students, many of the objections have been relegated to so much smoke and mirrors. Cross's prediction that selective private institutions are not likely litigation targets may add a level of comfort to those committed to continuing their student affirmative action policies and programs.

The Future of Affirmative Action in
College Admissions and Financial Aid

"The Quota Bashers Come in from the Cold" stated the article written by Brent Staples and published in *The New York Times* (1998). The author quoted a recent survey by *The Chronicle of Higher Education* that found legislatures from South Carolina to South Dakota back-pedaling furiously from California-style proposals in the wake of a feared and unintended "white out." The abrupt drop in Black and Latino enrollments in California raised the specter of a return to "whites only" times, not just on college campuses but also in the professions and in the next generation of state leadership. Californians themselves are looking for ways to undo the mess Proposition 209 created. According to the author, the emerging consensus is that special admissions measures must remain intact until urban schools do better by Black and brown students, who currently have little chance of first-rate preparation for college.

As further evidence of the changing tide of public perception, Staples notes the dramatic change in the viewpoints of ultra-conservative sociologist Nathan Glazer. Twenty years ago Glazer argued that taking race into account in hiring and college admissions was morally wrong and socially corrosive. Today Glazer has changed his mind about affirmative action, conceding that his presumption that African-Americans would soon be absorbed by the mainstream and afforded an equal opportunity at school proved false.

Katzenbach and Marshall argue in their article that the use of the term "preference" in relation to race is unfortunate because critics use it to imply that some kind of racial bias is used to reject better-qualified whites (Katzenbach & Marshall, 1998). In reality, of course, most of the students admitted are white. The authors candidly point out that the argument against "preferences" is that they are antimerit and discriminate against whites with higher scores on admissions tests. Only if admissions decisions were based solely on test scores would the argument have any real merit. Admissions decisions are rarely based exclusively on test scores, however, and whites would lose certain advantages, such as preferences for legacies, if such a limitation were ever imposed. Affirmative action programs, whether to correct present or past discrimination, are race-based. They have to be. The problems they seek to cure are, and always have been, race-based.

It should be understandably perplexing to African-Americans that the Fourteenth Amendment, which was designed to ensure that former slaves and their descendants would receive the same legal protection as white citizens, is now being used by affirmative action opponents to limit opportunities and to secure even more tightly the rights of whites. Reading the Equal Protection Clause of the Fourteenth Amendment as protecting whites as well as Blacks is to address a situation that never existed in America. "It is very nearly as if this Court has simply mandated that what is the country's historic struggle against racial oppression and racial prejudice cannot be acted upon in a race-conscious way—that the law must view racial problems observable by all as if oppression and prejudice did not exist and had never existed" (Katzenbach & Marshall, 1998, p. 45).

The University of Michigan is currently embroiled in two important court battles over affirmative action in admissions. One lawsuit, filed by Jennifer Gratz and Patrick Hamacher as a class action, is a complaint involving admission to the University of Michigan College of Literature, Science & Arts in Ann Arbor for the academic year 1995–1996 (*Gratz and Hamacher v. Bollinger*, 1997). The other lawsuit was filed by Barbara Grutter as a class action complaint involving admission to the University of Michigan Law School for the academic year 1997–1998 (*Grutter v. Bollinger*, 1997). The University has enlisted a large number of eminent scholars as expert witnesses in support of the need for and benefit derived from diversity. Current students have intervened to prove that the University of Michigan has a history of discrimination with effects that linger into the present. Lawsuits against the University are funded by the Center for Individual Rights, the organization that funded the *Hopwood* case in Texas. The University has vowed to defend its admissions practices vigorously. A great deal of up-to-date information on the cases can be found on its web site (University of Michigan, 2000). Proponents of affirmative action in admission are engaging in unprecedented collaboration to persuade the federal court in Michigan to rule favorably on the admissions programs at the University of Michigan.

Harvard University President Neil L. Rudenstine published a comprehensive report on diversity and learning. He argued that the most constructive and well-conceived admissions programs are those that view affirmative action in relation to the educational benefits of diversity. He acknowledged that they may take various characteristics such as race, ethnicity, or gender into account as potential "plus" factors (among many others) when evaluating candidates, but they do not assign such characteristics an overriding value. "Nor do they aim to achieve specific numerical targets, either through the use of set-asides or quotas. They involve energetic efforts in outreach, but not mandated outcomes. Programs of this kind, when they are carefully designed and implemented, preserve an institution's capacity—with considerable flexibility—to make its own determinations in admissions. This capacity and flexibility have been critical in the past, and will continue to be so in the future" (Rudenstine, 1996).

There is ample legal support for affirmative action in admission and financial aid to recruit and retain disadvantaged students of all races, to remedy the present effects of past discrimination, and to achieve racial and ethnic diversity. Title VI of the Civil Rights Act has, at its very core, the intent to prohibit discrimination on the basis of race and to promote the rights of racial minorities to educational opportunities that were historically denied outright or seriously restricted. According to OCR guidelines, states that practiced *de jure* segregation have an affirmative duty to eliminate past discrimination and all its vestiges. The Office for Civil Rights in the United States Department of Education has provided clear guidance as to what can and cannot be done within the law. Race and national origin may be taken into account as "plus" factors in admissions and financial aid programs at institutions of higher education, whether public or private, if the programs are:

- Narrowly tailored to achieve appropriate, flexible diversity goals
- Without unnecessarily trammeling the rights of others by eliminating or unduly restricting competition
- Where race or national origin are not the only factors used for decision-making purposes, but are included among other legitimate factors—such as test scores, grades, and economic need
- With fair assessment of applicants against established criteria
- And periodic program review and evaluation to determine continuing need with, or without, modification

Empirical evidence that a program in narrowly tailored to achieve a legitimate objective of the university will become increasingly important in defending student affirmative action programs against court challenges. In addition to the Bowen and Bok study, the American Council on Education (ACE) has published an important report of research studies. The report is entitled "Does Diversity Make a Difference? Three Research Studies on Diversity in College Classrooms" (American Council on Education, 2000, "Higher Education and National Affairs"). The evidence presented in the report demonstrates that campus diversity benefits all students, white as well as minority, and that those benefits cannot be duplicated in a racially and ethnically homogeneous academic environment. It concludes that efforts at diversity, therefore, can be viewed not only as a means of providing equal opportunity, but also as critical academic tools in providing students the best education possible. The report is cited in ACE's comprehensive publication, "Making the Case for Affirmative Action in Higher Education" (American Council on Education, 2000). That publication is a collection of research studies, surveys, advocacy letters, legal analyses, and position statements that support diversity and affirmative action in higher education.

ACE reports that diversity in student bodies, faculty and staff is essential to fulfill the primary mission of institutions of higher education, providing a high-quality education. Among the reasons given for such strong support of diversity are:

- Diversity enriches the educational experience. We learn from individuals with experiences, beliefs, and perspectives that are different from our own.
- Diversity promotes personal growth and a healthy society. It challenges stereotypes, promotes critical thinking, and encourages more effective communication.
- Diversity strengthens communities and the workplace. It prepares students to become good citizens in an increasingly complex and pluralistic society, fostering mutual respect and teamwork.
- Diversity enhances America's economic competitiveness. Making effective use of the talents and abilities of all citizens will be required to sustain the nation's prosperity into the twenty-first century.

ACE urges freedom for colleges and universities to continue to reach out and make a conscious effort to build healthy and diverse learning environments appropriate to their mission.

Building specific diversity programs must be tailored with due consideration to legal parameters and to the unique culture and academic considerations found at each individual institution. A detailed discussion of programs to achieve student diversity is beyond the scope of this chapter. Aside from the duly noted legal constraints, only the resources institutions are willing to commit to the effort limit the characteristics of individual programs. The literature is replete with examples of diversity programs. A search of ACE's web site and its links to others will yield a wealth of information on specific affirmative action programs to achieve diversity. So will conducting a search over the Internet of the key word "diversity."

While the future of affirmative action per se as a favored phrase may be uncertain, there appears to be a great deal of support in the public domain for racial and ethnic diversity. That there is value in learning about other cultures cannot be seriously disputed. That experience is a great teacher is still a truism. Eminent scholars have concluded that student diversity enriches the entire university community, with society the ultimate beneficiary. The difficulties with achieving diversity tend to lie, not in acknowledging its value, but in determining the manner in which it is to be achieved.

References

American Association of State Colleges and Universities. (1998, February). The move to end affirmative action: Making race a four-letter word. Retrieved February, 1998 from the World Wide Web: http://www.aascu. org/news/memo/archive/9802themove.html.

American Council on Education. (2000, June 15). Higher education and national affairs. Does diversity make a difference? Three research studies on diversity in college classrooms. Vol. 49, No. 10 (05/29/00). Retrieved June 15, 2000 from the World Wide Web: http://www. acenet.edu/hena/issues/2000/05_29_00/diversity.html.

American Council on Education. (2000, June 15). Making the case for affirmative action in higher education. ACEnet. Retrieved June 15, 2000 from the World Wide Web: http://www.acenet.edu/bookstore/descriptions/making_the_case/home.html.

Bowen, William G., & Bok, Derek. (1998). *The shape of the river: Long-term consequences of considering race in college and university admissions.* Princeton, NJ. Princeton University Press.

Bruni, Frank. (1998, May 3). Black students may prefer to say no to Berkeley. *The New York Times.*

Cantu, Norma (Assistant Secretary, U.S. Department of Education, Office for Civil Rights). (1997, April 11). Letter to the Honorable Rodney Ellis, U.S. Senator-Texas. Retrieved April 1997 from the World Wide Web: http://www.ed.gov/offices/OCR/hopwood.html.

Cross, Theodore. (1999, Summer). Why the opponents of racial preferences haven't taken America's private universities to court. *The Journal of Blacks in Higher Education.*

34 C. F. R. pt. 100. (1994).

59 Fed. Reg. 8756. (1994).

Georgia State Conference of Branches of NAACP v. State of Georgia, 775 F.2d 1403, 1418 11th Cir. (1985).

Gratz and Hamacher v. Bollinger. Civil Action #97-75231. USD.C., E.D. Mich. (1997).

Green v. County School Board of New Kent County, 391 U.S. 430, 438. (1968).

Grutter v. Bollinger. Civil Action #97-75928. USD.C., E.D. Mich. (1997).

Guardians Association v. Civil Service Commission of the City of New York, 463 U.S. 582. (1983); 34 CFR 100.3 (b) (2).

Hazelwood School District v. United States, 433 U.S. 299. (1977).

Hopwood v. Texas, 78 F. 3d 932 (5th Cir. 1996), cert. denied, 116 S. Ct. 2581. (1996).

Jackson, Gary D., OCR Region X Director. (1992, September 25). Letter: Attached Voluntary Conciliation and Settlement Agreement in OCR

Case No. 10906001 signed by the Assistant Secretary for Civil Rights, U.S. Department of Education, the Chancellor of the University of California at Berkeley, the Region X Director of OCR, and the Dean of the School of Law at the University of California at Berkeley.

Johnson, Constance A. (1999, July 22). Legal maneuvering: Law schools struggle to produce despite affirmative action bans. *Black Issues in Higher Education, 16*(10).

Katzenbach, Nicholas deB., & Marshall, Burke. (1998, February 22). Not color blind: Just blind. *The New York Times Magazine.*

McDaniel v. Barresi, 402 U.S. 39. (1971).

Minority numbers down at Washington law school. (1999, July 22). News brief in *Black Issues in Higher Education, 16*(10), 14.

Palomino, John E. (OCR Regional Director). (1995, September 8). Letter to UCLA Chancellor Charles E. Young. Docket No. 09-89-6003.

Podberesky v. Kirwan, 38 F. 3d 147 (4th Cir. 1994), *cert. den.,* 115 S. Ct. 2001. (1995).

Regents of the University of California v. Bakke, 265 U.S. 469. (1978).

Richmond v. J. A. Croson Co., 488 U.S. 469. (1989).

Riley, Richard (Secretary, U.S. Department of Education). (1997, March 19). Letter to "Dear Colleagues." Retrieved March 1997 from the World Wide Web: http://www.ed.gov/offices/OCR/prop209.html.

Rudenstine, Neil I. (1996, January). The president's report 1993–1995. Harvard University.

Shannon, Barbra (Acting Director, Atlanta Office Southern Division, Office for Civil Rights). (1997, February 2). Letter of Resolution to Mr. John C. Scully, Counsel, Washington Legal Foundation. Complaint # 04-90-2067. Retrieved February 1997 from the World Wide Web: http://www.ed.gov/offices/OCR/fau.html.

Singer Sutherland Statutory Construction. Section 46. 05, 5th ed. (1992).

Staples, Brent. (1998, April 12). The quota bashers come in from the cold. *The New York Times.*

Stephens, Angela. (1999, February 18). Fighting back the chill. *Black Issues in Higher Education, 15* (26).

Swan v. Charlotte-Mecklenburg Board of Education, 402 U.S. 1, 15-16 (1971).

Title VI, Civil Rights Act of 1964, 42 U.S.C. § 2000d *et seq.*

United States v. Fordice, 112 S. Ct. 2727. (1992).

United States v. Fordice, 505 U.S. 717. (1992).

United States v. Paradise, 480 U.S. 149, 167. (1987).

United Steelworkers v. Weber, 443 U.S. 193. (1979).

University of Michigan lawsuits. Retrieved May, 2000 from the World Wide Web: http://www.umich.edu/~urel/admissions/legal.

University of Texas system news and public information. (1999, September 3). Retrieved September 1999 from the World Wide Web: http://www.etsystem,edy/news/dailyclips/hopwood%20response.html.

U.S. Department of Education, Office for Civil Rights. (1994, January). F. R. Doc. 94-2042. Notice of application of Supreme Court decision. Retrieved January 1994 from the World Wide Web: http://www.ed.gov/offices/OCR/fordice.html.

Winston, Judith A. (General Counsel, U.S. Education Department, Office for Civil Rights). (1995, September 7). Letter to "Dear College and University Counsel." Retrieved September 1995 from the World Wide Web: http://www.nacua.org/documents/winston_letter.html.

Wygant v. Jackson Board of Education, 476 U.S. 267. (1986).

CHAPTER 3

Affirmative Action Retrenchment and Labor Market Outcomes for African-American Faculty

SAMUEL L. MYERS JR. AND CAROLINE S. TURNER

Introduction

Conventional wisdom has it that the growth in minority faculty hiring and promotion during the epoch of the 1970s can be attributed to affirmative action (Schneider, 1998). During the era of the 1980s, overall employment of faculty increased and the minority share of the total also increased. Specifically, the number of faculty in United States' institutions of higher education increased 14.2 percent between 1980 and 1990, while the representation of minorities (African American, Hispanic, American Indian, and Asian American) in the faculty population increased from 9 percent in 1980 to 11 percent in 1990 (National Center for Education Statistics, 1991, cited in Aguirre, 1995). The logic that affirmative action was one of the catalysts for this growth stems from the fact that many state institutions were under court orders to integrate their faculty, and the mechanism for implementing the court orders often was an explicit affirmative action plan. Following this logic, for example, the American Association of University Professors in 1973 endorsed affirmative action in faculty hiring and charged the professorate with promoting diversity to remedy past discrimination (Turner & Myers, 1997).

In recent years, however, there has been considerable retrenchment in support for affirmative action. Beginning with *City of Richmond v. J. A. Croson Co.* (1989) the Supreme Court's ruling dismantling affirmative action in public procurement and contracting, and followed by Court of Appeals reversals in the *Podberesky v. Kirwan* (1994) and *Hopwood v. Texas* (1996) cases, 25 states introduced anti–affirmative action legislation between 1992 and 1998. Such legislation has been designed to eliminate race-preferences in state employment, public contracting and procurement, and admissions and scholarships in higher education. Many of these were offered as constitutional amendments, and all included prohibitions on the use of race preferences in education. The retrenchment effort has also manifested itself in grassroots ballot initiatives, such as California's Proposition 209 and Washington State's ballot initiative, I-200, known as the Washington State Civil Rights Initiative. These ballot initiatives circumvent the legislative process and go directly to the voters in efforts to dismantle affirmative action and race preferences.

If conventional wisdom has it that affirmative action has helped to con-tribute to the increase in minority faculty during the 1970s and 1980s, what can be said about the potential impacts of affirmative action *retrenchment* on minority faculty prospects in the future? This chapter explores the question by looking both at the quantitative evidence on the determinants of minority faculty representation and at the qualitative evidence on the experiences that minority faculty are facing during the affirmative action retrenchment era.

We explore the question in some detail with respect to African American faculty and conclude that in states with anti–affirmative action retrenchment initiatives underway during the period of 1992–1996, the growth of Black faculty representation was lower than it was in those states without affirmative action retrenchment efforts. To reach this conclusion, however, we recognize that the ultimate issue is the role played by threats to white privilege as a contributing to factor in the dismantling of affirmative action and in the changing fortunes faced by minority faculty. Meaning is given to the empiri-cal evidence by our qualitative documentation of a rising hostile racial envi-ronment faced by faculty of color and the increasing perceptions by white scholars that minority faculty have gained unearned advantages. What is remarkable about our qualitative evidence is that many of the respondents are tenured faculty and thus are less likely to claim racial bias as an excuse for nonpromotion. Repeatedly, our respondents indicate that no matter how tal-ented, innovative, productive, or creative they may be, there remain doubts about their qualifications.

This essay is divided into six parts. The first part provides some back-ground context of the problems of hiring, tenure and promotion, and retention of faculty of color. The second section conjectures that the demand for mi-nority faculty is a function of minority student enrollments. If there were a decline in minority student enrollments, a reduced demand for minority fac-ulty would ensue. A third section explores the issue of a shortage of minority PhDs. If there were a decline in the production of minority doctorates, a shortage of minority faculty would arise. A fourth section examines empiri-cally the issue of anti–affirmative action initiatives and African-American tenure rates and African-American faculty representation. A penultimate sec-tion places the quantitative evidence into perspective, reporting results from interviews with minority faculty at a major research university. We conclude with our assessment of the overall impacts that affirmative action retrench-ment has had on minority faculty labor markets.

Background

Some would say that higher education has made significant progress in the promotion and tenure of faculty of color over the years. As a result, these voices claim, it does no good to hash over the past. These voices contend that they do not wish to revisit the historical legacy of exclusion. Such silence, however, obscures an important reality. Despite unambiguous improvements over the years, significant underrepresentation of faculty of color remains (Turner, Myers, & Creswell, 1998; Turner & Myers, 2000). The evidence shows that faculty of color continue to be persistently underrepresented among the professorate, and that subtle discrimination in the academic workplace is one of the proximate causes (Turner & Myers, 2000).

There are well-known exclusionary barriers to entry into higher education. Blauner (1972) and Weinberg (1977) and others point out that exclusion at the earliest stages of education carry forward to higher education. As Weinberg (1977) relates:

> Since its earliest beginnings, the American public school system has been deeply committed to the maintenance of racial and ethnic barriers. Higher education, both public and private, shared this outlook. Philosophers of the common schools remained silent about the education of minority children . . . White educators profited from the enforced absence of Black and other minority competitors for jobs. Planned deprivation became a norm of educational practice. (p. 1)

Robert Blauner characterized this exclusion as resulting from institutionalized racism. He contended that "the University is racist because people of color are and have been so systematically excluded from full and equal participation and power—as students, professors, administrators, and particularly, in the historical definition of the character of the institution and its curriculum" (1972, p. 277).

Not all analysts blame racism for the continued exclusion of racial and ethnic minority group members from higher education. But that has not prevented faculty of color from challenging what they perceive to be a racially hostile climate rooted in a newer form of racism that is less overt and more difficult to weed out. Continuing evidence of racially hostile campus incidents, repeated examples of hate speech on campus, and a significant minority of opposition to multicultural curricula have helped fuel lawsuits filed by faculty of color contesting tenure and promotion decisions (LaNoue & Lee, 1987; Leap, 1995). At least from the perspective of many faculty of color, the racially hostile campus climate can translate to adverse tenure and promotion decisions. Njeri (1989) relates one example of tenure denied on the basis of racial discrimination, *Clark v. Claremont University Center* (1992), in which a California court awarded the plaintiff $1.4 million—a verdict upheld by the state Court of Appeals. Leap (1995) calls this case "one of the most flagrant and costly examples of intentional discrimination" (p. 124). In his review of court cases relating to tenure and discrimination, Leap (1995) observes:

> The pressures associated with achieving tenure are even more intense for faculty who must deal with discrimination linked to racial, sexist, or other prejudices . . . The process of reappointment, promotion, and tenure at many colleges and universities is surrounded in uncertainty, a condition that is conducive to surreptitious discrimination. (p. 3)

The paradox here is that evidence of continuing racial discrimination and a racially hostile climate is matched by evidence of continued—although slight—growth in the representation of racial minority group members among tenured and tenure track faculty. Carter and Wilson (1996) document the increases in the number of full-time faculty of color since the mid-1980s, even while they caution "persons of color remain severely underrepresented among college and university faculty. They accounted for 12.2 percent of all full-time faculty and for just 9.2 percent of full professors in 1993" (p. 33). They also caution that tenure rates have declined in recent years. Thus, the evidence appears less to support the idea of total exclusion of racial and ethnic minority group members and more to support the idea that while they do have their feet in the academic door, their lives may be more miserable.

This is a paradox that we explore in the next sections of the chapter. Our exploration of how minority numbers can be increasing at the same time that there are intensified aspects of racism and a racially hostile climate are prompted by reports such as one entitled "Race and Ethnicity in the American Professorate, 1995–1996" by Astin et al. (1997) showing improvements in minority faculty representation. Astin, quoted in an article by Schneider (1997), added in surprise: "I was expecting the picture to look brighter . . . The proportion of minority professors is so small that they're invisible in so many ways" (p. A–13). She continued that, compared with white faculty, faculty of color, including Asian-American faculty, are "less satisfied" with nearly every aspect of their jobs—autonomy/independence, professional relations with faculty, overall job satisfaction, opportunity to develop new ideas (compared with all other respondents, Asian-Americans were least satisfied on this factor), job security, and quality of students. The analysis reveals continued experiences of workplace discrimination and concerns about racial discrimination in the tenure and promotion process. These factors, the authors contend, contribute to high levels of stress among faculty of color. The overwhelming consensus of these and other studies is that faculty of color experience (or believe they experience) subtle forms of discrimination in higher-education institutions (Carter & O'Brien, 1993; Milem & Astin, 1993; Pavel, Swisher, & Ward, 1994; Turner, Myers, & Creswell, 1999; Turner and Myers, 2000).

The Derived Demand for Minority Faculty

Consider this conceptual framework for characterizing minority faculty hiring in the affirmative action era: Colleges and universities, having opened their doors to members of historically underrepresented minority group members, were confronted with growing pressure—often from students themselves—to hire more minority faculty. These faculty were sought to provide role models, to enhance diversity, and to fulfill the University's commitment to employment equality. At the same time, increases in minority enrollments expand the pool of minority talent from which doctoral institutions can draw and thereby stimulate the production of minority PhDs. The resulting increase in minority PhDs. provides the supply from which hiring institutions can draw to meet their demand for minority faculty. This conceptual framework, depicted in Figure 3.1, suggests a feedback relationship between the growth in minority student populations and minority faculty representation. The factors that contribute to the gain in minority student presence on college campuses is also hypothesized to contribute to greater demand for minority faculty. Either directly or indirectly, presence of minority students ought to boost the numbers of minority faculty.

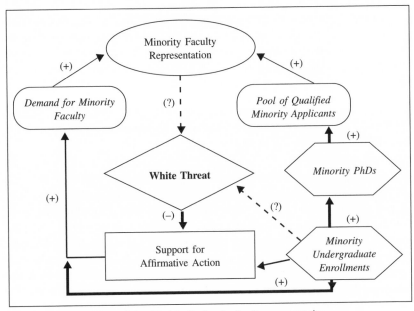

Figure 3.1.   Model of minority faculty representation.

One factor that may play an intervening role, however, is the threat to white male privilege associated with both the growth in minority enrollments and the rise in minority faculty representation. While a larger minority presence may increase greater awareness and understanding among students and faculty and promote diversity and cultural sensitivity, it is also possible that minority presence might stimulate greater hostility from whites that may perceive losses in their stronghold on the academy. For example, in an analysis of the 1993 National Study of Postsecondary Faculty Survey, Finkelstein, Seal, and Schuster (1998) note that new faculty cohorts are much more diverse than those of previous generations. They indicate that the most dramatic growth has not been in the numbers of women entering the professorate but a growth in the representation of faculty of color, especially Asian males, as well as an increase of foreign nationals that suggests the growing diversification of a once-homogenous faculty. They state, "For the senior cohort of faculty, 58.6 percent are native born white males...while the new faculty cohort consists of 43.2 percent native-born white males." This is significant because the new cohort is very large, constituting one third of the current faculty (p. 102). Thus, increased minority representation in theory could promote the very backlash that might contribute to reductions in support for affirmative action, thereby curtailing future growth in minority representation. Support for this thesis would come from evidence showing that affirmative action retrenchment efforts may be higher in places where there is a greater presence of minority faculty.

Another pathway toward the representation of minority faculty described in Figure 3.1 is the effect of minority student growth. The first question we descriptively ask is whether this linkage between minority student presence and minority faculty presence is weakened during the post–Affirmative Action era.

What Is the Effect of Minority Student Enrollments on Minority Faculty Presence?

There has been a steady rise in minority student enrollments since the 1970s. Minority student enrollment in institutions of higher education rose from 1.7 million in 1976 to 3.5 million in 1995 (U.S. Dept. of Education, 1997). The period from the 1970s until the 1990s reveals a more complex reality; however, Figure 3.2 plots the annual average rates of growth in enrollments for all minority students, and within each minority group. The Asian/Pacific Islander enrollment growth rate exceeds that of all other racial minority groups. Their high rates, in the range of 9 to 12 percent in the era before the 1990s, fell to around 3 percent by 1995. Hispanic enrollment growth rates also fell in the 1990s to around 5 percent after reaching 10 percent in the early 1990s. The Hispanic student annual average enrollment growth rate was 5.7 percent from 1976 to 1980, 6.6 percent from 1980 to 1990, and 10 percent from 1990 to 1991 and once again from 1991 to 1992. American Indian enrollment growth rates remained low throughout the period at around 3 percent, but with a surge between 1990 and 1991. African-American enrollment growth rates, the lowest of all, were less than 2 percent throughout the 1980s, saw a spurt to 7 percent in 1991, and then declined by 1995 to 1.7 percent. Overall, however, it is clear that the growth rates fell for all minority groups in the 1990s.

The onset of the decline, therefore, appears to be at the start of the dismantlement of affirmative action. Although many of the most important barriers to race-conscious admissions policies such as Washington State's affirmative action ballot initiative and California's Proposition 209 had not yet materialized by 1992, it is evident that the seeds of retrenchment had already taken place long before it was formalized in ballot initiatives.

Although enrollments were declining among minority students, degrees awarded continued unabated. Among whites, however, the growth in degrees awarded declined. This fall in the percentage rate of growth in white college degrees is central to understanding the backlash against affirmative action on college campuses. Whites perceived that they were losing ground.

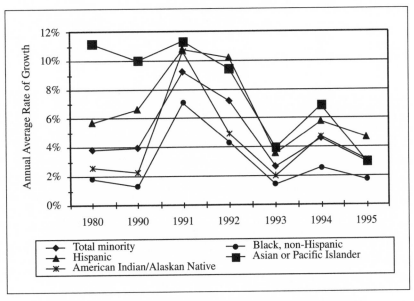

Figure 3.2. Declining growth in enrollments of minorities, 1976–1995.

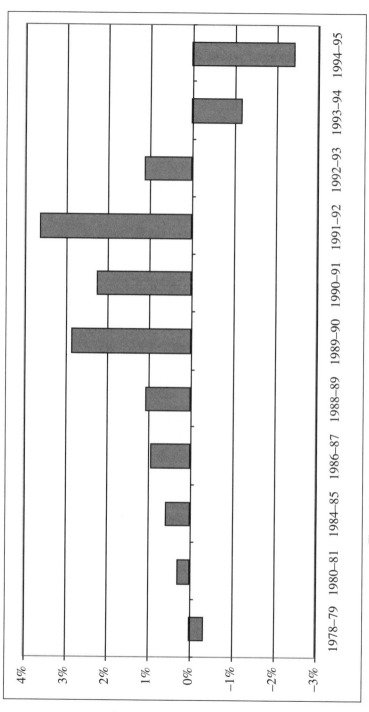

Figure 3.3. White bachelor's degrees awarded, annual rate of growth, 1976–1995.

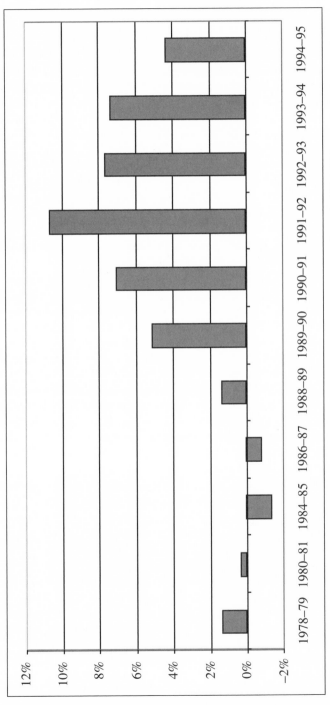

Figure 3.4. Black bachelor's degrees awarded annual, average rate of growth, 1976–1995.

White Threat

Figure 3.3 shows that from academic years 1976–77 to 1978–1979 the annual rate of growth in white bachelor's degrees awarded declined by about 3 percent. There were 807,688 white bachelor's degrees awarded in 1976–77; there were 802,542 white bachelor's degrees awarded in 1978–79. By 1980, graduations had recovered when 807,319 white bachelor's degrees were awarded. The numbers rose to 826,106 in 1984–1985 and again to 884,376 in 1989–1990. But by the early 1990s, the growth in bachelor's degrees declined. For the years 1991–1992 through 1994–1995 the numbers were: 936,771, 947,309, 936,227, and 913,377, reflecting annual average growth rates of 3.6, 1.1, –1.2, and –2.4 percent. Put simply, whites were falling behind during the early and mid-1990s.

It is important to appreciate this decline in white graduations from college when examining affirmative action retrenchment. Widening earnings gaps between those at the top and those at the bottom of the income distribution assure that significant premia persist for those with college degrees.[1]

For African-Americans, the situation was a bit different. Although they too saw a decline in the growth of bachelor's degrees awarded, the decline began later for them and the net effects of the declines were not as deleterious. For them, each year from the mid-1980s on saw higher numbers of graduates than the year before, as is seen in Figure 3.4. The annual average rate of growth in the award of bachelor's degrees to African-Americans, while negative in the 1980s, rose to a high of nearly 11 percent in the early 1990s, the years of the onset of the dismantling of affirmative action. Even though the rate of growth fell to around 4 percent by the mid-1990s, it still was positive in comparison with the declining fortunes of whites.

To understand more starkly the perceived threat to white economic security, observe in Figure 3.5 the rates of growth among non-Black minority bachelor's degrees. This figure shows that except for American Indians, a consistent positive rate of growth in the production of non-Black minorities persisted throughout the 1990s.

Thus, during a period when white fortunes were on the decline, there was a steady stream of minorities graduating from college. Even among Blacks, whose growth rates slowed, there continued to be a positive rate of growth in the production of bachelor's degrees in the midst of white declines. If whites perceived that affirmative action was robbing them of educational opportunities, they only had to look at the growth rates in degrees awarded by race. Asians, Hispanics, and to a lesser degree American Indians and African Americans were outpacing whites in the educational marketplace. White writers certainly acknowledged the decline in white bachelor's degrees.

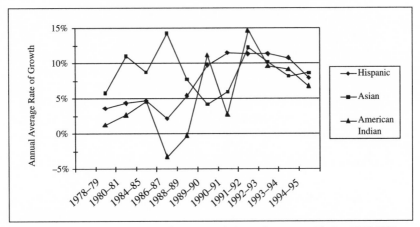

Figure 3.5. Minority bachelors degrees awarded growth rate, non-Blacks, 1976–1995.

The argument linking minority faculty hiring and promotion to the presence of minority students requires this important qualification concerning the feedback effects on white threat: Looking simply at the relationship between minority students and affirmative action is not enough. Increases in minority student enrollments occurred at precisely the time when there was a dampening of minority faculty hiring.

The Supply of PhDs: The Case of African-Americans

One of the most persistent myths about why there are so few minority faculty is that there are not enough qualified minority candidates because of an undersupply of minority PhDs. For years department chairs and deans have argued, particularly in the case of African-Americans, that there is a dearth of minority PhDs. With most hiring at the junior level and with most junior level candidates drawn from the pool of new or recent PhDs, it stands to reason that if there is a decline or nonincreasing supply of minority PhDs, there will remain small pools of new applicants drawn from minority populations. It is almost a universally held wisdom that the underrepresentation of minority faculty stems from the underrepresentation of minorities among PhDs. In our recent book, we asked the top administrators of more than 700 colleges and universities in the Midwest about their beliefs concerning low Black faculty representation in their institutions. For each of the broad areas of arts and humanities, science and technology, social sciences, and the professions, we asked: *For your institution, what are the obstacles you believe exist for the recruitment of minority faculty?*

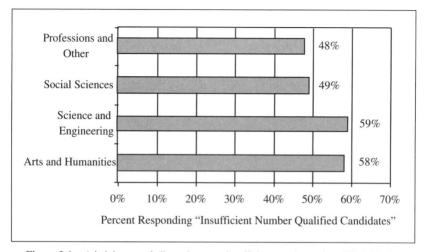

Figure 3.6. Administrators believe there are insufficient numbers of qualified Blacks. *Source: Turner and Myers, 2000.*

Overwhelmingly, administrators believe that the reason for the underrepresentation of African-American faculty is that there are an insufficient number of qualified Blacks. Whether the field is science and engineering, where 59 percent of respondents indicated there were insufficient numbers of qualified Blacks, or the professions, where 48 percent of respondents indicated that there were insufficient numbers of qualified Blacks, the same conclusion emerged. The top administrators at the Midwestern universities overwhelmingly believed that the reason for the difficulty in recruiting and retaining African-Americans was that there were too few qualified Blacks. This finding, which indeed is consistent with conventional beliefs about the underrepresentation of African-Americans in academia, must be tempered against recent evidence of a surge in the production of Black PhDs.

It is widely appreciated that from the 1970s until the 1980s there was a precipitous drop in the production of African-American doctorates. Total doctorate production among United States citizens in 1977 was 26,119. The African-American total was 1,113, or 4.3 percent of the total. The total production of African-American doctorates dropped to 771 in 1987, representing only 3.3 percent of all U.S. doctorates. In other words, the total and the share of Black doctorates fell during the 1980s.

What is much less well understood or appreciated is the resurgence in the numbers and share of African-Americans receiving doctorates during the 1990s. The total number of African-American PhDs awarded rose steadily during the late 1980s and early 1990s from 818 in 1988 to 1,010 in 1991. Moreover, the surge in African-American PhD production continued into the 1990s. From

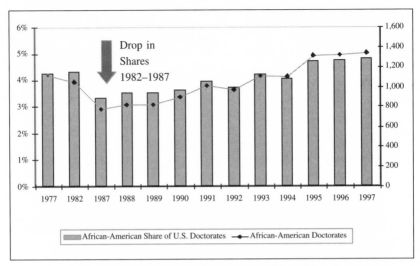

Figure 3.7.   African-American share and number of U.S. citizen doctorates.

1991 to 1997, the number of new Black PhDs increased from 1,010 to 1,335. Figure 3.7 shows that with only a slight drop in 1992, a recession year, the Black percentage of all U.S. citizen doctorates produced grew in the period 1991 to 1997, from 3.9 percent to 4.83 percent. While these numbers and percentages are still small, they do represent a significant rebounding during the 1990s, despite the nostalgic view held by administrators in our sample, who believed that there still were insufficient numbers of qualified African Americans. The inescapable conclusion emerging from Figure 3.7, showing the number and share of African-American doctorates among U.S. citizens, is that by the onset of the period of retrenchment in affirmative action, America was producing more and more Black scholars who were potential applicants for jobs in academia. Thus, the *excuse* often offered for the failure to recruit or retain Black faculty—that there are insufficient numbers of qualified applicants—is belied by the fact that Black doctorate production was on the upswing during the 1990s.

Possible Explanation for the Recent Growth in Black PhDs

Putting aside for the moment the fact that many administrators apparently were unaware of the surge in Black doctorate production, one plausible explanation for the upturn in Black PhD production is that it is a lagged response to the expansion in Black bachelor's degrees produced during the 1980s. Figures 3.8 and 3.9 show the production of Black male and female

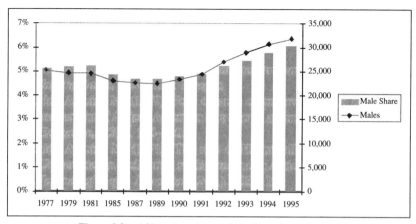

Figure 3.8.   African-American male undergraduate degrees.

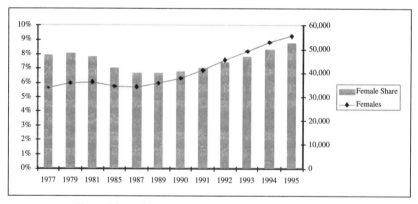

Figure 3.9.   African-American female undergraduate degrees.

undergraduate degrees from 1977 until 1995. Black male bachelor's degrees actually fell from 25,147 in 1977 to 22,370 in 1989. Their shares rose and then fell during the period of 1977–1989. Then their totals and shares rose during the 1990s, reaching 31,775 (6.1 percent of all male degrees) in 1995. Black female bachelor's degrees rose, leveled, and then rose again. The numbers were 33,489 in 1977, 36,162 in 1981, 35,708 in 1989, and 55,428 in 1995. Their shares fell and then rose again, reaching 8.7 percent in 1995.

Superimposing the undergraduate and graduate degree production graphs, we find that there is no discernable effect of *lagged* Black bachelor's degrees on Black PhDs. That is because the growth in PhDs occurred at approximately the same time as the upswing in bachelor's degrees for Black males and females. If the growth in Black bachelor's degrees were the cause of the

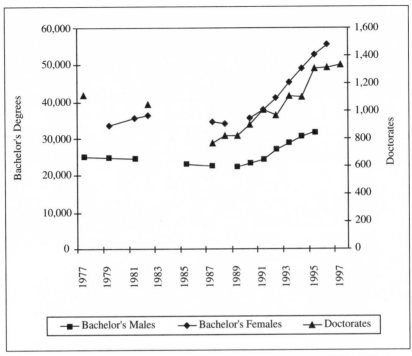

Figure 3.10. African-American bachelor's degrees and doctorates, 1977–1997.

growth in Black PhDs, and assuming it takes around 5 years to obtain a PhD, then the 5-year lagged bachelor's degree output should be positively corre-lated with the output of PhDs. As Figure 3.11 shows, however, the 5-year lagged bachelor's degree production is virtually unrelated to the PhD produc-tion. A linear regression reveals a coefficient not significantly different from zero.

The Underrepresentation of African-American Faculty

The largest number of faculty is found in public research universities. These universities represent both the standard-bearers for scholarship and research and the training grounds for most of the faculty in the next lower tiers of the academy. There were 107,358 faculty in these institutions in 1992. Only *1.5 percent* of these faculty were Black males; *1.2 percent* were Black females. These are the statistics that give rise to the claim of substantial underrepresentation of Blacks among faculty—given that together these groups account for nearly 5 percent of doctorates awarded in recent years.

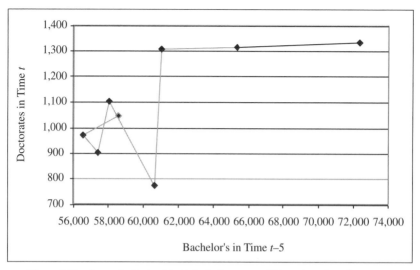

Figure 3.11. Lagged effects of bachelor's degrees on African-American doctorates.

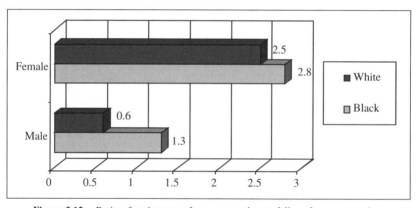

Figure 3.12. Ratio of assistant professor proportion to full professor proportion.

Source: U.S. Department of Education, National Center for Education Statistics, National Study of Postsecondary Faculty (NSOPF), 1993.

Shifting demographics within the academy, however, suggest a potential threat to white male dominance in higher education. Using data from the 1992 National Study of Postsecondary Faculty, it is possible to compute the relative representation of Blacks within the ranks by gender. Figure 3.12 shows the ratio of the proportion of female and male faculty by race that are assistant professors to their proportion among full professors. Black and white female faculty are several times more likely to be assistant professors than they are likely to be full professors. White male faculty are more likely to be full professors than they are likely to be assistant professors. While Black females are 2.8 times more likely to be assistant professors than full professors, white males are one-and-two-thirds times more likely to be full professors than assistant professors. In other words, despite the overall underrepresentation of African-American faculty, their underrepresentation is smaller at the lowest ranks. This reality must be understood when confronting the potential threats to white male dominance posed by affirmative action.

Affirmative Action Retrenchment and Minority Faculty

The potential threat to white male dominance that arises from affirmative action can be seen most easily by examining data on faculty age distributions in the 1992 National Study of Postsecondary Faculty. White males account for 70 percent of faculty over 60; they account for 39 percent of faculty under 30. That is to say, white males are concentrated among the older—and thus

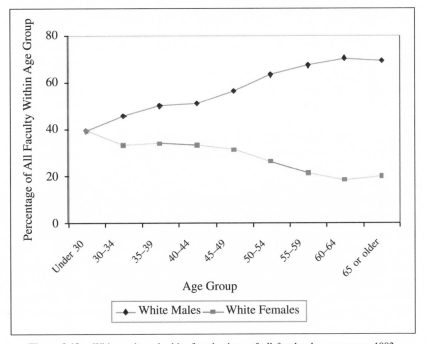

Figure 3.13.   White male and white female share of all faculty, by age group, 1992.

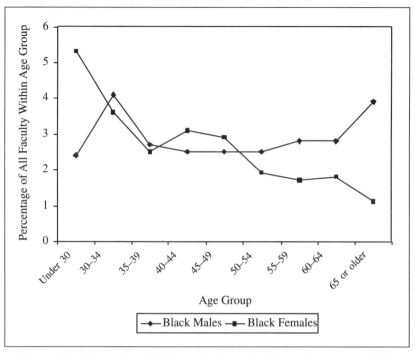

Figure 3.14.   Black male and Black female shares of all faculty, by age group, 1992.

more senior—members of the academy. They represent a *minority* among those at the other end of the distribution. White females, moreover, account for declining shares of older faculty and increasing shares of younger faculty. Figure 3.13 shows this pattern. Thus, although white males disproportionately occupy the most senior positions in the University, their share of all positions is declining. They are not poised to reproduce their historic hegemony in academia.

The age distribution for Blacks shows a similar pattern to that of white females. Figure 3.14 reveals that Black females make up disproportionately large numbers of younger faculty. If Black and white females get promoted, they—along with other nonwhite faculty—will displace white males in the years to come as tenured associate and full professors.

Figure 3.14 shows that Black females account for 5.3 percent of faculty under 30; they account for about 3 percent of faculty, age 30–40. Black males account for 2.4 percent of faculty under 30 and around 3 percent of faculty, age 30–40. Among older faculty, Black males account for larger shares (2.8 percent) and Black females account for declining shares (2.1 percent). Thus, the conclusion that Black and white women will largely replace white—and to a lesser extent—nonwhite males who occupy the upper reaches of the academy.

Affirmative Action Retrenchment

Is there any connection between the changing representation of African-American faculty and affirmative action retrenchment? Between 1992 and 1996, 16 states introduced anti–affirmative action legislation. Between 1997 and 1998 alone, 17 states introduced affirmative action retrenchment legislation. All told, 23 states introduced anti–affirmative action legislation between 1992 and 1998. Although the legislation failed in each of these states, the mere introduction of laws designed to dismantle race preferences in higher education and other spheres of public life threatened to change the landscape permanently. Many anti–affirmative action ballot initiatives arose as a direct response to the legislative efforts designed to eliminate affirmative action. In at least six states, ballot initiatives had been introduced by 1998. Ards and Myers (1997) examined the legislative initiatives from 1992 to 1996 and concluded that the main factors contributing to the dismantling of affirmative action were *economic factors*. While political factors such as the representation of African-American elected officials can help to thwart anti–affirmative action initiatives, economic factors explain why these initiatives come about in the first place. Economic distress faced by whites, particularly white males, is hypothesized to contribute to the demise of support for affirmative action. The logic is this: when white males feel their economic security is threatened, initiatives such as race-based hiring and college admissions are seen as "unfair" efforts designed to help undeserving women and minorities at the expense of whites.

We have performed the following test. We asked: What is the representation of African-American faculty in the 23 affirmative action retrenchment states versus the other nonretrenchment states in 1995 and 1997? We wanted to know whether retrenchment states have higher representation rates of Black faculty—and thus pose a greater threat to white dominance. We wanted to know whether retrenchment states saw slower growth between 1995 and 1997 in Black faculty representation.

Figure 3.15 shows the first of the results. Black faculty are more heavily represented in the retrenchment states than in the nonretrenchment states, a finding that supports the white threat hypothesis. In both 1995 and 1997, the share of faculty who were Black males or who were Black females was higher in retrenchment states than in the nonretrenchment states. The gap was larger for Black females. While Black females accounted in 1995 for nearly 7$\frac{1}{2}$ percent of female faculty in retrenchment states, they represented only a little more than 5$\frac{3}{4}$ percent of female faculty in nonretrenchment states. The

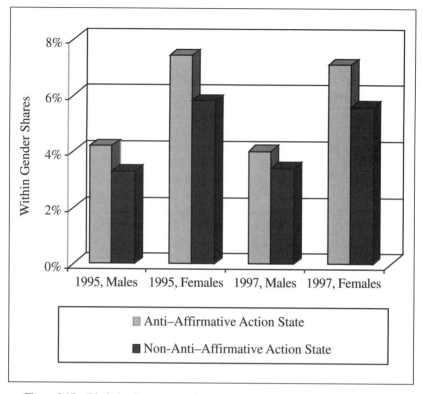

Figure 3.15. Black faculty representation in retrenchment vs. nonretrenchment states.

gaps between retrenchment and nonretrenchment states in the Black male and Black female shares of within-gender composition of faculty narrowed between 1995 and 1997, giving rise to the conclusions evident in Figure 3.16. Here we see that the share of Black male faculty fell between 1995 and 1997 in retrenchment states while it remained about the same in nonretrenchment states. The female share fell in both sets of states, but the Black female share fell more in the retrenchment states than in the nonretrenchment states. This evidence supports the view that affirmative action retrenchment has had a negative impact on changes in Black faculty employment, even though Black faculty representation seems to be higher in retrenchment states. The latter evidence is consistent with the perspective that retrenchment occurs where the threat to white male dominance is greatest. Of course, we have looked only at African-American faculty. Future research will permit us to extend this analysis to other faculty of color.

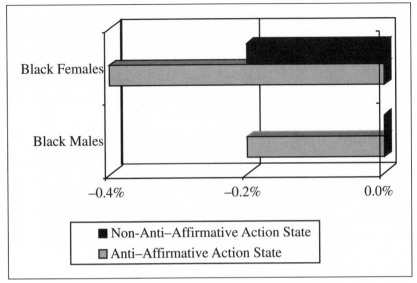

Figure 3.16.   Change in shares, 1995–1997.

A Case Study: Faculty and Administrator Perspectives

Another way to look at the issue of the changing environment faced by faculty of color is to explore intimately the experiences of a select group of faculty at a single institution. We asked tenured and tenure-track faculty and administrators at one major research university to comment on what departments do to successfully recruit and retain faculty of color and how new faculty learn "how to be faculty" in their department. We interviewed 21 administrators (9 deans and 12 chairs) and 18 faculty of color (12 tenured and 6 tenure-track). The number of administrators by race and gender were African-American, 1 (male); Hispanic, 1 (female); and non-Hispanic white, 19 (13 male, 6 female). The number of faculty by race and gender were American Indian, 1 (female); African-American, 5 (2 males, 3 females); Asian, 6 (3 male, 3 female); Hispanic, 5 (3 male, 2 female); and 1 male minority, specific race or ethnicity not identified.

The interviews were read and coded for emergent themes. Administrators identified some of the same issues as faculty of color. However, as a whole, they were not aware of the extent of the effects on the quality of life for faculty of color. Among other things, a negative workplace environment affects faculty performance and morale. Several previous studies provided the following background information for this study.

First, as part of the Midwestern Higher Education Commission Minority Faculty Development Project, Turner and Myers (2000) interviewed 64 faculty of color from seven Midwestern states—Illinois, Kansas, Michigan, Minnesota, Missouri, Nebraska, and Ohio. Through focus groups and individual interviews they found the following concerns expressed by faculty of color: race and ethnic bias, isolation, lack of information about tenure, an unsupportive work environment, gender bias, language barriers, lack of mentors, and lack of support from superiors. Our respondents cited as examples of racial and ethnic bias: problems of being denied tenure and promotion, being expected to work harder than whites, having their color given more attention than their credentials, feelings of being treated like a token, lack of support or validation of research on minority issues, being expected to handle minority affairs, and being in an environment where there were too few minorities on campus.

These examples of bias and of perceptions of differential treatment are classic examples of minorities' descriptions of racially hostile workplaces. While the racially hostile workplace of the 1990s certainly is not as abusive as that of the Jim Crow or pre–Civil Rights era, nor is it necessarily a throwback to the environment described earlier by Blauner, it nonetheless is a factor cited with continuing frequency by faculty of color in our examination of Midwestern universities (Turner & Myers, 2000).

A second source of evidence pointing to a racially hostile environment comes from an examination of majority (white) and minority faculty perceptions in academe at the University of Colorado (CU) System. Aguirre, Martinez, and Hernandez (1993) surveyed 73 minority faculty and 122 majority faculty. The study found that minority faculty were less satisfied than majority faculty with their employment, salary, promotion opportunities, performance evaluation, and everyday relations at the workplace. Female faculty were less satisfied with their salary and promotion opportunities than male faculty. Comparatively speaking, minority female faculty are even less satisfied with their promotion opportunities, performance evaluations, and everyday relations in the workplace. Female faculty and minority faculty were not compared to each other, but to the majority (white male) faculty.

A third piece of evidence comes from an examination of 35 white women, 7 minority women, 21 white men, and 4 minority men. Boice (1993), in an analysis of faculty involvement among women and minorities, found that minorities perceived that they needed to prove themselves by working harder than everyone else and by coping without complaining. The results showed that they felt their experience was marginalizing, making them feel like second-class citizens and leaving them alone to solve their problems where they were already peripheralized. The analysis also found that minority and women faculty ended up identifying with ethnically kindred students far more than with faculty colleagues. Thus, they found involvement in ways that would not pay dividends in campus decisions about retention and tenure. Women and minorities tended to be less immersed in their campuses and in self-help actions than were white males. The nontraditional newcomers who manage the highest levels of involvement (regularly socializing with the chair, participation in fine arts offerings, campus organizations and clubs, use of the library, involvement with colleagues and the campus) evidenced the most promise for successful careers.

In short, there exists ample literature pointing to the feelings of inadequacy, problems of marginalization, concerns about support from mentors and superiors, and perceptions of an unwelcome, chilly, or even a racially (or ethnically) hostile work environment among faculty of color. Against this backdrop we collected information from faculty at one major research institution in the Midwest.

Data Analysis

Each interview was tape-recorded and transcribed. Each transcript was read and emergent themes were coded and named by category. Emergent themes were put on two matrices, one for administrator and one for faculty responses. A matrix was used to organize the information in three areas: (a) emergent themes, (b) direct quotes of supporting examples, and (c) suggested solutions or implications. Suggested solutions were identified as either personal (P) or institutional (I). If a suggested solution to an identified issue was to be primarily implemented on an individual level, it was classified as personal. For example, taking a personal initiative to expand faculty networks by attending conferences would be classified as personal. An institutional solution would be a solution that must be implemented by the university, such as the university sponsoring events for faculty to network and share their research interests with each other.

One of the central findings of the interviews was intersection of the perceptions of faculty of color and that of administrators on issues of race and the status and standing of minority faculty. Faculty of color repeatedly identified concerns about racism and the marginalizing impacts of being deemed less qualified because some had been hired as affirmative action hires. Administrators, by way of contrast, saw problems as stemming from pipeline problems, not enough qualified minorities, the small numbers of minorities on campus and in the immediate geographical area, as well as the problem of possible racism in hiring and promotion. We do not conclude that this intersection reflects an agreement between faculty of color and administrators on the issue of race or racism. Rather, we conclude that both sides recognize the existence of the perception problem of race, even if the two sides do not converge in their interpretations of what race means for faculty of color.

Perspectives from Faculty of Color

Challenges that tenure-track and tenured faculty face at the study site are similar to challenges described by faculty of color in other studies. These are as follows:

Appendix Tables 1 and 2 display the results of categorizing the responses from the interviews. The main conclusion from the analysis confirms previous findings, showing that minority faculty feel they have to constantly prove themselves, that they must continuously confront subtle racism, and that they feel isolated and marginalized. The findings also show that they confronted unclear tenure expectations, a lack of proper mentoring, and a lack of support for minority concerns. Compounding the situation was the problem of tokenism. Many respondents perceived that they were often asked to provide the "minority perspective." This often resulted in their facing too many committee assignments and not enough time for their scholarly research or teaching.

Most telling, however, from the perspective of our previous empirical analysis, are perceptions about affirmative action. Aside from the belief by some respondents that covert racism seemed to creep into decision making in the evaluation of the research and teaching of faculty of color was the belief that they were not deemed equal to their peers, simply because they were hired—or thought to have been hired—under affirmative action mandates. The evident perception, expressed especially by Latino and African-American faculty, was that they had earned their positions because of affirmative action and not on their own merit.

The expression of concern about being perceived of as "affirmative action" hires and not as fully qualified candidates did not manifest itself as opposition to affirmative action. Rather, it found its voice in the perception that the racially hostile environment prevented faculty of color from rising above the *means* by which they may have been hired to assure that there was consensus among faculty about the positive *ends* occasioned by their being parts of the faculty. The failure to acknowledge the legitimacy of the research by minorities on problems confronting communities of color, the failure to validate the roles played by minority faculty in mentoring students and providing bridges to the community of color resulted in faculty of color feeling marginalized, unwanted, and undervalued. Whether they were hired via affirmative action or not, the label of "affirmative action hire" was almost synonymous with the label of "less qualified."

Not all faculty expressed negative views about their experiences. In some areas, faculty were split on their views regarding a particular issue. Some felt that their mentors had been helpful, that the tenure review process was fair, and that their departments offered supportive work environments. Many of the African-American faculty expressed considerable satisfaction with their jobs. What is particularly interesting, however, is the wide set of experiences with racism among Asian faculty members—the minority group often viewed as satisfied with their environment.

Administrator Perspectives

Administrators identified seven challenges to the recruitment and retention of minority faculty. First, they felt that faculty of color were in high demand to be represented on committees. As a result, these faculty can get too involved and neglect research and publications. A second challenge cited was the pipeline problem. Administrators felt that recruitment of faculty of color was hindered by the lack of enough qualified applicants. A third challenge was the problem of networking. Administrators pointed to the possible isolation of faculty of color and the absence of pools of other scholars with whom to interact in the fields and areas of interest of the minority faculty. This problem dovetailed with a fourth challenge raised: that the institution in question had few minority students, faculty or staff and was located in an area with few people of color. This challenge was cited along with a fifth problem of subtle racism in hiring procedures. A sixth challenge concerned the views of majority faculty: administrators interviewed admitted that majority faculty are oblivious of the problems that faculty of color feel need to be addressed. A seventh challenge identified was that of the disconnect between the University and the community of color. Administrators pointed to the fact that the University does not have an understanding of communities of color as a continuing impediment toward the recruitment and retention of faculty of color.

While our interviews focused on the four communities of color, with all four communities of color expressing concerns about racism on campus, African-Americans and Latinos specifically identified the issue of affirmative action as a challenge they faced. Both claimed that one of the barriers they faced was the perception that they earned their position because of affirmative action. It is particularly relevant to note, however, that the form of affirmative action implemented at the subject institution was of an odd variety. This program provided full central administration funding for "targets of opportunity" in the first year; partial funding in the second and third years; and required full departmental funding in subsequent years. Many white faculty at the institution (correctly) pointed out the disincentives to promote and retain minority faculty under this funding formula. They argued that if faculty of color were "fully qualified," they could (and should) be hired using regular funds. If they were hired instead using the "target of opportunity" funding, only if there were surplus departmental resources in the fourth year would tenured faculty feel supportive of renewing the contracts of probationary faculty.

It must be understood, moreover, that these are the views and experiences of faculty of color in the "post–Affirmative Action" era. While the university in question continues to employ "target of opportunity" funding strategies to attract minority faculty, white male faculty at that institution are becoming more and more vocal in their opposition to such funding. The direct attack on affirmative action, however, is matched in its vigor to the expressions of concerns by both white and nonwhite faculty about the unintended negative impacts of the specific brand of affirmative action at the subject institution. In essence, then, both faculty of color and white faculty have begun to retreat from the support for affirmative action funding initiatives that do not resolve the underlying problem of perceptions about the inferiority of people of color.

Summary and Conclusions

Simultaneously, as the United States approaches the twenty-first Century, the minority population is increasing. Academia must not only reflect the changing population, but it must incorporate the character within its domain. (Aguirre, 1995, p. 66)

We have argued that representation of faculty of color within the academy is both affected by and affects the threat to white male dominance. We discount the contention that the underrepresentation of Black faculty is due to the undersupply of Black PhDs. We show that there has been a recent surge in production of Black PhDs, hardly an outcome consistent with lingering perceptions that there are not enough qualified applicants for academic jobs. We also discount the view that the recent surge in Black PhDs is an artifact of a lagged production of Black bachelor's degrees. Something else is going on in the academic marketplace, and whatever it is, it is stimulating Blacks to complete the training and credentializing process that will make them qualified for tenure-track positions in colleges and universities.

Despite the evidence that there are willing, able, and qualified minorities interested in academic jobs, we find that affirmative action retrenchment efforts have had a negative effect on the representation of African-American faculty. This finding arises within the context of evidence showing that Black faculty are more heavily represented in states undergoing affirmative action retrenchment. There is no paradox here. In those states, the retrenchment itself may be a backlash against prior successes in affirmative action. Certainly it is conceivable that white males, who are holding relatively fewer and fewer positions at the lower rungs of the academic ladder, may feel threatened by initiatives such as affirmative action that may be perceived as the "cause" of their declining shares of the total academic pie. Coupled with the diversification of the undergraduate ranks—with nonwhite enrollments far outpacing white enrollments—the conclusion that affirmative action success contributes to white threat is plausible on its face. But, coupled with our qualitative evidence that faculty of color at one large research institution are facing increasingly hostile work environments due in part to the backlash against affirmative action, the conclusion becomes inescapable.

Previous research on the workplace environment for faculty of color has provided similar perspectives on issues described here. However, our qualitative analysis is unique because department chairs and college deans were also interviewed. Perspectives provided by these administrators can be very helpful in addressing the issue of recruitment and retention of faculty of color. Responses by administrators indicate that there is an awareness of some of the challenges faced by faculty of color, such as unreasonably excessive committee assignments, tokenism, and racism. However, administrators interviewed for this study, as a group, do not express an awareness of the detrimental effects that a stressful environment creates on faculty work, morale, and performance. For example, one faculty member of color described the following situation: "This is a big boy's club, they [associate dean and other faculty] are all in this plot of troubling me and harassing me and I don't know what to do. It's constant harassment."

Some administrators blame the faculty of color for leaving the institution. They blame competitive wages and attractive positions at other institutions, the state's weather, or other factors for the low numbers of faculty of color at the study site. They are very hesitant to put any responsibility on the University to address issues that could have been remedied. Some administrators even feel that they have done enough in recruiting faculty of color and are being pressured to hire faculty of color in their departments. "Because minority faculty in particular are in very much high demand nationally right now, because there are few of them and many places wanting them, they can pretty much write their own ticket, which they have . . . In terms of what we actually did to try to make a good situation for everyone who came, I think we did everything humanly possible." The perception that faculty of color can "write their own ticket" even in the face of the reality discussed by faulty of color shows the disconnect between administrators hiring minority faculty and providing a climate for retention and the actual life experiences of many faculty of color as noted in the growing literature on this issue.

This conclusion might reflect in a nutshell the double-edged sword of affirmative action. On the one hand, affirmative action may seem to be a viable tool for recruitment and retention of faculty of color. On the other hand, once used, the tool may absolve administrators of any culpability in resolving the underlying problems that make the work environment for faculty of color unpleasant or unwelcoming. Faculty leave; they express dissatisfaction. The response from administrators: "I think we did everything humanly possible."

It is clear that if the new realities of the faculty marketplace are to be consistent with retaining and continued recruitment of faculty of color, something beyond simple affirmative action hiring and funding plans must be implemented. The respondents in our interviews provided a number of valuable suggestions. They felt that there should be opportunities to network by establishing faculty of color caucuses. They urged better structuring of mentorship programs and better pretenure preparation. They urged administrators to recruit more people of color to create "critical masses" in all departments. Some respondents felt that more people of color should be placed at higher administration levels. But ultimately, the task is to produce a new generation of faculty of color who can survive as well as excel in the new environment where affirmative action is under attack and where there remains a perception that white males are losing ground.

In order to alleviate the situation generated by differing interpretations of the minority faculty experience as suggested by the qualitative data presented in this chapter,

- Universities and colleges should be at the forefront of preserving such legislative imperatives as affirmative action. Currently, external pressures have caused the institution to begin moving away from the goals of diversity for fear of lawsuits, and many academicians see little continued purpose to be served by affirmative action. While it is true that affirmative action policies have done little to change the overall pattern of hiring and retaining university faculty, they have still facilitated the entrance of a few faculty of color whose voices and contributions to the academic dialogue would not otherwise be there. If the programs that support the initiatives to recruit faculty of color are abandoned, many scholars see a trend back toward the pre–Civil Rights era. Creating a critical mass of scholars of color is vitally important in continuing to correct the underrepresentation of faculty of color, in retaining present faculty, and in enhancing their contributions to their respective disciplines. As an example, Harvard University's Afro-American Studies Department, though not representative of Harvard's other disciplines, shows the impact such an approach can make.
- Universities and colleges need to address directly the disconnect between the problems confronted by faculty of color and the perceptions of the problem by administrators interviewed for this chapter. Many of the administrative solutions are designed to fix the faculty of color rather than acknowledging the problem as an institutional issue. As one colleague observed, "A lot of time is spent on racial and ethnic bias. That's an institutional problem. The solutions . . . answer pipeline and access issues. We've got to figure out a way that the solutions answer what's found in the data."

- Designing and implementing mentor programs would help new faculty of color become acclimatized to academia and to the campus culture as a whole. Mechanisms must be created to enable department chairs and senior faculty to facilitate the success of new faculty of color. More opportunities for interaction, both formal and informal, between faculty of color and department/university level administrators need to be provided. For example, a national symposium entitled "Keeping Our Faculties," convened in 1998 at the University of Minnesota and attended by faculty of color as well as majority administrators and scholars, provided a platform for such discussions. More of these types of meetings need to take place and more follow up from such meetings is essential. Too often such meetings only begin the dialogue that must continue at faculty home institutions in order to begin to make a difference there.

- Colleges and universities are now in the process of designing faculty development leaves for tenured faculty. Such leaves might also include incentives for majority senior faculty and administrators to place themselves for a period of time in situations in which they are really a minority. One white senior faculty member (also an administrator) notes that whites "do not see color until they are in a position where they are in the minority and then you do see color." This faculty member goes on to state that she was placed in such a situation and learned "that I did not exactly know how to behave here—the rules might be different—I did not want to behave in ways in which I would be overly noticed." In her view, learning to live in a multicultural community "takes time and experience just like any other skill you might have. White faculty and administrators, who may be unaware of their own unconscious biases, must live through their own experience and acknowledge ignorance in this regard." To achieve a healthy, safe climate for growth, majority members must be willing to suspend their own quick judgments about what something means to them or how something looks from their perception, sincerely asking for more information and making the imaginative effort to exercise empathy.

- Universities and colleges need to address the subtle and subjective processes of creating a sense of belonging while dismantling the subtle and subjective processes of exclusion. An Asian-American tenured science professor observed, "As a somewhat overused African proverb goes, it takes a village to raise a child. It takes a department to nurture a junior faculty member . . . Some departments do that well and other ones don't . . . It's not really a programmatic thing, although I think one can move in that direction, because 'nurturing' comes more from how individuals relate to one another than the output of a program. We need to begin to look beyond the mechanical [such as campus orientations] and to develop a culture within the department in which [all] look out for each other. You can't program that . . . The point is not just to make the person feel comfortable. The goal is to allow the person to become productive. Usually a comfortable person is productive."

• Universities and colleges need to clearly articulate and find ways to move toward environments that honor diversity, not by creating homogeneous politically correct groupings, but by creating a community in which all groups can maintain integrity of identity while participating with equal power in the larger community. As Duster (1991) states, "It will mean knowing how to be 'different' and feeling comfortable about it; being able to be the 'insider' in one situation and the 'outsider' in another . . . Everyone [must do] some changing" (p. 54). Such changes would contribute to the creation of a university climate that is healthier for everyone.

No one knows for sure how to address these issues. But through compassion, understanding, and outreach, faculty of color themselves may serve as the new bridges to reassure white males, who now represent smaller shares of all faculty employment, that they too are valued and appreciated assets of the university.

Notes

The authors gratefully acknowledge the assistance of Maria M. Diaz in writing this chapter.

1. For more on premia to college education and the causes of widening earnings inequality, see Darity and Myers, *Persistent Disparity*, 1998.

References

Aguirre, Jr., Adalberto. (1995). The status of minority faculty in academe. *Equity and Excellence in Education 28*(1), 63–68.

Aguirre, Jr., Adalberto, Martinez, Ruben O., & Hernandez, Anthony. (1993). Majority and minority faculty perceptions in academe. *Research in Higher Education, 34*(3), 371–385.

Astin, Helen S., Antonio, Anthony L., Cress, Christine M., & Astin, Alexander W. (1997, April). *Race and ethnicity in the American professorate, 1995–96.* Los Angeles: Higher Education Research Institute, Graduate School of Education and Information Studies.

Blauner, Robert. (1972). *Racial oppression in America.* New York: Harper & Row.

Boice, Robert. (1993). New faculty involvement for women and minorities. *Research in Higher Education, 34*(3), 291–327.

Carter, Deborah J., & O'Brien, Eileen M. (1993). *Employment and hiring patterns for faculty of color.* (American Council on Education Research Briefs, Vol. 4, No. 6.) Washington, DC: American Council on Education, Division of Policy Analysis and Research.

Carter, Deborah J., & Wilson, Reginald. (1996). *Minorities in higher education: 1995–96 Fourteenth annual status report.* Washington, DC: American Council on Education, Office of Minority Concerns.

City of Richmond v. J.A. Croson, 488 U.S. 469 (1989).

Clark v. Claremont University Center, 6 Cal. App. 4th (1992).

Darity, William A., & Myers, Samuel L., Jr. (1998). *Persistent disparity: Race and economic inequality in the U.S. since 1945.* Cheltenham, UK; Northampton, MA: Edward Elgar.

Duster, Troy. (1991, November). *The diversity project: Final report.* Baltimore: Johns Hopkins University Press.

Finkelstein, Martin J., Seal, Robert K., & Schuster, Jack H. (1998). The new academic generation: A profession in transformation. Baltimore: Johns Hopkins University Press.

Hopwood v. Texas, 78 F. 3d 932 (5th Cir. 1996)

LaNoue, George R., & Lee, Barbara A. (1987). *Academics in court: The consequences of faculty discrimination litigation.* Ann Arbor: University of Michigan Press.

Leap, Terry L. (1995). *Tenure, discrimination, and the courts.* Ithaca, NY: ILR Press.

Milem, Jeffery F., & Astin, Helen S. (1993, March/April). The changing composition of faculty: What does it really mean for diversity? *Change 25*(2), 21–27.

Njeri, Itabari. (1989, September 20). Academic acrimony: Minority professors claim racism plays role in obtaining tenure. *Los Angeles Times* 1, 4.

Pavel, D. Michael, Swisher, Karen, & Ward, M. (1994). Special focus: American Indian and Alaska Native demographic and educational trends. *Minorities in Higher Education,* 13, 33–56. Washington, DC: American Council on Education: Office of Minorities in Higher Education.

Schneider, Alison. (1997, 20 June). Proportion of minority professors inches up to about 10 percent. *Chronicle of Higher Education 43*(41), A12–A13.

Schneider, Alison. (1998, November 20). What has happened to faculty diversity in California? *Chronicle of Higher Education 45*(13), A10–A12.

Turner, Caroline S. (2000). Defining success: Promotion and tenure—Planning for each career stage and beyond. In Mildred Garcia (Ed.), *Succeeding in an academic career: A guide for faculty of color* (pp. 111–140). Westport, CT: Greenwood Publishing Group.

Turner, Caroline S. (1999). Keeping our faculties: Executive summary. University of Minnesota: Office of the Associate Vice President for Multicultural and Academic Affairs.

Turner, Caroline S., & Myers, Samuel L., Jr. (2000). *Faculty of color in academe: Bittersweet success.* Needham Heights, MA: Allyn and Bacon.

Turner, Caroline S., & Myers, Samuel L., Jr. (1997). Faculty diversity and affirmative action. In Mildred Garcia (Ed.), *Affirmative action's testament of hope: Strategies for a new era in higher education* (pp. 131–148). Albany, NY: State University of New York Press.

Turner, Caroline S., Myers, Samuel L., Jr., & Creswell, John W. (1999, January/February). Exploring underrepresentation: The case of faculty of color in the Midwest. *Journal of Higher Education 70*(1), 27–59.

U.S. Department of Education, National Center for Education Statistics. (1997, January). Higher Education General Information Survey (HEGIS), "Fall Enrollment in Colleges and Universities" surveys; and Integrated Postsecondary Education Data System (IPEDS), "Fall Enrollment" surveys.

Villalpando, Octavio. (in press). Scholars of color: Are they really a part of the emerging composition of the professorates? *UCLA Journal of Education and Information Studies 6*(1). UCLA: Regents of the University of California.

Weinberg, Meyer. (1977). *A chance to learn: The history of race and education in the United States.* Cambridge, New York: Cambridge University Press.

APPENDIX TABLE 3.1
Faculty Perspectives

Issue	*Example*	*Solutions/Suggestions Personal (P)/Institutional (I)*
Department expectations	"My first few years here I had no sense of what was expected of me, no sense." (Female, Hispanic, Tenured)	"The way they learn is by informal conversation and observing, by talking to senior faculty members." (Male, Asian, Tenured) (P)
Tenured expectations evaluation	"Annual Review we do our own memo describing our year and our accomplishments and our supervisor does a memo and meets with us about it." (Male, African-American, Tenure-track)	"There was an orientation for new women faculty that was useful." (Female, Hispanic, Tenure-track) (I)
Committee and community work	"Because there are fewer faculty of color they get called upon to do committees over and over. It's not that you don't want to stop advising students or introducing issues . . . it [sitting on committees] isn't considered as important in the tenure process." (Female, African-American, Tenure-track)	"Take charge of your own intellectual direction, command respect in your area." (Male, Hispanic, Tenured) (P)
Support and mentoring	There should be a person to explain the system and also explain the culture and shepherd the person along and watch out for them. There isn't anyone like that." (Male, African-American, Tenure-track), (–) "For new faculty there is an enormous amount [of mentoring], we have our own mentoring comittee which is four people who help new faculty learn the ropes, the college is much better organized about informing new faculty of fellowship opportunities." (Male, Asian, Tenure-track), (+)	"McKnight Grants, graduate student grants." (Female, Hispanic, Tenured), (I) "We desperately need a liaison person with respect to fellowships both in house and beyond." (Male, Asian Tenured) (I)
Faculty relations	"We're a close-knit faculty." (Female, Hispanic, Tenure-track) (+) "[Insults regarded] Nothing about the field [they were] just making horrible remarks toward minority faculty members, poking them at their reputations, calling their publications not scholarly. We had a dozen minority faculty members. Ten of them left. . . . Our experience with white male faculty, all [minority] faculty members [in my department] felt that they were not respected. Absolutely the truth." (Female, Asian, Tenured) (–)	"In order for your colleagues to know what you are doing the chair should be responsible to organize activities to present your work to your colleagues, lunch bags, lunch meetings." (Male, Asian, Tenured) (I)

(continued)

APPENDIX TABLE 3.1
Faculty Perspectives

Issue	Example	Solutions/Suggestions Personal (P)/Institutional (I)
Dean support	"Doubting the competence of our administrators, I do a lot of that." (Male, Asian, Tenured), (–) "This is a big boy's club, they [associated dean and faculty] are all in this plot of troubling me and harassing me and I don't know what to do. It's constant harassment." (Female, Asian, Tenured) (–) "I would not have survived if I had not had (a professor) as a mentor for a long time and since she left my situation has become very bad." (Female, Asian, Tenured) (+, –)	"Try to make sure the administration knows you exist in positive ways. Broaden your network connections outside of your own department." (Male, Asian, Tenured) (P)
Recruiting challenges	"Not enough students in the mainstream, in the main pipeline of things. They [they system] are not interested in creating a healthy respectable, talented pool of intellectuals." (Male, Hispanic, Tenured)	"Our lack of middle-class background can create some very narrow perspectives and we have to wean our students from those perspectives, we have to challenge them and prepare them to compete at any level, at any given moment." (Male, Hispanic, Tenured) (P)
Other challenges	"As people of color, we have to be not only on our toes but occasionally we have to walk on water, a person of color has to do more than the average." (Male, Hispanic, Tenured) "My concerns are not at the core of what the school is all about. . . . Other people can come to school and most of their needs are being met. All their concerns are being addressed." (Female, African-American, tenure-track)	

APPENDIX TABLE 3.2
Administrators

Issue	*Example*	*Solutions/Suggestions* Personal *(P)/Institutional (I)*
Challenges for faculty of color	"An all-white or largely white faculty may not see the real problems that persons of color feel need to be addressed." "What's being said by the university doesn't match with the actions that we've had with the placement of funds for faculty of color."	"Organize professional organizations." (I) "Make them feel valued as part of the community and encourage them to have their own voice." (I) "[Faculty of color] must find a support system in the community." (P)
Tenure challenges	"Because faculty of color are in such demand to be represented on committees and other sorts of things . . . they can get too involved [and neglect research and publications]."	"As administrators it is our duty to . . . aid them in wise choices and being able to say no." (P)
Tenure support	"The formula for a successful evaluation of tenure is that 40 percent of your effort is research, 40 percent is teaching, and 20 percent is service. And 20 percent could be service to the College unit or to the profession. That's standard university-wide." "The mentoring committee ought to be initially helping the person develop trajectory for tenure." "Assistance in writing grants."	"Get new faculty into mentorship programs or educational programs, or professional development roundtable's or seminars." (I)
Need for faculty of color	"This department must be populated by more persons of color, if we do not we will be increasingly irrelevant in school situations. We're already irrelevant, we're all too old, we're all white, we're all boys." "There's a pipeline problem and there's an information, networking problem."	"I hope we're not sending the message that we just want people for the numbers. We want people because of what they contribute to some part of the academic community." (I)
Pretenure faculty support and development	"Teaching is crucial and there is the Bush Program, Workshop on how to give presentations, training sessions, conferences."	"A Black faculty union or a Latino faculty group might be useful to establish. It works in Congress, it can work here." (I)
Challenges for recruiting and retaining faculty of color	"This university is a bit racist in hiring procedures, I think there's a lot of subtle racism against different people in a lot of different capacities." "We're not very competitive in the salary area at the university so we . . . force people to explore other jobs." "This is not a university that has a large population of color."	"Targeted hire program bridging funding from central administration, if there is a scholar of color looking for a position, you can recruit and make a target opportunity hire." (I)

(continued)

APPENDIX TABLE 3.2
Administrators

Issue	Example	Solutions/Suggestions Personal (P)/Institutional (I)
Recruiting policies and practices	"This is a small town and is [open] to their leadership, so this would be a special kind of inducement to their coming here."	"Getting a critical mass, minority faculty members are going to feel more comfortable in situations where they aren't the only one." (I)
Retaining policies and practices	The university needs a "better understanding of the community," to be prepared to provide a receptive environment for faculty of color. "Personal contact, make him feel accepted, make him feel wanted, make him feel useful and productive and give him the space to be useful and productive." "For minority faculty members the only difference is that you want to get them into their own minority support network as well as introduce them to other people."	"In terms of retaining faculty of color, it would be important to have more faculty of color and more administrators of color. Positions should be filled at higher levels, not lower levels, that's not enough." (I)

CHAPTER 4

The Effects of Public Policy Conflicts and Resource Allocation Decisions on Higher-Education Desegregation Outcomes in Pennsylvania

JAMES B. STEWART

Contemporary public policy affecting Historically Black Colleges and Universities (HBCUs) reflects a continuing uncertainty regarding the role of these institutions in the changing U.S. higher education environment. Recent desegregation agreements typically include mandates to enhance public HBCUs through addition of new academic programs, upgrading of physical plant, and other initiatives. However, the stated purpose of such enhancements is to reduce or eliminate the racial identifiability of HBCUs rather than to improve their capacity to serve traditional constituencies. In contrast, a variety of federal initiatives have been undertaken with the goal of enabling HBCUs to expand their more traditional role through outreach to students and communities of color. This ambiguity in federal public policy is compounded by the lack of congruence between federal and state public policies affecting HBCUs.

This investigation explores the implications of these public policy conflicts by examining the desegregation process in the Commonwealth of Pennsylvania. An agreement between the Commonwealth of Pennsylvania and the United States Department of Education, Office for Civil Rights (Commonwealth of Pennsylvania and United States Department of Education, Office for Civil Rights, 1999) with its provisions to enhance Cheyney University is the focal point of the investigation. The judicial ruling in the highly publicized Mississippi desegregation litigation, typically referred to as *Fordice* (*United States v. Fordice*, 1992), serves as the frame of reference for examining the Pennsylvania settlement.

As indicated previously, specific attention is focused on conflicts between desegregation policies and other public policies targeted at HBCUs.

Current desegregation policy prioritizes the elimination of the racial identifiability of HBCUs by increasing enrollments of non-Black students. Independent of federal desegregation initiatives, the last three presidential administrations have issued executive orders designed to promote the enhancement of HBCUs. The types of programs introduced in response to these executive orders tend to strengthen the attractiveness of HBCUs to their traditional constituencies, rather than promoting desegregation, per se. As a consequence, there is policy conflict at the federal level regarding the expected role of HBCUs and the desired demographic composition of their student bodies. As suggested, this problem is compounded by the lack of interface between federal policies promoting either desegregation or enhancement and those policies implemented by state agencies to improve the functioning of public higher-education systems. The disconnection between federal and state polices has at least two potentially negative effects on HBCUs. First, the potential efficacy of federal policies, both desegregation and enhancement, is reduced because opportunities are lost to leverage state resources in support of common policy objectives. Second, the highly structured relationship between HBCUs and federal agencies reinforces the existing exclusion of HBCUs from involvement in the broad network of public-private partnerships that are being encouraged by states as a strategy to strengthen public higher education. There is a type of substitution effect at work whereby states feel justified in paying little attention to HBCUs because they anticipate that federal authorities will either impose funding requirements or make up for inadequate state-provided resources through special programs.

The examination of public higher-education desegregation in Pennsylvania has the potential to generate useful insights regarding the implications of the policy conflicts described above. Pennsylvania's geographical location (non-South) clearly differentiates it from most settings where higher-education desegregation litigation has occurred. Cheyney University and Lincoln University, Pennsylvania's two "public" HBCUs, have been the source of potential desegregation litigation. Cheyney, founded in 1837 as the Institute for Colored Youth, and Lincoln, founded in 1854, are unique in that they were the first HBCUs established in the United States (Office for Civil Rights, 1991).

The organization of the chapter is as follows. Selected aspects of the *Fordice* decision are reviewed in the next section to highlight the thrust of contemporary desegregation policy as it relates to the enhancement of HBCUs. Nondesegregation related Federal efforts to enhance HBCUs are then discussed, to underscore the disconnection with desegregation policy. The desegregation process in Pennsylvania prior to the decision in the *Fordice* case is then examined, highlighting parallels to the Mississippi case. The section after that presents the broad outlines of a framework for defining and assessing desegregation policy, with particular emphasis on the role of HBCUs in fostering economic and social development. This framework assesses the potential public policy implications of the Pennsylvania settlement, focusing on Cheyney University. The analysis concludes with a discussion of the broader public policy implications of the investigation.

The Fordice Case and Desegregation Policy

The segregated system of public higher education in the state of Mississippi was first addressed by the federal courts in *Meredith v. Fair* (1962). The segregative policies in question focused on: (a) student enrollment, (b) maintenance of branch centers by the historically white universities in close proximity to the Historically Black Universities, (c) employment of faculty and staff, (d) provision and condition of facilities, (e) allocation of financial resources, (f) academic program offerings, and (g) racial composition of the governing board and its staff.

Judge Neal Biggers's opinion in the *Fordice* case rearticulated the responsibilities of states to dismantle segregated systems of higher education and focused principally on two issues: (a) differential admissions standards at HBCUs and Traditionally White Institutions (TWIs), and (b) program duplication and its implications for enhancements to HBCUs versus closure/mergers with TWIs. The pronouncements on both issues are predicated on the following standard:

> If the State perpetuates policies and practices traceable to its prior system that continue to have segregative effects whether by influencing student enrollment decisions or by fostering segregation in other facets of the university system and such policies are without sound educational justification and can be practicably eliminated, the State has not satisfied its burden of proving that it has dismantled its prior system. Such policies run afoul of the Equal Protection Clause, even though the State has abolished the legal requirement that whites and blacks be educated separately and even though it has established racially neutral policies not animated by a discriminatory purpose. (United States v. Fordice, 1992)

Judge Biggers noted that *Fordice* requires that each challenged policy or practice of the State must be evaluated to determine "whether it is traceable to the prior *de jure* system, whether it continues to foster segregation, whether it lacks sound educational justification, and whether its elimination is practicable. [It] is the State's burden to show that it has dismantled its prior dual system at the liability stage" (*United States v. Louisiana*, 1993). The responsibility of the state depends on the effects of a challenged policy. To illustrate, Judge Biggers observed that:

Where the State proves that a challenged policy, shown by plaintiffs to be traceable to segregation, has no segregative effects, it is relieved of its duty to eliminate or modify the challenged policy (*Knight v. State of Alabama*, 1994). The State likewise has no obligation to modify or eliminate policies and practices traceable to *de jure* segregation that continue to manifest segregative effects where it is not possible to do so 'consistent with sound educational practices' (*Knight*, 1994). Because policies and practices traceable to the *de jure* era are the court's focus, '[t]hat an institution is predominately white or Black does not in itself make out a constitutional violation.' (*Fordice*, 1992)

Using this standard of review, differential admissions standards were deemed to be traceable to the *de jure* system and to have continuing discriminatory effects. Judge Biggers ordered that undergraduate admissions requirements be modified to eliminate the differential admissions standards between the HBCUs and TWIs.

Program duplication has been used as one indicator of "educational soundness" in desegregation oversight and it was found to be pervasive among Mississippi's public institutions of higher education. The effect of this duplication on academic program enhancement possibilities at Jackson State University (JSU) and Alcorn State University (ASU) was evaluated, as well as the state's proposal to merge Historically Black Mississippi Valley State University (MVSU) with nearby Delta State University (DSU). Using the articulated standard of review, Judge Biggers found a number of proposed enhancements to JSU and ASU capable of furthering desegregation and enhancing institutional prestige, consistent with sound educational practices.

For the purposes of brevity, the discussion of enhancements is restricted to JSU. Special funds were to be provided over a 5-year period to fund property acquisition, campus entrances, campus security and grounds enhancement at JSU's main campus up to an aggregate of $15 million. Academic program enhancements ordered by Judge Biggers consisted of selected nonduplicative programs in the fields of allied health, social work, urban planning, and business. An on-site institutional study of JSU was also ordered to determine the relative strengths and weaknesses of existing programs. Judge Biggers indicated that the study's purpose was to define the program areas and content associated with the urban emphasis of JSU's mission. Proposals to be reviewed included those for an engineering school, a law school, and a pharmacy program. He further directed that duplication with other institutions in the system be examined to determine if it would be educationally sound to increase white enrollments at JSU by introducing unique academic programs there through elimination and/or transfer of existing programs at other institutions.

Not only did Judge Biggers's language make it clear that the principal objective of the proposed enhancements was to make JSU more attractive to white students, the order included provisions for direct support of such efforts. One example was a mandated articulation agreement between JSU and surrounding community colleges to generate practices promoting racial diversity on the JSU campus. The state of Mississippi was also required to establish a $5 million endowment to be used to provide funds for continuing educational enhancement and racial diversity, including recruitment of white students and scholarships for white applicants.

No final decision was rendered regarding the state of Mississippi's proposal to merge MVSU and DSU. Mississippi authorities were directed to study program duplication between the two institutions to identify ways to eliminate segregative duplication consistent with sound educational practices. Embedded in these approaches to desegregation policy are several assumptions that inherently limit the capacity to conceive of HBCUs as other than a legacy of separate-but-equal educational policies. One key assumption is that the organization and operation of TWIs constitutes the paradigm for "educational soundness." Consequently, for HBCUs to have a legitimate role in the educational policy arena, they must look more like TWIs, both in a demographic sense and in an operational context. The current approach to the analysis of program duplication assumes that programs are totally interchangeable among locations. This approach ignores the possibility that there are some unique characteristics of a given environment that generate distinguishing educational outcomes. As a consequence, desegregation planners' emphasis on eradicating "racially identifiable" institutions has the potential to erode educational diversity in ways that reduce the capabilities of public systems to respond to new challenges—for example, major demographic changes anticipated in the next few decades. In contrast, interventions at TWIs are of insufficient magnitude to significantly affect these institutions' existing educational production function—that is, the manner in which resources are used to generate graduates, produce new knowledge, and serve local communities.

Some of these points are raised, albeit using slightly different language, in the report entitled "The Historically Black Colleges and Universities: A Future in the Balance" (Committee L on the Historically Black Institutions and the Status of Minorities in the Profession, 1995). The report, commissioned by the American Association of University Professors (AAUP), makes a powerful case for the continuing social efficacy of HBCUs. Several types of evidence are presented including information about the achievements of HBCU graduates, successes of HBCUs despite limitations in funding and resources, recent gains in enrollments, special efforts in the sciences and, descriptions of research and outreach activities in both domestic and international settings.

The report highlights the critical and disproportionate role of HBCUs in producing the current generation of black leaders in a variety of fields. However, more important for present purposes is the evidence that the production function and educational outcomes generated by HBCUs are distinguishable from those associated with TWIs. As an example, the report emphasizes that HBCUs serve a disproportionately disadvantaged clientele while maintaining low tuition and, despite these hurdles, have higher retention and graduation rates of black students than TWIs. Various factors are identified as contributing to these successes, including: (a) expertise in providing remedial preparation for students who start out with weak high-school backgrounds; (b) provision of a supportive social, cultural, and racial environment, (c) greater involvement of students in campus activities; and (d) a high level of interaction with faculty, particularly black role models (Committee L on the Historically Black Institutions and the Status of Minorities in the Profession, 1995).

In economic terms, there is a bias in current desegregation policy that presumes HBCUs are a source of systemic inefficiency. Academic programs, or entire HBCUs, located in close proximity to TWIs are treated as excess capacity that can be eliminated or modified to alter student body demographic profiles. TWIs are assumed to have sufficient capacity to accommodate displaced Black students. The quality of the educational experience (product quality) received by Black students at TWIs is assumed to be at least as good as, if not better than, that provided by HBCUs. Enhancements of HBCUs are designed to minimize quality losses that might be imposed on white students attending HBCUs.

As suggested in the introduction, the alternative federal policy embodies an entirely different set of assumptions, although enhancement is also the desired policy outcome. These policies are described below.

Alternative Enhancement Models for HBCUs

Two of the earliest federal initiatives to enhance HBCUs are found in the *Strengthening Historically Black Colleges and Universities Program* and the *Strengthening Historically Black Graduate Institutions Program* authorized in Title III of the Higher Education Act of 1965. These precedents were reaffirmed in 1980 when President Jimmy Carter signed Executive Order 12232, which established a federal program to overcome the effects of discriminatory treatment and to strengthen the capacity of HBCUs to provide quality education. A similar executive order was signed by President Ronald Reagan (12320), and President George Bush issued Executive Order 12677 (1989) mandating that federal agencies take positive steps to increase participation of HBCUs. In 1993 President William Clinton issued Executive Order 12876 that, in part, directed federal agencies to increase contract and grant awards to, as well as establish cooperative agreements with, HBCUs. Each agency was directed to establish annual goals and the Department of Education and other agencies were directed to encourage private sector assistance in carrying out the mandates contained in the order. The types of programs emerging from these initiatives were summarized previously (Committee L on the Historically Black Institutions and the Status of Minorities in the Profession, 1995).

In part as a result of this policy thrust, at least 52 HBCUs are actively involved in community outreach and development efforts. Many of these projects are associated with grants made by the Department of Housing and Urban Development to help revitalize communities around HBCU campuses. A few HBCUs have also received grants from the Department of Energy to increase the numbers of minority science students and to retrain workers for jobs in high-tech fields. The Department of Energy has also funded a consortium, made up of 12 HBCUs and 6 institutions with substantial enrollments of other minorities, to perform environmental research and technological development. The consortium is also charged with developing degree programs in these fields and increasing environmental literacy by working with community groups (Committee L on the Historically Black Institutions and the Status of Minorities in the Profession, 1995).

A number of HBCUs have also formed partnerships with urban elementary and secondary schools. Some HBCUs, including Jackson State, are expanding curricula to pursue a distinctive urban educational and outreach mission. International linkages are also highlighted, with several long-standing initiatives noted, including those at Lincoln University. In fact, the report observes that approximately 50 HBCUs are taking part in international projects, many working under a NAFEO-U.S. Agency for International Development Cooperative Agreement (Committee L on the Historically Black Institutions and the Status of Minorities in the Profession, 1995).

The types of activities described are examples of what the Kellogg Commission on the Future of State and Land-Grant Universities (1999) has described as "engaged institutions." The Commission (1999, 7) argues that:

> Engagement goes well beyond extension, conventional outreach, and even most conceptions of public service. . . . Embedded in the engagement ideal is a commitment to sharing and reciprocity. By engagement the Commission envisions, partnerships, two-way streets defined by mutual respect among the partners for what each brings to the table.

In many respects, then, this alternative federal enhancement policy is increasing the "value-added" by HBCUs as role models for the type of engagement proposed for all state universities and land-grant institutions. Although this vanguard role is not explicitly acknowledged, it is clear that this function would support a very different HBCU enhancement strategy and set of policy outcome expectations than those associated with desegregation policy. Two of the critical issues to be addressed are: (a) which federal policy objective does or should have priority? And (b) are there ways to align the two policies in ways that optimize the public policy outcomes of HBCUs?

A third issue of particular concern is how to harmonize federal policies with state policies. As an example, consider the designation of a unique urban mission for JSU. Specification of a "unique" urban mission seems to provide a means to allow JSU to serve its traditional constituency while also introducing programs that can reduce racial identifiability. Moreover, this role also provides a special opportunity for JSU to contribute to overall development efforts within the state. However, this role was imposed on Mississippi officials rather than reflecting their own assessment of JSU's potential involvement in statewide and regional development initiatives. This disjunction between federal and state mission expectations suggests that another critical issue is the extent to which federal support for enhancements contributes to the isolation of HBCUs from the larger arena of government-institutional partnerships. In general, state support for HBCUs has been largely defensive or reactive, undertaken as responses to desegregation lawsuits, rather than as proactive efforts to involve HBCUs in the broader network of development initiatives. There appears to be no mechanism to coordinate federal desegregation-related enhancements with other federal enhancement initiatives, much less with state-level development projects.

These issues provide the context for the exploration of the desegregation process in Pennsylvania.

Higher-Education Desegregation in Pennsylvania

Although Pennsylvania was found to be one of 10 states operating a racially segregated system of higher education in 1969, the submission of a formal desegregation plan did not occur until 1983. And it was not until 1999 that the Office for Civil Rights (OCR) of the U.S. Department of Education determined Pennsylvania's status vis-à-vis compliance with Title VI of the Civil Rights Act of 1964. In that year it brokered a new agreement specifying activities to be undertaken during the next phase of the desegregation process (Commonwealth of Pennsylvania and United States Department of Education, Office for Civil Rights, 1999). The process used to develop the new desegregation plan departed significantly from the adversarial enforcement model traditionally employed by OCR. In its stead, a "partnership" process was utilized similar to that implemented in Florida, in which various stakeholders were charged with conducting an assessment and generating suggestions for future initiatives.

The original delay in submitting a desegregation plan resulted from uncertainty regarding which institutions would be required to participate in the desegregation process. Pennsylvania has a unique multitiered system of public institutions that has evolved into three distinct sectors: the State System of Higher Education universities (SSHE); the state-related universities (SRIs); and the community colleges. Each of these three sectors is independently governed, although the State Board of Education is charged with providing periodic guidance to all institutions financed to any degree by state appropriations.

The SSHE was established by statute in 1983 (24 P.S. 020-2002-A) and consists of 14 institutions including Cheyney University. Another SSHE institution, West Chester University, is located relatively close to Cheyney. The SRIs are Lincoln University (an HBCU), the Pennsylvania State University, Temple University, and the University of Pittsburgh. Each of these universities operates under a separate, nonprofit corporate charter and independent governing board. However, state law recognizes these institutions as "an integral part of a system of higher education in Pennsylvania" (24 P.S. 2510-2, 2510-202, 2510-402, 1983) and State government officials sit on their Boards of Trustees in various capacities. Each SRI receives an annual appropriation that provides only partial support for specific line items. Lincoln was a private institution prior to receiving designation as an SRI, as were Temple University and the University of Pittsburgh. Since receiving SRI status, several unsuccessful attempts have been made to have Lincoln designated as a land-grant institution, equivalent to the 1890 public HBCU land-grant institutions.

There are also 15 community colleges in Pennsylvania. Although frequently referred to as public institutions, they are neither owned nor controlled by the Commonwealth of Pennsylvania. Each college operates under an approved plan and is governed by a local board of trustees accountable to the local government sponsor of the college. Generally, one third of their funding is furnished by the Commonwealth (see 24 P.S. '19-1913-A, 22 Pa. Code '35.62).

The 1983 desegregation order mandated that all three public sectors participate in the desegregation process. OCR accepted the Commonwealth's plan entitled, "The Commonwealth of Pennsylvania Plan for Equal Opportunity in the State-Supported Institutions of Higher Education" in July 1983. The Plan covered the period 1983–1988 and specified the remediation activities that would be undertaken to meet the mandates of Title VI. These included a wide range of measures and activities, like enhancing Lincoln and Cheyney, desegregating student enrollments through increased recruitment of African-American students and improved retention programs, and desegregating faculties, staffs and governing boards (Commonwealth of Pennsylvania and United States Department of Education, Office for Civil Rights, 1999).

Pennsylvania officials submitted annual progress reports to OCR as well as a "Five Year Summary" of the Plan's accomplishments in November 1988. As noted previously, OCR never formally responded concerning Pennsylvania's compliance with the Plan. Following the Plan's expiration in 1988, the PDE assumed oversight responsibility for desegregation activities without OCR guidance. Each public institution was requested to submit new 3- to 5-year plans. Updated goals were distributed in 1989, followed by an action plan, released in January 1993, entitled "Plan to Improve Minority Student Achievement in Higher Education" (Commonwealth of Pennsylvania and United States Department of Education Office for Civil Rights, 1999).

The principal support provided for Lincoln and Cheyney in the original desegregation plan consisted of "The Equal Opportunity Professional Education Program," a scholarship program initiated in 1983 for graduate and professional education for students graduating from the two institutions. The Commonwealth designed this program to advance two goals: (a) the strengthening and enhancement of the Commonwealth's two traditional Black institutions, Cheyney University of Pennsylvania and Lincoln University, and (b) the elimination of the disparity in the proportion of entering Black and white graduate students in the state-supported institutions (Commonwealth of Pennsylvania and United States Department of Education, Office for Civil Rights, 1999).

Subsequent to the expiration of the original desegregation plan, a new equity plan was adopted by the State System Board of Governors in 1988 entitled, "The Affirmative Action and Equal Opportunity Plan: A Prospectus." An updated plan was adopted in July 1994 entitled, "Excellence and Equity—A Plan for Building Community in Pennsylvania's State System of Higher Education" (Commonwealth of Pennsylvania and United States Department of Education Office for Civil Rights, 1999).

As a component of the State System, Cheyney's role is described in these documents. However, concerns about the vitality of Cheyney were expressed in a 1993 study, which found serious concerns in numerous areas, such as governance, institutional advancement, fiscal affairs and physical plant (Commonwealth of Pennsylvania and United States Department of Education Office for Civil Rights, 1999). This report did not serve as the impetus for any major initiatives to address these problems.

The preceding discussion suggests that following expiration of the original desegregation plan and prior to the issuance of the order in *Fordice*, Pennsylvania was largely allowed to determine its own priorities and pace of activity vis-à-vis desegregation. Following the decision in *Fordice*, Pennsylvania was informed that OCR would be renewing its oversight of desegregation activities.

The partnership between Pennsylvania and OCR was formalized in May 1996. Individuals representing various interested constituencies were asked to serve as members of a "Partnership Working Group" charged with conducting an examination of issues of access, enrollment, retention, and graduation of African-American students. This body engaged in sporadic deliberations over the next year and a half. Then, in March 1998, OCR informed Pennsylvania that it was narrowing the scope of its concerns to three issues: (a) Cheyney University facilities; (b) the reservation of unique academic program areas for Cheyney; and (c) the enhancement of initiatives at selected TWIs in the areas of campus climate, student recruitment, and student retention (Commonwealth of Pennsylvania and United States Department of Education Office for Civil Rights, 1999). The focus on Cheyney University reflected, in part, the findings of a 1997 follow-up report to the 1993 study that identified some progress in correcting deficiencies, but few items that were actually completed (Commonwealth of Pennsylvania and United States Department of Education Office for Civil Rights, 1999).

Assessing Public Policy Affecting HBCUs

The public policy benefits generated by public institutions of higher education are typically discussed in three general categories—teaching, research, and service. Supporters of HBCUs have organized their cases for the continuing importance of these institutions around these three themes. In particular, as noted previously, it has been argued that HBCUs (a) provide academic and career preparation of an historically underserved population, (b) generate a distinct body of knowledge arising from the experiences of a distinct population, and (c) provide high levels of support to traditionally underserved communities.

The principal economic impact of instructional activities derives from the training of highly skilled workers. In economic terminology, universities provide an efficient method for students to augment their human capital in ways that increase both their earnings and the production of goods and services. Although the connection between the instructional activities of 4-year institutions and labor market outcomes is not as direct as is the case for vocational training enterprises and community colleges, the rationale for public support is still based, to a significant extent, on expected employment effects. Consequently, developing a more systematic approach to promoting synergies between the activities of public institutions of higher education and local, state, and regional labor market needs is a desirable public policy objective.

In the arena of vocational education, there has been a long-standing recognition of the need for a planned approach to matching supply and demand of human resources. As an example, in the early 1980s the National Center for Research in Vocational Education sponsored several forums focusing on how to determine the types of information needed by educational institutions and public policy makers to adjust activities to meet societal needs for skilled workers (Taylor, Rosen, & Pratzner, 1983). Similar perspectives have been applied to 4-year institutions as well.

Since the early 1980s the growing importance of the service sector as the core of the U.S. economy has contributed to expanded options for obtaining training for future employment. As an example, proprietary institutions are increasingly perceived by many prospective students as viable alternatives to traditional institutions of higher education. Faced with a continually shifting landscape, the decision-making process that policy makers must employ in making resource allocation decisions becomes ever more complex. Competition has intensified, not only among postsecondary institutions, but also between different segments of the educational pipeline. Moreover, policy makers must find ways to create incentives for collaboration among institutions to foster more efficient use of scarce resources.

A similar perspective can be applied to research and outreach activities. Policy makers must first decide how to allocate resources between theoretical and applied research. That decision will have differential impacts across institutions. Contemporary public policy prioritizes research that has concrete applications with respect to enhancing the public welfare. This type of research allows for greater collaboration among institutions with both similar and different research capacities. Such collaboration can, in many cases, produce more efficient outcomes than unbridled competition. In a parallel manner, decisions about support for outreach activities should take into account which institutions are best positioned to work most effectively in those communities with the greatest needs, and the allocation of resources should reflect those assessments.

In such a complex environment, how can policy makers approach the Herculean task of allocating resources in a way that optimizes outcomes in terms of levels of output, efficiency of resource use, and equity? The criteria listed below, suggested both by the preceding discussion and the earlier discussion of public policies focusing on HBCUs, are proposed as a starting point:

1. Uniqueness/overlap of institutional missions
2. Quantity/quality of human capital outputs (number of graduates, placement rates, earnings profiles)
3. Efficiency of resource use/absorptive capacity vis-à-vis new resources (educational production function—that is, enrollments, faculty resources, budgets)
4. Current versus potential institutional contributions to local, regional, and state economic development initiatives (quantity, quality, and distribution of benefits flowing from research and outreach activities)
5. Institution-specific characteristics that contribute uniquely to higher-education outcomes (e.g., service to disadvantaged populations and/or communities, higher retention rates, empowering institutional climate)

These criteria are clarified and used to examine the Pennsylvania deseg-regation agreement below.

1. Mission Definition

The historically circumscribed missions of public HBCUs and the tradi-tionally low priority assigned by state officials to the education of African-American students have created a policy dilemma. The education of black students has been the raison d'être for HBCUs, while it has been no more than a peripheral concern for TWIs. Moreover, the size imbalance between HBCUs and TWIs leads to disproportionate effects on the former when ef-forts are undertaken to adjust institutional missions.

Efforts by desegregation planners to reduce concentrations of African-American students at HBCUs run the risk of forcing undesirable changes in institutional culture. In particular, increasing enrollments of white students is a relatively new challenge for HBCUs and may require alteration of some institutional characteristics that have contributed to their success in educating Black students and may be incompatible with the traditional HBCU mission.

Program reservation, as a component of desegregation intervention, en-tails externally manipulated mission realignment among institutions. As noted previously, such realignments are designed principally to reduce racial identifiability, rather than optimizing educational outcomes. Planners appar-ently assume that an efficient and effective program is location independent, and that sufficient investments in infrastructure will enable recruitment of more diverse student bodies.

The approach to targeting enhancements at JSU included an effort to ensure that new programs would contribute directly to the urban dimension of JSU's mission, while also minimizing duplication of offerings at other institutions. In the case of Cheyney and Lincoln universities, the type of focus reflected in JSU's "urban mission" is not feasible, in part, because neither institution is located in close proximity to central city of Philadelphia. As part of the Pennsylvania settlement, the development and strengthening of several academic programs at Cheyney are to occur, with a particular empha-sis on computer science, middle school certification, geographic information systems, emerging technology, preprofessional programs and hotel, restau-rant, and institutional management programs. These program areas had been identified as priorities by Cheyney in its institutional strategic plan. Thus, similar to the JSU case, there was an effort to align program expansion plans with the institution's core mission. However, these programs will not be the exclusive province of Cheyney, although expansion within the State System's other universities will be limited, as a form of program reservation. Other universities located in close proximity to Cheyney already offer some of these programs (Commonwealth of Pennsylvania and United States Department of Education Office for Civil Rights, 1999). In addition, because Cheyney is not located in an urban setting, per se, it is unlikely to be able to take advantage of metropolitan economies of scale in attracting students to the new programs. As a consequence, programmatic overlap and possible duplication is likely to increase rather than decrease, and the short and intermediate term effects on Cheyney's racial identifiability are likely to be small.

2. Output of HBCUs

Over the last two decades there has been a marked shift in the production of African-American baccalaureate recipients away from HBCUs and toward TWIs. The proportion of baccalaureate degrees awarded to African-American students by HBCUs fell from 35.4 percent in 1976–1977 to 28.0 percent in 1993–1994 (National Center for Education Statistics, 1996). HBCUs contribute a significantly greater proportion of baccalaureate recipients in Mississippi than in Pennsylvania. In 1993–1994, Mississippi HBCUs produced 1,635 baccalaureate recipients, or 15.5 percent of all baccalaureate recipients. The comparable figures for Lincoln and Cheyney were 381 recipients, or 0.6 percent of all baccalaureate recipients (Calculated from data contained in National Center for Education Statistics, 1996; 1998). It is also useful to compare baccalaureate degree production in Pennsylvania and Mississippi with all HBCUs nationally. Relevant data are provided below in Table 4.1. The general trends in Pennsylvania and Mississippi follow the national pattern, that is, steady declines through 1990–1991 and increases in 1993–1994. Because some Mississippi HBCUs are much larger than their Pennsylvania counterparts, proportional relationships are the most appropriate comparison. In 1976–1977, Lincoln and Cheyney produced 32 percent as many degree recipients as Mississippi HBCUs. This figure fell to 29 percent, 28 percent, and 23 percent in subsequent periods. The percentage increase from 1990–1991 to 1993–1994 for Lincoln and Cheyney was 12 percent, compared to 25 percent for Mississippi HBCUs, 32 percent for all public HBCUs, and 27 percent for all HBCUs. These data suggest that Lincoln and Cheyney have not been able to maintain "production" levels comparable to other HBCUs.

While the number of graduates provides a quantitative measure of the output of HBCUs, it is also important to assess the quality of output. One measure of output is the earnings of Black graduates of HBCUs compared to Black graduates of TWIs. While specific studies for Mississippi and Pennsylvania graduates are not available, it is possible to extrapolate from other investigations. There are two major studies comparing outcomes for graduates of HBCUs and TWIs (Constantine, 1995; Ehrenberg and Rothstein, 1994). Ehrenberg and Rothstein's study focuses on African-American students who graduated from high school in 1972 and attended either a 4-year HBCU or

TABLE 4.1
Bachelor's Degrees Conferred by HBCUs: Pennsylvania, Mississippi,
4-Year Public and Total Selected Years, 1976–1994

Year	Pennsylvania HBCUs	Mississippi HBCUs	4-Year Public HBCUs	All HBCUs
1976–1977	550	1,695	15,591	23,551
1983–1984	409	1,405	13,990	21,430
1990–1991	341	1,225	13,947	21,627
1993–1994	381	1,635	18,390	27,425

Source: National Center for Education Statistics, U.S. Department of Education (1996). *Historically Black Colleges and Universities, 1976–1994.* NCES 96-902, by C. Hoffman, T. Snyder, and B. Sonnenberg. Washington, D.C.: National Center for Education Statistics, Tables 27, 30, 31, 32, 33, pp. 52–55.

another 4-year institution. Controlling for both college and individual characteristics they found that African-American students who attended HBCUs were more likely to receive a bachelor's degree than African-American students attending other institutions. However, they also found that HBCU attendees gained no future labor market benefits compared to other students (based on analysis of earnings in 1979). This resulted primarily because nongraduating attendees of HBCUs earned less than other nongraduates. To the extent that a similar pattern was found to characterize the contemporary social setting, public policy should reflect the reality that HBCUs appear to produce graduates of the same quality as non-HBCUs, but more efficiently. This evidence contradicts one of the key assumptions underlying contemporary desegregation policy—that is, that educational outcomes are improved if African-American students attend TWIs as opposed to HBCUs.

Constantine (1995) reexamined the experiences of this cohort, but focused on labor market outcomes in 1986 (when the average age of the sample was 32 compared to approximately 25 in the previous study). Her methodology incorporated a more detailed examination of enrollment options. The results indicated that HBCU graduates earned about 8 percent more than graduates of other institutions. Constantine (1995) also found evidence that public HBCUs appeared to increase enrollment at 4-year institutions for students who otherwise would have attended a 2-year institution or not attended college. Finally, unlike the previous study, there was no difference in earnings between nongraduating attendees of HBCUs and TWIs. Constantine's results reinforce the conclusion that the assumptions underlying contemporary desegregation policy may be flawed and that policy outcomes resulting from shifting enrollments of black students from HBCUs to TWIs may be suboptimal.

One of the key considerations in assessing the public policy implications of enrollment patterns is whether HBCUs and TWIs are attracting the African-American students with similar background characteristics. There were clear differences between the cohorts examined in the two studies reviewed above. However, desegregation policy includes efforts to reduce differences in the characteristics of white and black students entering public higher education. In Mississippi, this public policy objective was pursued by raising entrance requirements at HBCUs. In Pennsylvania, one component of the proposed desegregation settlement is continuing support for the Cheyney University Keystone Academy for honors students. In support of this commitment, the Commonwealth will include a special line item for $500,000 in the State System's 1999–2000 appropriations request to cover the cost of the Academy's pilot cohort, and subsequent appropriations will be $1 million for year two, $1.5 million for year three, and $2 million for all subsequent years. The level of funding from the Commonwealth will be reduced proportionately as the University succeeds in building an adequate endowment to support this program (Commonwealth of Pennsylvania and United States Department of Education, Office for Civil Rights, 1999).

3. Efficiency of Resource Use

The assessment of the efficiency with which higher-education institutions produce outputs is a complex undertaking. Enrollment levels drive many indicators that attempt to measure higher-education outputs (graduates) per unit of inputs. Enrollments can be treated as both outputs and inputs. As an output, enrollments are an indicator of the effectiveness of institutional recruitment and marketing efforts as well as the relative valuation of potential clients. As an input, enrollments measure the amount of raw material available for transformation into outputs (graduates) through the institution's educational production function. This educational production function is the mix of various labor, knowledge, and infrastructure inputs employed in the educational process. Concrete measures usually focus on faculty size, composition, and salary levels as well as total employment and budgetary expenditures.

One of the critical public policy questions is the extent to which the educational production functions of HBCUs are different from those of TWIs. If so, do these differences result from the relative efficiencies or inefficiencies of each? Alternatively, if the production functions differ, does the variety provide value for the overall system?

A. Enrollment Patterns

Table 4.2 below provides comparative enrollment data for HBCUs in Pennsylvania and Mississippi, as well as for all HBCUs. The general pattern can be described as declining enrollments from 1976 to 1984, followed by an

TABLE 4.2
Fall Enrollments, Selected HBCUs and Total Selected Years, 1976–1994

Year	Cheyney	Lincoln	Alcorn	Jackson State	MVSU	All HBCUs
1976	2,848	1,104	2,603	7,928	3,228	222,613
1980	2,426	1,294	2.341	7,099	2,564	233,537
1984	1,795	1,167	2,395	6,088	2,396	227,519
1988	1,361	1,251	2,757	6,777	1,756	239,755
1990	1,738	1,374	2,863	6,837	1,873	257,152
1991	1,477	1,458	3,244	6,639	2,059	269,335
1992	1,548	1,476	2,919	6,203	2,213	279,541
1993	1,519	1,445	2,712	6,346	2,330	282,856
1994	1,357	1,371	2,742	6,224	2,182	280,071

Source: National Center for Education Statistics, U.S. Department of Education. (1996). *Historically Black Colleges and Universities, 1976–1994.* NCES 96-902, by C. Hoffman, T. Snyder, and B. Sonnenberg. Washington, D.C.: National Center for Education Statistics, Table 8, pp. 28–31.

upward trend that continued into the early 1990s. There is some variation among the individual institutions, but the general pattern is fairly consistent.

Between 1984 and 1994, all of the institutions except Cheyney experienced enrollment growth. However, none matched the 23 percent enrollment growth for all HBCUs. The growth rates for Lincoln, Alcorn, Jackson State, and Mississippi Valley State were, respectively, 17 percent, 14 percent, 2 percent, and 9 percent. Cheyney lost 24 percent of its enrollment. Only Mississippi Valley State experienced enrollment growth between 1990 and 1994, and its growth rate of 16 percent exceeded that for all HBCUs of 9 percent. Lincoln's enrollment was virtually flat, while Alcorn and Jackson State experienced declines of 4 percent and 9 percent, respectively. Cheyney lost another 22 percent of its enrollment. The data indicate that Cheyney's enrollment pattern is the least stable of the HBCUs for which data are presented. This would suggest that interventions should prioritize the stabilization of Cheyney's enrollment. However, this focus, per se, is outside the scope of desegregation policy.

The suboptimality of desegregation policy vis-à-vis enrollments is evidenced by the fact that the declining proportion of African-American students enrolled at HBCUs has not resulted in sufficient enrollment growth of African-American students at TWIs to meet the expectations of desegregation planners. As an example, Penn State University enrolled about 350 fewer African-American residents of Pennsylvania in both 1994 and 1995 than necessary to meet enrollment goals based on criteria established by OCR (Enrollment Disparities and Enrollment Goals, 1994).

Despite desegregation interventions, the racial identifiability of HBCUs in both Mississippi and Pennsylvania is not in question. In fall 1994, 93.2 percent of Alcorn's enrollment was African-American and 6.0 percent was white. The comparable figures for Jackson State were 94.5 percent and 2.7 percent, and for Mississippi Valley State 99.3 percent and .6 percent, respectively. These figures can be compared to 95.0 percent and 2.9 percent for Cheyney and 90.1 percent and 6.1 percent for Lincoln. (Calculated from data in National Center for Education Statistics, 1996, Table 9, pp. 34–35).

B. Faculty and Staff Inputs

Table 4.3 below provides comparative data describing the employment profiles of the HBCUs in Pennsylvania and Mississippi, for all public 4-year institutions in both states, and for all HBCUs. As can be seen from the table, Cheyney's educational production function makes much more extensive use of full-time faculty than other institutions. This phenomenon is driven by the unionized status of its faculty. Thus, decision makers have much less flexibility in adjusting this component of Cheyney's educational production function than is the case for most HBCUs. The more general conclusion that can de drawn from Table 4.3 is that the human resource component of HBCUs'

TABLE 4.3
Faculty and Staff Employment: Selected HBCUs, Pennsylvania (PA), and Mississippi (MS) 4-Year Public Institutions, and All HBCUs (1993)

Category	Cheyney	Lincoln	PA 4-Year Public	Alcorn	Jackson State	MVSU	MS 4-Year Public	All HBCUs
Full-time faculty	96	85	15,180	163	320	106	3,389	13,406
Part-time faculty	5	293		34	123	26		4,194
Full-time faculty/ Total faculty (%)	95.0	77.5		82.7	72.2	80.3		76.2
Full-time employees	254	375		580	636	368		44,087
Total employees	309	745		653	1,110	404		52,154
Full-time faculty/ Full-time employees (%)	37.8	22.7	22.8	28.1	50.3	28.8	18.9	30.4
Total faculty/ Total employees	32.7	50.7		30.1	39.9	32.7		33.7

Source: National Center for Education Statistics, U.S. Department of Education (1996). *Historically Black Colleges and Universities, 1976–1994.* NCES 96-902, by C. Hoffman, T. Snyder, and B. Sonnenberg. Washington, DC: National Center for Education Statistics, Table 8, pp. 28–31; National Center for Education Statistics, U.S. Department of Education (1998). *Digest of Educational Statistics 1997.* NCES 98-015. Washington, DC: National Center for Education Statistics.

educational production functions exhibits wide variation. As a consequence, no single algorithm can be used to generate recommendations regarding optimal staffing levels and composition.

C. Revenue and Expenditure Patterns

Public HBCUs exhibit similar patterns of revenue sources as other public colleges and universities, although the proportion derived from endowments, private gifts, grants, and contracts are slightly smaller. Public HBCUs receive a higher proportion of revenue from government sources than other institutions. Expenditure patterns are similar to other public institutions, with about the same proportion spent on instruction, less on research, and more on institutional support and on operation and maintenance of plant (National Center for Education Statistics, 1996, pp. 14–15). In the absence of desegregation interventions, resource reallocations by states have favored TWIs. To illustrate, according to the National Center for Education Statistics (1996, p. 15), "increases in expenditure for students at both public and private HBCUs lagged behind increases in expenditures for student at all public and private

TABLE 4.4
Current Fund Revenues and Expenditures: Total and Percentage Changes Selected HBCUs and Total ($000—Selected Years)

Indicator	Cheyney	Lincoln	Alcorn	Jackson State	MVSU	All HBCUs
Current Fund Revenues (1976–1977)	11,922	9,293	13,201	27,106	9,083	984,241
Percent change (1983–1984/1976–1977)	45.3	52.1	64.7	37.2	74.0	85.9
Percent change (1989–1990/1983–1984)	25.7	50.2	21.6	52.5	11.3	48.1
Percent change (1993–1994/1989–1990)	15.9	21.5	24.8	20.3	33.2	28.9
Educational and General Expenditures (1976–1977)	10,982	7,673	10,366	24,081	6,657	783,927
Percent change (1983–1984/1976–1977)	40.2	54.6	68.9	31.5	43.6	84.9
Percent change (1989–1990/1983–1984)	24.6	55.3	21.6	43.2	51.0	47.8
Percent change (1993–1994/1989–1990)	16.1	22.2	35.6	19.9	26.5	32.0

Source: National Center for Education Statistics, U.S. Department of Education (1996). *Historically Black Colleges and Universities, 1976–1994.* NCES 96-902, by C. Hoffman, T. Snyder, and B. Sonnenberg. Washington, D.C.: National Center for Education Statistics, Table 8, pp. 28–31.

institutions between 1976–77 and 1993–94." Over the entire 1976–1977 to 1993–1994 periods, educational and general expenditures per student at HBCUs rose 4 percent (after adjustment for inflation) compared to 11 percent for all public colleges (National Center for Education Statistics, 1996, p. 15). Thus, as suggested previously, federal enhancement funding has served largely as a partial replacement for relative declines in state funding.

Table 4.4 provides comparative revenue and expenditure data for Pennsylvania and Mississippi HBCUs. Cheyney has consistently had growth rates among the lowest for the institutions. The principal public policy implication is that changes in Cheyney's educational production function may have been disproportionately constrained by budgetary limitations compared to the other HBCUs.

D. Comparative Performance Indicators

The imbalances in Cheyney's educational production function suggested by the data discussed above are confirmed when selected performance indicators are compared as in Table 4.5 below.

The data indicate that Cheyney and especially Lincoln have lower outputs per faculty member and per employee and lower outputs per thousand dollars of general fund expenditures. Lincoln has apparently been able to

TABLE 4.5
Performance Indicators, Selected HBCUs, and Total

Indicator	Cheyney	Lincoln	Alcorn	Jackson State	MVSU	All HBCUs
Enrollment/ total faculty (1993)	15.0	3.8	13.8	14.3	17.7	16.1
Baccalaureate degrees/ total faculty (1993)	1.6	.58	2.1	1.7	1.5	1.6
Enrollment/ total employees (1993)	4.9	1.9	4.2	5.7	5.8	5.4
Baccalaureate degrees/ total employees (1993)	.52	.30	.62	.66	.50	.53
Enrollment/($000) general fund expenditures						
1990–1991	.09	.07	.12	.15	.12	.11
1993–1994	.07	.06	.09	.12	.13	.10
Average faculty salary (1994–1995)	$56,348	$39,503	$34,238	$38,848	$33,797	$38,472

Source: Computed from data contained in various tables included in National Center for Education Statistics, U.S. Department of Education (1996). *Historically Black Colleges and Universities, 1976–1994.* NCES 96-902, by C. Hoffman, T. Snyder, and B. Sonnenberg. Washington, DC: National Center for Education Statistics.

offset its financial constraints by extensive use of part-time faculty and other employees. Cheyney has a disproportionately high-salary structure, reflecting the unionization of faculty in the State System of Higher Education (SSHE). This compounds the problems created by the slow growth in revenues and general fund expenditures discussed previously.

Although the desegregation agreement mandates additional funding for Cheyney, improvements in infrastructure are prioritized. As discussed previously, this pattern is consistent with the desegregation policy emphasis on increasing attractiveness of HBCUs to white students. The level of funding involved is substantial. The Commonwealth of Pennsylvania is committing to fund five capital projects totaling approximately $10.4 million. Funding for five additional authorized capital projects, totaling approximately $10.3 million, will be requested from the state legislature within the next five years. New authorization and funding for four additional new projects, totaling approximately $24.9 million, will also be sought to renovate existing facilities on the Cheyney campus by the start of the 2002–2003 academic year (Commonwealth of Pennsylvania and United States Department of Education, Office for Civil Rights, 1999). While these budgetary reallocations are likely to ameliorate the infrastructure problems at Cheyney, they do not address the basic imbalances in Cheyney's educational production function described previously.

4. Contributions to Local, Regional, and State Economic Development

There are few precedents available to provide guidance in assessing the impact of HBCUs on community development efforts. One study of special relevance was undertaken by Morse, Sakano, & Price (1996) and involved comparing the economic impact of three public institutions in North Carolina: North Carolina A & T (NCAT)—an HBCU, the University of North Carolina at Greensboro, and the University of North Carolina–Chapel Hill. The measures of impact used in the study are the dollar value of university, student, and visitor expenditures and the derivative effects of these expenditures on earnings, output and employment of residents. The authors found that NCAT generated the second-largest surplus per dollar of state appropriations and generated the largest relative impact on labor earnings. This study suggests at least the possibility that Cheyney and Lincoln could contribute significantly to development efforts. In fact, the authors conclude that "HBCUs have a social value in the sense that in their absence, the stock of human capital would be lower" and "where social welfare is an increasing function of output, an economy with HBCUs is better off than one without them" (Morse et al., 1996, p. 73).

Unfortunately, there is no direct evidence regarding the impact of Cheyney and Lincoln on the regional economy. It is clear, however, that the original desegregation plan did not include provisions for a greater participatory role for Cheyney or Lincoln universities in publicly supported development projects. Nor, as described later in this section, does the new agreement propose new initiatives in this area.

One of the most feasible approaches for increasing HBCU involvement in development projects is through collaboration with TWIs. However, the formal relationships between HBCUs and TWIs are generally focused elsewhere. As an example, in Pennsylvania formal linkages have focused primarily on cooperative degree programs and provision of opportunities for HBCU faculty, alumni, or both to obtain terminal degrees. The latter program was, in fact, mandated in the original desegregation plan.

Under the new agreement, Penn State would work with Cheyney to develop collaborative academic programs. Opportunities for Lincoln and Cheyney graduates to obtain advanced degrees would continue under the auspices of the Equal Opportunity Professional Education Program. In 1998, this program was restructured to further enhance these goals and the name was changed to the Horace Mann Bond-Leslie Pinckney Hill Scholarship, commemorating the first African-American presidents of Lincoln and Cheyney, respectively. The program now provides full scholarships for medical, dental, or law school education at Temple University, Pennsylvania State University, and the University of Pittsburgh to eligible graduates of Lincoln University and Cheyney University of Pennsylvania (Commonwealth of Pennsylvania and United States Department of Education, Office for Civil Rights, 1999).

In addition, under the proposed agreement a number of new initiatives would be established to facilitate student transfer among institutions in the southeastern quadrant of the state including Cheyney, West Chester, Penn State (including the Delaware County and Abington-Ogontz campuses), the Community College of Philadelphia, and the Delaware County Community College. Opportunities for student movement among institutions across the state would be expanded through an Academic Passport available to community college students who have earned an associate degree that allows transfer to any State System University and receive credit toward graduation for all coursework successfully completed for credit for the associate degree (Commonwealth of Pennsylvania and United States Department of Education Office for Civil Rights, 1999). These initiatives are clearly consistent with the desegregation policy objectives of promoting integrated learning environments and reducing the racial identifiability of institutions based on demographic characteristics of students.

While the proposals put forward to improve collaboration among higher-education institutions and across stages in the educational pipeline in Pennsylvania constitute an improvement over the design of the original desegregation plan, they are largely traditional. There are no concrete designs for interinstitutional collaboration on degree offerings and no mention of collaborative research and outreach initiatives.

At the same time, some of the proposed changes at Cheyney are likely to increase its capacity to participate in a broader range of publicly supported ventures. As an example, some new appointments are to be made to Cheyney's Council of Trustees to improve oversight and strengthen connections to potential sources of external support. In addition, special support is being provided to upgrade Cheyney's institutional advancement capabilities (Commonwealth of Pennsylvania and United States Department of Education Office for Civil Rights, 1999). What is missing is a mechanism to transform this potential into direct involvement in economic development projects.

The difficulties associated with engaging in a high level of outreach for institutions like Cheyney and Lincoln should not be minimized. To illustrate, a few years ago Lincoln and Cheyney universities were given possession of a major facility located in the inner-city area of West Philadelphia. Efforts to use this facility to build a stronger urban presence were largely unsuccessful, even after Penn State University relocated some offices to the facility. Lincoln and Cheyney have largely abandoned this initiative due to funding constraints.

5. *Effects of Institution-Specific Culture on Student Experiences*

As noted previously, one of the claims advanced by supporters of HBCUs is that these institutions offer a more positive learning environment for African-American students that contribute to positive retention and graduation outcomes. Presumably, these positive outcomes are especially salient for students from disadvantaged backgrounds. Consequently, in comparing retention and graduation rates between HBCUs and TWIs it is important to control for student background. Unfortunately, detailed studies comparing the academic progression of African-American students in HBCUs and TWIs in Pennsylvania are not available. However, summary statistics are available for the period during which the first desegregation order was in effect and are presented in Table 4.6.

While the data seem to suggest that the claims of supporters have some validity for Lincoln University, this does not appear to be the case for Cheyney. Differences in the backgrounds of students may account, in part, for this difference but it is not clear that this is the primary cause. Additional insights can be generated by examining information about campus climate and faculty characteristics.

A. Institutional Climate

Although current information is not available, the study by Cheatham, Slaney, & Moses (1990) comparing the psychosocial development of African-American students at Penn State University and Lincoln University is directly relevant. In contrast to the claims of HBCU advocates, the authors found that

TABLE 4.6
Retention and Graduation Rates for Black Students in Selected Pennsylvania Universities—
Selected Years

Institution	Black freshmen (1986)	Retained (1991)	Retention rate	5-year graduation rate (1983 cohort)	5-year graduation rate (1984 cohort)
Lincoln				34%	31%
Cheyney	321	87	27%	25%	16%
SSHE—					
excluding Cheyney	895	397	44%	25%	19%
SSHE total	1216	484	40%	25%	18%
Penn State	265	93	35%	33%	31%
Temple	489	169	35%	20%	23%
University of					
Pittsburgh	307	93	30%	31%	42%

Source: The Pennsylvania Legislative Black Caucus (1992). Report, The African-American Reality in Higher Education in Pennsylvania: Opportunities Denied!, 1980–1990. Harrisburg, PA: The Pennsylvania Legislative Black Caucus (June).

African-American students attending Lincoln did not appear to be benefiting from a more positive climate than those attending Penn State. Students attending Penn State reported more involvement in cultural activities and exhibited greater emotional autonomy—that is, freedom from the need for others' approval. Students at Lincoln scored higher on a scale that is designed to measure whether a student's lifestyle is consistent with good health and wellness practices. Lower participation in cultural activities may simply reflect the overall cultural ambience of the institution. The variance between these findings and the claims of supporters of HBCUs may result, in part, from regional cultural differences. Whatever the reason for the discrepancy, however, it does not appear that the educational production functions of Lincoln and Cheyney are as successful in creating a climate that yields positive educational outcomes as would be anticipated from the claims of supporters.

B. Faculty Composition

Proponents of HBCUs have also maintained that one reason for the more positive experiences of students at HBCUs is the greater availability of Black faculty role models Table 4.7 below provides comparative information on the composition of faculty at selected Mississippi HBCUs, Lincoln and Cheyney universities, and all HBCUs. The percentage of Black full-time faculty members at Lincoln and Cheyney is in line with the national average, while those

TABLE 4.7
Instructional Faculty—Black and Total Selected HBCUs and All HBCUs
1993 and 1994–1995

Institution	Total full-time faculty	Black full-time faculty	Percent Black	Total part-time faculty	Black part-time faculty	Percent Black
Cheyney	96	55	57.2	5	4	80.0
Lincoln	85	49	57.6	293	232	79.1
Alcorn State	163	102	62.6	34	26	76.4
Jackson State	320	201	62.8	123	79	64.2
MVSU	106	75	70.8	26	23	88.5
All HBCUs	13,406	7,777	58.0	4,194	2,339	55.8

Source: National Center for Education Statistics, U.S. Department of Education (1996). *Historically Black Colleges and Universities, 1976–1994.* NCES 96-902, by C. Hoffman, T. Snyder, and B. Sonnenberg. Washington, D.C.: National Center for Education Statistics, Table 40, pp. 68–69.

at the Mississippi HBCUs are slightly above average. The percentage of Black part-time faculty is higher at all of the institutions than the national average. The percentages at Cheyney and Lincoln are almost identical. Consequently, differences in the retention and graduation rates cannot be attributed to faculty demographic variation.

The examination of the available information about institutional climate, faculty demographic characteristics, and persistence and graduation patterns suggests that if Cheyney is indeed providing an especially nurturing environment for black students, then it is manifested in ways not captured by traditional indicators.

Summary

Based on the criteria examined above, the following conclusions can be drawn regarding the desegregation outcomes in Pennsylvania:

1. As is the case for all public HBCUs, policy makers operating from contradictory orientations have widely varying perceptions of the appropriate mission of Cheyney University. There is continuing overlap of institutional missions across public institutions that will persist even after complete implementation of the new desegregation agreement. Unlike the situation of JSU in Mississippi, the nonurban location of Cheyney increases the difficulty of defining a unique mission within the SSHE.

There is currently no mechanism to harmonize conflicting role expectations. The situation facing Lincoln University is even more problematic. The origin of Lincoln as a private institution and its current status as an SRI preclude its participation in the reallocation process mandated by the desegregation agreement. Thus, it is in a state of limbo vis-à-vis its role within the SSHE, since it is largely ignored by both desegregation planners and state policy makers.

2. Direct information about the career profiles of Cheyney graduates is currently unavailable. Information from various research studies suggests that Black graduates of HBCUs generally have greater earnings potential than Black graduates of TWIs. However, there are obvious variations across individual institutions. A study of the earnings profiles of black graduates of HBCUs and TWIs in Pennsylvania would provide useful information for determining the extent to which Pennsylvania HBCUs provide students with unique educational experiences that translate into future earnings premiums.

3. The educational production function of Cheyney is significantly dissimilar from that of other HBCUs. These differences contribute to suboptimal outcomes in various areas because of Cheyney's enrollment instability. The problematic dimensions of Cheyney's educational production function appear to result from a combination of distinctive institutional characteristics such as size and budgetary limitations deriving from relatively parsimonious allocations from state sources. Institutional research should be conducted to identify strategies to bolster Cheyney's educational activities. Without careful planning, efforts to increase the enrollment of white students through program enhancements have the potential to further distort Cheyney's educational production function.

4. The size and location of Cheyney create difficulties with respect to active involvement in state and regional economic development initiatives. Existing and emerging partnerships with TWIs and other organizations are not operative in this area. There is a need for new types of partnerships formed around the Kellogg Commission's model of the engaged institution. In particular, the possibility of forming a network of engaged institutions comprised of Pennsylvania's HBCUs and selected TWIs should be explored. It is significant that Penn State University is identified in the Kellogg report as one of the models of an engaged institution. It is acknowledged for its engagement with business, with communities, and with the future (distance education initiatives). Partnerships with Cheyney and Lincoln universities in these areas would enable Pennsylvania's HBCUs to become more active players in statewide, national, and international venues. Policy makers in various state agencies should establish a plan to ensure participation of HBCUs in major development initiatives. This could be accomplished via a state equivalent to the Executive

Order issued by President Clinton. There are good reasons to believe that changes in the administrative structure at Cheyney will facilitate greater participation in economic development networks in the future.

5. Direct evidence regarding unique institutional characteristics at Cheyney that provide a distinctly positive environment for Black students does not exist. However, the limited information available that focuses on other HBCUs suggests that identifying these characteristics may be difficult. Comparative case studies examining the experiences of Black students at Pennsylvania HBCUs and comparing the experiences of Black students at HBCUs and TWIs in Pennsylvania could yield important information that could lead to enhanced environments for all students in both types of institutions.

In general, the desegregation process in Pennsylvania is not likely to result in significant reductions in the racial identifiability of Cheyney. In fact, it is not clear from the evidence considered in this investigation that this is an appropriate public policy objective at this point in time. Before such a policy thrust can have a reasonable chance of success, a concerted effort must be undertaken to stabilize Cheyney's enrollment, which has been improving in recent years. However, these gains have come from Cheyney's traditional constituency, not the illusive body of prospective white students that deseg-regation planners envision. To build on its recent momentum, Cheyney needs resources to shore up its current educational production function in addition to the resources committed to establish new programs. In short, there is a need for an approach to institutional enhancement that balances competing policy objectives more effectively than is currently the case.

The preceding observations and recommendations have implications beyond the boundaries of Pennsylvania as discussed below.

Public Policy Implications

Current public policy toward HBCUs is highly fragmented. If public HBCUs are to play a major role in the higher-education arena during the next century, there is a critical need to resolve the policy conflicts explored in this investigation. Resolution will require policy makers at the various levels, leaders of public HBCUs, and various stakeholders to reach a consensus regarding the mission of public HBCUs. Particular emphasis must be placed on which constituents they are expected to serve. There will, of course, be variation in the individual missions of institutions, but there must be a general agreement regarding, for example, whether high levels of racial identifiability are acceptable if institutions are actively engaged in serving particular com-munities. Reaching such a consensus will require more detailed institutional studies than are currently available. As an example, there is a need to know much more about the operation of public HBCUs and how they achieve the disproportionately positive outcomes for African-American students claimed by proponents. Special funding should be provided to enable public HBCUs to undertake the type of institutional self-studies required to generate the necessary information. These case studies can then be compared and synthesized to provide a more accurate picture of the educational production functions of HBCUs.

Assuming that a policy consensus can be reached, policy makers at the various levels must coordinate policies to maximize the likelihood of success of public HBCUs in realizing their missions. As a first step, conflicting signals and incentives emanating from desegregation and enhancement policies must be reconciled. This would enable states to approach the issue of integrating HBCUs into the fabric of overall educational planning with greater assurance that their efforts would not be stymied by federal policies.

As suggested previously, achieving greater involvement of public HBCUs in state development initiatives will require an emphasis on partnerships with TWIs and other major actors reflecting the Kellogg Commission's model of engaged institutions. Such partnerships could be structured on a more egalitarian foundation than existing relationships. States are in the position to mandate greater collaboration between public HBCUs and public TWIs. Such an initiative is absolutely critical, because the relationship between public colleges and universities and other societal institutions is being altered significantly through a growing number of bilateral and multilateral partnerships and consortia. Although so-called public-private partnerships have received the most attention, these alliances take many forms and include a variety of types of actors (see, e.g., Clark, 1997; Ryan and Heim, 1997; and Usnick, Shove, and Gissy, 1997). The Kellogg Commission would do well to undertake a special study to explore how HBCUs can become full partners in the process of promoting institutional engagement.

Current consternation regarding the role of public HBCUs has its origins in this nation's distasteful history of race relations. There is no better time than now to resolve ongoing policy conflicts. Major anticipated changes in U.S. demographics will require a more sophisticated approach to understanding the role of different types of institutions in the overall system of higher education. Policy makers must avoid knee-jerk reactions based on a nebulous vision of nonracialism. The diversity of the U.S. population and the unique culturally influenced knowledge sets associated with each of the U.S.'s population groups constitute a major resource for addressing the challenges that will emerge during the next century. All institutions of higher education must find ways to synthesize such knowledge. Some institutions will specialize in developing and disseminating knowledge and insights associated with particular cultural traditions. Public HBCUs can play a vital role in this process.

However, more informed and consistent public polices will be required for HBCUs to maximize their contribution.

References

Cheatham, Harold E., Slaney, Robert B., & Moses, Nancy. (1990). Institutional effects on psychosocial development of African American college students. *Journal of Counseling Psychology 37*, 453–458.

Clark, Will. (1997). The global information economy and its effect on local economic development. In James Pappas (Ed.), *The university's role in economic development: From research to outreach* (*New directions for higher education, 97*, 25(1) (pp. 51–61).

Committee L on the Historically Black Institutions and the Status of Minorities in the Profession. (1995, January/February). The Historically Black Colleges and Universities: A future in the balance. *Academe.*

Commonwealth of Pennsylvania and United States Department of Education, Office for Civil Rights. (1999). *Partnership report and commitments.* Harrisburg, PA: Department of Education.

Constantine, Jill. (1995). The effect of attending Historically Black Colleges and Universities on future wages of Black students. *Industrial and Labor Relations Review 48*(3), 531–546.

Ehrenberg, Ronald, & Rothstein, D. (1994). Do Historically Black institutions of higher education confer unique advantages on Black students? An initial analysis. In Ronald Ehrenberg (Ed.), *Choices and consequences: Contemporary policy issues in education.* Ithaca, NY: ILR Press.

Enrollment disparities and enrollment goals, Pennsylvania State University 1994–1995. (1994). [Mimeo].

Kellogg Commission on the Future of State and Land-Grant Universities. (1999*). Returning to our roots: The engaged institution.* Washington, DC: National Association of State Universities and Land-Grant Colleges.

Knight v. State of Alabama, 14 F.3d 1534, 1541 (11th Cir. 1994).

Meredith v. Fair, 305 F. 2d 343 (5th Cir. 1962).

Morse, Lawrence, Sakano, Ryoichi, & Price, Gregory. (1996). Black public colleges and universities as projects: How do they rank relative to white public colleges and universities? *The Review of Black Political Economy 24*(4), 65–79.

National Center for Education Statistics, U.S. Department of Education. (1996). *Historically Black Colleges and Universities, 1976–1994.* NCES 96-902, by C. Hoffman, T. Snyder, and B. Sonnenberg. Washington, D.C.: National Center for Education Statistics.

National Center for Education Statistics, U.S. Department of Education. (1998). *Digest of Educational Statistics 1997*. NCES 98-015. Washington, D.C.: National Center for Education Statistics.

Office for Civil Rights, U.S. Department of Education. (1991). *Historically Black Colleges and Universities and higher education desegregation*. Washington, D.C.: U.S. Department of Education, January.

The Pennsylvania Legislative Black Caucus. (1992, June). *Report, the African-American reality in higher education in Pennsylvania: Opportunities denied, 1980–1990*. Harrisburg, PA: The Pennsylvania Legislative Black Caucus.

Pennsylvania statute, 24 P.S. 020-2002-A. (1983).

Ryan, James, & Heim, Arthur. (1997). Promoting economic development through university and industry partnerships. In James Pappas (Ed.), *The university's role in economic development: from research to outreach* (*New directions for higher education*, No. 97, 25(1) (pp. 42–50).

Taylor, Robert, Rosen, Howard, & Pratzner, Frank (Eds.). (1983). *Responsiveness of training institutions to changing labor market demands*. Columbus, OH: The National Center for Research in Vocational Education.

United States v. Fordice, 505 U.S. 717, 112 S.Ct. 2727, (1992).

United States v. Louisiana, 9 F.3d 1159, 1164 (5th Cir. 1993).

Usnick, Russell, Shove, Chris, & Gissy, Francine. (1997). Maximizing community development through collaboration. In James Pappas (Ed.), *The university's role in economic development: from research to outreach* (*New directions for higher education*, 97, 25(1) (pp. 51–61).

The Threatened Future of Affirmative Action and the Search for Alternatives

REGINALD WILSON

Introduction

Since the *Bakke* decision was rendered over twenty years ago (*Regents of the University of California v. Bakke*, 1978), colleges and universities have been using its guidance to allow consideration of race and gender as a "plus factor" in their admissions policies to boost the number of minorities and women in their student bodies and to overcome the effects of past sexual exclusion and racial discrimination. The *Bakke* decision, in conjunction with the Civil Rights Act of 1964 and Executive Order 11246 of 1965 (affirmative action), gave academia powerful legal tools to use in correcting discriminatory practices that have kept women and minorities artificially underrepresented in many academic and professional fields. Today, women outnumber men in college enrollment, and have done so since the mid-1980s. Minorities have increased their numbers in graduate school during the same period, from 167,000 to 286,000 in 1998 (Wilds & Wilson, 1997–1998).

This chapter will trace the increasing limitations placed on the use of affirmative action by the recent rulings of the courts. It will also discuss some of the alternative methods and programs used by a variety of colleges and universities to cope with these restrictions in an effort to maintain minority enrollment and student diversity.

Court Decisions and Their Effects

Despite the impact of affirmative action overall and the remarkable, but modest, success stories alluded to above, the public and the courts have become convinced that the strategy of affirmative action gives minorities unfair advantages in college admissions and jobs. Despite the fact that minorities and women have only recently begun to overcome the barriers of the past, the drumbeat of incessant negative media attention and the increasingly restrictive decisions by a conservative federal judiciary have tightened the strictures of permissible affirmative action and have soured the public on continued efforts to improve the status of minorities.

The *Hopwood v. Texas* (1996) decision and the passage of Proposition 209 in California are portents of the conservative mood of the federal courts and the equally conservative mood of the public respectively. Cheryl Hopwood and her three male codefendants sued the University of Texas Law School for denying them admission while accepting several Black applicants with lower scores than she obtained. (It should be noted that there were 103 white applicants with *higher* scores than she had who also were rejected and several whites with *lower* scores who were accepted.) The district court ruled that she had no case, gave her $1 in damages, and said she could reapply without paying an additional fee. However, on appeal to the Fifth Circuit Court, a three-judge panel ruled that she had been discriminated against and that race could not be used as a factor in admission. In the opinion of the court, "race has no more meaning than height or weight" when it comes to admissions decisions. Two of the judges (*Hopwood*, 1996) went even further, declaring that Justice Lewis Powell's controlling opinion in the *Bakke* case—stating that race could be used as a plus factor in college admissions—was merely his opinion and did not have the force of law! The case was appealed to the Supreme Court. Many legal experts thought that the Supreme Court would hear the appeal, if for no other reason than the temerity of a lower court declaration that a ruling of the Supreme Court is not binding law! But to the surprise of many, the Supreme Court denied *certiorari* on the narrow ground that since the University of Texas Law School no longer used the admission criteria that had resulted in the denial of Hopwood, the case was moot. Thus, *Hopwood* is law in only the three states covered by the Fifth Circuit—Texas, Louisiana, and Mississippi. That presents a unique problem for Mississippi, which is covered by an earlier Supreme Court ruling; in *United States v. Fordice* (1992), the court ruled that racial counts *must* be considered in reducing Mississippi's previously segregated public higher education system. Obviously, the contradictory rulings in *Fordice* and *Hopwood* will eventually have to be reconciled. For the time being, however, the rulings have caused confusion and some legal head scratching.

Compounding the problem of *Hopwood* has been the ruling of Texas Attorney General Dan Morales. His interpretation, which is binding on all public colleges and universities in Texas, is that by implication, the *Hopwood* ruling on admissions extends also to race specific scholarships, recruitment, and financial aid. Such an interpretation further restricts valuable tools used in recruiting minority students. The decline in minority enrollment with the imposition of the *Hopwood* ruling is testimony to the devastating effect of Morales's sweeping decision.

The effect of the passage of Proposition 209 (1995) in California had an equally devastating effect. Originally the Board of Regents of the University of California System had been successful, after rancorous debate, in passing Board of Regents Order SP-1 (1994), which prohibited the University from using affirmative action in student admissions, financial aid, and the awarding of contracts for work at the University. Regent Ward Connerly, who took the lead in the regents' successful action, then led an effort (backed by the governor of California and partially financed by the conservative Center for Individual Rights) to include Proposition 209, calling for the same restriction as SP-1, as an amendment to the state constitution. Although it lagged in early balloting, the infusion of considerable funds paved the way for the measure to be successful in garnering 54 percent approval by the electorate, thus making the exclusion of affirmative action effective throughout the state of California.

The decline of minority admissions was as drastic in the University of California System (particularly at the UCLA and Berkeley campuses) as it had been in Texas. The decline is especially threatening to the production of minority lawyers and doctors, since among the top five producers of minority graduates in these professions were the University of California, Berkeley, UCLA, and the University of Texas-Austin (Karabel, 1998), the other two being Howard and Xavier.

The precipitous decline of minority admissions in these two states has had ramifications far beyond their boundaries and has alarmed higher education administrators. The state of Washington, for example, has passed Proposition 200, which has had the same effect as 209 had in the state of California (and was financed and led by the same forces). And college administrators have become reluctant to vigorously pursue the implementation of affirmative action for fear of lawsuits and the negative implications of recent federal court decisions. During their tenures, Presidents Reagan and Bush appointed the majority of sitting federal judges whose narrow vision is reflected in the increasing restrictions on affirmative action (Orfield, 1998).

Given the limited range of allowable actions that can now be taken to increase the presence of minorities on college campuses, administrators have increasingly relied on a variety of non-race-conscious measures to achieve the desired results. The first thing they have discovered is that race-conscious remedies are the most effective means of overcoming racially restrictive policies. What we often forget is that race restrictive policies did not just restrict minority access to predominantly white universities, they also restricted their *preparation* for college and, indeed, their consideration of the *possibility* of even going to college. Thus, true affirmative action not only vigorously recruits minorities to college, it also helps them overcome their

deficiencies with remedial classes and provides scholarships for their economic limitations. Such measures have been shown to work where implemented, most notably in the case of the City University of New York with its
open admissions policies (which have now been restricted by Mayor Guiliani).
Given the realities of current court decisions and state initiatives, the search
for race neutral alternatives continues, while allowing for their deficiencies in
achieving the maximum result. Race-blind admission procedures have just
begun in the light of the *Hopwood* decision and Proposition 209. They are
tentative, new, and experimental, and their results cannot be accurately measured just yet. A description of their efforts follows.

In Texas, on the one hand, following the court decision, the state legislature provided automatic access to the University of Texas "for any student
finishing in the top 10 percent of his or her high school class" (Orfield, 1998).
Black and Hispanic numbers did not improve, only Asian numbers increased.
A similar plan is being considered in California, allowing the top 4 percent
access. However, any plan that lets in a certain number of high school graduates without modifying the admission process is likely to have a similar
result. The University of Houston Law School, on the other hand, maintained
its minority enrollment by a combination of aggressive recruitment and less
reliance on the Law School Admission Test (LSAT), which suggests a strategy that might be considered by other colleges and universities.

The experiment at the University of California, Irvine (UC-Irvine) bears
some watching. In the wake of the University of California Regents vote
ending affirmative action, the UC-Irvine admissions committee expanded their
criteria beyond just grades and test scores to include several multidimensional aspects of student strengths, like leadership, overcoming adversity,
coming from a deprived area, and so on. (Wilbur & Bonous-Hammarth,
1998).

The University of Michigan also broadened its admission criteria while
enhancing its recruitment efforts and establishing a number of special programs, all of which led to its achieving the top graduation rate of minority
students among the Big Ten Schools. It must be remembered, however, that
the University of Michigan is being sued for allegedly giving minorities
inappropriate advantages in admission by the same Center for Individual
Rights that has been successful in California and Washington. The University
is aggressively challenging this suit and believes it can win. The case is to
be decided shortly.

Another initiative being tried in a few states is one where the University
reaches out to one or more elementary and secondary schools and intervenes
in their curriculum and teacher skill development to prepare younger students
for admission to college.

In addition to the use of the various "race neutral" methods in admissions
practices, some colleges and universities have experimented with a variety of

strategies in an attempt to maintain their student diversity while at the same time complying with the strictures imposed by the limitations on affirmative action. The search for alternatives has taken several directions.

Not all diversity efforts have stressed the same tactics. Some have benefited from earlier efforts that were not as successful or efficient. Some institutions have been drawn to certain methods because they were more compatible with their mission. Other institutions have combined several methods to enhance their students' retention and success. Daryl Smith suggests, "[b]ecause of the inherent complexity of the topic, we believe it is necessary to examine multiple dimensions of diversity in higher education" (Smith, Gerbick, Figueroa, Watkins, Levitan, Moore, Merchant, Bellak, & Figueroa, 1997, p. 8).

Diversity efforts can generally be placed under four broad categories: inclusion, student relations, academics, and institutional change, with the understanding, of course, that institutions may have more than one or two of these methodologies operating at the same time.

Inclusion

Inclusion represents all institutional efforts to increase underrepresented students enrolling at a university or college. Probably all institutions, at one time or another, practiced some form of vigorous recruitment as a part of their inclusion efforts. Unfortunately, many of these schools thought, naively, that all they had to do was get the bodies on campus and the rest would take care of itself. They soon found out—as minority students dropped out—that admission alone is often not enough. On the other hand, elite universities like Princeton and Harvard do little besides recruiting the very best minority students. They have found that "graduation rates rise as the selectivity of the colleges rises . . . carefully chosen minority students have not suffered from attending colleges heavily populated by white and Asian classmates with higher standardized test scores" (Bowen & Bok, 1998). Thus, it is important to distinguish between highly selective colleges and those more general institutions that admit most students who apply, although it is equally important to remember that some of the latter institutions have compensatory programs that enhance minority students' chances of success (Richardson and Skinner, 1990). Typical of the highly selective schools are the privates, like Princeton University and Columbia University, and the equally elite publics, like the University of Michigan and Miami University that were included in a massive study by William Bowen and Derek Bok entitled *The Shape of the River: Long-term Consequences of Considering Race in College and University Admissions* (1998).

In *The Shape of the River*, Bowen and Bok show how, collectively, 25 leading, selective universities have succeeded with minority students in their postgraduate careers. Indeed, the minority students exceed their white peers in graduating from law and medical schools despite suffering disadvantages in their undergraduate preparation (such as low SAT scores and low GPAs). Conversely, Richardson and Skinner document in their book *Achieving Quality and Diversity* (1990) that some public and less selective universities that devote their resources to enhancing student achievement are able to succeed in increasing the graduation of minority students while maintaining high standards. Ultimately, the answer to underpreparation will lie with improvement in the elementary and secondary schooling provided in inner-city areas. But as long as Americans are wedded to locally funded school districts, the disparity between rich and poor districts will be stubbornly maintained. Thus, efforts to bridge the gap in minority preparation will rely on programs such as James Comer's and Xavier University's (described later in this chapter).

Student Relations

   Student relations refers to all those programs intended to lessen the "chilling" effect of college environments that can cause alienation, poor group relations, hostility, lower grades, and dropping out. This can encompass a multiplicity of programs such as mentoring programs, acculturation programs, centers for students, campus activities, intergroup programs, and so forth. A study by Sedlacek showed that when minority students belonged to campus organizations, their retention and feelings of belonging were significantly enhanced (Sedlacek, 1995). At the University of Michigan, there were several programs that enhanced the efforts of the University to retain minority students and graduate them successfully (Moody, 1990). Among them were the Leadership Development Program, the Women in Science Program, the Mandela Anti-Racist Education Center, and the Quality of Life Program. These programs are partly responsible for the fact that the University of Michigan has the highest graduation rate for minority students of all the Big Ten schools.
   A student peer-mentoring program was initiated at the University of North Carolina–Greensboro. Results from a survey instrument that measures the positive purpose of participants and good interpersonal relations revealed that minority participants in the program were significantly less likely to drop out than students not in the program (Bell & Drakeford, 1992). Davine (1994) studied 342 white students enrolled in a required course at the University of Iowa whose theme was affirmative action and increasing diversity on their campus. The results indicated that students' attitudes moved in a positive direction after the course (Davine, 1994). Both of these efforts stress the effect on students' attitudes and feelings, with the intent of strengthening positive feelings about life on campus and enhancing good relations with diverse students.

Academics

Academics stresses the enhancement of the teaching/learning process in order to improve students' mastery of the curriculum. This is especially important for minority students, who often come from impoverished educational backgrounds and who sometimes suffer a wide academic performance gap in relation to their student peers. That gap can be overcome, as evidenced in some of the innovative programs described below.

The Mathematics Workshop Program (MWP) developed by Phillip Uri Treisman at the University of California, Berkeley (Treisman & Fullilove, 1990), was one such innovative program that achieved remarkable results in calculus performance. The African-American and Latino participants in the MWP earned grades of B-minus or better at a significantly greater rate then the grades earned by their white and Asian peers who were not in the MWP, despite the minority students having lower math SAT scores. Professor Treisman, who is now at the University of Texas at Austin, has replicated his success at over 25 other institutions. Henry Frierson, at the University of North Carolina at Chapel Hill, has achieved similar results using the Treisman model with African-American nursing and medical students (Frierson, Malone, & Shelton, 1990). He was able to significantly improve their scores on nursing and medical exams from what they had been before his intervention.

Lewis Kleinsmith, a biology professor at the University of Michigan, introduced a computer training program in his introductory biology classes. The innovation not only raised the minority students' scores to those of the white students, but also raised both groups' scores to over 80 percent mastery of the materials (Kleinsmith & Johnston, 1991).

These successes in academic improvement have also been achieved at the elementary school level where, quite properly, they ought to begin. James Comer's remarkable work in the New Haven schools is instructive. Introducing his parenting, instructional, and counseling teams to the mostly African-American, poor, single-parent students at two elementary schools, he was able to improve their achievement levels to number two and three in the district. His work has been widely publicized (Comer, 1988). Not as well known but equally striking in results is Barbara Sizemore's study of the Madison Elementary School in Pittsburgh (Sizemore, 1988). This school, like James Comer's in New Haven, was predominantly African-American (94 percent), poor (86 percent), and single parented (60 percent). With her strong leadership and her stress on holding teachers accountable for the achievement of their students, the principal was able to raise Madison School to number one among the thirty-three elementary schools in Pittsburgh in math and reading achievement, as measured by the California Achievement Test. These case studies are all the more remarkable because they are contrary to the conventional wisdom that children with the demographic characteristics described above are doomed to school failure or, at best, substantial under-achievement. It is this powerful hold of conventional wisdom on most educators that prevents them from adopting the successful mechanisms of Comer and Sizemore.

Institutional Change

Institutional change is both the most radical and the rarest of the inclusion methodologies. Unlike the methods described above, which are characterized by one or two courageous faculty successfully trying out an innovative approach, institutional change means the *entire* college transforms itself to meet the unique educational needs of its minority students.

Mount St. Mary's college is a Catholic, women's college in Los Angeles that is now 70 percent Latino and 10 percent Black (Mount St. Mary's, 1995). It has two campuses, a junior campus and a senior campus. It admits women who have low-test scores or poor high school grades to its junior campus. It has an over 70 percent transfer rate from its junior to its senior campus, attesting to a rigorous course of study at its junior campus. And it enjoys a 69 percent graduation rate from its senior campus, which is nearly twice the rate for minority students nationally. These results were brought about by changes on the campus, in the curriculum, and with the introduction of a new freshman seminar. In addition, the entire faculty developed new teaching techniques. Similarly, Xavier University (a Historically Black College) has undergone a radical transformation of its teaching methods to accommodate the underpreparation of its students, most of whom come from the New Orleans public schools ("Tiny Black College," 1990). It begins with the preparation of its future students before they enter college by educating them in summer courses in math, chemistry, and biology in the 9th, 10th, and 11th grades respectively. And the summer before they arrive on campus, they take a 4-week course in analytical reasoning. After they matriculate, their textbooks are rewritten to cover just the material they need to know in order to grasp the concepts, and they have vocabulary drill every day. Such rigorous preparation pays off in that Xavier, with just 2900 students, sends more of its Black graduates to medical school than any other college. And over 55 percent of its students are majoring in a science—more than any other liberal arts institution. It also produces the largest number of Black pharmacists.

Admittedly, the two schools described above are both small, private colleges, which makes their transformation easier. But we should recognize that it is their commitment to educating *all* of their students and convincing their faculty to radically alter their teaching methods that makes them uniquely successful in their transformation, not simply the fact of their size.

In another example of attempted institutional transformation, the City University of New York's (CUNY) experiment with open admissions revealed remarkable, but complex, indications of success (Lavin, Alba & Silberstein, 1979). A lengthy analysis of the program concluded that it "was aimed at minority students, primarily lower-class Blacks and Hispanics, but to a degree not generally recognized, it also benefited working- and middle-class whites." Despite its benefit to whites, "Blacks and Hispanics in large proportions would not have enrolled [in CUNY] had it not been for open admissions" (p. 85). Not only did large numbers enroll, but also, with targeted remedial programs, equally large numbers of minorities were graduating. Coming at the same time as the *Coleman Report* (Coleman, Campbell, Hobson, McPartland, Mood, Weinfield, & York, 1966) and Christopher Jencks's study of *Inequality* (Jencks, Smith, Acland, Bane, Cohen, Gintis, Heyns, & Michelson, 1972), which cast doubt on the ability of students to overcome their disadvantaged background, the open admissions policy at CUNY did much to dispute these influential studies. New York Mayor Guiliani's reported plans to end remedial education classes and introduce stringent entrance requirements may diminish much of this progress.

Variations of the above described methods and programs are being tried by a number of colleges and universities in their increasing recognition of the fact that boosting minority enrollment and achievement is a long-term project and not the result of a quick fix.

Conclusion

In conclusion, it cannot be stated strongly enough that the successful, race specific strategies of the past will no longer be practicable if the federal courts continue toward eliminating or severely restricting affirmative action. This means that if colleges and universities are to continue their efforts to increase, or even maintain, a diverse student body that reflects the population of the country, they will have to try out many alternative strategies and schemes. At the same time, they will also have to aggressively challenge the legal tactics that are currently being used successfully to defeat affirmative action methods that have been used in the past. The efforts of consortia like the Harvard Civil Rights Project (Orfield, 1998) to bring college administrators and legal counsels together to share their expertise is a step in the right direction. But we need many more of these groups with sympathetic foundations providing some support. As Christopher Edley, Jr., law professor at Harvard University, has so eloquently said:

> While the struggle to repair the pipeline continues toward uncertain and perhaps distant success, we cannot allow the nation's leading institutions to undermine

their educational and social missions by excluding capable underrepresented minorities. They must not return to their 1950 demographics while the face of twenty-first-century America becomes so radically different. (Edley, 1998)

Policies that embrace African-Americans, Latinos, Native Americans, and Asian-Americans must become evident.

References

Bell, Edward D., & Drakeford, Robert W. (1992). A case study of the Black student peer mentor program at the University of North Carolina-Greensboro. *College Student Journal, 26,* 381–386.

Bowen, William, & Bok, Derek. (1998). *The shape of the river: Long-term consequences of considering race in college and university admissions.* Princeton, NJ: Princeton University Press.

Comer, James, (1988, November). Educating poor minority children. *Scientific American, 259*(5).

Coleman, James, Campbell, E., Hobson, C., McPartland, J., Mood, A., Weinfield, F., & York, R. (1966). *Equality of educational opportunity.* Washington, DC: U.S. Government Printing Office.

Davine, Victoria R. (1994). Multicultural instruction and attitude change. PhD. dissertation, University of Iowa. *Dissertation Abstracts International, 55*(12), 3767A.

Edley, Christopher, Jr. (1998). Foreword. In Gary Orfield & Edward Miller (Eds.), *Chilling admissions: The affirmative action crisis and the search for alternatives.* Cambridge, MA: Harvard Education Publishing Group.

Frierson, Henry, Malone, Beverly, & Shelton, Phillip. (1990). Related effects of intervention on the NCLEX-RN. Unpublished paper.

Hopwood v. Texas. (1996). 78 F. 3d 923 (5th Cir. March 8, 1996). Cert. Denied 116 S. Ct. 2581.

Jencks, Christopher, Smith, M., Acland, H., Bane, M. J., Cohen, D., Gintis, H., Heyns, B., & Michelson, R. (1972). *Inequality: A reassessment of the effect of family and schooling in America.* New York: Basic Books.

Karabel, Jerome. (1998). No alternative: The effect of color-blind admissions in California. In Gary Orfield & Edward Miller (Eds.), *Chilling admissions: The affirmative action crisis and the search for alternatives.* Cambridge, MA: Harvard Education Publishing Group.

Kleinsmith, Lewis, & Johnston, Jerome. (1991). Tackling the fear of science: The impact of a computer-based study center on minority students' achievement in biology. In Walter R. Allen & Edgar Epps (Eds.), *Colleges in Black and white: Black students on Black and white campuses.* Albany: State University of New York Press.

Lavin, David, Alba, Richard D., & Silberstein, Richard A. (1979, February). Open admissions and equal access: A study of ethnic groups in the City University of New York. *Harvard Educational Review*, 49(1), 53–93.

Moody, Charles, Sr. (1990, October 3–5). A case study: The University of Michigan's approach to multicultural excellence: Access, progress, achievement and transfer. Unpublished paper presented at the Michigan Association for Institutional Research.

Mount Saint Mary's College. (1995). *Many voices*. The newsletter of Mount Saint Mary's Multicultural Advisory Council, Vol. 4, No. 2.

Orfield, Gary. (1998). Campus resegregation and its alternatives. In Gary Orfield & Edward Miller (Eds.), *Chilling admissions: The affirmative action crisis and the search for alternatives*. Cambridge, MA: Harvard Education Publishing Group.

Regents of the University of California v. Bakke, 438 U.S. 265. (1978).

Richardson, Richard C., Jr., & Skinner, Edward F. (1990). *Achieving quality and diversity: Universities in a multicultural society*. New York: Macmillan.

Sedlacek, William E. (1995). Improving racial and ethnic diversity and campus climate at four-year independent midwest colleges: An evaluation report of the Lilly Endowment Grant Program. College Park, MD: University of Maryland.

Sizemore, Barbara. (1988). The Madison Elementary School: A turnaround case. *Journal of Negro Education, 57*(3), 247–266.

Smith, Daryl G., with Gerbick, G. L., Figueroa, M. A., Watkins, G. H., Levitan, T., Moore, L. C., Merchant, D. A., Bellak, H. D., & Figueroa, B. (1997). *Diversity works: The emerging picture of how students benefit*. Association of American College and Universities.

Tiny Black college takes the high road in sciences. (1990, March 28). *The New York Times*, p. C1.

Treisman, Phillip U., & Fullilove, Robert. (1990). Mathematics achievement among African American undergraduates at the University of California, Berkeley: An evaluation of the mathematics workshop program. *Journal of Negro Education, 39*(3), 463–478.

United States v. Fordice. (1992). 505 U.S. 717.

Wilbur, Susan A., & Bonous-Hammarth, Margaret. (1998). Testing a new approach to admissions: The Irvine experience. In Gary Orfield & Edward Miller (Eds.), *Chilling admissions: The affirmative action crisis and the search for alternatives*. Cambridge, MA: Harvard Education Publishing Group.

Wilds, Deborah J., & Wilson, Reginald. (1997–1998). *Minorities in higher education: Sixteenth annual status report, American Council on Education*. Washington, DC: American Council on Education.

P A R T III

Interrogation of Public and Education Policies

The Real Question after *Hopwood*: Why Equity in the K–12 Pipeline Will Change Our University Campuses for the Better and Help Preserve a Citizen Democracy

MANUEL J. JUSTIZ AND MARILYN C. KAMEEN

Introduction

California and Texas have provided endless debate about affirmative action issues nationwide, but the challenge of access to a quality education for all Americans, whether it be K–12 or a college degree, remains. The ban on affirmative action by the University of California Regents took effect in 1998, inseparably linked to national media coverage about Propositions 187 and 209—California legislative initiatives that prevented undocumented immigrants from receiving state services, and banned race and gender considerations from all state outreach programs.

The Fifth Circuit Court of Appeals effectively wiped out race-based admissions in Texas with its 1996 *Hopwood* decision against the University of Texas (UT) at Austin law school admission process. Although the effect was somewhat different for Louisiana and Mississippi, the other Fifth Circuit states, the *Hopwood* decision ultimately led to the dismantling of all other affirmative action in state education throughout Texas, based on the legal interpretation of Dan Morales, Texas's Attorney General. A new Texas attorney general, John Cornyn, rescinded his predecessor's opinion, but warned the state's public higher education institutions not to change post-*Hopwood* policies, particularly in terms of minority financial aid, until a federal court appeal of a decision barring racial preferences was completed. Additional lawsuits were also possible, Cornyn added (Selingo & Burd, 1999).

This controversy occurred just as the nation moved into a new millennium, at a time when post–World War II Baby Boomers ranged in age between 35 and 53. And it paralleled the coming wave of Baby Boom II—as the U.S. educational system braces against K–12 enrollment climbing every year until at least 2006. At that point about 54.6 million students—just less than a million from the first post–World War II population explosion—will challenge the education pipeline at all levels (Martinez & Day, 1999). At the same time, bidding wars over growing demand for new teachers have accelerated nationwide, emphasizing that an estimated 2.5 million new teachers will be needed in the next two decades. Student population explosions, which vied with teacher scarcity crises, stimulated media coverage. Just as the year 2000 began, for example, more affluent school districts began raiding poorer neighbors for their experienced teachers. Indeed California, confronting the demand for about 250,000 to 300,000 new teachers by 2008, became painfully aware that low-income and minority schools were forced to hire less qualified, noncredentialed instructors (Smith, 2000).

The demography thesis contributed even more tension in terms of cultural diversity. U.S. Census data revealed that in 1972, just after the crest of the post–World War II Baby Boom, 85 percent of all students were white and 14 percent Black; the remaining 1 percent were mostly Asian. Twenty-five years, later with the children of Baby Boom II, the totals had changed dramatically: 78 percent white, 17 percent Black, and 4 percent Asians. Hispanics, who can be counted by the Census Bureau as members of any race, jumped from 1972's 6 percent to 14 percent in 1997, although this figure may always be contested as "undercounting" by some Latino civil rights organizations (Martinez & Day, 1999).

Hispanics will become the nation's largest minority population block by 2020, and probably sooner; three fifths of all Hispanics will attend school in either California or Texas, states in which they will become the dominant population group (Orfield & Miller, 1988), participating in the world's 7th and 11th largest economies, respectively. Clearly, Baby Boom II is very different in terms of diversity from its predecessor (Martinez & Day, 1999; Sorensen, Brewer, Carroll, & Bryton, 1995), particularly when high school dropout figures for Hispanic and African-American youth are factored into the equation.

Predictably, media reports compress this information, if covered at all, to focus on the litigation conflicts of affirmative action (Jackson, 1995): one side competes with the other in almost a stylized litany, reflecting the nation's adversarial legal tradition. At the University of Texas at Austin, we watched the *Hopwood* case begin with a 2-week trial in May 1994, and continue to the final August 21, 1996, interpretation by former Texas Attorney General Dan Morales, which effectively halted affirmative action programs (D. Morales, letter to L. Rauch, August 21, 1996). In the daily news focus on conflicting views about race, ethnicity, and gender, the shift to a new paradigm—helping students to succeed without special allocations—has become obscured.

At the root of our observations about educational equity lie a number of core beliefs. First, U.S. schools must be able to create a sophisticated, well-trained work force. Second, the future of the economy and its global role will be influenced by quality pre-K to K–12 teaching, regardless of whether in a disadvantaged environment or not. Third, today's citizens should recognize their self-interest in making sure social security retirement benefits are protected by successive replacement waves of highly educated workers. And finally, the nation's future as a democracy depends on how well we share the responsibility of creating the world's best system of public education. Failure is simply not an option for any of these challenges.

While the reform initiative in educational policy moved from federal actors to state governors and other policy makers in the mid-1980s (Justiz & Bjork, 1988), the fundamental questions about educational equity did not change. All schools are not created equal; however, each student and his or her family inherits the burden of these common queries:

- Will this country be able to field a technologically literate society and sustain its quality of life in a twenty-first century global economy?
- Will *all* of the nation's children have mastered early reading, writing, and arithmetic by the third grade so that they have an equal shot at a college degree?
- Will access to higher education for all segments of our population be recognized as critical to national security, economic self-interest, and defense of the basic mission of American colleges and universities in contributing to a healthy democracy?

Discussion

In the wake of the 1996 *Hopwood* interpretation by the Texas attorney general, many dire predictions followed, alleging the death of any future diversity at our campus, the University of Texas at Austin, the nation's largest public research university (usually between 47–50,000 students). Enrollment for African-Americans and Hispanics dropped the next year, but after a searingly difficult period for UT-Austin, applications actually began to rise once again. The *New York Times* initiated a front-page story on November 24, 1999, describing how a Texas legislative initiative—the 10 percent admissions rule—allowed the son of an immigrant construction worker with low standardized test scores to enter one of the most selective campuses in the state (Wilgoren, 1999). Florida also proposed automatic admission for the top 20 percent of its graduates, and California approved opening about 3,600 more slots at the University of California for the top 4 percent of its high school students, although not at any specific UC campus.

The authors, however, are well aware that unhappiness continues about plummeting minority admissions at graduate/professional schools in the wake of *Hopwood*. Atlanta's highly respected Southern Education Foundation, which annually surveys the 19 U.S. states that once operated dual (and racially segregated) systems of higher education, saw *Hopwood* as deeply affecting the entire region (SEF, 1998):

> Yet Texas' restricted ability to address the needs of minority students may resonate throughout the region. For example, in 1995, 733 blacks earned law degrees from public institutions in the 19 states. With almost 20 percent of these law graduates, Texas was the largest producer of new black attorneys among these states. The University of Texas at Austin alone produced more black law graduates than 10 of these states, including Alabama, Georgia and Mississippi, where blacks make up much larger percentages of the population than in Texas . . . the representation of black law students in the region is almost certain to fall.

The literature review in this volume should leave little doubt in any reader's mind about how opposing views would react to the above analysis. Lemann's work further emphasizes the dilemma for both educators and state officials (Lemann, 1999):

> The reason for the crush at the gates of selective universities is that people believe admission can confer lifelong prestige, comfort, and safety, not just access to jobs with specific functions. . . . There is now a sturdy and well-established conservative defense of the system, which argues that however odd its evolution, it now works just fine: we're right to assign economic destinies through education and test scores, because that's the fairest way and the one most likely to promote the quality of sheer brain power that fuels the modern American economy. . . . The arguments of both sides have something important in common, though, which is that they presume (as most discussions of meritocracy in America presume) that it's good for the country to have a designated, educationally derived elite. The question is whether to have one with a conservative or liberal design.

Indeed, critics of both Texas' 10 percent and California's 4 percent admissions plans quickly pointed out that students, particularly from low-income and minority schools, would not be able to compete at selective college campuses, even though they ranked in the upper percentages of their respective high schools. Parental complaints, particularly when children have not been admitted to the UT-Austin campus, are rising, and we believe that lawsuits will follow.

While the media focused on the differences between Texas's school achievements and California's—thanks to the 2000 presidential primaries—it largely overlooked the more stringent requirements that the UC Regents had imposed on its 4 percent admissions plan. Set to take effect in 2001, it would only add about 3,600 more students to the current eligibility pool of 28,400. Nearly 60 percent would come from rural and urban high schools, which only send small numbers to any of the UC campuses, if at all. Minimal requirements for all students embrace a 3.3 grade-point average in high school, satisfactory completion of all required college prep courses, and taking the SAT and SAT II achievement tests (Healy, 1999; Weiss, 1999). "Although it will bring only a slight increase in Blacks and Latinos, UC officials hope it will inspire more of these minority students to view UC as within reach. Furthermore, they hope the plan will stimulate lagging high schools to improve their programs for university-bound students" (Weiss, 1999b).

State coverage about admissions at UC Berkeley, UCLA and UC San Diego routinely refers to high-intensity competition for places. UC Riverside, which has shown strong leadership in encouraging diversity (Traub, 1999), accepts all eligible students who apply. Riverside and UC Santa Cruz are growing, but the others refuse thousands of applicants yearly. In 1998, for example, UC Berkeley turned away 22,000 out of a 30,000-applicant total, ultimately enrolling a freshman class of about 3,500. Of those denied admission, 7,200—including 800 underrepresented minority students—had GPAs of 4.0 (Berdahl, 1998a, b). Referring to the Berkeley Pledge program, Dr. Robert Berdahl, UC Berkeley chancellor, emphasized that its goal aimed to develop an outreach model for how universities could help improve K–12 schooling. "It will not, in and of itself, solve the problem of inequalities of educational opportunity in California schools," he said. "Leveling the playing field of educational opportunity must start in first grade, not when students apply to college" (Berdahl, 1998b).

Predictably, the California 4-percent plan also worried many middle class students and their parents, who charged that those students already attending competitive schools but who are not in the top 4 percent would be unfairly affected. "How are you going to defend one kid with high grades and SAT scores not getting in, when another kid with lower grades and SAT scores gets in just because he goes to another school? It's an unbelievable concession to failure in the school systems," said Sen. Steve Peace, D-San Diego (Healy, 1999).

Just 4 months later, members of the Latino Legislative Caucus, pointing out that Hispanics would become California's largest worker group by 2025 (from 28 percent currently to more than 50 percent), if not earlier, issued a special report about wage gaps. The California Research Bureau determined that the median state Latino income was $14,560, significantly less than any other ethnic or racial group. Even more troubling was the conclusion that new immigrants were not the only low-earning Latino group: "low levels of educational attainment persist for even third-generation Latinos . . . and the main reason was lack of education" (Rojas, 1999).

Only 8 percent of all California Latino workers have a BA degree or more, compared to 33 percent of whites, 24 percent of African-Americans, and 43 percent of Asian-Americans. Out of 4.4 million Latino workers in California, 45 percent have not graduated from high school; another 41 percent have only a high school diploma. "This report alerts policy makers to the fact that the wages of Latinos are not in parity with their numbers; therefore, neither are their tax contributions . . . the most important reason for Latinos earning relatively less is that they have lower levels of educational attainment . . . relying on time alone to take care of the problem does not appear to be the best prescription" (Lopez, Ramirez, & Rochin, 1999).

These controversies occur within the context of the world's 7th largest economy and are comparably evident in Texas, the 11th largest global economy. Indeed, there are critical implications for the nation's twenty-first-century's knowledge-based society, where the creation of wealth will depend on the influences of new knowledge, often in science or technology. School inequality directly affects nation-state performance in the global economy—a byproduct of the Third Industrial Revolution. The same economic performance also affects the "social peace in rich and poor countries alike," not to mention the quality of life for all Americans (Greider, 1997).

Competition between nations to maintain their educational systems as the fuel powering economic vitality also remains a constant pressure on how U.S. states confront their K–12 school system inequalities. The question of making college admissions a more equal process for all Americans, particularly in the overheated arena of socially prestigious campuses, is only the tip of the proverbial iceberg. Massachusetts, for example, already faces litigation challenges over how fairly it allocates revenues for K–12 education. More specifically, the reappearance of its highly publicized early 1990s "McDuffy" case, named after a sixth-grader in a working-class school district, focuses on whether contemporary reforms have done enough to close the gap between affluent and nonaffluent school districts—in this instance, Brockton versus top performers such as Harvard, Newton, and Wellesley (Vigue, 2000). Similar efforts can be found in a majority of American states.

But it is the world's seventh largest economy again, California, that provides the most telling range of conflicts in the post-*Hopwood* era. Although its controversial Proposition 209 banned any state program targeting students by race, the University of California was allowed to expend $180 million in 2000 on outreach efforts to help public school students. In 2001, Governor Gray Davis has proposed that funding be increased to $250 million; and the University can focus on poor inner-city schools, where most students are either Latino or African-American—the two groups most underrepresented on UC's campuses (Weiss, 2000c). At the same time as race-based admissions are prevented nationwide by successive court rulings, one study claims that only a small percentage of the 1,000 pre-college U.S. outreach programs have produced "reliable evaluations," adding that only one third of students enrolled in these efforts actually complete them (Blair, 2000).

To make the scenario more complex, the American Civil Liberties Union of Southern California and the Mexican American Legal Defense and Educational Fund both mounted significant legal challenges based on allegations of educational inequality in California and Texas. The latter, filed in 1997, argued that Texas's standardized exit test (Texas Assessment of Academic Skills, or TAAS) to receive a high school diploma discriminated against minority students who were generally clustered in low-income schools with few resources and poorly qualified teachers.

These students, the suit added, failed the exam in disproportionate numbers; about 100,000 students had already been denied secondary diplomas (Stutz, 1999). In January 2000, a federal judge, Edward C. Prado disagreed, ruling that the TAAS did not violate Title VI of the Civil Rights Act of 1964. "While the TAAS test does adversely affect minority students in significant numbers, the TEA has demonstrated an educational necessity for the test, and the plaintiffs have failed to identify equally effective alternatives. In addition, the Court concludes that the TAAS test violates neither the procedural nor the substantive due process rights of the Plaintiffs" (*GI Forum v. Texas Education Agency*, 2000).

In comparison, the ACLU initiative in California focused exclusively on the University of California admissions process, arguing that inequalities in access to high school Advanced Placement (AP) classes violated the state's constitution, which identifies public education as a fundamental right. California, therefore, has an obligation to correct inequities in its school systems. "This is a two-tiered educational system," argued Mark Rosenbaum, ACLU legal director. "One is designed to intellectually challenge students and prepare them for college. The other offers least-common denominator courses that disadvantage its most promising students" (Sahagun & Weiss, 1999a).

The civil rights class-action lawsuit was filed in state superior court on behalf of four minority Inglewood High School students against the California Department of Education and the local Inglewood Unified School District. The suit charged that the Department of Education and the School District had marginalized these students in the statewide competition to enter the most desirable state universities. With only 3 AP classes at minority Inglewood High School (none in math or science) as opposed to Beverly Hills High School's 14 different AP subjects and 45 AP classes, the students were clearly disadvantaged in UC admissions, which awards AP class completion an extra point in grade point average calculations. For example, successful AP grades can allow students to enter UC admissions competition with a GPA above a 4.0 "perfect score" (ACLU, 1999). Last year's entering UCLA class students had taken an average of 16.8 Advanced Placement classes with an average GPA of 4.19 (Sahagun, 1999).

Designed as a test case in the aftermath of the UC Regents' decision to end all race-based admissions, the lawsuit focused on the 40-year history of Advanced Placement (AP) classes. Such classes were developed by the College Board, a national nonprofit organization administered by the Educational Testing Service of Princeton, New Jersey—the same entity that also creates the SAT and GRE examinations, among others. AP classes allow high school students to tackle more rigorous college-level material, and they must pass an exam at the end of the class to obtain credit. They "are traditionally more challenging and demanding than regular and honors (high school) courses, providing for greater intellectual and scientific development," asserted the ACLU of Southern California.

Rosenbaum later added that his Inglewood High plaintiffs "have no shot at competing with kids in more affluent white schools" (Sahagun & Weiss, 1999). Wade Curry, a College Board representative, later told journalists "a lot of people with low expectations of their students think it's impossible to mount an AP offering. It's not. It just requires some commitment and a few thousand dollars, which doesn't sound like a lot" (Sahagun & Weiss, 1999).

Seventeen years earlier, minority students at Garfield High School in East Los Angeles were accused of cheating on an AP calculus exam taught by a then-unknown teacher, Jaime Escalante. The Educational Testing Service simply did not believe that this high school could produce so many students capable of taking such a test. The accomplishments of this 43-year-old Bolivian immigrant, who refused to accept that disadvantaged youths could not learn, mounted a popular culture attack on diluted curriculums and poor teaching in "warehouse" minority school districts. Escalante's work was later dramatized in the movie, *Stand and Deliver*; a book by *The Washington Post* education writer Jay Mathews, *Escalante—The Best Teacher in America*, also debuted in 1988. We should note that at the time, there were 2.2 million teachers nationwide—a little less than the 2.5 million needed in the next two decades.

While truly inspirational, Escalante was only an early entrant in the complex issue of whether "demography is not destiny. Some poor children will, with effort, natural ability and good schooling, achieve more than most privileged children," argued *The New York Times* essayist Richard Rothstein. "Rags to riches" stories abound—some disadvantaged children excel in school and become leaders. But these stories are not universal. On average, with more equal school quality, children with more academic support at home will have higher achievement. The power of social class will not disappear if we pretend it does not exist" (Rothstein, 1999).

Let's examine California's AP classes with a stronger lens. By the state's Department of Education report in 1997–1998, 129 out of 870 high schools offered no AP classes. Just 333 offered four or less; these high schools are usually inner-city or rural campuses. Nationwide, about 25 percent of all high schools do not offer AP classes. In Texas, Governor George W. Bush pushed through a $19 million package designed to bring AP courses to every high school in the state during the most recent biennial legislative session; currently, only 60 percent of Texas high schools offer AP classes.

California, however, increased its Advanced Placement offerings statewide, although early data tend to reinforce the argument that these curricular improvements occurred in more affluent environments. For example, in 1988, about 39,000 public high school students took more than 56,600 AP exams. A decade later, more than 87,600 students were tackling an excess of 145,000 exams—reflecting the importance of gaining admission to a selective UC campus. AP success at the secondary level also allows a student "to leapfrog" over basic college introductory classes, which speeds progress toward a 4-year degree ("The Advanced Placement Program," 1999). Availability and access for all the state's students, particularly in rural and minority populations, remained a significant equity problem, and of course, the future implications for any state economy are obvious.

Conclusion

Inequity problems in the K–12 pipeline presage problems for higher education, including underprepared college applicants, a need for remedial education in some form at the postsecondary level, and underrepresentation of minorities on campus. If only for their own self-preservation—a view developed further in this book's last summary chapter—colleges and universities must demonstrate an active commitment to education at all levels. And it should include all groups and races—simply because the knowledge-based society of the future will be driven by powerful social, economic, and scientific/technological forces. We stress that educated minds will be able to participate in the knowledge-based initiatives driving the nation's constant economic transformation; uneducated minds will not be included.

We have offered some blunt commentary about a suggested action plan, or "new paradigm." However, we emphasize that there is very little "new" in our analysis; instead, we consider action steps designed for accountability rather than the empty constructs currently littering policy discussion today. In short, we believe that the post-*Hopwood* era offers all educational providers a fresh opportunity to attack inequity throughout the K–16 pipeline, and to implement meaningful programs that will not only improve educational quality for all our citizens, but also increase the vitality of this nation's citizen democracy.

As we completed a draft of this chapter, California released a $242 million statewide attempt at increasing accountability for its 6,700 K–12 schools. In just the first moments of the Academic Performance Index (API)—the state's first-ever performance ranking of elementary, middle, and high schools—the web site at the State Education headquarters in Sacramento collapsed after 4,000 hits (www.cde.ca.gov/psaa) (Groves, 2000a). But even more telling, only 12 percent of the state's schools met an 800-point target in the first-ever baseline exam. "Schools that fail to meet improvement targets could have remedies forced on them and, in extreme cases, face takeover by the state" (Groves, 2000b). Most observers, including the *San Francisco Chronicle*, acknowledged that the scores required a broad range of perspectives ("School Academic Index," 2000):

> The rankings are based on the results of one test taken last spring, and kids who come to school hungry, who have little support at home, whose English is weak—in general, the disadvantaged—will as a group score lower than kids who are well-nourished, whose parents graduated from college and whose native tongue is English. The fact that wealthy South Bay and Peninsula Schools emerged as some of the highest performers in the state should come as no surprise.

Sacramento Bee columnist Peter Schrag, who formerly ran that paper's opinion-editorial pages, said flatly that the API provided a guide to the state's hottest real estate markets. "Every educator worth her Ed.D. could tell you that more than 80 percent of school test scores, which is what the API is based on, can be explained by socioeconomic class, particularly by the educational level of the parents" (Schrag, 2000). Without delving too heavily into state economic development, we should add that research also indicates that the new knowledge economy businesses are highly mobile; they can move easily—not just from one state to another, but globally.

If fabled Silicon Valley, for example, cannot produce the labor force necessary for business expansion, which is strongly linked to that area's educational achievements, then out-of-state migration of wealth and business occurs. This hypercompetitiveness has already pitted "neighbor against neighbor, region against region, and state against state. . . . We're able to entice workers for three to four years, but employees are leaving when they become most productive," said one Bay Area high-tech CEO. "We're training people for other areas like Austin, Colorado and Seattle, where housing costs are lower and the quality of life is better" (O'Connell & King, 2000).

Almost everyone has heard about one potential solution of the last decade—partnerships between schools, businesses, universities, and government. Many of these alliances have contributed greatly to K–12 reform, and many fall into the realm of hype without substance. But it is parents, we argue, who often constitute "the missing link" in the pipeline. Educational providers can set higher standards and increase the rigor of curricula at all levels, but we agree with Loveless's contention that parents are absent from educational reform. In short, they exist as ghostly assumptions—"Parents will do whatever is necessary to raise children's levels of achievement. But will they?"

(Loveless, 1999). Studies point out that teenagers today are consumed by extracurricular activities (sports), part- to full-time employment, and social activities; they spend an average of 4 hours weekly on homework. Suffice it to say that teens in comparable Asian or European nations have one primary goal: to learn, and they devote 4 hours every day to homework.

If educational reform is to work nationwide, more must be done to integrate parents into the educational system. Most students are no longer labor extensions of the family farm. Today, a successful college graduate must first have arrived in college classrooms with highly evolved computer literacy skills, which then enhance a strong foundation in verbal and mathematical ability, presumably imparted by a rigorous K–12 school district. We recognize that parents are already overworked, and a huge proportion hold down the equivalent of at least two jobs. This leaves little time to invest in one's children, let alone when the tough reality of social promotion hits with full force.

We should add that too many parents remain oblivious to the rising literacy requirements of college today—another reason why tougher admissions standards will affect younger siblings in entirely different ways from their older counterparts, who graduated in the last decade. For the first-generation students heading toward college, the two-tier economy can also translate into "the digital divide"—only 8 percent of families earning less than $10,000 a year have computers, and only 3 percent of this group even have an Internet connection (May, 2000). Minority children tend to become the majority in this grouping.

We argue that parents are really the unseen force behind our educational system, along with very good teachers. However, the reform movement, coupled with global economic competition, has increased pressures on parental roles. Largely traditional dyads at the top of the nation's two-tier income system have only begun to feel the full effect as they advocate for their children to be admitted to selective colleges or universities. For example, some Virginia high schools now offer classes to parents on how to handle the stress of impending standardized testing. By 2004, students who fail that state's Standard of Learning (SOL) exam will not receive diplomas. By 2007, schools failing to meet state passage standards could lose their accreditation. More important, the sessions teach parents how to better counsel their own children (Wax, 2000). Once again, it is the tip of the proverbial iceberg.

More pressures are clearly on the way for all levels of the educational system, suggesting an era of tougher interaction between elected state officials, policy makers, and federal administrators. Better counseling, better school-to-college transition programs, and greater involvement of all family units will be required—much more so than the K–12 pipeline has seen in recent decades. As UC Berkeley's Chancellor said bluntly in an earlier passage: "Leveling the playing field of educational opportunity must start in first grade, not when students apply to college" (Berdahl, 1998).

Critics have charged that partnerships between education, politics, business, and parents too easily lapse into meaningless clichés. As deans of a public College of Education, we too have participated in our share of good and bad partnerships. But the purpose remains essential in the post-*Hopwood* era, particularly since this can be one of the few organized motivations for improving schools that still "warehouse" poorer, disadvantaged children.

Partnerships almost always constitute a direct cultural challenge for their participants. It is not easy to bridge the gap, for example, between K–12 school districts, parents, and a large public research university such as the University of Texas at Austin. Each institution has its own set of competing priorities. We write from difficult, yet productive experience. Our College of Education, for example, works collaboratively with the local Austin Independent School District, or AISD. The partnership is an emerging concept, requiring sustained effort over time. We expected that issues of trust, respect, and competence would be raised, particularly when hard discussions occurred about tangible rewards, benefits, and shared goals of the partnership. Yes, we ultimately managed to create significant achievements in educational technology, teacher training/mentoring, and professional development—to name but a few arenas. But partnerships are really about beginning a journey that does not end. There is always more left to do.

Nevertheless, many university faculty balk at working in these joint collaborative efforts. The academic culture and its focus on research tell them it is a poor time investment, because such activities are undervalued by top administrators and lack tangible rewards. Getting beyond lip service is not easy, but the College's leadership has fought—literally fought—to provide incentives for tenured faculty to participate (Justiz, 1997). Once again, more needs to be done to increase the resource sharing between businesses, parents, and policy leaders—not to mention each state's legislatures, complete with committee structures of elected representatives who make critical decisions about increasing educational resources amid rising competition from other competing budget sectors.

Keep in mind that as school boards confront the inevitable pressures of educational reform, local citizens can expect significant change at all levels of school leadership. At any given time, at least a dozen major U.S. school districts are desperately seeking new school superintendents, including New York, Los Angeles, Detroit, Baltimore, and San Francisco as we write. Each candidate must propose a solution to chronically low urban school performances. Mayoral takeovers have already occurred in Chicago, Cleveland, Detroit, and Boston, and currently, Washington, D.C. is under consideration. In light of our earlier reference to regional economic competitiveness, we argue that it is in no one's interest to abandon whole generations of less affluent children to minimum wage futures.

Until the K–12 pipeline improves radically, we can also expect students to arrive on college campuses unprepared or under prepared in certain disciplines. As the literature review indicates, the pre-*Hopwood* era often left American minority students, whether admitted under race-sensitive plans or not, open to the ideological conflict generated by both sides of the affirmative action chasm. We have found that students from all groups can arrive at the University of Texas at Austin needing serious remediation to survive what has become a 6-year bachelor's degree for two thirds of our 50,000-student campus. Yet public universities are already under attack for offering what are termed "remedial classes," which allegedly charge taxpayers more than once for education that should already have occurred (Roueche & Roueche, 1999). We believe that the problem is much worse than is currently reported; it will improve only as the pre-K to K–12 pipeline improves.

Future students at UT-Austin or the University of California campuses, to cite two familiar examples, will enter campuses struggling to service impressive growth. We earlier referred to this societal phenomenon as Baby Boom II. If admitted, we inherit a moral responsibility to offer them pragmatic counseling about their academic futures. Too often we see students fall victim to what UCLA education professor, Alexander W. Astin, calls the cult of "smartness"; that is, where the "mere demonstration of intellect is valued more than its cultivation" (Astin, 1997). True, on our own campus, admissions are becoming more selective each year, and as deans, we already encounter families whose older children were easily admitted in the early 1990s, but whose later sons and daughters—often judged better students than their older siblings—cannot easily gain admission under rising standards. Listen to Astin's main points:

> But perhaps the most serious consequences of our unexamined emphasis on smartness falls on students. Most of us clearly favor the brightest students, not only in admissions and financial aid, but also in the classroom. If bright students enroll at our institution and take our classes, we believe that this reflects well on our own brightness. . . . But if our students are not topnotch, we think that this reflects poorly on us . . .
>
> The real problem is that we value being smart much more than we do developing smartness. We forget that our institution's primary mission *is to expand students' intellectual capacities,* not merely to select and certify those whose intellectual talents are already well developed by the time they reach us. (Astin, 1997)

Astin is, of course, not calling for relaxed standards, but his argument synthesizes the controversies revolving around remediation today. We need effective, pragmatic counseling at the K–12 grades so that parents and students better understand the tough realities of academic competition stemming from educational reform—ever-increasing standards, regular testing, and the attempted end of social promotion in most states. Students and their parents can then realistically consider at least one possible creative solution to this complex problem: high-quality community colleges.

We should emphasize, however, that the national "California model" (a three-tiered system of K–12 schools, community colleges as a second chance for students who did not perform well at the secondary level, and a state university system combined with an even more prestigious, highly selective University of California) no longer works as well as it once did. For example, in 1996 the University of California and the state's community colleges agreed to increase the number of students transferring to the UC system by 33 percent. In the last 5 years, however, the numbers have either dropped or risen slightly. This year showed a 12-student increase, even though UC administrators emphasized that transfers might provide increased diversity on their respective campuses because minority student enrollment is sizable at 2-year community colleges (Leovy & Weiss, 2000).

We believe that our educational partnerships must also insist on strong reforms at the community college level. Some campuses have lapsed in their original dedication to remedial and developmental instruction, and few measurements exist nationwide to provide convincing accountability for this critical mission. In short, community colleges also need to take educational reform much more seriously. There are excellent examples of highly successful community colleges, but we continue to observe a wide disparity in national results—much the same effect shows in our K–12 school pipeline.

If states like Texas and California are to increase the number of college graduates in their citizen base and continue to maintain their competitive standing in the global economy, then they first must realize that it is no longer "business as usual." As we completed this chapter, studies emerged declaring that despite a booming economy, a two-tier social system was hardening— that is, an "hourglass economy" characterized by high-wage professions at one end versus a growing base of low-paying, unskilled jobs at the other. Remarkably, the studies showed that California was one of the wealthiest states in America, and also one of the poorest.

> In another era, when California manufactured cars and airplanes in great numbers, it was possible to scratch out a middle-class living by the sweat of one's brow. Now many good blue-collar jobs have been shipped abroad or retooled in a way that they command smaller paychecks. California's new manufacturing industries—electronics and computers—reward the white-collar workers handsomely but generally don't pay good assembly line wages as in an auto plant. (Kasler & Rojas, 2000)

Just three decades ago, male high school graduates in California earned nearly $395-a-week less than college graduates. Today, the disparity begins immediately at $475-a-week, and it continues to rise exponentially.

Public universities can seize a major opportunity to massively upgrade service to their respective states by helping to improve the K–12 pipeline. Experienced observers can usually analyze a campus's commitment by surveying which administrators manage auxiliary developmental programs and financial aid. More important, they can easily perceive whether top administrators are truly committed or simply going through the proverbial motions. Our conclusions stress that the roles of public universities are changing as we write. Indeed, as productivity rises in our global economy, is it too unusual to believe that similar expectations would emerge about campuses?

We are also reminded of massive change when scanning a recent *New York Times Education Life* tabloid section. The cover page's headlines focused on "Higher ed at age 14; Dorm life at 40-plus; and Starting over at 56" (Harden, Rimer, & Trimpe, 2000). And if readers doubted that access to education would be affected by telecommunications and computer technologies, there was one other headline: "It's Year 2000. We're Wired. Now What?" (Guernsey, 2000).

A knowledge-based society and economy means just that—citizens engaged in a lifetime of learning, a seamless web if you will. The traditions of higher education have deeply enriched this nation; however, a new era of market forces carries both the potential of rewards and punishments. The *Hopwood* decision may have ended a 30-year process in college admissions, but it was only an early warning that higher education needed to reinvent itself. Jaime Escalante's 1982 AP barrio high school calculus class offers a somewhat dated example today, but 15 out of his original 18 students went to college. Five years later, at least half had entered the knowledge society with BA degrees. Hundreds more followed from successive AP classes.

Note

The authors gratefully acknowledge the assistance of Chuck Halloran in writing this chapter.

References

American Civil Liberties Union. (1999, July 27). In class-action lawsuit, ACLU says CA students are denied equal access to Advanced Placement courses [press release]. Los Angeles: Author. Retrieved July 28, 1999 from the World Wide Web: http://aclu.org/congress/ccpa_analysis. html.

Astin, Alexander W. (1997, September 26). Our obsession with being "smart" is distorting intellectual life. *Chronicle of Higher Education*, A60.

Retrieved June 18, 1999 from Nexis database on the World Wide Web: http://web.lexis-nexis.com.

Berdahl, Robert. (1998a, March 31). Fall '98 freshman admissions results: A message to the campus community. Berkeley, CA: University of California. Retrieved October 20, 1999 from the World Wide Web: http://www.chance.berkeley.edu/cio/chancellor/ar/admismes.html.

Berdahl, Robert. (1998b, April 24). Bringing the best of UC Berkeley. Berkeley, CA: University of California. Retrieved October 20, 1999 from the World Wide Web: http://www.chance.berkeley.edu/cio/chancellor/ar/chronop.html.

Blair, Julie. (2000, January 19). Minorities need path to top schools, report finds. *Education Week*. Retrieved January 19, 2000 from the World Wide Web: http://www.edweek.org/ew/ewstory.cfm?slug=19affirm.h19.

GI Forum v. Texas Education Agency, No. SA-97-CA-1278 (W. D. Tex. Jan. 7, 2000).

Greider, William. (1997). *One world, ready or not: The manic logic of global capitalism*. New York: Simon & Schuster.

Groves, Martha. (2000a, January 26). Vast majority of state's schools lag in new index. *Los Angeles Times*. Retrieved January 26, 2000 from the World Wide Web: http://www.latimes.com/news/learning/20000126/t000008189.html.

Groves, Martha. (2000b, January 27). Lowest scorers predict progress—and more work. *Los Angeles Times*. Retrieved January 27, 2000 from the World Wide Web: http://www.latimes.com/news/learning/20000127/t000008524.html.

Guernsey, Lisa. (2000, January 9). The wiring of America. *The New York Times*. Education life, Section 4A, p. 32–38.

Harden, Blaine. (2000, January 9). Transitions. *The New York Times*. Education life, Section 4A, p. 28–31.

Healy, Patrick. (1999, April 2). U. of California to admit top 4 percent from every high school. *Chronicle of Higher Education 45* (30) A36. Retrieved June 15, 1999 from the World Wide Web: http://chronicle.com/weekly/v45/i30/30a03601.htm.

Jackson, J. (1995, September–October). White man's burden: how the press frames affirmative action. *Extra!*, 7–9.

Justiz, Manuel J. (1997, Spring). Collaborating for success: Case history of a school-college partnership. *Educational Record*, 31–38.

Justiz, Manuel J., & Björk, Lars G. (1988). *Higher education research and public policy*. New York: American Council on Education/Macmillan.

Justiz, Manuel J., Wilson, Reginald, & Björk, Lars G. (1994). *Minorities in higher education*. Phoenix, AZ: Oryx Press.

Kasler, Dale, & Rojas, Aurelio. (2000, January 23). Left behind: Good times barely touch state's poor. *Sacramento Bee.* Retrieved January 24, 2000 from the World Wide Web: http://www.sacbee.com.

Lemann, Nicholas. (1999). *The big test: The secret history of the American meritocracy.* New York: Farrar, Straus and Giroux.

Leovy, Jill, & Weiss, Kenneth. (2000, January 28). Applications to transfer to UC level off. *Los Angeles Times.* Retrieved January 28, 2000 from the World Wide Web: http://www.latimes.com/news/learning/20000128/t000008904.html.

Lopez, Elias, Ramirez, Enrique, & Rochin, Refugio I. (1999, June). *Latinos and economic development in California* (Publication No. CRB-99-008). Sacramento, CA: California Research Bureau.

Loveless, Tom. (1999, Autumn). The parent trap. *The Wilson Quarterly, 23*(4), 37–43.

Martinez, Gladys M., & Day, Jennifer C. (1999, July). *School enrollment—social and economic characteristics of students. October 1997* (USCB Publication No. P20-516). Washington, DC: U.S. Census Bureau.

Mathews, Jay. (1998). *Escalate—The best teacher in America.* New York: Henry Holt.

May, M. (2000, January 18). Push on to get home computers to poor students. *San Francisco Chronicle.* Retrieved January 18, 2000 from the World Wide Web: http://www.sfgate.com/cgi-bin/article.cgi?file=chronicle/archive/2000/01/18/MN99736.DTL.

Morales, Dan (1996, August 21). [Personal communication.]

O'Connell, Jock, & King, James R. (2000, January 30). A high-tech exodus looms as growth chokes state. *Sacramento Bee.* Retrieved January 30, 2000 from the World Wide Web: http://sacbee.com.

Orfield, Gary, & Miller, Edward (Eds.). (1998). *Chilling admissions: The affirmative action crisis and the search for alternatives.* Cambridge, MA: Harvard Education Publishing Group.

Rimer, Sara. (2000, January 9). Campus life. *The New York Times.* Education life, Section 4A, pp. 21–23 and 40–41.

Rojas, Aurelio. (1999, August 19). Latino incomes lagging—education gap blamed. *Sacramento Bee.* Retrieved August 20, 1999 from Nexis database on the World Wide Web: http://web.lexis-nexis.com.

Rothstein, Richard. (1999, November 10). Does poverty at home mean low achievement? *The New York Times.* Retrieved November 10, 1999 from the World Wide Web: http://www.nyt/com/library/national/110999/lessons-edu.html.

Rothstein, Richard. (2000, January 19). Inner-city nomads: route to low grades. *The New York Times.* Retrieved January 19, 2000 from the World Wide Web: http://www.nyt/com/library/national/011900lessons-edu.html.

Roueche, John E., & Roueche, Suanne D. (1999). *High stakes, high performance: Making remedial education work.* Washington, DC: Community College Press.

Sahagun, Louis. (1999, August 4). Students in lawsuit are cast as heroes. *Los Angeles Times.* Retrieved August 4, 1999 from the World Wide Web: http://www.latimes.com/HOME/NEWS/STATE/t000069269.html.

Sahagun, Louis, & Weiss, Kenneth R. (1999, July 28). Bias suit targets schools without adavanced classes. *The Los Angeles Times.* Retrieved July 28, 1999 from the World Wide Web: http://www.latimes.com/HOME/NEWS/STATE/t000067039.html.

School academic index a force for improvement [Editorial]. (2000, January 27). *The San Francisco Chronicle.* Retrieved January 27, 2000 from the World Wide Web: http://www.sfgate.com/cgi-bin/article.cgi?file=/chronicle/archive/2000/01/27/ED47889.DTL.

Schrag, Peter. (2000, February 2). The API guide to state's hottest real estate markets. [Column]. *The Sacramento Bee.* Retrieved February 8, 2000 from the World Wide Web: http://www.sacbee.com.

Schrag, Peter. (1999a, March–April). Muddy Waters. [Review of the book *The shape of the river*]. *The American Prospect.* Retrieved October 28, 1999 from the World Wide Web: http://epn.org/prospect/43/43schrag.html.

Schrag, Peter. (1999b, July 28). Doctor Unz's magical elixir for learning [Column]. *Sacramento Bee.* Retrieved July 28, 1999 from the World Wide Web: http://www.sacbee.com.

Selingo, Jeffrey. (2000, January 20). Education dept. disavows approval of Florida governor's plan to end race-based admissions. *Chronicle of Higher Education.* Retrieved January 24, 2000 from the World Wide Web: http://www.chronicle.com/daily/2000/01/2000012406.htm.

Selingo, Jeffrey, & Burd, Stephen. (1999, September 17). Texas attorney general rescinds opinion barring race-exclusive scholarships. *Chronicle of Higher Education 46* (4). Retrieved January 11, 2000 from the World Wide Web: http://www.chronicle.com/weekly/v46/i04/04a04401.htm.

Smith, D. (2000, January 6). David sets battle plan for schools: Incentives for teachers proposed. *Sacramento Bee.* Retrieved January 6, 2000 from the World Wide Web: http://www.sacbee.com.

Sorensen, Stephen, Brewer, Dominic J., Carroll, Stephen J., & Bryton, Eugene. (1995). *Increasing Hispanic participation in higher education: A desirable public investment* [Issue paper]. Santa Monica, CA: RAND. Retrieved March 8, 1999 from the World Wide Web: http://www.rand.org/publications/IP/IP152/index.html.

Stutz, Terrence. (1999, October 26). Judge weighs arguments in TAAS lawsuit. *Dallas Morning News.* Retrieved November 3, 1999 from the World Wide Web: http://www.dallasnews.com/education/1026edu1taas.htm.

Traub, James. (1999, May 2). The class of prop. 209. *The New York Times Magazine*, pp. 44–51, 76–79.

Trimpe, Herb. (2000, January 9). Starting over. *The New York Times*. Education life, Section 4A, p. 24–26 and 42–46.

Vigue, Doreen I. (2000, January 13). Class action: Student-parent lawsuit alleges education reform failures. *The Boston Globe*. Retrieved January 13, 2000 from the World Wide Web: http://www.boston.com/dailyglobe2/013/metro/Class_actionP.shtml.

Wax, Emily. (2000, January 30). Virginia parents cope with test stress. *The Washington Post*. Retrieved January 30, 2000 from the World Wide Web: http://www.washingtonpost.com/wp-spv/WPlate/2000-01/30/2141-013000-idx.html.

Weiss, Kenneth. (1999a, April 21). Easing the fears surrounding UC's 4 percent solution. *Los Angeles Times*. Retrieved June 15, 1999 from Nexis database on the World Wide Web: http://web.lexis-nexis.com.

Weiss, Kenneth. (1999b, October 6). An insider view of UC admissions. *Los Angeles Times*. Retrieved October 6, 1999 from the World Wide Web: http://www.latimes.com/HOME/NEWS/STATE/t000089984.html.

Weiss, Kenneth. (2000a, January 9). New test-taking skill: working the system. *Los Angeles Times*. Retrieved January 10, 2000 from the World Wide Web: http://www.latimes.com/news/learning/20000109/t000002866.html.

Weiss, Kenneth. (2000b, January 21). Race query affects tests, regents told. *Los Angeles Times*. Retrieved January 21, 2000 from the World Wide Web: http://www.latimes.com/news/learning/20000121/t000006720.html.

Weiss, Kenneth. (2000c, January 27). Blacks, Latinos post gains in applying to UC. *Los Angeles Times*. Retrieved January 27, 2000 from the World Wide Web: http://www.latimes.com/news/front/20000127/t000008521.html.

Wilgoren, Jodi. (1999a, October 17). Report calls for new focus on aid for minority students. *New York Times*. Retrieved October 18, 1999 from the World Wide Web: http://www.nytimes.com/library/national/101799college-race-edu.html.

Wilgoren, Jodi. (1999b, November 24). Texas top 10 percent law appears to preserve college racial mix. *New York Times,* A1, A18.

Wilgoren, Jodi. (1999c, December 3). Credit given to failed education goals. *New York Times*. Retrieved December 4, 1999 from the World Wide Web: http://www.nytimes.com/library/national/120399national-goals-edu.html.

Forces Eroding Affirmative Action in Higher Education: The California-Hawai'i Distinction

JOANNE COOPER, KATHLEEN KANE, AND JOANNE GISSELQUIST

As the introduction to this volume points out, considerations of the role of affirmative action in diverse geographic settings, such as California, and Hawai'i, are of utmost importance as we move into the next century. The current changes in affirmative action policy around the country create questions about the status of women and minorities and about the complexities of the country's changing demographic and economic conditions. Higher education in particular, grapples with issues of equity, access, and the racial, ethnic, and gender struggles from which those issues arise.

This chapter will examine the status of women in higher education, the events surrounding affirmative action in California, and the situation for women and minorities in another highly diverse state with a different history, Hawai'i. While affirmative action in California has been under direct attack through its dismantling in the University of California system, Hawai'i has encountered a more subtle erosion of such policies through the destructive force of continual budget cuts. Considering these divergent histories, we find it unlikely that the political environment around affirmative action in California can be used to predict future changes in Hawai'i. Indeed, it is possible that Hawai'i may be in a strong position to avoid the contentious struggle over affirmative action in higher education that California has experienced during the last 5 years. Troy Duster articulated this conclusion during a presentation at the University of Hawai'i at Manoa (UHM) in the spring of 1999 (University of Hawai'i President's Commission on Diversity, Ku Lama, March 5, 1999). Duster (1999), who serves as Chancellor's Professor of Sociology at University of California, Berkeley, outlines a three-stage view of diversity, framed in the context of education. In stage 1, one group dominates and holds

163

unchallenged authority, with perhaps a small representation of other groups—a constrained number with discreet ability to affect broad change. In stage 2, challenge to this authority takes the form of admitting significant numbers of different groups, with contestation arising over the nature of every aspect of education, from pedagogy to curriculum. In stage 3, different versions of human experience, expression, and knowledge are valued and shared. Duster stated that Hawai'i may be well-positioned to avoid the stage 2 contestations of California. The authors hope that the history of ethnicity and culture in Hawai'i will indeed continue to provide support for affirmative action policy and practice in Hawai'i. Unfortunately, this possibility is currently threatened by continuing fiscal constraints in the state's higher education system.

Duster's projections depart from the common way of anticipating political, social, and economic patterns in Hawai'i which has been to expect that events on the continental United States will reverberate into the Pacific and impact the state of Hawai'i. Because both California and Hawai'i are states of great racial and ethnic diversity, with California currently the site of much turmoil surrounding affirmative action policies, Hawai'i must consider the same possibilities in contemplating its future. Changes in affirmative action policy create deep and difficult questions about the status of women and minorities and about the complex entanglement of the country's changing demographics and economics. Thus, questions about the future of Hawai'i in the next 5 to 10 years are inevitable. With this concern and with Duster's analysis as a backdrop, this chapter presents a closer examination of the situation in Hawai'i, illuminating a particular cultural history and an accompanying commitment to community. We then examine the impact of fiscal constraints on that commitment, providing additional information about the complex forces that come to bear on affirmative action policies and procedures as we enter the millennium.

We have chosen to focus our work on women in higher education in part because, in the 24 years since the full implementation of affirmative action measures in academe, women have made more progress than minority groups. However, Busenberg and Smith (1997, p. 162) caution, "It is critical to realize that the progress which has been made has benefited predominantly white women."

We are also compelled by ways in which women understand themselves as a part of the educational enterprise, as distinct from the hegemony of masculinist traditions of education. Much of what concerns women who are involved in teaching and learning is an awareness that "the forms of our social and individual existences are not merely imposed upon us but sustained by us with our tacit if not explicit consent" (Grumet, 1998, p. 4). For many women, education is the site where resistance to the hegemony of privilege is exercised on behalf of themselves and their students. For this reason, "it is common for women in general, and for women from working-class backgrounds in particular, to put high value on advising and teaching. They often devote what some might judge to be disproportionate time to these activities, believing they are doing their jobs. When these faculty come up for tenure or reappointment, they learn that their colleagues do not judge the labor of pedagogy as highly as they have" (Tokarczyk & Fay, 1993, p. 9). This chapter examines the ways in which women toiling in higher education in Hawai'i today both understand and resist the forces that shape their work as educators.

Women, especially minority women, could be described as "historically, quite recent immigrants to the academic groves" (Griffin, 1992). The workloads of these recent immigrants to academe represent expectations of others on them, as well as their own "desire to reinvoke [a] transformational experience, their own experience of growth and change, for others. It is not . . . simply an extension of the nonintellectual gifts of mothering transplanted to another professional scene, but something far more radical—women invoking change in others" (Aisenberg & Harrington, 1988, p. 39). Thus, women in academe are often confronted by conflicting forces and desires. As Glazer-Raymo (1999) has stated, they often desire growth and change for themselves and others. Yet they find themselves conforming to institutional norms in order to gain acceptance. Following traditional career paths, in their efforts to be taken seriously, they "have anticipated rewards, acceptance and recognition for their conscientious work and their acceptance of institutional norms" (Glazer-Raymo, 1999, p. 24). Instead, they are unable to escape the stereotypes that are still pervasive in the society and the academy today.

We will present the experiences of individual women in higher education from across the University of Hawai'i (UH) system, at 4-year and 2-year colleges and universities. We include UH community colleges, as they share a strong history of commitment to serving marginalized student populations within their communities. Our study reveals the pressures, struggles and frustrations of women faculty and administrators committed to the values of affirmative action, yet thwarted in their efforts to actualize their professional responsibility in the face of severe fiscal constraints. We conclude with a discussion of the complex connections between Hawai'i's history of commitment to diversity and community and the impact of fiscal constraints on that commitment.

Affirmative Action and Women in Higher Education

President Clinton commented on the intent of bills passed by Presidents Roosevelt in 1941 and Johnson in 1965 and 1967 as the means to "give our nation a way to finally address the systemic exclusion of individuals of talent, on the basis of their gender or race, from opportunities to develop, perform, achieve, and contribute" ("Excerpts from Clinton talk on affirmative action,"

1995). There is little doubt that these bills paved the way for today's affirmative action policies. The initial act in a series of orders came in 1941, when President Roosevelt issued an executive order barring defense contractors from discriminating against minorities (Garcia, 1997). Next came the passage of the Civil Rights Act of 1964, which was much more sweeping. Title II prohibited racial discrimination in public accommodations. Title VI, which later became one of the grounds for Alan Bakke's suit against the University of California at Davis's affirmative action program, barred discrimination by educational institutions receiving federal monies. And Title VII protected plaintiffs alleging discrimination in employment (Howard, 1997). In 1965 President Johnson issued Executive Order 11246, which prohibited contractors from discriminating against any employees and applicants for employment by requiring that contractors take affirmative action "to ensure that applicants are employed and treated during their employment without regard to race, color, religion or national origin." Two years later, in 1967, President Johnson signed Executive Order 11375, which included sex as a protected class. The intent was—and still is—to boost the number of minority and women employees in employment settings that receive federal funding" (Garcia, 1997, p. 4).

In some ways, women are seen as the stepchildren of affirmative action policies, given that it took 2 long years of hard lobbying by feminists to include "sex" as a discrimination category after Executive Order 11246 was issued by President Johnson on September 24, 1965. Five years later in 1972, the effect of this policy was felt in the academic world, when Title VII of the Civil Rights Act was extended to include all educational institutions.[1] From that point, colleges and universities have had an obligation to ensure that their hiring practices are in line with the availability of women and minorities in the labor pools from which their employees are drawn (Busenberg & Smith, 1997).

In the 24 years since the full implementation of affirmative action measures in academe, women viewed broadly as a category would seem to have made progress. But a closer examination of the conditions in which women in academe work reveals that women continue to hold a much higher percentage of part-time and non-tenure-track positions than men and experience salary inequities within and across academic disciplines. In the fall of 1992, 41 percent of all female faculty were employed part-time, while only 29 percent of their male counterparts were part-time employees. In 1996, 22 percent of full-time women faculty were nontenure track, bringing the total of either nontenure track or part-time female faculty to 62.4 percent (Glazer-Raymo, 1999). Today women remain disproportionately located in the less prestigious community colleges (37.6 percent) and 4-year colleges (29.3 percent). Across the country, the number of female professors has increased since the early 1970s, but the proportion of female faculty has remained the same since the total number of faculty has also increased (Blum, 1991).

When women do advance to the rank of full professor, the average salary of male faculty was 13 percent higher than the average female faculty salary (Busenberg & Smith, 1997). Women are clustered in fields such as the health professions and education, where in 1995 women made up nearly all (98 percent) of the faculty in nursing and more than one half (56 percent) of the faculty in education. In contrast, women make up only 6 percent of the nation's engineering faculty and 23 percent of the natural sciences faculty.

Furthermore, a definitive look at increased equity for women as a category reveals that over the past two decades, it has been white women who have predominately benefited. Within the 36 percent of female instructional faculty employed by colleges and universities, 32 percent were white women and only 4 percent were women of color. While minority women students in colleges and universities constitute 13 percent of the student body today, they make up only 4 percent of the faculty, providing few who might serve as role models to encourage female students of color in their chosen professions (Busenberg & Smith, 1997). The picture for women in administration is not much better than that for women faculty. "Among presidents and chief executive officers, 84 percent are white women, while only 16 percent are women of color, including 39 African Americans, 24 Hispanics, 2 Asian Americans and 7 American Indians. Clearly," state Busenberg and Smith (1997, p. 163), "to be a woman and to be a minority member is a double jeopardy for those seeking a career in academia." Thus, in spite of the progress that has been made, it is obvious that equity across the nation has not been achieved for women faculty in general nor for women faculty of color in particular.

The Case of California

Despite such failures in reaching equity, both the executive and the legislative branches of government are engaged in efforts to dismantle the laws and programs meant to support the nation's struggle against discrimination. Opponents have argued against affirmative action, in some cases asserting that affirmative action programs represent a form of "reverse discrimination." In an old but continuing opposition, there is the assertion that affirmative action stigmatizes potential beneficiaries in a manner that they would never be able to overcome. These arguments represent features of a discourse designed to dissolve support for affirmative action among women and minority scholars, particularly among those faculty of color and white middle-class women who feel they have not experienced the discrimination practices that drove the politics of affirmative action in the 1970s.

California has been the site of much of the turmoil surrounding affirmative action policies, in part because of its history of racial and ethnic diversity. "The rollback of affirmative action by the University of California Regents and the voters of California mark two of the most dramatic events in the history of affirmative action" (Smelser, 1999, p. 181). Several factors, both nationally and locally, contributed to the dramatic events in California. Nationally, the real wages of Americans have remained virtually stagnant since 1973. In addition, as companies began to downsize as a competitive strategy, middle-class positions became less secure. Second, the stagnation of American wages was aggravated by a regressive movement in the distribution of income from the early 1980s on, due to a complex set of causes, including technological changes and international wage competition. This was accompanied by increases in poverty and homelessness, exaggerated further by the economic recession of the early 1990s. During this same time, the country experienced the greatest increase in foreign immigration since the late nineteenth and early twentieth centuries (Smelser, 1999), creating a situation for Californians in which there were fewer jobs along with an increase of immigrant workers competing for those jobs and willing to work for less. In a political context dominated by the right and the Republican Party through the administrations of Nixon, Reagan, and Bush, and the election of a Republican Congress in 1994, politicians began a campaign to radically revise or abolish affirmative action as a governmental policy (Smelser, 1999).

At the same time, forces in the state of California converged to intensify these national developments. Immigration rates in California were higher than for the rest of the nation. The recession of the early 1990s was more severe in California than it was in the rest of the nation. California politics had been dominated since the early 1980s by the Republican governorships of George Dukemejian and Pete Wilson, both of whom carried out extensive antiwelfare and anti-immigration campaigns. Anti–affirmative action was added to this list, when on June 1, 1995, Governor Wilson issued an executive order to "End Preferential Treatment and to Promote Individual Opportunity Based on Merit" (Smelser, 1999, p. 185). In addition, there was the tendency for California politics to result in what Smelser (1999, p. 186) has termed public "free-for-alls." Because California has institutionalized many features of direct democracy, including provisions for initiatives, referenda, and the recall of public officials, state officials on occasion pass difficult and explosive issues on to the voting public. In addition, California's political parties, in comparison with states to the east, are weak in structure and in capacity to control and discipline their members, leading to many political mavericks and unpredictable elections. In large part due to the conditions described above, political issues are frequently fought out in the public media rather than negotiated in party caucuses and meetings. All of this, including the debate over affirmative action by the University of California Regents in 1995, has been subject to public airing by the mass media.

Finally, the appointment of Ward Connerly, a conservative African-American businessman from Sacramento, to the University of California system

Board of Regents, has been of crucial significance (Smelser, 1999). Without his determined action, the issue might never have reached the voting public. Although Connerly was the recipient of contracts under affirmative-action provisions for minority businessmen, he has held antagonistic views toward affirmative action since the beginning of his term. His decision to "increase [the issue's] public visibility" in January of 1995 brought the matter to the attention of the entire state and subsequently the nation (Smelser, 1999, p. 186). Connerly's status as a minority sharpens the debate about affirmative action because the opposition can no longer claim that the desire to abolish affirmative action is simply another case of discrimination by whites. In addition, Connerly's belief that "the university did not take his concern seriously (he spoke of his 'Lone Ranger' image)" led him to bring the debate to the attention of the public (Smelser, 1999, p. 186).

By July of 1995 the University's Regents had adopted a resolution turning back affirmative action policy, despite the protests of administrators, faculty, and students. In November of 1996, the voters of the state passed an anti–affirmative action initiative, the California Civil Rights Initiative, which was similar to the wording of the Regents' resolutions. Thus, despite the ambivalence of the university toward its new policy, the matter has now been propelled into state and national arenas and is headed for the United States Supreme Court. Ironically, the measure's passage has had an interesting consequence for the University of California. "Every constituency in the University, save the Board of Regents, [has] gone on record as favoring affirmative action for the University, i.e. opposing the initiative" (Smelser, 1999, p. 191).

While affirmative action seems to be the focal point of this current debate, scholars agree that it is the underlying issues of racial, ethnic, and gender struggles that the country must come to terms with (Smelser, 1999; Tien, 1999). For despite the advances affirmative action has secured for both minorities and women, "neither its adoption nor its implementation nor the efforts to reverse it seems to have had—or will have—a calming effect on the racial, ethnic and gender politics of the country" according to Smelser (1999, p. 197). However, agreement on the underlying issue does not mean agreement about the character of that issue. As Tien states (1999, p. 197), "Where [Smelser] sees problems and conflict, I see opportunities and even progress." Whether the struggles in California constitute continuing problems or continuing opportunities, or both, it is obvious that the issues in California will remain key to the questions about affirmative action nationwide.

The Case of Hawai'i

Although Hawai'i has not taken the path of California in rolling back affirmative action policy, it faces similar questions, given its diversity and its experience of economic recession, including continuing stagnant or shrinking wages. In fact, while California seems to have pulled out of its economic slump of the early 1990s, Hawai'i continues to grapple with a sluggish economy. Thus, the case of Hawai'i presents a counterpoint of possible responses to a somewhat similar set of racial and economic conditions.

The University of Hawai'i has experienced more than 5 years of extremely tight budgetary constraints. In the last 10 years, state financial support of the university system has dropped by a total of 19 percent. State lawmakers added less than 1 percent to the 1999–2001 budget for the university system and froze all government workers' salaries, including those of university professors and staff members (*Chronicle of Higher Education*, 1999). The Western Association of Schools and Colleges, the system's chief accreditor, called the financial situation at the flagship campus, at Manoa, "serious and immediate," after its visit in the Spring of 1999. The agency warned that the university's "accreditation will soon be endangered" if it does not make efforts by 2002 to reverse declines in budgets, among other things (*Chronicle of Higher Education*, 1999, p. 74).

Two current responses to the budget crunch were a reduction in tuition waivers given to students for public service and the state legislature's rejection of a proposal to waive tuition for all Native Hawai'ian students (*Chronicle of Higher Education*, 1999). These services directly affect low income and minority populations and are examples of the ways in which budgetary constraints undermine affirmative action.

Another way in which fiscal constraints function to dismantle policies and procedures that uphold affirmative action's intent is the demise of the Office for Women's Research on the University of Hawai'i Manoa campus. This office, whose work has provided invaluable information as well as opportunities for research on and support to the work of women in academe, has slid silently from our view. A letter dated June 14, 1999, was sent from the Office for Women's Research, which supported this project on women and budget cuts at its inception. It stated:

> We at the Office for Women's Research (OWR) at the University of Hawai'i at Manoa regret to announce that due to severe budget cuts and restructuring, OWR has lost complete funding, including unit operations, two graduate research assistantships, and the directorship. As a result, we do not have any other option but to significantly curtail our activities. . . . While we hope to maintain a minimal level of activity, the future of OWR is uncertain. . . . Established in 1990, OWR has worked towards maintaining a mission to promote interdisciplinary work that . . . provided research and community initiatives for women and men in Hawai'i, Asia and the larger Pacific region. Our focus of activities have included not only issues concerning gender, but sexuality, race, ethnicity, class and nationality.

The higher education system of the state of Hawai'i is a place that holds a stunning range of Asian and Pacific ethnic diversity. University of Hawai'i EEOAA statistics for 1994–1995 indicate that 76.4 percent of the student population is Asian/Pacific (Japanese 25.8 percent; Chinese 12.3 percent; Filipino 9.2 percent; Hawai'ian 7.0 percent; Korean 3.4 percent; East Indian, mixed, and other Asian/Pacific 18.7 percent); 21.8 percent of the students are Caucasian, 1.0 percent are Hispanic, and 0.8 percent are African-American. Class and economic status are not specifically articulated in these statistics, but configurations of ethnicity and class have been extensively and histori- cally determined through the plantation system of labor and immigration. That history inhabits the present through the great numbers of students at the University of Hawai'i at Manoa, and indeed across the UH system on all islands, whose knowledge of the plantation derives directly from the life experiences of their grandparents. The era of the plantation in Hawai'i has passed, but its intersecting social constructs of ethnicity, gender, and class remain and are present in the classrooms of the university system today (Kane, 1992).

Although faculty at UH are not as diverse as students, when the faculty at community colleges are included, there are growing numbers of women and minorities. In the fall of 1998, faculty across the entire higher education system were 58 percent Caucasian, 19 percent Japanese, 10 percent Chinese/ Korean, 4 percent Hawai'ian, 2 percent Filipino, and 7 percent other (Univer- sity of Hawai'i Fact Sheet, 1998). Although women comprise 51 percent of the general population at both the national and state levels, only 32 percent of full-time faculty nationally and 30 percent of full-time faculty at Manoa are women (Office for Women's Research, 1995). At the full professor level at the University of Hawai'i Manoa, 87 percent are men and 13 percent are women. In contrast, at the instructor level, women outnumber men at Manoa (Office for Women's Research, 1995).

California and Hawai'i, holding similarly diverse populations, thus present two different examples of how affirmative action is challenged. While Cali- fornia played out its public debate over the fate of affirmative action policies in its university system, affirmative action in Hawai'i and its university sys- tem has suffered a more silent budgetary demise.

The Women and Budget Cuts Project: History and Methodology

During the Fall of 1995 and Spring of 1996, which followed a 3-year period of profound and continual budget cuts at the University of Hawai'i, two panels were organized and convened by one of the authors at the Office of Faculty Development and Academic Support (OFDAS) and the UH

Commission on the Status of Women (UHCSW), respectively. Women from diverse locations within the university system gave testimony about how these cuts were affecting women on several campuses. Ways in which progress regarding women's issues has been made over the last 10 years in the UH system were discussed. These included programs like the Women's Program at the Health Center, sexual harassment awareness, Center for Adults Returning to Education, and support for child care. In juxtaposition, there was discussion about how this progress had been threatened in the last 3–5 years by difficulties in attracting and retaining talented women faculty. Travel and sabbatical leave freezes have been detrimental to junior faculty (many of whom are women, due to preaffirmative action policies and practices) in their promotion and tenure process. Counseling services have been reduced and tuition waivers have decreased at a time that tuition was also dramatically increasing.

These panels were drawn from women across the spectrum of the University of Hawai'i, women whose labor includes teaching, research and learning, guarding and securing university properties, managing offices and programs, and maintaining grounds and buildings. These panels were themselves very diverse by ethnicity, race, and class. It was through this process of testimony from women who occupy very different places within the system that we identified threats to the goals of diversity and equity. These two panels suggested a relationship between a climate of budget crisis and a negative impact on diversity and equity issues. Participants and attendees felt that by gathering narratives across the UH system, it would be possible to discover a more enriched, complex illumination of affirmative action's successes and failures in the educational community. Of concern during these discussions was the possibility that actual program or overall budget cuts were disproportionately affecting women, most particularly women of color.

The Project

From these initial events grew a small grant from the Office for Women's Research at UH Manoa to further investigate the effects that budget cuts may have had on the goals of diversity, with gender as a broad frame of reference that intersects with other dimensions of diversity—particularly ethnicity, culture, age, and class. We sought narratives from women across the UH system about their experiences and understanding of the conditions of their work in both universities and community colleges. Our work, rather than addressing macropolitical issues, focused on narratives of individual experience. The research was exploratory in nature. It asked, "What happens to women who work in the academy as systems begin to shrink budgetarily?" Everyone is affected in a fiscal crisis, but specifically, how are women affected? How are minority women affected? As Glazer-Raymo (1999) has suggested, women in higher education, both faculty and administrators, experience frustrated ambitions and a sense of backlash. We wanted to know if these experiences were exacerbated under reduced fiscal conditions. These narratives were audiotaped and transcribed to generate multiple themes and issues of concern.

We conducted seven focus groups and two private interviews at eight campuses in a statewide system. Two of the campuses were 4-year campuses, and six were 2-year colleges. In all, 41 women participated. Of these women, 14 were tenured faculty or administrators, four were nontenured faculty, two were professional staff, and four were state civil service support staff. Data was unavailable for 17 participants. Ten of the 41 participants were Caucasian, 16 were Asian/Pacific Islander or had mixed ethnicity, and 15 did not report their ethnic backgrounds. Thirteen of the participants were born and raised in Hawai'i, eight were born and raised in other states, one was born and raised abroad, and data was unavailable for 19 participants.

Participants were asked about their experiences during the years leading up to and including the period of system wide budget cuts. They were asked to provide narratives about how their own work was affected, whether positively or negatively, and observations about work in their own departments or campuses. Participants were also asked about their expectations of the university as an institution in creating a climate that expects and promotes diversity and equity. They also discussed their expectations of their own roles in creating a collegial and productive university climate.

The Impact of Budget Cuts in the Context of Social Responsibility

The voices of the women in this study reveal a diversity of personal and professional experiences. They clearly articulate their expectations that the academy must be a responsible member of the local community. They bring, as well, a strong sense of commitment to the academy and a sense of how their own contributions make a difference in the lives of the students they serve. Hearing these voices compels us to reflect on our *own* assumptions about the role of the university in our communities and about the responsibility of the university toward social change. If, as Duster suggests, stage 3 is a less contentious period in which diverse experiences and expressions will share space in the academy, then it is incumbent on us to attend to these voices now and ensure their participation in the life of the academy.

Despite the great diversity of cultures and ethnicities found in Hawai'i, the predominant culture of the academy is similar to the rest of the United States, in that it is dominated at the faculty ranks by white males (Glazer-Raymo, 1999; University of Hawai'i Fact Sheet, 1998). Women administrators and faculty from colleges and universities throughout the state of Hawai'i thus toil in circumstances that are demographically similar to the rest of the nation at the faculty and administrative ranks. Yet they serve populations that are more diverse than many parts of the nation. These women articulate clear norms and expectations about the responsibilities of institutions of higher education to their students, and they express frustration at the ways in which the realization of equity and access to the academy have been thwarted by the current fiscal restraints of the university system.

Three major themes emerged from an analysis of the data. First, these women demonstrate a keen awareness of the impact of budget cuts on their institutions and the state in general. Their response was generally to redouble their efforts to serve students in any way possible. Second, their willingness to work harder seemed tied to their strong sense of community and their desire to serve the local community in Hawai'i. Third, within the context of a web of relationships and a dynamic reciprocity that created and strengthened community, there were embedded assumptions about the university and its responsibilities to social equity in general and to diverse constituents in particular.

The women in this study have been firsthand witnesses to the impact of budget cuts on students and on the sometimes complex web of interactions between a reduced number of course offerings and the ability of the academy to uphold its commitments to equity and social justice. They spoke, for example, of entry-level courses that had been cut, restricting the ability of marginalized groups to enter higher education. "What's happened here is that a lot of women are coming back to school. They tend to walk in the door at the last minute because it is so intimidating to come in, and the last week, because our courses [are so] minimal . . . the only ones that will be left are those instructors who create an intimidating and hostile environment in the classroom."

On the job, the response of these women to the cuts in work hours of temporary help was to increase their own workloads to meet student needs. They described their efforts to "help out" the university during times of economic duress. "Women tend to just sort of take on more. We just do more, we organize ourselves a little better, we adjust here, we adjust there. We try to meet whatever perceived need we see." Some women tied this tendency to ethnicity and to cultures in which relationships of reciprocity were expected.

For these women, their connection to the community precedes their work on the campus. Their work on behalf of the institution has a quality of *accompaniment*, that is to say, they bring to their work, or are accompanied by, a personal history with both the institution and the community that hosts it. This feature of accompaniment is a strength they bring to their work at the institution and the source from which they draw a sense of purpose and focus in their work. "As women we make do, we do more. As *local women* we place great emphasis on community. As *local Asian women*, we give, we

give . . ." " We were trained and raised to be flexible, and [not] to be takers."
"And [if given a gift] you don't forget to pay back." Women recognized the
difference between their "work more" approach to scarcity and the responses
of others on campus. "It's a whole different approach to the same problem. . . . I
think about our campus . . . who [are] the . . . hard workers versus [the]
grumblers."

The decision taken by many women to work harder is related to a deep
sense of commitment to an island community in which relationships are very
much contextualized by a small landmass on a remote island chain, which
defines the relations between people (and therefore, relations of knowledge)
as circular or weblike, reciprocal, and in continual return— rather than on a
landmass that extends in straight lines and ever-outward and away. There is
a very strong history of community building through social and familial alliances "as members of an extensive and untangled net which represents
security and coherence" (Hopkins 1992). One woman said, "I have a sense
of . . . responsibility to the community. I was born and raised in a plantation
camp, so community is very important to me . . . I was fortunate enough to
play in a camp with all of the children and that's where you learn your
values. . . . I think it's mainly a sense of family which is a major part of the
community and also a sense of tradition." To work under the harsh conditions
of plantation life with a variety of peoples underscored a sense of the importance of working together despite cultural and ethnic differences.

Local Asian and part-Hawai'ian women who have entered the academy
in Hawai'i recognize the potential of higher education to change lives, while
they in turn bring their own values into the academic workplace. These women
had expectations of the university's role and responsibility within the larger
community. As part of the university, one woman felt that, "because you're
in education you can have a major role in transmission of culture, of history."
At the same time, one faculty member expressed a belief that the university's
mission is tied to the local community. "This is the only university here. And
it is established for the people who live here. . . . We have to be able to take
care of the local people."

These convictions about the role of the university in the life of the community led to another source of tension: the changing expectations from the
academy for the women who worked there. For example, women observed
that more emphasis is being placed on fund-raising. One faculty woman
explained that "this huge emphasis on fund raising is just a whole shift [in
priorities]." Another stated, "Suddenly it's how you maintain self-support . . .
[and] I'm not prepared [for] . . . that."

In addition to conflicts about one's role in the university, the women in
this study voiced the conflicts they felt between the values of the community
and the values of the academic workplace. One woman stated that she looked
"for the tradition . . . the family . . . the same values, but when I don't see it,

then I have to realize that I'm in the workplace and it's a different world." Several women reflected on how they felt less satisfaction as they kept taking on more and more roles and working a greater number of hours. One woman stated, "I think there's a lot of stress . . . on the body."

Having brought particular community-based values into the academy and redoubled their efforts to translate those values into action, these women came face-to-face with the realization that the culture of higher education may thwart those same values and desires. The women talked about their sense of community and its disjuncture with a white western culture that places emphasis on individual achievement. One woman stated, "Reality hits you when you go through the tenure process . . . because it's . . . very much a male oriented process. . . . It's very hard for you to put yourself down on paper in such a manner that is advantageous to you in that process."

Other faculty described the very real impact of budget cuts on their work as scholars. A faculty member from an English department stated, "One of the arguments that is being used against arguments for decentering and more diverse faculty is that we're in the middle of a . . . budget crisis. And the state legislature must see that English is doing its job that means that English is teaching Chaucer, Milton, and Shakespeare. [They say,] 'We don't want any of this new-fangled Tony Morrison, Alice Walker stuff . . . and now is not the time to propose . . . these other classes that are really marginal.'" In addition, the budget cuts have affected the availability of on-campus resources for women scholars engaged in feminist research; "you know when there is no money to buy journals and a lot of the women's journals are not available electronically because it's very expensive and only the big journals are available electronically, you have a lot of problems." As research scholars at a large 4-year public university, the budget cuts affect the very core of professional activity, the ability to do research and interact in the ongoing dialogue among scholars. "With respect to faculty, I think the cuts can be painful in ways of developing interaction, physical interaction with colleagues outside of the state." One woman stated that "the worst part of my experience here was not having the money to continue my research." The isolation from colleagues and from new developments in their fields brought frustration and a sense of disadvantage. "This isn't a women's issue, but I've heard so many other people comment that they have colleagues that come here from the mainland and they start talking about . . . some old computer program that they aren't using anymore, and we are still four generations behind them. It's insane . . . I go to conferences and I don't know what they are talking about because I haven't read the articles. I mean, it's embarrassing."

Academic women interviewed across the state of Hawai'i thus demonstrated a keen awareness of the impact of budgetary constraints on their work and their professional lives. They exhibit a number of responses to these growing pressures, including an effort to work harder to meet increasing demands, a response they report emerges directly from their values and commitment to "help out" the higher-education community. Their commitment to the care of local populations is clearly evident. Yet these women are caught between cultures in many ways. They are squeezed between the culture of higher education, which is steeped in white, Western, male traditions and bureaucratic functions, and their own local cultures, which value community and service. These conflicts give rise to frustration, exhaustion, and discouragement, especially when programs or services are cut during times of budget constraints.

Women working in higher education across the state of Hawai'i are the beneficiaries of an affirmative action system already viewed as passé in some parts of the nation.[2] Yet, these women have just begun to make a place for the generations that will come after them. They are at this point in dire need of policies, procedures and the fiscal resources to do the job they believe must be done, the work that Garcia (1997, p. 249) asserts is vital, "if we are to be members of a just and democratic society."

Considerations for Policy Makers

Our exploratory research on the experiences of women during a severe fiscal crisis in the academy indicates that there is a threat to the goal of maintaining equity and diversity during times of exigency. The threat may not be a direct one, as in the case of California and its rollback of affirmative action policies. Indirect but nevertheless damaging effects can result from decisions to cut programs or staffing of activities that affect women and minorities once they are members of the academy. These decisions, such as reducing support staff, or cutting an Office for Women's Research, can act to stifle the voices of women in the higher-education community.

It is beyond the scope of this chapter to discuss criteria for program retention or reduction based on an equity agenda. However, our research and our review of recent literature suggest that, whether affirmative action policies are rescinded or not, policy makers, and all of us within the academy, must develop new paradigms in pursuing the goals of diversity and equity.

First, we can renew our understanding that diversity contributes to successful educational outcomes. In 1996, the ad hoc Commission on Governance and Affirmative Action Policy of the AAUP issued a report commenting on the July 20, 1995, decision by the Board of Regents of the University of California to end affirmative action. The report noted that the decision of the Regents violated the tradition of shared governance in higher education by ignoring the input of faculty who have "unique expertise" on educational matters (AAUP, 1996). The Commission recognized that the motives for affirmative action were tied to the University's responsibility to provide access to higher education, to remedy discrimination, and to provide students with the educational benefits of diversity. Furthermore, the report observes that these anticipated educational benefits were realized by the increase in measures of student success at Berkeley between 1964 and 1990, following the implementation of affirmative action.

Research has shown that an environment of diversity on campuses has a positive relationship to college student development (Astin, 1993). The positive effects on development of knowledge and satisfaction with the college experience were related to institutional policies and practices, such as the existence of women's studies programs, faculty engagement in diversity in their teaching and research, and student involvement in diversity activities (Astin, 1993).

Second, we can establish and maintain programs that support women and minority students and faculty once they become members of a higher-education institution. We might begin by examining the research that has suggested that students at predominantly Black or single-sex institutions have higher educational achievements than students at other institutions (Pascarella & Terenzini, 1991). Based on that research, we can then ask what support mechanisms we might replicate for minorities and women on campuses with more heterogeneous faculty and student populations.

Third, we can explore and strengthen the dimension of public responsibility of our institutions of higher learning. Recent research has identified characteristics of campuses that produce successful outcomes for women, measured by large proportions of women graduating with baccalaureates and earning doctorates (Wolf-Wendel, 2000). These institutions have high expectations for women within a climate of support that provides a strong peer culture and role models and gives students leadership opportunities. The institutions have a clear sense of mission. And, directly related to our own research, the campuses studied by Wolf-Wendel encourage a commitment to the community "as a crucial factor underlying student success" (Wolf-Wendel, 2000, p. 340). Wolf-Wendel's finding that women-friendly campuses see themselves as part of the social context of families and communities suggests to us that we turn from images of universities as ivory-towered bastions and move toward a vision of centers of learning with porous boundaries encouraging inclusion and participatory commitment to the larger environment.

Fourth, individual voice and agency may become vital tools in support of diversity and equity, especially in climates where policy may be threatened by fiscal or political issues. A study of higher-education administrators concludes that, in the absence of policy, administrators may have to more clearly articulate their own commitment to diversity when difficult hiring or other decisions are faced (Vozzola, Hatfield, Hatfield, 1998).

Conclusion

We began this chapter with the observation that it may be useful to examine the experiences of women in higher education in the very diverse context of Hawai'i. The discussions in the focus groups conducted at campuses across the University of Hawai'i system indicate that years after the implementation of affirmative action policy, issues of equity and opportunity are continuing concerns for women in the academy. While the women who participated in the focus groups are active members of their campuses, their words reveal a conflict of cultures, between local island culture(s) and education culture, and an accompanying sense of marginality. Their viewpoints and experiences diverge from the mainstream academic discourse on equity—a divergence that creates for them situations of tension, frustration, and conflict.

The authors do not anticipate that the spectacle of politics that is characteristic of California will be reenacted in Hawai'i. What we have been witnessing is that a politics of fiscal pragmatism is one in which it is expedient to eliminate that which has less longevity, less infrastructure, and less institutional history. It is expedient to do so because of deep resistance to dismantling all that is older, richer, and more embedded—certainly, it seems true that when dealing with the most entrenched aspects of the educational institution, it would, indeed, be easier to move a graveyard.

It may not be possible for commitment and support of the goals of affirmative action to thrive or even survive in an environment where fiscal constraints are permitted to stand in for policy. Rather than the frontal attacks seen in the case of California, Hawai'i suffers slowly and silently from continual, incremental, and profound retraction of resources to do the kind of work to which the women in our study are so committed. Duster (1999) may be right that Hawai'i's situation provides hope for an avoidance of stage 2 conflict and a movement directly to a space that welcomes different versions of human experience, expression, and knowledge. However, this potential may be squelched by fiscal policies that function to simply exhaust the women who have previously benefited from and are most dedicated to affirmative action and its values. If accrediting bodies like the Western Association of Schools and Colleges (*Chronicle of Higher Education,* 1999) demonstrate concern over the impact of budgetary constraints on the quality of higher education in Hawai'i, it is less likely that these same fiscal policies would undermine the current quality of commitment to diversity and equity.

This examination demonstrates that while ethnic/racial/gender relations in Hawai'i sometimes diverge in very specific ways from those of California and the rest of the continent, diversity and equity within higher education may not follow the hopeful path suggested by Duster when subjected to continual and pervasive fiscal assault. In Hawai'i, budgetary constraints may dismantle the work of those dedicated to equity within institutions of higher education as effectively as the political climate of California.

Notes

1. In addition, Title IX of the Educational Amendments of 1972 was enacted. It prohibits sex discrimination in all educational institutions that receive federal funding and applies to the employment of workers as well as the admission of students (Garcia, 1997).

2. At present, of the nine issues listed as affecting higher education across the nation, one is new restrictions on affirmative action. California, Maine, Mississippi, Texas, and Washington are currently prohibited, by legislation, court order, or statewide policy, from using affirmative action in some or all admissions, financial-aid, or hiring decisions.

References

AAUP ad hoc Commission on Governance and Affirmative Action Policy. (1996, July–August). Report: The Board of Regents of the University of California, Governance, and Affirmative Action. *Academe, 82*(4), 61–66.

Aisenberg, Nadya, & Harrington, Mona. (1988). *Women of academe: Outsiders in the sacred grove.* Amherst: University of Massachusetts Press.

Astin, Alexander W. (1993). *What matters in college? Four critical years revisited.* San Francisco: Jossey-Bass.

Blum, Debra E. (1991). Environment still hostile to women in academe, new evidence indicates. *Chronicle of Higher Education, XXXVIII*(7).

Busenberg, Bonnie, & Smith, Daryl. (1997). Affirmative action and beyond: The woman's perspective. In Mildred Garcia (Ed.), *Affirmative action's testament of hope: Strategies for a new era in higher education* (pp. 149–180). Albany, NY: State University of New York Press.

Chronicle of Higher Education Almanac Issue. (1999, August 27). *XLVI*(1).

Duster, Troy. (1999, February 12). Affirmative action in higher education: The California experience and implications for Hawai'i. [Speech] University of Hawai'i at Manoa campus.

Equal Employment Opportunity and Affirmative Action Office (UH EEOAA). (1993–1994). Unpublished data. Honolulu: University of Hawai'i at Manoa.

Excerpts from Clinton talk on affirmative action. (1995, July 20). *New York Times,* p. A10.

Garcia, Mildred. (1997). *Affirmative action's testament of hope: Strategies for a new era in higher education.* Albany, NY: State University of New York Press.

Glazer-Raymo, Judith. (1999). *Shattering the myths: Women in academe.* Baltimore, MD: Johns Hopkins University Press.

Griffin, Gail. (1992). *Calling: Essays on teaching in the mother tongue.* CA: Trilogy Books.

Grumet, Madeleine. (1988). *Bitter milk: Women and teaching.* Amherst: University of Massachusetts Press.

Hopkins, Pua. (1992). Contemporary Hawai'ian culture workshop notes. Unpublished. Hopkins' private archives.

Howard, John R. (1997). Affirmative action in historical perspective. In Mildred Garcia (Ed.), *Affirmative action's testament of hope: Strategies for a new era in higher education* (pp. 19–46). Albany, NY: State University of New York Press.

Kane, Kathleen. (Ed.). (1992). In celebration of students: Reflections on learning at the University of Hawai'i at Manoa. Honolulu: University of Hawai'i at Manoa, Center for Teaching Excellence.

Office for Women's Research (1995, Fall). Fact Sheet Series, No. 4. Reprint. Honolulu: University of Hawai'i at Manoa.

Pascarella, Ernest T., & Terenzini, Patrick T. (1991). *How college affects students: Findings and insights from twenty years of research.* San Francisco: Jossey-Bass.

Smelser, Neil. (1999). Problematics of affirmative action: A view from California. In Eugene Y. Lowe (Ed.), *Promise and dilemma: Perspectives on racial diversity and higher education* (pp. 169–192). NJ: Princeton University Press.

Tien, Chang-Lin. (1999). What a university can learn and teach about conflict and difference. In Eugene Y. Lowe (Ed.), *Promise and dilemma: Perspectives on racial diversity and higher education* (pp. 193–198). NJ: Princeton University Press.

Tokarczyk, Michelle, & Fay, Elizabeth. (1993). *Working class women in the academy: Laborers in the knowledge factory.* Amherst: University of Massachusetts Press.

University of Hawai'i fact sheet. (1998, Fall). Retrieved from the World Wide Web: www.hawaii.edu/iro/facts/fs1998.htm.

Vozzola, Elizabeth, Hatfield, Timothy, & Hatfield, Susan Rickey. (Fall 1997/ Winter 1998). Practice and principles: University administrators reflect on affirmative action. *CUPA Journal, 48*(3, 4), 11–15.

Wolf-Wendel, Lisa E. (Spring 2000). Women friendly campuses: What five institutions are doing right. *The Review of Higher Education, 23*(3), 319–345.

CHAPTER 8

The Continuing and Expanding Roles of Historically Black Colleges and Universities in an Era of Affirmative Action and Diversity in Higher Education

ANTOINE M. GARIBALDI, HORACE G. DAWSON JR.
AND RICHARD A. ENGLISH

The majority of the more than 100 Historically Black Colleges and Universities (HBCUs) were founded more than a century ago, and the oldest of these institutions have been in existence for more than 130 years. In general, though, the public knows very little about most of these institutions—except for the fact that they enroll predominantly African-American students. But when one reviews the unique histories and the composition of the faculty and administration of these colleges and universities in their early years, a picture emerges of America's first true models of diversity in higher education. Despite legally mandated separation of the races in many societal contexts, including education, many of these colleges and universities were established primarily by whites. In several instances, this was done in collaboration with African-Americans or with missionary and abolitionist groups that were sympathetic to the needs of newly emancipated slaves. Additionally, administrators and faculty of these institutions were usually white, as were their governing boards. But the mission of these schools was unequivocally focused on providing educational opportunities for African-American students. Given this long-standing history of diversity within HBCUs, the term "equity" that is used in the context of many of the chapters in this book has a very different meaning for this discussion of the continuing and expanding role of Historically Black Colleges and Universities in their third century.

Beginning with the premise that HBCUs are and have always been diverse, this chapter describes some of the contributions that this select group of institutions has made to society and to higher education. First, the authors emphasize that HBCUs continue to play a pivotal role in educating and graduating a disproportionately higher share of African-Americans. This is in spite of the fact that HBCUs represent a small percentage of the total number of higher education institutions in this country, and despite 3½ decades of legislative action to increase minority access to postsecondary institutions generally. Second, the authors argue that the majority of the nation's colleges and universities in general should be enrolling and graduating more African-American students today. This is based on the larger number of students graduating from high school and the fact that more institutional choices for nonwhite students were made available by post-1960s open admissions policies and affirmative action initiatives. Third, the authors remind the reader that HBCUs enroll a modest but representative proportion of white students in comparison to African-Americans' share of the enrollment at predominantly white institutions. And, fourth, the authors provide historical examples and perspectives on how African-American faculty and students have assumed leadership roles in two academic areas—international education and the social sciences. This chapter's overall purposes, therefore, are to demonstrate not only that HBCUs have epitomized the kind of multicultural environments to which most institutions should aspire, but also to reinforce the point that many of America's other 3,500 institutions of higher education can learn a great deal from HBCUs.

HBCUs' Roles in Increasing Access Since 1960

After more than 3½ decades of court-mandated integration, voluntary affirmative action, and legislative action to increase minority access to higher education, HBCUs' role in the education of all Americans, but African-Americans especially, is still prominent. Over the last 40 years, many have questioned whether there is a need for these institutions to continue to exist. After the signing of the Civil Rights Act of 1964, the public belief was that HBCUs would not be needed after states implemented open admissions policies in their public colleges and universities and when predominantly white institutions, primarily located in the South, desegregated. In spite of that legislation, it became necessary in 1969 for a suit to be filed, with the assistance of the NAACP Legal Defense Fund, compelling the Office of Civil Rights in the United States Department of Health, Education and Welfare to dismantle dual systems of higher education in nine Southern states and Pennsylvania. Named after the Secretary of HEW at that time and successive secretaries thereafter (i.e., *Adams v. Richardson, Adams v. Califano,* and *Adams v. Weinberger,* etc.), the suit focused on the need to bring about more access in traditionally white institutions of higher education and Historically Black

Colleges and Universities in Arkansas, Florida, Georgia, Louisiana, Maryland, Mississippi, North Carolina, Oklahoma, Pennsylvania, and Virginia. More specifically, as Blackwell notes in 1981:

> These States were required to submit plans for dismantling their dual systems, and for demonstrating substantial movement toward assuring equality of opportunity in access, distribution, and retention of students, faculty, and administrators in state systems. (p. 30)

Thirty years later, several of the original Adams states are still engaged in active litigation as attempts are being made to create more diverse student bodies and to provide adequate financial support for HBCUs. As an indication of how long these protracted cases have lasted, the lead author has served as an expert witness and consultant for cases in two of the Adams states within the last 5 years. Another legal landmark in the struggle to achieve equity in access came with the Supreme Court's 1978 ruling to admit Allan Bakke to the University of California at Davis Medical School (*Regents of the University of California v. Bakke,* 1978). With its support of the consideration of "race" in admissions decisions, it became permissible for colleges and universities to utilize goals in their voluntary affirmative action programs. However, they had to be "flexible goals" rather than "rigid, fixed quotas" in order to comply with Title VI of the Civil Rights Act of 1964 (Blackwell, 1981, p. 86). As a result of the *Bakke* decision, the same question about the need for HBCUs was raised, since most individuals believed that many more opportunities would be made available to underrepresented minorities, especially in professional and graduate programs. As will be described shortly, however, enrollment data in the late 1990s indicate that the enrollment growth of African-Americans has been modest, at best, at the other approximately 3,500 colleges and universities in this country. Thus, the slightly more than one hundred HBCUs still contribute disproportionately to the enrollment and educational attainment of African-Americans. Unfortunately, most of these colleges and universities are limited in their ability to accept many more students, because they have already reached their enrollment capacity.

In 1996, HBCUs accounted for slightly more than 15 percent of all African-American students attending college (225,886 of 1,499,000), compared to a little more than 16 percent in 1986 (176,610 of 1,082,000). These institutions' total enrollment in 1996, however, was 277,974 students compared to 213,000 in 1986—a 30 percent increase over that 10-year period (Wilds & Wilson, 1998). Yet these slightly more than 100 Historically Black institutions awarded over one fourth (28 percent) of all baccalaureate degrees, 15 percent of all master's degrees, 9 percent of doctorates, and 17 percent of first-professional degrees. While the majority of these degrees were awarded to African-American students, the data show that white students accounted for 13 percent of HBCUs' total enrollment in 1996 (37,013 of 277, 974) compared to almost 11 percent in 1986 (22,784 of 213,114). Thus, HBCUs continue to fulfill their historical missions while simultaneously expanding their student bodies' diversity as they enroll a sizable number of white students and another 5 percent of Hispanic, Asian-America, American Indian, and nonresident alien students.

These patterns of attendance and educational attainment have occurred as the nation's other 3,500 colleges and universities have "opened their doors" to more underrepresented minorities over the last three decades. It is important to note, however, that similar to 1976, 42 percent (629,000) of African-Americans were in 2-year colleges in 1996, while 43 percent were enrolled at 4-year predominantly white universities (644,000). In 1976, almost 604,000 African-American students, or 59 percent, attended 4-year institutions, while a little more than 429,000, or 41 percent, attended 2-year institutions (Wilds & Wilson, 1998).

These institutions have made a major impact on the preparation of their graduates to pursue and obtain doctoral degrees. The National Academy of Science Summary Report of 1996 Doctorate Recipients indicates that 11 HBCUs and 2 predominantly Black institutions were responsible for the undergraduate preparation of almost 20 percent of African-American doctorate recipients between 1992 and 1996 (Henderson, Clarke, & Woods, 1998). Additionally, these 13 institutions were among the top 18 institutions that awarded baccalaureate degrees to those African-American doctoral recipients. Even though these figures are not as high as the 50 percent recorded in the 1950s and 1960s, the contributions of these institutions to the postsecondary education of African-Americans are still significant. Coupled with this is the fact that among the top 20 institutions that awarded doctorate degrees to African-Americans between 1992 and 1996, three of those institutions were HBCUs—Howard University (209), Clark Atlanta University (103), and Texas Southern University (69). And given the more than 100 percent increase in the overall number of institutions awarding the doctorate from 1964 (174) to 1991 (367), there should be even greater opportunities for minority students to earn terminal degrees at the other American institutions that award doctorates.

It is obvious that HBCUs continue to be environments where individuals can succeed and fulfill their aspirations to pursue graduate and professional opportunities. To assure that graduates from these colleges and universities will be able to compete in the world, as well as in this country, several of these institutions have expanded or developed new international initiatives to provide more opportunities for both students and faculty. And, due to HBCUs' significant role in advancing the nation's civil rights agenda and in addressing the social and economic needs of African-Americans in particular and other minorities in general, these institutions have continued to strengthen their programs in the social sciences. The following discussion of HBCUs' past and current roles in advancing these two critical areas—namely, international affairs and the social sciences—demonstrates how extensive that involvement has been and will continue to be in the future.

HBCUs' Expanding Involvement in the International Arena

Any discussion of the expansion of employment opportunities in international affairs for Blacks and other minorities must occur within the proper context. Among government agencies, the U.S. Foreign Service has been viewed as among the least receptive to racial diversity. Since 1845, the date Dawson (1993) establishes for the appointment of the first African-American diplomat, there have been a limited number of African-Americans in the Foreign Service, and many of them were, in the early days, political appointees.[1] In more recent years, beginning with the Kennedy administration, the numbers increased significantly, and leadership positions, including ambassadorships, began to be offered to African-Americans and other minorities. These declined under Presidents Reagan and Bush but rose significantly once again under President Clinton. Even so, there can be no real discussion of "equity" in this area of government employment of African-Americans who, even today, number only about 5 to 6 percent of foreign service personnel at all levels. For the most part, the policies—and the results—of private business in this area have not differed significantly from those of government.

HBCUs have traditionally produced the majority of African-Americans preparing for leadership positions in international affairs, as illustrated by the first U.S. ambassador of color, Edward R. Dudley, who was a product of Virginia Union University. Nevertheless, the actual numbers of African-Americans engaged as professionals in international affairs continue to be a matter of serious concern. African-American leaders view the relatively small numbers as a manifestation of limited opportunity related to the existence of racial barriers in such institutions as the American foreign service, economic development agencies, and the private sector. These agencies, in turn, complain of a supposed dearth of interest among African-Americans and other minorities and of a lack of qualified applicants.

Denying both assertions, most HBCUs pride themselves on their historical legacies in international affairs. The first such institution, Lincoln University (Pennsylvania), founded in 1854, notes that training young men for service abroad was one of its original objectives. Similarly, Florida A&M University has embraced, as a part of its historical mission, an "international commitment" coincident with its founding in 1887. And Howard University, with one of the most diverse student populations among higher education institutions in the United States, admitted international students as early as 1870 (Logan, 1969). While these examples certainly do not represent the norm, they reflect a tradition of openness and diversity that is common among HBCUs. As Stent (1984) observed correctly, although HBCUs were founded primarily for Black Americans, their charters, in most instances, were not "exclusionary." This accounts for the presence of international students on the campuses of almost all HBCUs, which is a reflection of these institutions' interest in this area, and for the significant growth in their numbers in recent years.

In refuting the apparent "lack of interest" among HBCU students and faculty, Howard University alone can document a rich legacy of foreign affairs involvement. Former law faculty dean, Richard T. Greener, became in 1898 the first U.S. Consul and Trade Representative in Vladivostok (Logan & Winston, 1982). One of the University's most renowned figures in the medical field was Dr. Hildrus Poindexter who, in a career which began in 1927, made outstanding contributions to public health in Africa, Asia, the Caribbean, Central and South America, and Australia. In the 1940s, his name was virtually synonymous with malarial research and the study of other tropical diseases. Dr. Poindexter's pioneering work, chiefly in Liberia but also in other parts of Africa, marked the beginning of President Truman's Point Four Program on that continent. It also paved the way for extensive work abroad by members of the medical school faculty and hospital staff that continues today.

Other members of the Howard University faculty, beginning with former President Mordecai Wyatt Johnson, were associated with various research and political interests abroad, notably Dr. Rayford Logan, who published extensively on U.S.-Haitian relations and on agrarian conditions in Cuba, Haiti, and the Dominican Republic. President Johnson was a delegate in San Francisco at the birth of the United Nations. So also was Dr. Ralph Johnson Bunche, who became a member of the Howard faculty in political science in 1927. He subsequently went on leave to take positions in the U.S. State Department in 1941, and later, in 1946, joined the staff of the UN Secretariat, rising ultimately to the position of Under Secretary for Special Political Affairs. In 1948, Bunche was awarded the Nobel Peace Prize for his mediation of the agreement between Arab states and Israel (Urquhart, 1993).

Contributions of this type over the years symbolize Howard University's involvement and leadership in international affairs. It should be noted also that the University to date has graduated three heads of state—Keith Mitchell (Grenada), Melvin Evans (Virgin Islands), and Roy Schneider (Virgin Islands). At least seven Howard graduates have received U.S. ambassadorial appointments—Patricia Roberts Harris (Luxembourg); Samuel Z. Westerfield (Liberia); Andrew Young (United Nations); Melvin Evans (Trinidad and Tobago); Maurice Bean (Burma); Ronald D. Palmer (Malaysia, Togo, and

Mauritius); and William Clark (Eritrea).[2] In the Agency for International Development (AID), Howard University alumnus Irvin Coker attained that agency's highest foreign service rank, Career Minister, while contributing to economic development in three geographic areas. Howard University faculty and alumni have achieved distinction as well at both the staff and volunteer levels of the Peace Corps.

In varying degrees, and in many different ways, virtually all Historically Black Colleges and Universities have made contributions in the international arena. Lincoln University and Spelman College, for example, have produced several U.S. ambassadors, despite their relatively small size. In 1999 Tuskegee University celebrated 100 years of providing technical assistance to Togo (formerly Togoland). Howard University and Morehouse College have produced Rhodes Scholars also. Almost without exception, HBCUs have contributed to leadership cadres in foreign countries through their training of international students. Constrained mainly by the lack of resources, these educational institutions have adopted numerous techniques of instruction and innovation to compete with more well-endowed colleges and universities in international affairs and education.

Indeed, in the various instructional and non-instructional areas identified with international affairs (i.e., study abroad, student and faculty exchange programs, diplomatic and security studies, the teaching of foreign languages, and international visitors), there has been a steady upward trend within HBCUs over the years. In general, the response from government and private sector agencies has been positive, but slow. Despite progress, the United States still does not have a foreign service—nor American business a cadre of workers abroad—that is reflective of America's diverse society. As in other areas, HBCUs are providing the leadership not only in preparing students for service but also in reminding the society of the need for greater access and expanded employment opportunity.

As HBCUs have prepared leaders for international service, they have been challenged over the past 30 to 40 years by the emergence and growth of schools of foreign affairs. By long-standing tradition, foreign affairs practitioners have been drawn from the ranks of liberal arts graduates in such fields as political science, economics, history, English, and foreign languages. These "generalists" were then trained on the job in specialties as required, whereas the products of foreign affairs schools, mainly graduate level institutions, come with degrees as specialists in such areas as diplomatic practices, security, and international business. There have been very few African-American graduates of such institutions. With only one recent exception, HBCUs follow the traditional "generalist" model of a broadly based liberal arts education in preparing students for careers in international affairs.

Clark Atlanta University is that exception. In the fall of 1992, Clark Atlanta opened the School of International Affairs and Development—a graduate-level, degree-granting entity, the first of its kind at an HBCU. The mission statement reads, in part:

> The mission of the School of International Affairs and Development (SIAD) is to provide a professional education that adheres to the highest standard of scholarship and that, at the same time, is relevant to contemporary problems in international affairs. The primary objective of the SIAD is to produce graduates, particularly those of African descent, who will be prepared to exercise leadership in international affairs and development in the public and private sectors, including international public service, business, banking, journalism, teaching, and research. The School also recognizes the importance of class and gender in the study of international affairs and encourages incorporating analyses of both in all areas of study (International Politics, Diplomatic History, and International Economics). "The academic program takes into account the nature of the contemporary international system and the trans-territorial nature of such global challenges as environmental pollution, ethnic particularism, the transition to democracy, ensuring respect for human rights, increases in refugees and displaced persons, international terrorism, and the widening economic disparity between rich and poor nations." (Clark Atlanta University, 1998, pp. 233–234)

The new unit at Clark Atlanta, partially funded through its W. K. Kellogg Excellence Grant to the University, began with a 2-year professional master's degree program and the proposed development of a doctoral program. Due to limited enrollment and other factors, the school was transferred to departmental status by 2000. Nevertheless, by offering training in international affairs at the graduate level, the Clark Atlanta program broadens opportunities for African-Americans and other minorities seeking to prepare for careers in various fields abroad. It responds also to an unmet need, as the 17 other existing institutions that have U.S. foreign affairs schools specializing in this area traditionally enroll only a limited number of African-American students. Those seventeen other institutions, which professionally belong to the Association of Professional Schools of International Affairs (APSIA), include: American University, University of California (San Diego), Columbia University, University of Denver, Georgetown University, George Washington University, Harvard University, Johns Hopkins University, University of Maryland (College Park), University of Michigan, University of Pittsburgh, Princeton University, University of Southern California, Syracuse University, Tufts University, University of Washington, and Yale University.[3] It is from these institutions, notably Harvard, Georgetown, Yale, Princeton, and Tufts, that large numbers of foreign service officers and candidates for careers in international banking, business, law, and economics traditionally are selected. This applies with particular relevance to the U.S. Foreign Service, to which admission is based on rigorous written and oral examinations that receive special attention in these foreign affairs institutions.

The availability and magnitude of resources impact the production of candidates at the undergraduate level for the study of international affairs in Historically Black Colleges and Universities. Unable to provide academic majors in what is regarded normally as a "subset" area, the institutions instead offer students in traditional liberal arts fields the opportunity to "specialize" in international affairs by supplementing standard programs. Students may take specialized courses (e.g., "International Economics" or "International Business") or find a highly specialized offering, such as "Diplomatic History" at Howard. However, discrete academic majors in international affairs have yet to be developed at HBCUs.

Instead, programs and activities supplement course offerings and, in the long run, may assist in advancing them. As resources permit, these are enhanced with a view toward strengthening programs and, thereby, broadening opportunities. Traditional among HBCUs, such offerings as study abroad, international visitor programs, and economic development, have undergone significant expansion in recent years. This is particularly true in the area of economic development.

Until its demise officially in fiscal year 1996, the Gray Amendment to the Economic Assistance Act proved exceedingly beneficial to HBCUs in extending, far more widely than in the past, opportunities for participation under United States Agency for International Development (AID) contracts in economic development projects in Africa.[4] Essentially established as a "set aside program" with the requirement that at least 10 percent of federal economic assistance funds be allocated to minority contractors, this initiative paved the way for participation by colleges and universities that had not been involved heretofore in overseas activities and facilitated expanded opportunities for institutions with a longer history in managing such projects. Central State University and Morehouse Medical School are examples of the former, and Tuskegee, Prairie View, and Southern universities are three prime examples where HBCUs developed increased overseas activities in the second category.

With a view toward improving their ability to compete for AID-type contracts, some institutions (e.g., Alcorn State University, Jackson State University, and Tougaloo College) entered into consortia arrangements. And especially for the smaller HBCUs, "linkage" agreements with majority group institutions, typically the "prime" contractors, account for yet another dimension of increased activity in this area by African-American colleges and universities. The result has been greater exposure for students and increased professional experience for faculty members and administrators in this aspect of international affairs.

It is perhaps fair to say that growth in other areas, such as foreign student enrollment, study abroad, student and faculty exchange programs, the teaching of foreign languages, and international visitor programs, has more or less followed national trends in higher education, as American colleges and universities attempt to respond to growing internationalism within the society. While the majority of international students who attend HBCUs come from African and Caribbean countries, most HBCUs, given their traditional "open admission" policies, have hosted students from various countries around the world. Founded in 1867, Howard University, for example, admitted three Chinese students in 1870 and graduated a Canadian student in 1873 (Logan, 1969). Today, approximately 84 percent of its student body of more than 10,000 is African-American, with the majority of the remaining 16 percent coming from more than 115 foreign countries.

Similar patterns of diversity can be seen at other HBCUs. In 1993, Clark Atlanta University reported an enrollment of 19 percent international students in its student body of 4,400. Oakwood College's enrollment of 1,336 students included an international student population of 15 percent. Tuskegee had an 8 percent enrollment of these students among its 3,700 total. Overall, international student enrollment in the majority of HBCUs averages about 2 to 3 percent. Together with other factors, this diversity is regarded as contributing to a favorable foreign affairs environment.

In achieving this end and, in the process, providing leadership in international affairs, HBCUs employ various techniques and promote numerous international affairs activities. Typical of the previously mentioned consortium arrangement, especially in the area of economic development, is the Mississippi Consortium for International Development (MCID), involving Alcorn State University, Jackson State University, and Tougaloo College. Established in 1989, MCID is designed to collaborate in developing and implementing international development projects and exchange programs. The group has pursued these objectives in countries of Africa, Asia, Central and Eastern Europe, Latin America, the Newly Independent States (NIS) of the former Soviet Union, and the Middle East.

Both singly and in cooperation with other institutions (as subcontractors), Southern University has implemented a number of development projects over the past 8 to 10 years. The University established in 1993 a Center for International Development Programs for this purpose, drawing on a limited amount of overseas experience, a relatively large international faculty and student population, and extensive Washington contacts. Projects have been developed in fields as diverse as agriculture, law, public administration, and education; and both faculty and student exchanges have occurred between the Baton Rouge, Louisiana, institution and colleges and universities in such countries as Belize, Brazil, Nigeria, Pakistan, South Africa, Vietnam, and Zimbabwe.

Similarly, Florida A&M University (FAMU) collaborates with many different institutions in overseas projects, in addition to conducting some projects unilaterally. Some of the primary areas of involvement have been in African countries, the Caribbean, South America, Asia, and Russia. FAMU has implemented short-term training projects for professionals from Belize, Grenada, Haiti, and South Africa. For the most part, these have been technically oriented projects consistent with the Florida institution's A&M status. The units that have been involved primarily are the School of Agriculture and Home Economics, and the College of Engineering Sciences and Technology. Some of the cooperating institutions include the University of Florida, Florida Atlantic University, and the University of Central Florida.

Whereas HBCUs such as the foregoing present excellent examples of expansion primarily in economic development areas, institutions such as Lincoln University (Pennsylvania), Spelman College, and Howard University are more typical of institutions with a more academically oriented focus. Lincoln was among the first of the HBCUs to establish in 1991–1992 an international affairs program center. The Center for Public Policy and Diplomacy was designed to promote public service and international affairs among students and prospective students through training and research. Prefreshman summer institutes in international affairs are examples of the first programs sponsored by the Center in 1992 and 1993. With assistance from the Woodrow Wilson National Fellowship Foundation, a student exchange program was established between Lincoln University and the Fletcher School of Law and Diplomacy at Tufts University, an APSIA institution. The grant also enabled a Lincoln University professor to spend one semester annually conducting research in international affairs at the Fletcher School.

Lincoln's Center for Public Policy and Diplomacy developed rapidly as a conference center concentrating primarily on Africa and African issues. Government leaders such as former President Nnamdi Azikiwe of Nigeria, King Moshoeshoe II of Lesotho, and former Prime Minister Julius Nyerere of Tanzania are among numerous African leaders who have participated in seminars there. Such exposure is considered valuable for students who also are provided numerous opportunities for foreign travel and foreign language study.

Spelman College established its International Affairs Center (IAC) in 1989. Designed to "further enhance internationalization of the college," IAC works cooperatively with the already well-established study abroad program, which has been a prominent feature of the academic programs at Spelman for over 20 years. Established in the 1970s in honor of Charles Merrill, Spelman College's study abroad programs, as well as its international exchanges, are perhaps the most extensive among African-American institutions. Through cooperative arrangements with major study abroad organizations in the United States and overseas, Spelman has provided overseas study opportunities for its students in Australia, Austria, Belgium, Brazil, Chile, China, Ghana, Costa Rica, Czech Republic, Dominican Republic, Ecuador, England, France, Germany, Greece, Israel, Italy, Japan, Kenya, Mexico, Namibia, Scotland, Senegal, Singapore, South Africa, Spain, and Zimbabwe.

In addition, language and cultural training experiences are available to Spelman students through programs the college conducts jointly each summer with Morehouse College and the Atlanta University Center. The month-long Spanish program with Morehouse takes place in Oalaca, Mexico; and for a similar period, there is a French-oriented program with the AU Center in Martinique as well as another Spanish-based one with the Center in the Dominican Republic. The language departments of the cooperating institutions arrange and operate these overseas enrichment experiences for the Atlanta-based students.

As the flagship institution among HBCUs, Howard University has a long and unique history of involvement in international affairs. It is the only predominantly African-American university with Research I status. It has a multinational faculty and a student body representing more than 120 countries. Howard's strong curricular offerings at both undergraduate and graduate levels best exemplify the academic programs that lead to "specialization" in various areas of public policy and international affairs. Academic areas with the highest degrees of concentration are the arts and sciences, especially the fields of political science, economics, history, modern foreign languages and literatures (which offers instruction in Spanish, French, German, Russian, Japanese, Swahili, Zulu, and Arabic), and communications. Professional and graduate schools, which offer curricula in the areas of medicine, engineering, architecture, computer sciences, divinity, social work, and allied health, as well as continuing education, are committed also to teaching, research, and exchanges in these areas.

In addition to course offerings, Howard University has a variety of internationally oriented projects and programs across its 12 colleges and schools. Many of these were catalogued in a study commissioned by the administration in 1986 to determine and assess "Howard University's international activities."[5] This was followed in 1990 by the appointment of a faculty committee and the establishment, in 1993, of an international affairs program in the Office of the Vice President for Academic Affairs. Funded in large part with one of the 10 W. K. Kellogg Foundation "Centers of Excellence" grants, the program spawned in 1995 an international affairs center which, in the following year, was named formally in honor of Dr. Ralph J. Bunche. Today, this Center serves as a focal point for the University community's numerous international activities, complementing academic offerings with a variety of lectures, symposia, workshops, exchanges, internships, and other public policy and international affairs programs.

The Center also houses the Diplomat-in-Residence Program, an arrangement whereby the Department of State assigns one of its senior officers for a year-long stay at the University. The only such full-time appointment at an HBCU, the officer is available for lectures in foreign policy, diplomacy, and the officer's own academic area of specialization, as well as for consultation with students regarding careers in international affairs. Howard has had senior diplomats in residence for 15 years. The University also has an Office of International Student Services and an Office of Domestic and International Exchanges.

Reflective of the type of overseas assistance in which the institution engages is the "Diplomats Training Program" conducted over 4 months in 1992–1993. In cooperation with Georgetown University's School of Diplomacy, Creative Associates, and the University of the Western Cape, Howard University assisted in the training of 30 Africans, Indians, and "Coloureds" for South Africa's diplomatic service. Their "graduation" was timed to coincide with South Africa's independence and the need at that time to integrate that country's diplomatic representation abroad.

Like other HBCUs, Howard receives funding for its assistance programs from both government and private sources. Whereas the diplomatic training program was funded by USAID, the Minority International Research Training Project is financed by the National Institutes of Health/Fogarty International Center. Additionally, the Pew Charitable Trusts has provided some resources for an ongoing project of continuing contacts with institutions of higher learning in South Africa.

Many HBCUs continue to adjust, as resources permit, to requirements of an increasingly diverse and internationally interdependent world. Notwithstanding their increased involvement in international affairs, the underrepresentation of minorities in this important area remains an issue of concern. Unfortunately, the pace of change has not been as rapid as it should be and fails to presage the "sea change" that President Clinton envisioned in his call for a foreign affairs presence which "looks more like America." To accomplish this goal, change in the political environment, including opening wider the doors of opportunity and equity, will be necessary. Historically Black Colleges and Universities, therefore, will continue to provide the training of African-Americans and other minorities who will assume even more and greater leadership roles in foreign affairs in the next millennium, in the same way that these institutions have succeeded in this area over the past century.

Past, Current, and Future Roles of the Social Sciences in Historically Black Colleges and Universities

The three academic fields in which African-Americans receive their highest proportions of undergraduate degrees are business (24.2 percent) and the social sciences, including history and psychology (18.8 percent) and education (7.6 percent). These trends have not changed significantly over the last 20 years (Garibaldi, 1991), and the ratio of baccalaureates awarded in these disciplines are almost equal for African-Americans at all colleges and universities and at Historically Black Colleges and Universities. Even though fewer African-American students receive undergraduate degrees in education, a field in which most HBCUs have had undergraduate programs because of their original founding as normal schools, HBCUs still continued to prepare a large share of the nation's African-American teachers in the last decade of this century. As an example, almost one fifth of the undergraduate education degrees awarded in 1994 were from HBCUs—that is, 2,420 of 10,207 (Frederick D. Patterson Research Institute, 1997). Similarly, HBCUs accounted for 17 percent, or almost 4,000, of all undergraduate degrees awarded to African-Americans in the social sciences and history in 1994. In 1985, 6,100 undergraduate degrees in the social sciences were awarded to African-Americans in all colleges and universities. But in 1995, this number had risen to 10,586—an increase of 73 percent between 1985 and 1995 (Wilds & Wilson, 1998). At the master's level, the corresponding figures were 422 and 874 between 1985 and 1995—an increase of 107 percent. These significant increases demonstrate a renewed interest by African-Americans in social science disciplines, and HBCUs are contributing significantly to this upswing as they have consciously strengthened and expanded their undergraduate and graduate programs in these fields.

As has been pointed out earlier in this chapter, HBCUs have maintained their fundamental missions, many after more than 100 years of existence. In particular, these institutions have espoused, almost uniformly, the goal of educating and preparing African-American students who come from all socioeconomic backgrounds and who have varied levels of academic abilities and secondary preparation. However, as Thompson (1986) confirmed in his 1982–1985 study of Black graduates of United Negro College Fund institutions, 74 percent of those who had obtained doctoral degrees had received them from prestigious universities. While HBCUs have always had a strong emphasis in the liberal arts, a major in the social sciences was always viewed as a means to furthering a student's education and as ideal training for his or her eventual leadership in the community. In particular, sociology, political science, and psychology were the disciplines of preference for those who would pursue future graduate and professional education. Thus, faculty at HBCUs developed programs that incorporated the social sciences into their liberal arts core curricula.

The teaching of sociology in the privately supported HBCUs dates back to the turn of the last century (1897) at Atlanta University where W. E. B. DuBois began studies of African Americans and their families in the city. In the early years of sociological education, great emphasis was placed on developing solutions for numerous social problems and race relations issues in the United States. In 1910 Fisk University established a department of social science, which later added a research program that focused on race relations and the history and conditions of African-Americans. The program at Fisk was organized by George Edmund Haynes, who received his PhD in sociology from Columbia University. The goal of this program was the education of future generations of African-American students for research and teaching careers. Graduate education at the master's level was established in 1927, but it was discontinued in 1945. The expectation was that graduates would continue their education in the prestigious departments of sociology located at Michigan, Chicago, Columbia, Ohio State, the University of Washington, and Harvard.

The social sciences, and especially sociological research, at HBCUs were conceived as important because studies in those areas could help to solve the race problem in American society (Hudgins, 1994). Thus, many faculty at HBCUs began to devote more attention to societal issues rather than concentrating on the disciplines in which they were trained. A notable example of this was Kelly Miller, who left his professorship in mathematics at Howard University in 1918 and shifted his attention to sociology. Miller organized Howard's Department of Sociology and chaired the department until he turned it over to Professor E. Franklin Frazier (Logan, 1969).

Walter R. Chivers was responsible for the pioneering work in sociology at Morehouse College. With a social work degree from the New York School of Social Work (which later became the Columbia University School of Social Work), Chivers organized the Annual Institute of Successful Marriage and Family Life and a Visiting Lectureship Program in Sociology. The Institute began in 1946 and was aimed at strengthening the African-American family. The Institute has continued to thrive and still exists today. The Visiting Professorship program was designed to expose successful graduates who had completed their social science doctoral degrees as well as other distinguished sociologists to the young Morehouse sociology major. The lectureship was intended to be both intellectually stimulating and inspirational. However, during the 1960s, the program was modified to include politically oriented topics, which diluted Chivers's original purposes. Many of Chivers's students continued their graduate education and obtained doctoral and master's degrees in sociology, social science, and social work.

Social science and sociological education were also developed and expanded at Tuskegee University by Charles G. Gomillion, who came to the campus in 1928. During his 40-year career at Tuskegee, he chaired the Social Science Division and served as professor of sociology. Along with Monroe Work, a historian-sociologist, they began a repository of research data and records of the general activities of Black persons all over the world, but especially in the United States. Through these efforts the Tuskegee Bureau of Records and Research was founded and still maintains its present distinction as an important source of information and materials on the lives of African-Americans. Additionally, Professor Gomillion organized the Tuskegee Civic Association in 1947. The association was a political organization of rural African-Americans that later emerged as an effective organization that assisted in the election of its members to "every elective political office in the city and county" (Jones, 1974). As a result of the election of more African-Americans to political offices, Gomillion and his colleagues at Tuskegee provided many more field opportunities for their sociology students, several of whom continued their graduate education in sociology.

The above mentioned pioneering programs in sociology and the social sciences are illustrative of the kinds of programs that several HBCUs established to prepare future generations of African-Americans for training in fields that had heretofore been offered only in northern majority institutions. With the addition of some of those programs at HBCUs, a larger cohort of African-Americans were trained in these disciplines and many pursued terminal degrees in the social sciences at other predominantly white institutions. However, many of the graduates returned to HBCU campuses—in part because of discriminatory faculty hiring practices even at the institutions where they were trained—and they continued teaching and conducting research in sociology and other related social science disciplines.

Mid-Twentieth-Century Developments in the Social Sciences at HBCUs

As is obvious from the previous discussion, HBCUs, in their early years, laid the foundation for the education of social science scholars whose applied and policy-related research on the African-American experience would influence major changes in American society. After most of these individuals obtained their undergraduate education at HBCUs, these scholars received their graduate education, primarily, in majority institutions in the Northeast, Midwest, and the Far West. Most of them focused their attention on addressing and, in many instances, countering the emerging paradigms and research that were used to characterize the "African-American experience" as deviant, marginal and dysfunctional, especially when compared with the majority population. They also worked vigorously to bring about societal and political changes to improve the conditions and participation of African-Americans in the United States.

Professor E. Franklin Frazier, whose academic career began at Atlanta University and ended at Howard University with many other visiting appointments at major institutions in between, is credited with establishing the framework for the contemporary study of the family. His seminal study on *The Negro Family in the United States,* published in 1939, provided an empirical historical perspective on the African-American family from slavery to the middle of the twentieth century. Dr. Frazier's work was preceded by the pioneering research of Dr. W. E. B. DuBois who had conducted a study on

The Negro American Family that was published in 1909. Like Frazier, who was educated at Howard University, DuBois received his undergraduate training at Fisk University. Both of these scholars spent their entire careers addressing issues affecting Black people in the United State and throughout the world through their research and scholarly pursuits.

Over the next 50 years and even today, African American and other scholars, public policy makers, and others have been preoccupied with issues brought to the forefront by Professor Frazier. These issues included: the legacy of slavery and its impact on family life and organization among African-Americans; the role of women in family life; households headed by women; the role of the Black male in the family; and the Black middle class. Professor Frazier's work has remained a model for research on the family today, despite the criticism of his research perspective—especially following then Assistant Secretary (now Senator) Daniel P. Moynihan's 1965 report on the emerging single parent African American household headed by women, *The Negro Family: The Case for National Action.*

Professor Andrew Billingsley pioneered the development of the first major revisionist perspective of the Black family in his study, *Black Families in White America* (1968). Billingsley's study paved the way for the subsequent emergence of a large body of social science literature on African-American families. These studies emphasized, specifically, the strengths of African-American families, rather than their so-called "weaknesses" (Hill, 1977; Allen, English, & Hall, 1986). Additionally, other scholars focused on the "historical connections" of the African past that African-American families shared rather than their supposed discontinuities (Allen, English, & Hall, 1986).

Joyce Ladner, another leader in this research genre and a graduate of Tougaloo College, questioned the traditional paradigms for studying the Black American experience, as well. She proposed, for example, the development of a new framework that would transcend mainstream majority concepts and the view of Black-Americans as a minority group that could only survive and succeed by immersing themselves into the nation's "melting pot," as other European ethnic groups did after coming to this country. Ladner developed this work and *Tomorrow's Tomorrow: The Black Woman* (1971) while on the faculty at Howard University.

Professor Lawrence E. Gary, a graduate of Tuskegee University and a faculty member in Howard's School of Social Work, is considered the pioneer in the social science inquiry on African-American males. His book, *Black Men* (1981), was the first empirical research study focusing on the conditions of African-American males. Professor Edgar G. Epps, who received his undergraduate education in sociology at Talladega College, concentrated his research on issues of racial identity and racial socialization in his book, *Black Consciousness, Identity and Achievement* (Gurin & Epps, 1975). In that coauthored study with Professor Patricia Gurin, Epps examined Black consciousness among African-American college students at Historically Black and predominately white colleges and universities and found minimal differences between the two groups. The extensive literature developed by the aforementioned scholars and many others changed significantly the direction, foci and emphases of future conceptual and empirical studies, particularly in the area of studies on families and about African-American life in the United States. Those pioneering social science scholars, the majority of whom spent their entire careers in Historically Black Colleges and Universities, left legacies to build on and influenced an impressive array of contemporary African-American social scientists.

Increased Diversity in Social Science Programs

In recent years education in the social sciences at HBCUs has been augmented and further diversified by new academic programs, including social work, women's studies, and the African Diaspora. The continuation of these programs at the undergraduate and graduate levels is essential to the training of future leaders and scholars for addressing and providing remedies for the attainment of social justice, leadership, community development, and expanded opportunities for African-American students (Icard, Spearman, Curry-Jackson, 1996).

Social work education's roots are deeply embedded in the social sciences. Most programs, undergraduate and graduate, originated in social science departments, usually sociology. Social work curricula are highly infused by social science content. While social work education has a long history in HBCUs, only a few programs were in Black schools at the turn of the century, notably Atlanta University. The second graduate program in an HBCU began at Howard University in 1935 and was accredited in 1940. In 1998 there were 358 Council on Social Work Education accredited baccalaureate social work degree programs, of which 25 were in HBCUs (Council on Social Work Education, 1998). These programs are producing graduates for entry-level professional careers in social work practice and for graduate-level education at a time when cities and communities need more social service personnel.

Founded in 1993, the African American Women's Institute in the Department of Sociology and Anthropology at Howard University sponsored in 1999 the 2nd National and International Conference on Black Women in the Academy. This successful conference focused on interdisciplinary topics in an attempt to link the social sciences with the physical and life sciences, technology, and humanities. This effort, focused heavily on cross-cultural studies of women of color, was accomplished through collaborations with faculty at Spelman College, the Massachusetts Institute of Technology, and other institutions, and with funding from Howard University, the Ford Foundation, and the National Science Foundation. Spelman College has also introduced a new course on the African Diaspora. This course is a world civilization course that highlights the perspective of people of African descent. Various other collaborations are occurring with majority institutions and HBCUs. For example, at Morgan State University, a collaborative study is underway with Michigan State University on the study of Black women, and Clark Atlanta University and Georgia Tech are engaged in a joint venture focusing on the physical and natural sciences.

These developments at HBCUs are occurring during a period of societal change and shifting values on affirmative action. Nevertheless, Historically Black Colleges and Universities are developing creative ways to respond to affirmative action, gender studies, and other related topics. It is important to recognize that the institutions are shifting their foci and are responding to new demands and challenges, rather than changing their missions. As HBCUs continue to educate large numbers of students in the social sciences, they will be able to maintain their historic mission of preparing each student for a life focused on a commitment to service and leadership in improving the educational, economic, and social conditions of their communities and the nation. Those disciplines, perhaps more than any others, have the greatest potential for not only increasing equity in education but also in improving the entire society.

Conclusion

As the authors of this chapter reflect on whether affirmative action and desegregation have had a significant impact on increasing the educational access and attainment of African-Americans in higher education, it is their judgment that progress has been made. However, they concur strongly that majority institutions that enroll the largest numbers of nonwhite students must do more. While HBCUs have graduated large numbers of African-American students and a representative proportion of white students over the last 30 years, majority institutions have widened opportunities and access in a number of specialized fields. But more increases in enrollment and degree attainment are necessary if this "equity gap" is to be closed. Additionally, more articulation agreements between 4-year colleges and community colleges are imperative, especially given the fact that more than 45 percent of every minority group is enrolled in a 2-year college.

Among the top 18 institutions from which African-American doctoral recipients obtained their undergraduate degrees between 1992 and 1996, eleven were HBCUs and two were predominantly Black institutions (Henderson, Clarke, & Woods, 1998). This is a clear sign that students at HBCUs are more likely to continue their education in graduate or professional schools than African-Americans who attend non-HBCUs (Nettles, Perna, & Edelin, 1999). This chapter has briefly treated the historical development of international affairs and social science programs at HBCUs. These institutions will continue to contribute to the undergraduate and graduate preparation of future African-American scholars and foreign service officers, but they will not be able to do it alone. Over its own short 40 years of awarding the doctorate, Howard has awarded more than 1600 terminal degrees since 1958. But as pointed out by its President, H. Patrick Swygert, at a National Symposium on Affirmative Action held at the University in 1998: "Howard University and its sister institutions that offer advanced degrees do not have the capacity to absorb those hundreds of thousands of students who need to pursue and, indeed, through their talent and hard work, should be encouraged to pursue graduate and professional education wherever they choose."

The missions of HBCUs will not change significantly in the next century, even if affirmative action remains in its present form. These institutions will not only play a major role in producing future African-American leaders in the fields of international affairs and the social sciences; they will also take the lead in closing the gap in numerous fields of study where African-Americans continue to be underrepresented. If the majority of the nation's colleges and universities are seriously interested in advancing equity in their institutions, they would benefit tremendously from a review of some of the HBCUs' histories. They would also be able to make a significant contribution by forming collaborations with HBCUs, where many innovative academic programs have been developed and where faculty, administrators, staff, and students of all races, creeds, and nationalities have worked harmoniously together to advance educational equity for more than a century.

Notes

1. Dawson (1993) identifies William Alexander Leidesdorf, not Ebenezer Don Carlos Bassett, as previously believed, as the first diplomat of color in the U.S. Foreign Service.

2. The number of ambassadors produced would increase to 12 if 5 individuals involved in the special Foreign Affairs Scholars Program were included. On a Ford Foundation grant, 40 outstanding African-American and other minority youth in their junior and senior years were enrolled at Howard between 1963 and 1967 in a special program designed to assist them in qualifying for Foreign Service careers. Those who have since become ambassadors include: Aurelia Brazeal (Kenya); Ruth Davis (Benin); George Moose (Benin,

Senegal, and U.S. Mission to the European Office of the UN, Geneva); Robert Perry (Central African Republic); and Sharon Wilkinson (Burkina Faso).

3. In addition to member institutions in the U.S., there are 5 associate members abroad (Canada, France, Russia, and Japan), and 13 affiliated member institutions, including Howard University.

4. Section 567 (a) of the FY 1991 Appropriation Act, entitled "Disadvantaged Enterprises" (more commonly known as the "Gray Amendment").

5. This survey was conducted by Ambassador O. Rudolph Aggrey at the request of Dr. Michael Winston, then Vice President for Academic Affairs; the results were reported in a 1987 document titled "Howard University and International Affairs: A Study."

References

Adams v. Califano, 430 F. Supp. 118 (D.C. 1977).

Adams v. Richardson, 480, F.2d 1159 (D.C. Cir. 1973).

Adams v. Weinberger, 391 F. Supp. 269 (D.C. Cir. 1975).

Aggrey, Rudolph O. (1987). Howard University and international affairs: A study. Howard University.

Allen, Walter R., English, Richard A., & Hall, Jo Ann. (1986). *Black American families, 1965–1984.* New York: Greenwood Press.

Billingsley, Andrew. (1968). *Black families in white America.* Englewood Cliffs, NJ: Prentice-Hall.

Blackwell, James E. (1981). *Mainstreaming outsiders: The production of Black professionals.* Bayside, NY: General Hall Publishers.

Blackwell, James E., & Janowitz, Morris. 1974. *Black sociologists: Historical and contemporary perspectives.* IL: The University of Chicago Press.

Carter, Deborah J., & Wilson, Reginald. (1997). Minorities in higher education 1996–97: Fifteenth annual status report. Washington, DC: American Council on Education.

Clark Atlanta University Graduate Catalogue: Celebrating a Heritage, 1995–98. (1998). Atlanta: Clark Atlanta University.

Council on Social Work Education. (1998). *Statistics on social work education in the United States: 1998.*

Dawson, Horace G., Jr. (1993). First African American diplomat. *Foreign Service Journal, 70*(1), 42–45.

DuBois, William E. B. (Ed.) (1909). *The Negro American family.* Atlanta University Publication Series.

Frazier, E. Franklin. (1939). *The Negro family in the United States.* Chicago: The University of Chicago Press.

Frederick D. Patterson Research Institute of the College Fund/UNCF. (1997). *The African American education data book, Volume I: Higher and adult education.* Fairfax,VA: Author.

Garibaldi, Antoine (Ed.). 1984. *Black colleges and universities: Challenges for the future.* New York: Praeger.

Garibaldi, Antoine M. (1997). Four decades of progress . . . and decline: An assessment of African American educational attainment. *Journal of Negro Education, 66*(2), 105–120.

Garibaldi, Antoine M. (1991). The role of Historically Black Colleges and Universities in facilitating resilience among African American students. *Journal of Negro Education, 24*(1), 103–112.

Gary, Lawrence E. (Ed.). (1981). *Black men.* Beverly Hills, CA: Sage Publications.

Gurin, Patricia, & Epps, Edgar. (1975). *Black consciousness, identity and achievement.* New York: John Wiley & Sons,

Henderson, Peter H., Clarke, Julie E., & Woods, Cynthia. (1998). Summary report 1996: Doctorate recipients from United States universities. Washington, DC: National Academy Press.

Hill, Robert B. (1977). *Informal adoption among Black families.* Washington, DC: National Urban League Research Department.

Hudgins, John L. (1994). The segmentation of Southern sociology? Social research at Historically Black Colleges and Universities. *Social Forces, 72*(3), 885–893.

Icard, L. D., Spearman, Margaret, & Curry-Jackson, Anita. (1996). B.S.W. programs in Black colleges: Building on the strengths of tradition. *Journal of Social Work Education, 32*, 227–235.

Jones, Butler A. (1974). The tradition of sociology teaching in black colleges: The unheralded professionals. In James Blackwell & Morris Janowitz (Eds.), *Black sociologists: historical and contemporary perspectives* (pp. 121–163). Chicago: The University of Chicago Press.

Ladner, Joyce A. (1971). *Tomorrow's tomorrow: The Black woman.* New York: Doubleday and Company.

Ladner, Joyce A. (Ed.). (1973). *The death of white sociology.* New York: Vintage Books.

Logan, Rayford W. (1969). *Howard University: The first hundred years, 1867–1967,* New York: New York University Press.

Logan, Rayford, W., & Winston, Michael (Eds.). (1982). *Dictionary of American Negro biography.* New York: Norton.

Moynihan, Daniel P. (1965). *The Negro family: The case for national action.* Washington, DC: U.S. Department of Labor, Office of Planning and Research.

Nettles, Michael T., Perna, Laura W., & Edelin, Kimberley C. (1999). *African Americans moving up in higher education: Southern states are leading the way*. Fairfax, VA: Frederick D. Patterson Research Institute of the United Negro College Fund.

Regents of the University of California v. Bakke, 438 U.S. 265 (1978).

Stent, Madelon Delany. (1984). Black college involvement in international and cross-cultural affairs. In Antoine M. Garibaldi (Ed.), *Black colleges and universities: Challenges for the future* (pp. 93–115). New York: Praeger.

Thompson, Daniel C. (1986). *A Black elite: A profile of graduates of UNCF colleges*. New York: Greenwood Press.

Urquhart, Brian. (1993). *Ralph Bunche: An American odyssey*. New York: W. W. Norton & Company

Wilds, Deborah J., & Wilson, Reginald. (1998). *Minorities in higher education 1997–98: Sixteenth annual status report*. Washington, DC: American Council on Education.

Executive Initiatives and International Perspectives

CHAPTER 9

Equity in the Contemporary University

GRAHAM B. SPANIER AND MARY BETH CROWE

At the Pennsylvania State University, as at every college and university, issues of equity arise out of educational, economic, and ethical concerns that confront higher education in our nation. Our institutions embrace diversity as an integral component of the learning environment in which all students are prepared for life in a pluralistic society. Access for all segments of the population is essential to the success with which higher education addresses growing workforce needs for the high-level skills required by the information age. We have a special obligation to champion the ideal of equal opportunity to which our nation aspires and to maximize the economic and social impact of higher education throughout society. In short, our role in promoting human, economic, and cultural development compels universities to open our doors wide to qualified individuals. Yet barriers of many kinds can and do limit the broad-based participation we seek.

The inclusivity of our institutions is clearly a measure by which equity in the research university ultimately must be judged. The extent to which a cross-section of the population comprises our academic communities not only is a reflection of the equality of opportunity within our institutions but is also the best predictor of the widespread distribution of the benefits research universities bring to society. However, creating inclusive universities is in itself a challenge that raises numerous and often difficult questions of fairness and appropriateness.

At the heart of these questions is the apparent contradiction of the goal of nondiscrimination and the means to achieve it. We are required by law to ensure that individuals are not denied access to our institutions because of race, religion, ethnic background, sex, age, natural origin, veteran status, or disability; many institutions have added sexual orientation to this list as well. Equal opportunity ideally is neutral with regard to such characteristics. Yet efforts to increase the participation of individuals historically excluded from higher education and, more broadly to establish a supportive environment for

209

all within the academic community, are conscious of such differences. The current debate about affirmative action in higher education is a highly salient example of the dilemmas that result in attempting to adjust programs and procedures without introducing additional bias.

There are many points within the contemporary research university where such questions of equity occur. The continuing advancement of under-represented minorities is a fundamental priority. However, a commitment to educational equity must be sensitive also to the many factors that affect the involvement of qualified individuals from any group. These include barriers to access that systematically deter some from joining our learning communities. They also concern the comparability of the experiences of different groups within a diverse student body, faculty, and staff.

Pursuing educational equity within this framework of perspectives and issues is helpful in three ways. First, in taking a comprehensive approach, it promotes broad institutional ownership of the values and actions necessary to create an inclusive university. Second, it is sensitive to the best interests of all members of the university community, providing a uniform standard of responsiveness against which the fairness of specific initiatives may be judged. And third, it assures that the underlying reason for educational equity—equal academic success—is addressed.

The contemporary research university, by virtue of its comprehensive mission and academic competitiveness, confronts the full range of equity issues challenging higher education today. In this chapter, we look at the advancement of educational equity within such institutions, considering first the landscape of concerns that delineate opportunity within our universities and their related policy and program implications. We then draw on Penn State's comprehensive framework for fostering diversity to illustrate how these issues can come together in the effort to create inclusive institutions.

Dimensions of Educational Equity

Educational equity is a multidimensional quality that is articulated in a variety of institutional contexts. The equity issues universities confront reflect the diverse challenges and concerns of underserved and nontraditional groups as well as those of persons whose identities, interests, and abilities differ from the mainstream. Underlying the many specific concerns of these different groups are a number of fundamental equity considerations that circumscribe the policy issues and programmatic and procedural needs that must be addressed to successfully and fairly open our universities to diverse audiences. These issues fall into two broad categories: equity in access and equity in experience. In this section we highlight the barriers that inhibit membership in the academic community and limit full participation in university life, look at the equity questions involved in removing these barriers, and point to the bases for setting related policy and program directions.

Equity in Access

The Kellogg Commission on the Future of State and Land-Grant Universities, convened to identify how public universities must change in response to societal changes, identified educational access as one of the key domestic policy issues in the years ahead. In looking at access, the commission cited both the existing inequities in higher education participation in our nation and the added challenges of the need to serve growing numbers of increasingly diverse students, including adult and part-time learners and those from expanding minority populations (Kellogg Commission, 1998). The commission's observation underscores both the importance to the future of our nation of increasing access for those groups historically underrepresented in higher education and the range of groups for whom equal access is an issue.

Minority participation continues to be a special concern given the history of racial and ethnic discrimination in our nation and the critical social and economic implications of educationally enfranchising those who still tend to be excluded from our midst (Sable, 1998; Sable & Stennett, 1998). The trajectory for women's participation in higher education has been steeper, yet access issues remain in certain disciplines within science and engineering (National Center for Education Statistics (NCES), 1997), in progress through faculty ranks (NCES, 1999), and in leadership positions (Characteristics, 1999). Gender equity in sports is also a continuing concern (NCAA, 1999a). Low-income and first-generation college students may find more selective institutions, in particular, beyond their reach (Choy, 1998). Our institutions must be opened up to persons with disabilities, not just visible physical handicaps, but also hidden learning disabilities and health problems (Scott, 1997). Many adult and part-time students find traditional academic schedules incompatible with work and family responsibilities. Although not all of these groups are protected from discrimination under the law, all face obstacles that have tended to exclude them categorically from our academic communities. An equitable commitment to access will be responsive to all such concerns.

Within this broad commitment to open up the university to diverse audiences, three areas serve to highlight the scope and complexity of equity issues pertaining to access. The first concerns the selection decisions made in admissions and hiring. Second is the comparability of available opportunities for different groups. A third area relates to physical and organizational barriers that can discourage membership in the academic community.

Selectivity and Access

Admissions and hiring decisions made by selective universities impact significantly on the representation of minorities, economically disadvantaged individuals, and women within the student body and faculty and staff. The challenge for these institutions is to expand the pool of eligible individuals from these underrepresented groups. Three courses of action exist: altering the criteria of eligibility that are used, pursuing aggressive recruiting programs to identify available talent, and addressing pipeline concerns to increase the number of appropriately prepared individuals.

Much has been written documenting the difficulties of advancing the participation of underrepresented minority groups within selective universities while making case-by-case judgments of merit that are race blind. These analyses (see, e.g., Bowen & Bok, 1998, and the volume edited by Orfield & Miller, 1998) point to inequities in precollege education, possible bias in standardized tests, and inadequacy of alternative criteria (such as socioeconomic status) as some of the factors that inhibit racial diversity among students. Only one third of campus administrators surveyed at research universities considered their institutions high in the ability to attract African-American students; about one-fifth said so in regard to Hispanic students (El-Khawas, 1995). The meager progress in the growth of minority faculty, to just 13 percent nationwide in 1995 (NCES, 1999), suggests a parallel challenge in drawing diverse talent to the professorial ranks.

Affirmative action that uses race or ethnicity as a factor in making admissions decisions has been a successful approach to increasing minority enrollments. However, legal and political developments in several states have challenged the use of such practices, leading many universities to seek new ways to identify diverse pools of eligible students. Nearly 30 percent of the presidents responding to the 1998 state issues survey of the American Association of State Colleges and Universities (AASCU) indicated that public institutions in their states were currently reviewing or revising admissions policies (AASCU, 1999). A variety of alternative approaches has been suggested, including adjusting the relative weights of standardized test scores and high school grades, adding new academic criteria (such as the number and level of high school courses), considering a wide range of personal factors as predictors of educational success, basing admissions decisions on class rank, and expanding recruiting activities in targeted communities (see, e.g., Karabel, 1998; Wilbur & Bonous-Hammarth, 1998; Healy, 1999).

Although these efforts promise in the long run to achieve a more valid admissions process for all students, many of these approaches are themselves problematic. For example, although race-blind, admissions plans that select a specified percentage of the top graduates of each high school in a state can disadvantage students with more rigorous course work. Some alternative selection practices, such as the review of expanded student profiles by more than one reviewer, bear substantial financial costs. With always-strained budgets, universities must judge how much of a financial commitment to these and other equity initiatives is appropriate compared to investments in other institutional priorities.

An appropriate commitment of resources is also an issue in forms of affirmative action that reach out to underrepresented groups, either through aggressive recruiting efforts or initiatives to expand the pipeline of appropriately prepared candidates. Community recruiting centers and partnerships with high schools can be highly effective in identifying potential minority and low income students, but building and maintaining a local presence and community relationships takes time. Working to strengthen the quality of precollege education in communities with less rigorous schools or to increase minority or women's interest and preparation in fields that tend not to include them requires an even longer term investment.

In deciding where they stand on the continuum of activities that represent affirmative action in admissions and hiring, universities must weigh both potential legal risks and financial costs.

Comparable Opportunities

Questions of equity in access arise when the same opportunities simply are not available to all groups. The area of financial aid, a critical consideration in opening doors to a college education, offers one example. Race-exclusive financial aid programs, struck down in 1994 by the Fourth Circuit Court of Appeals *(Podberesky v. Kirwin)*, underscore the inherent tension between the goal of equal access and the means to obtain it.

Another interesting example is gender equity in sports where men and women are not necessarily seeking access to the same programs, but to comparable opportunities. In 1971, prior to the Title IX legislation that prohibits discrimination in education based on gender, women comprised just 2 percent of college athletes. As a result of Title IX initiatives that have increased the number of sports and sports scholarships available to women, their participation in Division I sports of the National Collegiate Athletic Association (NCAA) in 1997–1998 was 40 percent (NCAA, 1999b). Women clearly have much greater access to intercollegiate sports today, although there remains a need for continuing progress toward the goal of gender equity endorsed by the NCAA. Progress also remains to be made in increasing women's leadership in intercollegiate athletics through their representation in coaching and administrative positions.

Ideally women's gains come as a result of new opportunities added. But in some cases, gender equity in sports has been pursued by cutting back programs for men, leading to charges in some quarters of discrimination against men. This is a scenario that promises to loom even larger for the future as the bar for proportionality is raised by increasing enrollments of women in higher education, in some cases to more than half of an institution's students.

The challenge of attaining gender equity in sports highlights a fundamental policy question concerning the role of expanding capacity in increasing access to university opportunities.

Structural Barriers

A third source of access inequities stems from physical or organizational barriers that make if difficult if not impossible for persons with special needs to participate in the academic community. Our society has been greatly opened up to persons with disabilities through the Americans with Disabilities Act (ADA). Under this legal mandate, campuses have been visibly transformed to accommodate physical handicaps. Less visible and far more ambiguous is how we adjust jobs, teaching practices, and testing procedures to make them accessible to persons with disabilities. Particularly difficult equity questions occur concerning what constitutes a reasonable accommodation to provide access for persons whose special needs may impact negatively on others, for example, individuals with mental health problems. Not only are there many judgments to be made in these areas, such accommodations are prone to misperceptions of unfairness, as they are not widely understood. While from a policy viewpoint universities have no choice but to address barriers to participation covered by ADA, such efforts can be enhanced by increasing familiarity with various disability services.

Other barriers to access include such elements as flexibility in scheduling and convenience of program sites to students. These are factors particularly important to working adults who comprise an increasing segment of the market for learning. Happily, responsiveness to such needs is supportive of all students.

Achieving equity in access is a complex task that requires vigilance in balancing many different objectives, perspectives, and approaches to create institutions that fulfill the multiple missions of higher education. As daunting as the challenges of access are, they are only a first step in achieving educational equity. Many factors differentially shape the nature of the experience afforded by an institution to persons of different identities and, in influencing retention, impact on long-term prospects for increasing diversity.

Equity in Experience

Institutional environments can be markedly different for different groups. A "chilly" climate for women in higher education refers to dozens of ways women students are treated differently from their male peers in the classroom (Sandler, Silverberg, & Hall, 1996). Structural (defined as the number of racial/ethnic group members present), psychological, and behavioral dimensions of campus climate can adversely affect minority students (Hurtado, Milem, Clayton-Pederson, & Allen, 1998). Incidents of intolerance based on race or ethnicity, gender, sexual orientation, and religion curtail citizenship in campus life for those whose hurt and fear displace freedom to live and learn.

There are numerous ways a campus environment can disadvantage certain members of an academic community, creating inequities in academic experiences and more broadly, in the full enjoyment of university life. Four areas speak to the range of these concerns: the availability of appropriate support services, the inclusion of diverse perspectives in curricula and scholarship, campus climate, and policies and practices that relate to institutional life.

Support Services

Once accepted into an academic community, students and faculty have a right to be supported in their endeavors. For institutions to do otherwise would be to defeat their reason for existence. Our support systems and services must diversify with the broader range of needs inclusivity brings. There is ample precedent for making special efforts in this domain. Student athletes, for example, customarily receive tutoring and other academic support to help make up for the time commitment they make to their sport. Honors students often have access to some restricted academic resources and may be granted such privileges as priority in registration in order that they might most fully develop their special potential.

The substantial disparity in graduation rates for minority students compared to whites—19 percentage points less for African-Americans and 15 percentage points less for Hispanics nationally in 1995 (Carter & Wilson, 1997)—underscores the need for support programs to assist at-risk students in these groups. This does not necessarily mean remediation, an effort under national scrutiny as being counterproductive to the need to improve the academic preparation of students from disadvantaged schools. Yet tutoring, guidance, and social support will help students unfamiliar with the culture of the university to understand and negotiate expectations better. Similarly, programs to help retain and promote minority and women faculty can improve progress in an area where gains have been slow and that has substantial implications for reinforcing diversity in the student body. While such special support services find an important audience in underserved groups, help most equitably is made available to anyone who needs it.

Intellectual Diversity

Our institutions will not be successful in educating students for participation in a diverse and multicultural world unless our academic enterprises are diverse and multicultural as well. The inclusion of such perspectives affirms the identities of those who join our ranks, a critical factor in determining status within our campus communities. Moreover, no vision of educational equity would be complete without developing the full armament of ideas with which society must move forward. Yet we face the dilemma of having many more intellectual works available than can be practically incorporated into our general education programs. There is also resistance within faculties to work that is out of the academic mainstream.

Our basic policy of academic freedom is not enough to open the university to intellectual diversity. Policy and practice in the areas of curriculum and faculty reward systems are relevant, as are institutional program priorities. In our shared governance systems, where substantial decision-making responsibility lies in the hands of faculties primarily representing traditional academic backgrounds, there can be little impetus for change. Leadership is particularly important in this area.

Closely related is the right of free speech, which is one of the least understood privileges in our society and one of the most contentious points about which questions of equity revolve in our campus communities. Universities are most appropriately champions of first amendment rights. Yet at the same time, finding a balance between the rights of those who engage in speech that is disagreeable or hurtful to others and the rights of individuals thereby victimized and alienated is a particularly important expression of equal opportunity in our society. While controversial speakers cannot be banned from campus, institutions can provide opportunities to ensure the expression of other points of view.

Climate

The single most important factor in opening our doors wider is to create a climate in which all students, faculty, and staff feel welcome. Yet the reality is that indifference, intolerance, and harassment continue to exist in our campus communities. At Penn State, more than 60 percent of undergraduate and graduate students surveyed reported they had witnessed or experienced an act of intolerance and nearly one fourth a racial or ethnic insult (Penn State Pulse Survey, 1998). A university committed to equity in experience will articulate expectations concerning such behaviors, and when they occur confront them through established procedures. Furthermore, it will be proactive in anticipating climate concerns and in taking initiatives that improve the environment for diversity rather than merely being reactive to incidents that occur. To wait until something negative happens is to devalue the identities of those who are different and likely to be victimized. To welcome, through educational, cultural, and social events that celebrate differences and forge understanding, not only heads off possible incidents but affirms the value of all who join our academic community (Spanier, 1995).

Work Environment

Finally, another important component of opportunity within the university relates to institutional policies and practices that characterize the work environment. These include fundamental equity issues such as those related to pay. Also of concern are factors that humanize the university and enable all members of the campus community to focus equally on their work. Family friendly policies, flexible benefits, and employee assistance programs are some examples of ways institutions can be supportive of individuals with differing needs, including women, adult students, and persons with disabilities (Spanier, 1996). A major issue of equity on some campuses today is the provision of domestic partner benefits. The importance of such considerations should not be underestimated.

Setting Policy and Program Directions

Faced with often imperfect solutions, sometimes strongly opposing positions, and potentially substantial costs surrounding issues related to equity in educational access and experience, universities must somehow chart a course toward the goal of greater inclusivity. Aside from legal requirements, institutional mission, standards, and values offer the most reasoned and defensible bases for policy and program directions that seek to open our doors wider. These are elements that apply equally to all members of the academic community. On a more practical level, it is helpful also sometimes to disaggregate groups to ensure that actions are appropriately targeted.

Mission

Institutional mission and admissions policies and practices go hand-in-hand. Admissions requirements may differ by educational program and by institutional priorities and circumstances (Coleman, 1998). Different academic programs look for different qualities in their students; some emphasize quantitative skills, others verbal skills, still others artistic skills. Special consideration is given to talents that relate to well institutionalized activities such as the band, choir, or sports. Market forces may lead to enrollment controls that drive up the standard for entrance to a program, limiting entry for students who previously would have been judged acceptable, an interesting question of equity in itself, but one that goes largely ignored.

Other mission-related concerns include commitment to access and the importance of a diverse student body to the quality of education provided to all students. Empirical support for the positive impact of mission-based admission decisions is found in the study by Bowen and Bok (1998), that addressed the question of whether affirmative action admissions are successful in spreading the benefits of higher education more broadly in our society. This analysis demonstrated a positive academic, professional, and personal impact of the enrollment of minority students at selective colleges and universities. Evidence of the impact of admissions decisions on the fulfillment of the instructional mission may be found in documentation of the importance of diversity, including racial and ethnic diversity, to the quality of education for all students (Astin, 1993; Gurin, 1999; Milem, 1999). Clearly articulating the relationship of admissions policies and practices to attainment of institutional mission can provide justification for an institutional use of race, ethnicity, or educational disadvantage as one of the factors in making admissions decisions. This relationship also provides a basis for funding priorities that allocate resources to support affirmative action.

The educational mission of research universities further provides the foundation for academic and climate initiatives that are supportive of the diverse viewpoints that contribute to effective learning in a pluralistic society. For land-grant universities and others whose mission includes an historic commitment to access, there is, in addition, a special impetus for making investments that promote wider participation in higher education.

Standards

Selection criteria in admissions or hiring must honor some predictor of academic success within the university environment. It is simply unfair to admit students who are not capable of benefiting from a university education or to hire faculty who cannot expect to achieve tenure and promotion.

One arena in which this point has been illustrated for students is intercollegiate athletics, where some students charged they were unfairly denied eligibility to play sports because they failed to achieve the minimum test scores required by the National Collegiate Athletic Association (*Cureton v. NCAA*, 1999). Since the NCAA introduced academic eligibility standards in the 1980s, the graduation rate for student athletes has risen, student athletes in many sports graduate at a higher rate than the general student population, and recruited prospective student athletes are taking more core academic courses in high school. For example, for first-year students entering Division I schools in 1985, the year before new NCAA academic regulations were put in place, 52 percent of all athletes and 36 percent of black athletes graduated within 6 years. For student athletes entering in 1991, the comparable figures were 57 percent and 44 percent respectively (Suggs, 1999). The overall student body graduation rate after 6 years for students entering in 1985 was 54 percent; for students entering in 1991, it was 56 percent (NCAA, 1999c).

However, minority student athletes and low-income student athletes are impacted to a greater degree by initial eligibility standards. The NCAA continues to study initial eligibility rules, seeking enlightened practices that meet the test of fair treatment, the mission of higher education for academic success, and the desire of individuals for athletic access and opportunity. Similarly, an ongoing commitment to the development of improved admissions criteria is important to maintaining standards while improving access.

Values

The university's values of academic freedom and freedom of speech grant everyone the right to bring their voices to our academic communities. While these values are supportive of intellectual endeavors outside of the academic mainstream, they inevitably open our doors to speech that is considered offensive and harmful by some. While limitations of "time, place, and manner" can be imposed legally, such speech cannot be totally curtailed. In our university communities, we are fortunate to be able to call on our value of learning and use these situations as teachable moments, countering them with other points of view.

There are other values associated with an enlightened community that the university must claim if it is to be successful in a leadership role for society. Among them are humanity, compassion, and justice. These values go far in justifying a broad range of initiatives that promote diversity in our learning communities.

Targeting Actions

In moving forward from mission, standards, and values to create policies and programs that promote greater inclusivity in research universities, it is helpful also from an equity point of view to target initiatives carefully to those who can benefit. For example, although Asian-Americans, broadly defined, have achieved parity in higher education nationwide, this development overshadows the fact that many Asian-American students are the first in their families to attend college or come from certain Asian-American groups that are still significantly underrepresented (Wilds & Wilson, 1998). While it may be inappropriate to target Asian Americans in general for affirmative action in higher education, it would also be unfair to dismiss them categorically from special recruiting and retention initiatives. Another example lies in the area of financial aid. Although there is a strong correlation between minority status and low income, not all minority group members are economically disadvantaged and therefore may not need access to special scholarship programs. Still another example concerns equity issues for women that can vary greatly by field.

It is helpful to pull these diverse equity concerns together in a unified plan to underscore institutional commitment and ensure that efforts to address them are mutually reinforcing. Penn State's comprehensive framework to foster diversity offers one illustration of how these diverse policy and program considerations come together to address the equity issues that promote the broad goal of inclusivity for our learning community.

A Framework to Foster Diversity

Beginning in 1998, Penn State undertook a 5-year plan to continue the progress our university has realized in minority representation and retention, the status of women, and the quality of the climate at the University's 24 campuses throughout Pennsylvania (Penn State University, 1998). We have had many successes; for example, minority enrollments at Penn State have increased steadily over the last decade and a half, from 4.8 percent of total enrollments in 1982 to 10.3 percent in 1998. The graduation rate after six years for African-American students increased by 11 percentage points for freshmen that began their studies in 1992 compared to those entering in 1978. In 1988, women held 19 percent of the University's executive, administrative, and managerial positions; in 1998, they held 33 percent. Dozens of climate initiatives have been implemented that strengthen the environment for diversity. Yet there remains room for improvement in addressing our strategic goal to become "a caring university community that provides leadership for constructive participation in a diverse, multicultural world" (Penn State University, 1997).

Seven goals provide our framework to foster diversity at Penn State.[1] Key program and policy issues are highlighted under each one below.

Developing a Shared Understanding of Diversity

We believe it is important to promote the development and collective acceptance of an inclusive understanding of diversity to provide the foundation for efforts to integrate traditionally underrepresented groups more fully into the life and fabric of the university. This serves both to underscore that progress in any one arena does not forego progress in another and to correct misunderstandings regarding diversity initiatives that can fuel nonacceptance and hostility.

Attaining this goal is a process of education that calls for persistence and consistency in disseminating information about relevant policies and diversity initiatives. While the leadership of the Vice Provost for Educational Equity and units such as the Affirmative Action Office and Human Resources is important, we expect the responsibility for such efforts to be broadly shared by executives and administrators throughout the university to ensure that they reach all students, faculty, and staff.

Creating a Welcoming Campus Climate

Building on the foundation of a shared understanding of diversity, we seek to create a welcoming and inclusive campus climate, grounded in respect for others, nurtured by dialogue among individuals of differing perspectives, and evidenced by a norm of civil interaction among community members. Civility has been a major theme in student programming on our campuses in recent years.

To strengthen the policy foundations for the environment for diversity at Penn State, we recently added a statement on harassment to the university's policy on nondiscrimination. While policy statements on intolerance and sexual harassment had been in place, there was nothing explicitly stated about other forms of harassment. This addition is an important clarification of the university's position on such behavior.

We also have recently added a policy on the use of outdoor areas for expressive activities. While encouraging and protecting the right to express divergent viewpoints and opinions on matters of concern, the University expects that persons engaging in expressive activity will demonstrate civility, concern for the safety of persons and property, and respect for university activities and for those who may disagree with their message, and that they will comply with university rules. The purpose of this policy is to provide for expressive activity to be conducted on the grounds of the university in a manner consistent with these principles. Not surprisingly, the policy has been protested by some as interfering with first amendment rights. However, it does not seek to prohibit expressive activity but rather to limit time, place, and manner as allowed under the law.

Such policies are reinforced by systematic climate improvement initiatives that provide social and cultural support for groups historically excluded from the mainstream of campus life, raise awareness of all students, faculty, and staff on diversity concerns, and increase communication and understanding among individuals of diverse backgrounds. Penn State's Campus Environment Team brings together the perspectives of high-ranking administrative staff representing student affairs, affirmative action, educational equity, university safety, public information, human resources, and the president's office. The Team monitors problematic aspects of the university climate for diversity and promotes proactive efforts to raise awareness, communicate institutional problems, and address potential problems before they arise. In addition, Penn State's diversity strategic planning process has led to a more systematic focus on climate assessment and enhancement in academic and support units.

Recruiting and Retaining a Diverse Student Body

Among our most fundamental equity goals is reducing intergroup disparities in enrollment, retention, and graduation rates. Penn State also seeks to develop and implement proactive strategies to recruit and retain adult students.

Desegregation directives, described elsewhere in this volume, have mandated focused efforts for Pennsylvania's public institutions of higher education to recruit larger numbers of African-American students. Aggressive outreach is Penn State's primary means to this goal and to the goal of increasing minority enrollments generally. The university does not use race as a factor in admissions decisions, although it may be used in campus assignment in keeping with our desire to create a diverse student community to enhance the education of all students. Our minority admissions staff maintain community recruitment centers in the three major metropolitan areas of the state, make high school visits, bring prospective minority students to campus, and keep in touch with students after applications have been submitted. The directors of minority programs in each of Penn State's academic colleges also play an active outreach role in supporting graduate minority recruitment. As a result of this constellation of efforts, minority undergraduate applications to Penn State have increased 23 percent in the last 5 years.

Personal relationships have proven to be a key not only in admissions, but also in retention for underrepresented and nontraditional students. A second strategy to reduce retention disparities centers on specialized forms of academic support to meet the specific needs of different constituencies. A third strategy involves special instructional initiatives targeted to reducing academic performance disparities. For example, responding to evidence that students of color were disproportionately failing calculus taught in large sections, a pilot program offered calculus to some minority students in small sections. This led to a significant improvement in grades. As a result of this targeted initiative, calculus instruction in small sections is now the experience of most Penn State students.

In the long term, Penn State's goal of diversifying the student body requires increasing involvement in early intervention programs to expand the pool of prospective students. A major effort, focusing primarily on middle school students, is the Penn State Educational Partnership Program, a collaboration with local school districts in four urban communities aimed at helping disadvantaged students develop the necessary skills and aspirations to attend college. Many of our colleges offer summer programs dedicated to the same objectives.

Recruiting and Retaining a Diverse Workforce

Progress in diversifying the university's workforce has been limited. This is in spite of affirmative action search procedures, special recruitment initiatives that provide for competitive offers to minority and women faculty candidates, collaborative efforts with other institutions belonging to the Committee on Institutional Cooperation (CIC—the academic arm of the Big Ten) to increase the numbers of minority PhD graduates from CIC universities who move into faculty positions at other CIC institutions, and professional development experiences designed to attract members of underrepresented groups to staff employment opportunities at Penn State.

We are focusing on improving search processes, expanding faculty and staff retention programs, accelerating the introduction of family friendly policies and programs, and expanding personal and professional development opportunities to attract and retain a more diverse faculty and staff. We are especially concerned that the search processes used by committees may inadvertently screen out well-qualified women and minority candidates and that there may be several stages in the hiring process at which women and minorities may become discouraged. This can happen, for example, because of the candidate's perceptions that the university and surrounding community are insensitive to women or people of color, lack of special encouragement to remain a candidate, or unresponsiveness to the employment needs of a partner. Efforts to counter these possibilities include improved instructions for search committees and the development of a wide range of informational resources about the working and community environment at Penn State.

Developing a Curriculum that is Supportive of Diversity

Penn State's new general education curriculum, implemented in fall 1999, includes components in cultural diversity skills and international competence. In addition, changes in the foreign language proficiency expected of entering undergraduate students will facilitate cultural competence skills, as will plans to increase enrollments in study abroad programs.

Another essential ingredient in a multicultural academic environment is the presence of viable and visible units engaged in instruction and research examining the experiences of groups historically ignored or stereotyped in the curriculum. Expanding such venues for multicultural scholarship and teaching is a particularly difficult challenge.

Diversifying University Leadership and Management

The development of a diverse and multicultural management team is closely related to the recruitment and retention of a diverse student body and workforce and the advancement of multicultural curricula and scholarship. The commitment to diversity must be visible in its most public face, that of the senior managers and leaders of the university.

Penn State's Administrative Fellows program offers an avenue for women and minorities to develop administrative interests and talents, but it is limited to just a few individuals each year who are mentored by senior executives. Structured mentoring programs at other levels that promote similar objectives are being developed. Penn State's management team also will be shaped by a new Leadership and Management curriculum that both provides professional development opportunities that are responsive to retention concerns and incorporates a component on managing diversity.

Coordinating Organizational Change

Successful implementation of our Framework to Foster Diversity requires a solid fiscal resource base and an effective institutional infrastructure. Making funds available to support diversity initiatives is an especially difficult challenge in a public university such as Penn State, where funding is highly constrained. In some areas, such as compliance with ADA regulations, significant additional expenditures are mandated. It is imperative that creative strategies be developed to meet critical needs and that duplication of effort be avoided to make the most of available resources.

Penn State's Equal Opportunity Planning Committee (EOPC) has been a primary avenue for funding unit diversity initiatives. EOPC funds were meant to serve as start-up funds or seed money, with units taking over full fiscal responsibility for programs after a period of time. However, this transfer for fiscal responsibility has rarely occurred, with the result that funding of new programs has been increasingly limited. Increasingly stringent criteria have been applied to renewal requests, collaboration across units is being encouraged, and funding is being reoriented to address innovative programs to enhance recruitment and retention of undergraduate students.

There is also a need to ensure that the infrastructure supporting diversity initiatives is organized appropriately and is functioning in an efficient manner. We have attempted to strike a balance between centralized activities where collaboration and efficiency is maximized and decentralized activities that require critical functional areas to assume direct responsibility for ensuring equitable delivery of services to all constituents. But units serving underrepresented groups within larger organizational structures often have few resources at their disposal. Our goal is to institute the necessary organizational realignments, systems of accountability, resource mobilization and allocation strategies, and long-term planning strategies necessary to realize Penn State's diversity goals.

Achieving Educational Equity: Policy and Progress

Ultimately, educational equity in the research university must be judged by results that reflect inclusivity of diverse students, faculty, and staff. Yet for a host of reasons, many of which involve societal factors beyond our control, progress by numbers takes time and cannot be the sole measure of equity within our institutions.

What, then, constitutes equity in the contemporary research university? From a policy perspective, five considerations are essential.

Universities must take a comprehensive approach to the pursuit of equity to ensure that all barriers to participation are addressed. It is not sufficient to focus merely on access or to construe equity in terms of a general context established through policies on equal opportunity, nondiscrimination, and harassment. The wide range of educational and climate issues that pertain to equity in experience within our learning communities also must be addressed through policy and related program initiatives. In matters of access, institutions should consider the range of activities that constitutes affirmative action.

In making the difficult judgments of fairness that inevitably arise with equity issues, universities are well advised to remain true to their missions, standards, and values. These are the defining characteristics of our institutions and offer a solid rationale for the decisions we make. This will leave us vulnerable at times to situations that in the short run appear counterproductive to the goal of inclusivity but that in the long run uphold the principle of equal opportunity.

To the extent possible and appropriate, universities should emphasize expanding opportunities rather than divvying up existing resources and programs to accommodate an increased number of interests. While demand will always exceed supply, efforts to ease competition can be helpful in reducing disparities in participation across groups and in avoiding perceptions of reverse discrimination.

For this reason, and in support of the many initiatives that promote equity in experience, equity and diversity must be budget priorities. Need-based financial aid is a critical focus in increasing access for underserved populations. The commitment to equity also is made evident through investments in outreach, programming, and support services. To institutionalize ownership of equity issues, these investments must come not only from centralized sources but also, where appropriate, from academic and support units as well.

Finally, procedures and programs must be proactive and results oriented. Policy backed by ineffective practices or inadequate support is likely to have little impact on the progress we seek. Institutional priority is essential to the advancement of educational equity. This priority begins with the leadership of the university letting it be known where they stand on issues of equity through their own statements and actions, including the hiring decisions they make and the commitment of resources to advance equity goals.

No single policy, action or program will achieve educational equity in our research universities. Sensitivity, flexibility, and perseverance in a constellation of efforts will take us closer to the goal of equal educational opportunity for all.

Note

1. The authors acknowledge the contributions of the staff in the Office of the Vice Provost for Educational Equity, particularly Associate Vice Provost Thomas Poole, to this section that summarizes Penn State's *Framework to Foster Diversity.*

References

American Association of State Colleges and University. (1999). *State Issues Digest.* Washington, DC: Author.

Astin, Alexander. (1993, March/April). Diversity and multiculturalism on the campus. How are students affected. *Change,* 44–49.

Bowen, William G., & Bok, Derek. (1998). *The shape of the river: Long-term consequences of considering race in college and university admissions.* NJ: Princeton University Press.

Carter, Deborah J., & Wilson, Reginald. (1997). *Minorities in higher education. 1996–97 fifteenth annual status report.* Washington, DC: American Council on Education.

Characteristics of college presidents 1995. (1999, August 27). *Almanac Issue, Chronicle of Higher Education,* 38.

Choy, Susan P. (1998). Issues in focus. College access and affordability. In National Center for Education Statistics, *The condition of education 1998,* pp. 20–29. NCES98-013. Washington, DC: U.S. Government Printing Office.

Coleman, Arthur. (1998). Live by the score, die by the score: Academic freedom and responsibility in admissions decisions. *Diversity Digest.* Retrieved December 15, 1998 from the World Wide Web: http://www.inform.umd.edu/diversityweb/Digest/Sm98/score.htm.

Cureton v. NCAA, 37 F. Supp. 2d 687 (E.D. Pa. 1999).

El-Khawas, Elaine. (1995). *Campus trends 1995.* Washington, DC: American Council on Education.

Gurin, Patricia. (1999). *Expert report. Gratz, et al. v. Bollinger et al. No. 97-75321 (E.D. Mich.) Grutter, et al. v. Bollinger, et al. No. 97-75928 (E.D. Mich.).* Retrieved April 14, 1999 from the World Wide Web: http://www.umich.edu/~newsinfo/Admission/Expert/opinion.html.

Healy, Patrick. (1999, April 2). University of California to admit top 4 percent from every high school. *Chronicle of Higher Education.* Retrieved March 29, 1999 from the World Wide Web: http://chronicle.com/weekly/v45/i30/30a03601.htm.

Hurtado, Sylvia, Milem, Jeffrey F., Clayton-Pederson, Alma R., & Allen, Walter R. (1998). Enhancing campus climates for racial/ethnic diversity: Educational policy and practice. *The Review of Higher Education, 21*(3) 279–302.

Karabel, Jerome. (1998). No alternative: The effects of color blind admissions in California. In Gary Orfield & Edward Miller (Eds.), *Chilling admissions. The affirmative action crisis and the search for alternatives* (pp. 33–50). Cambridge, MA: Harvard Education Publishing Group.

Kellogg Commission on the Future of State and Land-Grant Universities. (1998) *Student access.* Washington, DC: National Association of State Universities and Land-Grant Colleges.

Milem, Jeffrey F. (1999). The educational benefits of diversity: Evidence from multiple sectors. In Mitchell Chang, Daria Witt, James Jones, & Kenji Hakuta (Eds.), *Compelling interest. Examining the evidence on racial dynamics in higher education.* Prepublication draft of a report of the American Educational Research Association Panel on Racial Dynamics in Colleges and Universities. Stanford, CA: Center for the Comparative Studies on Race and Ethnicity. Retrieved May, 1999 from the World Wide Web: http://www.stanford.edu/~hakuta/ racial_dynamics/ Compelling1.pdf.

National Center for Education Statistics. (1999). *Digest of Education Statistics 1998.* NCES1999–36. Washington, DC: U.S. Government Printing Office.

National Center for Education Statistics. (1997). *Findings from the condition of education 1997. Women in mathematics and science.* NCES97-982. Washington, DC: U.S. Government Printing Office.

National Collegiate Athletic Association. (1999a, August 16). Committee on Women's Athletics seeks quicker solutions for gender-equity issues. *NCAA News.* Retrieved September 28, 1999 from the World Wide Web: http://www.ncaa.org/news/19990816/active/3617no7.html.

National Collegiate Athletic Association. (1999b, October 25). Report shows women trailing in participation and resources. *NCAA News Digest.* Retrieved June 14, 2000 from the World Wide Web: http://www.ncaa.org/ news/19991025/digest.html.

National Collegiate Athletic Association. (1999c). *1999 NCAA graduation rates summary.* Retrieved September 26, 1999 from the World Wide Web: http://www.ncaa.org/grad_rates/.

Orfield, Gary, & Miller, Edward (Eds.). (1998). *Chilling admissions: The affirmative action crisis and the search for alternatives.* Cambridge, MA: Harvard Education Publishing Group.

Penn State Pulse Survey. (1998, May). *Diversity climate.* University Park, PA: Penn State University Division of Student Affairs.

Penn State University. (1998). *A framework to foster diversity.* University Park, PA: Office of the Vice Provost for Educational Equity.

Penn State University. (1997). *Academic excellence. Planning for the twenty-first century.* University Park, PA: Center for Quality and Planning.

Podberesky v. Kirwin, 38 F.2d 147 (4th Cir.1994).

Sable, Jennifer. (1998). Issues in focus. The educational progress of Black students. In National Center for Education Statistics, *The condition of education 1998* (pp. 2–10). NCES98-013. Washington, DC: U.S. Government Printing Office.

Sable, Jennifer, & Stennett, Janis. (1998). Issues in focus. The educational progress of Hispanic students. In National Center for Education Statistics, *The condition of education 1998,* pp. 11–18. NCES98-013. Washington, DC: U.S. Government Printing Office.

Sandler, Bernice, Silverberg, Lisa A., & Hall, Roberta M. (1996). *The chilly classroom climate: A guide to improve the education of women.* Washington, DC: National Association for Women in Education.

Scott, Sally S. (1997). Accommodating college students with learning disabilities: How much is enough? *Innovative Higher Education, 22*(2), 85–99.

Spanier, Graham B. (1995). *Inaugural state of the university address.* University Park, PA: The Pennsylvania State University, Office of the President.

Spanier, Graham B. (1996). Humanizing the university. *Journal of Family and Consumer Sciences, 88*(1), 3–5.

Suggs, Welch. (1999, April 9). Fight over NCAA standards reelects long-standing dilemma. *Chronicle of Higher Education.* Retried April 9, 1999 from the World Wide Web: http://www.chronicle.com/weekly/r45/31/31a04801.htm.

Wilbur, Susan A., & Bonous-Hammarth, Marguerite. (1998). Testing a new approach to admissions: The Irvine experience. In Gary Orfield & Edward Miller (Eds.), *Chilling admissions. The affirmative action crisis and the search for alternatives* (pp. 111–122). Cambridge, MA: Harvard Education Publishing Group.

Wilds, Deborah J., & Wilson, Reginald. (1998). *Sixteenth annual status report on minorities in higher education.* Washington, DC: American Council on Education.

C H A P T E R   1 0

Forging New University Initiatives in the Twenty-first Century: Women Executives and Equity

BEVERLY LINDSAY

> Part of affirmative action . . . I have not resolved. Absent affirmative action, would there be any consideration, any consciousness to include minorities in the pool?—in the interviews? How do we do this?
>
> —Ward Connerly, 1998

Extensive sociopolitical changes generated by social and political movements and by subsequent civil rights legislation external to the university community, necessitated changes within the walls of academe during the 1960s and 1970s. Social and political pressure caused universities to become more inclusive of various demographic groups within the general population. During this era, salient socioeducational policies emerged in an effort to ensure educational equity and diversity within the academic community—namely, forms of affirmative action. The 1980s ushered in a presidential administration that was instrumental in increasing the level of scrutiny for all federal affirmative action cases. The 1990s generated animated debates in the public at large, and among national legislators in particular, regarding the continuation, collapse, or both of affirmative action as a legal tool for achieving equity.

President William Jefferson Clinton announced *One America in the Twenty-first Century: The President's Initiative on Race* on June 14, 1997. The report generated by this initiative, released in September 1998, was viewed as a document raising the consciousness of a racially divided America (Fletcher, 1998). The tides, however, are shifting as anti–affirmative action efforts attempt to roll back the various measures that were designed to provide educational

229

equity. Voters in California, the state of Washington, and various cities across the nation have passed laws banning race and gender preferences in public hiring, contracting, and university admissions. Although the momentum of this movement may have slowed temporarily as the result of voter rejection of similar measures in Houston, other states are considering whether to pursue the California or Washington approach.

The objective of this chapter is to examine institutional policies initiated specifically by female university presidents—women who were students and in the early stages of their careers at the dawn of the contemporary affirmative action era in the 1960s and 1970s. Their careers evolved, in contrast to men, when a range of primarily Federal (and some State and local) executive and legislative initiatives commenced. Today, are these women (some of the early pioneers affected by evolving policies) able to counteract the rollback effect of anti–affirmative action measures in their current presidencies? Can they maintain educational equity via affirmative action, diversity, and other voluntary means? Pivotal perspectives and initiatives will be articulated that portray the contemporary contributions of female executives in higher education, while simultaneously responding to urban, state, and national legislation. These external policies influence internal institutional policies, which can, in turn, impact external policies, creating an interactive nexus. What is exceedingly important regarding this select group of women is their essential role in promoting and maintaining a steady state for educational equity in their universities. Of particular note will be their impact in changing institutional initiatives in an era of shifting state and federal policies.

To begin our analysis, descriptive statistics regarding the interrelations among university enrollments, faculty profiles, and university women presidents are presented. A conceptual framework based on the literature from sociology, social psychology, political science, administration, and management will provide insight into the importance of women in executive positions. Pivotal barriers such as mentoring, stereotypes, power, institutional climate, and leadership are posited via the several disciplines (Collins, Chrisler, & Quina, 1998; Benjamin, 1997; Hacker, 1992; Welch, 1992). After discussing conceptual tenets, the responses of women in executive positions will be examined, as they foster institutional changes and policies for educational equity via affirmative action and other measures.

Profile of Minorities and Women in Academia

Due in part to affirmative action, minorities and women hold more college presidencies today than in previous years. The past two decades have shown increases for women and minorities in enrollment gains, increased undergraduate and graduate degree attainment, and in faculty and administrative employment. However, white males continue to be the favored group in all areas of higher education (American Council on Education (ACE), 1998). The following statistics summarize the demographic backgrounds of students, faculty, and administrators in higher education, with specific focus on race and gender.

The decade between 1986 and 1995 revealed a modest growth in the percentage of minorities in the college-age population (ages 18–24). Information from the 1998 American Council on Education (ACE) *Status Report on Minorities on Higher Education* shows that the number of African-American, Hispanic, Asian-American, and American Indian students enrolled in college increased by 2.7 percent from 1986 to 1995. Despite this modest enrollment growth, minorities are still underrepresented on college campuses. Statistics from the same ACE Report show that African-Americans and Hispanics are less likely to attend college than whites in the same age group: 44 percent of white high school graduates ages 18–24 enrolled in college in 1996, compared with 35.9 percent of Blacks, and 35 percent of Hispanics the same year.

College participation rates among all high school graduates ages 18–24 reached its highest point in 1996, 43.5 percent (ACE, 1998). Yet a breakdown from the same report reveals a racial imbalance wherein undergraduate enrollment comprised approximately 10 percent African-American, 8 percent Hispanic, 6 percent Asian, 1 percent American Indian, and over 71 percent European-American. Overall rates in 1996 were nearly the same for entering freshman. However, of the total undergraduate student population, women made up more than 52 percent (Chilwniak, 1997).

While minority students complete college at substantially lower rates than whites, students of color have progressed in the number of undergraduate and graduate degrees they receive. Between 1986 and 1996 the number of bachelor degree awards increased for African-Americans 42.8 percent, 65 percent for Hispanics, 50.4 percent for American Indians, and 54.1 percent for Asian-Americans (ACE, 1998). Progress can also be seen in terms of graduate school enrollment. In 1996, 14 percent of all doctorates awarded to U.S. citizens went to minorities, compared to 9 percent in 1985 (ACE, 1998). Although progress has occurred, persons of color remain underrepresented at the doctoral level.

The gender split in faculty parallels that of the student population, but only at the instructor and assistant professor levels. For the 1995–1996 academic year, more than 40 percent of all male faculty members held the rank of full professor, which is more than double the 17.5 percent of female faculty who attained this position (Turner & Myers, 1999). Adding race to the equation, the demographics become more critical. The racial makeup of faculty at American research universities was 66.5 percent white male, 21 percent white women, 3.2 percent African-American (men and women), and 1.9 percent Hispanics (men and women) (ACE, 1998). J. K. Wilson (1996) noted that between 1981 and 1991 affirmative action was instrumental in increasing the numbers of minority faculty at research institutions.

Minority faculty, particularly women, are typically found at the lower levels of the professorate as assistant professors and non–tenure track lecturers. Without some impetus to help move them beyond that nontenured level, they have failed to gain a permanent foothold in the academic profession. As suggested by the ACE, "The possibility of their developing a critical mass and thereby becoming a permanent presence can be ensured . . . with the continuation of some form of affirmative action" (ACE, 1998). Although advancements have been made, equity has not been established, and women continue to hold inferior roles to men (Gorena, 1996).

Further, men in academe continue to out-earn women. Survey results reported by the American Association of University Professors in their 1998 annual report indicate the average salary for a female full professor as $65,365, compared with $74,515 for male colleagues. The survey also found that the pay gap between men and women is widest at research universities. The average salary of a female full professor at a private, nonsectarian institution was $90,611, while a man of the same rank at the same type of institution made an average of $99,979. Public research institutions revealed the same trend, where female full professors earned an average of $72,885, and men $80,379.

According to an ACE report on American college presidents (1998), female presidents increased by 61 percent between 1986 and 1995. However, women continue to hold fewer than one in five presidencies of over 3,000 colleges and universities. Approximately 16.5 percent of all college presidents were women in 1995, roughly the same percentage as those in the National Association of State Universities and Land-Grant Colleges (NASULGC), which are among the most prestigious public research and comprehensive doctoral institutions in the country. Of 113 NASULGC presidents that joined together to fight underage drinking on campus in a national ad campaign in the fall of 1999, 18 were women. Although the gap is narrowing, it is unlikely that women will achieve parity in the near future. The data in the 1998 ACE report suggests that men are more likely than women to serve in more than one presidency. Slightly more than 13 percent of women serve a second consecutive presidency, compared to 21.3 percent of men; 4.9 percent of women were in their third presidency, compared to 8.5 percent of men.

While women serve as presidents in all types of institutions, they have made the greatest strides at 2-year colleges, and master- and doctorate-granting institutions. In 1995, 25 percent of all presidents at 2-year colleges were women. The actual number increased from 74 to 148 between 1986 and 1995. During the same time period, the number of women leading doctoral institutions increased from 8 to 22. African-American women made up more than

8 percent of women presidents in 1995. This was an increase from 3.9 percent in 1986. Asian-Americans and American Indians each accounted for 1 percent of women college presidents in both 1986 and 1995. The proportion of women presidents who were Hispanic/Latina decreased during the period, from 5.1 percent to 2.4 percent (ACE, 1998). No minority women were presidents of Research I universities in the late 1990s.

At the dawn of the twenty-first century, demographic trends are shifting. It is projected that immigrants, women, and minorities will account for more than 80 percent of the net growth in the labor force. Projections show that women and minorities will comprise the majority of the U.S. workforce between the year 2000 and 2025 (U.S. Department of Labor, 1998; U.S. Bureau of Census 1996). These projections will have a direct impact on higher education, which intensifies the need for continued awareness of equity and diversity issues in higher education. The statistics show that the faces of the student body, faculty, and administration will become more colorful and include more women. But will authentic diversity be seen in university executive offices?

Diversity in higher education is important and needs to be recognized as part of the academy's mission. In *Making the Case for Affirmative Action in Higher Education,* ACE (1999) states that "each of our more than 3,000 colleges and universities has its own specific and distinct mission. This collective diversity among institutions is one of the great strengths of America's higher education system. Preserving that diversity is essential if we hope to serve the needs of our democratic society" (p. 1). Women executives of various demographic backgrounds have the opportunity and the obligation to enhance diversity in their institutions.

Conceptual Tenets for Affecting Equity and Affirmative Action

Equity undergirds and is linked to race, ethnicity, economic status, disability, and other special group concerns. Educational equity, for the purpose of this chapter, is a set of premises, plans, and programmatic actions that provide educational opportunities and create expectations for and about individuals, regardless of race, gender, ethnicity, economic status, disability, or other special group differences. Although affirmative action—a key plan and program of equity—has been a positive influence on the employment options of women in higher education, there continue to be factors that hinder the career advancement of women. Some of these factors are sex-based discrimination, lack of pay equity, fewer opportunities for career development, and an unfavorable institutional climate (Gorena, 1996; Quina, Cotter, & Romenesko, 1998). Gorena (1996) asserts that equity has not been established and that women continue to hold inferior roles to men.

Research done by Quina, Cotter, and Romenesko (1998) found that, years after Title IX legislated sex equity in education, there are significant areas where little has changed. They conducted an intensive case study of a large Midwestern public university and supplemented their study by collecting data from participants in a working seminar. Their findings revealed institutional barriers to promotion for women throughout the university. Faculty, academic staff, and administrators, despite widely disparate job classifications, listed similar barriers to advancement. These obstacles impede the careers of women, reinforcing terms such as "glass ceiling," "Plexiglas ceiling," and "concrete wall," used to describe the phenomenon by Chilwniak (1997), Daniel (1997), and Quina, Cotter, and Romenesko (1998). Thus employment equity in higher education remains an unachieved goal.

A common reason cited for the absence of females in executive positions in higher education is that there are not enough women candidates in the pool of senior faculty (Collins, Chrisler, & Quina, 1998). Although the use of this excuse is fading, it still applies in the case of ethnic minority applicants. Since nearly half of Americans receiving doctorates are women (NCES, 1996), it is understandable that in the past 40 years the proportion of women in faculty positions has steadily increased (Bellas, 1994). Despite efforts to hire more women, results are not reflected in female representation in senior faculty. Bentley and Blackburn (1992) attribute the absence of women in the tenured positions to their relatively recent entry into the workforce. However, women have been represented significantly in academic doctoral programs for over a quarter century. During the mid-1980s women received 31.5 percent of doctorates granted; 15 years later they should be in the senior professional ranks. This reveals a clear discrepancy between their availability and their presence in the upper ranks. Collins et al. state that the "availability of women with doctorates who are interested in academe is not commensurate with the current prevalence rates for women full professors, even when a time delay is added to allow for promotion" (p. 47).

Minority women often confront a combination of racism, sexism, and socioeconomic differentials termed "multiple jeopardy" or "triple jeopardy" (King, 1990; Lindsay, 1980 & 1997). Creating obstacles, these multiple forms of discrimination obstruct the careers of minority women in faculty positions, which, in turn, reduce diversity in higher education. Overt discrimination against minorities and women in the work environment and elsewhere is prohibited. Although institutions have a set of informal and formal rules that create an environmental culture, the institutional climate can enhance or create barriers for women and minorities in their quest for promotions to senior levels.

Individual prejudices become part of the institutional climate, forming norms that are reinforced within the organizational structure. These institutional norms display the sometimes-subtle ways in which women are treated differently, as Sandler (1986) notes, "ways that communicate to women that they are not quite first-class citizens in the academic community" (p. 175). The organizational climate and structure create barriers that laws alone cannot remedy. Often, the usual ways in which men and women relate to each other, ways that the organization considers "normal," go unnoticed. One example is inadvertently treating women in a way that indicates that somehow women are not as serious professionally or as capable as their male peers. Sandler (1986) found that,

> While policies—and even attitudes—concerning women may be quite favorable, subtle behavior discrimination toward women may abound. Often these behaviors are not seen as discrimination even though they frequently make women feel uncomfortable and put them at a disadvantage. Frequently, neither women nor those who treat them differently are aware of what has occurred; indeed, the possible lack of awareness by both parties is what makes the behavior and its impact so insidious.

Kanter (1993) theorizes that white males (seen as the dominant group) resist infiltration by the minority group. Thus, as women enter the male-dominated work environment, they encounter different and subtle forms of discrimination. Hacker (1992) adds that the desire to maintain and enhance power is a basis for discrimination. Power enables gender and racial discrimination to continue by the ongoing legitimization of policies and practices.

Kanter (1993) clearly articulates the centrality of power within formal organizations. Her study shows that maintaining positions within the power structure is the goal of most white men and demonstrates this point in the following candid statement made by a white male: "It's okay for women to have these jobs, as long as they don't go zooming by me" (Kanter, 1993, p. 218). Males often feel uncomfortable and threatened when they do not maintain position and status or when they report to a woman in a more powerful role. Official and nonofficial political structures within institutions and organizations provide the means whereby power via resources is mobilized and distributed. According to Hacker (1992), the desire to maintain and enhance power is a basis for discrimination. The hiring and promotion of a limited number of minorities and women due to discriminatory practices simply enables white males to maintain their power and position. In order to acquire power, women must form alliances with sponsors, peers, and subordinates. Sponsors support and speak on behalf of their protégées. For women, sponsors are exceedingly important, since their alliances or networks with peers are often more limited than those of males. In effect, sponsors and mentors bring women into networks and facilitate their relations with coworkers.

According to Eberspacher and Sisler (1988) mentors (and sponsors) may be the single most important factor in the career development of administrators. In recent years, academic literatures have drawn attention to the advantages that mentoring relationships can offer to protégés, mentors, and organizations (Kram, 1988). Mentors can be linked to career advancement, higher pay, and greater career satisfaction (Scandura, 1992), and the mentoring relationship may be critical to the advancement of women in organizations (Dreher & Ash, 1990). Sosik and Godshalk (2000) define mentoring as a relationship in which individuals with advanced experience or knowledge support, and assist or help, the upward mobility of junior group members. Mentors may be teachers who enhance administrative and intellectual skills, sponsors who facilitate entry and mobility, hosts and guides who welcome the novice into the profession, and exemplars that serve as role models. As Christiansen, Macagno-Shang, Staley, Stamler, and Johnson (1989) assert, "success in academia depends not only on what you know but also who you know for support, guidance, and advocacy" (p. 58).

The influence of women is often limited by casting them into stereotypic gender roles. Gender stereotypes, where women are seen as communal or relational and men as emissary or instrumental, have an effect on the types of opportunities offered to faculty (Chrisler, Herr, & Murstein, 1998). The female role is characterized as that of mother, one who nurtures and tends to emotional needs. Thus, Twale and Shannon (1996) found that women faculty are more likely to be asked to do "mom" work (dealing with student concerns, social issues, or routine matters), while male faculty are more likely to handle policy making and its implementation, faculty status, or grievances.

Biernet and Kobrynowicz (1997) conducted a series of experiments on how stereotypes affect judgments. They found that people set lower minimum competency standards but higher ability standards for women and Blacks than for men and whites in general. Therefore, it is easier for low-status groups to meet minimum standards, but harder to prove that their performance is based on their abilities. This explains why women are seen as appropriate for stereotypical tasks, yet, despite their successes, not good enough for leadership positions. When women are not expected to be leaders, their voices go unheard. A suggestion made by a woman may be ignored, but applauded when stated by a man. A similar phenomenon occurs when, after a meeting, comments made by a woman are attributed to a man (Chrisler, Herr, & Murstein, 1998). In reviewing linguistic research, North (1991) found that individual and group perceptions and norms put women in the position of listening more and speaking less than men. She also found that women who use language comparable to that of men are judged differently—that is, more harshly than their male peers.

Conditions favorable to equity and affirmative action require strong support from institutional leadership. The ability of a leader to set an institutional agenda is a powerful tool in shaping the values of an institution (Hanna, 1988). As the affirmative action debate continues on legal, political, and social levels, much of the attention in the past decade has focused on higher education (AAUP, 1999). Affirmative action plays a role on university campuses across the nation. It is seen as a way to redress past discrimination and to improve the quality of higher education by promoting diversity in the faculty, the student body, and society at large.

Peter Flawn (President Emeritus of University of Texas at Austin) notes, "universities are in the knowledge business—generating it, transmitting it, and disseminating it" (p. 107). The primary goal is to develop students academically. Of equal importance, and vital to the survival of the university, is the intellectual development of the faculty. To meet these needs, a leader of a college or university must be capable of monitoring ideas, trends, and research; should participate in the development and support of a strong faculty; and must act as the chief disseminator of knowledge (DeFleur, 1992).

It is the responsibility of an executive at an institution of higher education to create an environment that will facilitate the building of knowledge while ensuring that the needs of a diverse faculty, student body, and constituency are met. A fundamental question is, Who is capable of handling such a challenging portfolio? With a projected increase of minorities and women in the workforce during the next 20 years, a closer look at contemporary African-American and European-American women university leaders suggests answers to this question.

Methodology and Profiles of Institutions

To explore the current impact of university women executives on equity (especially affirmative action), qualitative case studies were conducted. An interpretive, naturalistic approach enabled the researcher to conduct semistructured interviews with six women who were, at the time of the interviews, university presidents and tenured professors. The respondents in the study were awarded degrees by top Research I university programs in the United States. Their doctoral degrees were in educational administration and curriculum, counseling psychology, foreign language and comparative literature, anthropology, political science, and biochemistry. Several of them participated in postdoctoral programs, fellowships, or leadership programs at some of the very top universities.

Interviews and campus visits began in 1997 and concluded in 1999. Three of the women are African-American and three are European-American. To ensure anonymity of the institutions involved and professionals interviewed, the six institutions will be referred to by pseudonyms: Wood University, Granite University, Plains University, Ravine University, Ivy College, and Lake University. Interviews with the presidents were recorded and transcribed. Information was gathered from in-depth participant observations at three universities and reviews of all the institutions' strategic plans, mission statements, catalogs, and World Wide Web sites. These written sources are not cited in the reference list in order to preserve anonymity of the professionals and institutions participating in this study.

Wood University is a comprehensive public university located near a growing city of approximately 200,000 in the western region of the United States Wood has a diverse student body of over 6,000 students. Slightly more than 50 percent of the University's students are Caucasian, approximately 16 percent are Hispanic, roughly 4 percent African-American, and about 10 percent of the student population is made up of international students. The university notes in its mission statement that faculty, staff, administrators, and students are committed to creating a learning environment that "encourages all members of the campus community to expand their intellectual, creative, and social horizons." To facilitate this mission, they "promote academic excellence in the teaching and scholarly activities of their faculty, encourage personalized student learning, foster interactions and partnerships with our surrounding communities, and provide opportunities for the intellectual, cultural, and artistic enrichment of the region."

Granite University, a public university located in the Northeast, has a student body of approximately 12,000 students, 32 percent of whom are Black, 31 percent Caucasian, 25 percent Hispanic, and 12 percent Asian. Granite University notes in its mission statement that it aims to offer educational opportunities to students of promise who may be of modest means and whose families may have little history of higher education. The university "encourages its students and faculty to contribute new knowledge and methods in scholarly and professional disciplines and to engage in the solution of important intellectual and social challenges through distinguished teaching, research and service."

Plains University is a public research university located in the central region of the United States. Enrollment at Plains is over 28,000. It has a minority student population of less than 10 percent; 2.5 percent of the students are African-American, 0.05 percent are American Indian, 4.1 percent Asian, and 2.2 percent Hispanic. The Plains University mission statement notes that an "environment that promotes free inquiry and ethical behavior, which fosters the qualities of mind that lead to mature, independent, informed, and humane judgment" is required if students are to reach their educational goals. In fulfilling its teaching, research, and service mission, Plains University strives to "provide a full range of high quality educational opportunities to citizens" of their state.

Ravine University is a public research school with an enrollment of just under 10,000. Located in the northwestern region of the country, Ravine University boasts a 13:1 student/faculty ratio. The student body at Ravine is 59 percent female. Fourteen percent of the student population is indigenous to the state and 6 percent is made up of other American minority groups. Approximately 80 percent of the student population is European-American. An important strategic goal at Ravine is to create a "model that demonstrates how gender, racial, and cultural diversity strengthen a university and society." Noting that faculty and staff should mirror the diversity found in American society, Ravine has pledged to achieve this objective on their campus by the year 2000.

Ivy College is a private institution located at the edge of a large East Coast city with a population of over three million. A small women's college, Ivy has an undergraduate enrollment of 1,226 and graduate enrollment of 510. Ivy College has a diverse population; minority groups account for 27.9 percent of its students with 4.3 percent African-American, 17.5 percent Asian-American, 3.8 percent Latino, 0.16 percent Native American, and 2.1 percent multiracial. Of the 99 full-time undergraduate faculty at Ivy, 45 are women. The school has a 10:1 student/faculty ratio. The mission of Ivy is to provide a rigorous education and to encourage the pursuit of knowledge as preparation for life and work. Ivy also focuses on "encouraging students to be responsible citizens who provide service to and leadership for an increasingly interdependent world."

Lake University is a public, urban institution located in the Midwest. Enrollment at Lake University was just under 9,000 for the fall of 1998. Classified as a comprehensive urban university, 85 percent of the population is African-American, 10 percent Hispanic, and 5 percent European-American. Lake University's mission is to provide access to higher education for residents of the region, the state and beyond, and to produce graduates who are responsible, discerning, and informed citizens with a commitment to lifelong learning and service. One way in which the university hopes to accomplish its mission is by recruiting, retaining, and graduating a culturally and economically diverse student body.

The protocol questions guiding the interviews included the following:

1. What types of education credentials or qualifications prepared you for your current position?
2. Did you participate in a fellowship or similar program that contributed to your current role?
3. Did you have mentors? If so, what roles did they play?
4. What are two or three of your most salient administrative experiences that contributed to your current position?
5. What problems/issues impeded your career (temporarily or permanently) as a Dean, Associate Dean, Department Chair, or similar position? Salient issues/factors? How did you address the issues/factors?
6. What do you do when your supervisor or the person to whom you report does not support you? When similar issues/factors occurred for European-American males and/or females, what was the result or outcome? Why do you think this was the reality? What would you recommend to another minority female in a comparable situation?

7. When you interviewed for your current position, how did you address the following:
   a. Areas where you did not have administrative experience?
   b. Areas where you had not conducted research or served as a consultant?
   c. Negative comments from your immediate supervisor or others?
   d. Negative comments from colleagues and others at your home institution or elsewhere?[1]
8. Do you envision a more senior or comprehensive administrative experience? What type? What kind of institution?
9. What is educational equity?
10. What is affirmative action to you, personally?
11. What, if any, is the role of affirmative action in today's universities?
12. How is affirmative action manifest on your campus? (Also, behind the scenes, e.g., subtleties of the faculty and administrative search.)
13. How is diversity manifest at your campus?
14. What do you still plan to achieve during the next 3 to 5 years at your university in terms of equity and diversity?
15. What are the major internal pressures that influence equity and affirmative action?
16. What are the major external pressures that influence equity and affirmative action?
17. How has affirmative action influenced your hiring practices?
18. How many/what percentage of students transfer to your institution, versus how many begin at your institution?
19. How important is internationalizing your campus?
20. Are there issues or areas that were not covered in our interview and discussion which you would like to address?

Detailed information from the interviews, participant observations, mission statements and strategic plans are depicted in Table 10.1. Questions 1 and 2 are discussed in the methodological section. Responses to protocol questions focused on 1–4, 9–18, and 20. Initial foci concentrate on mentors and leadership. Table 10.1 emphasizes educational equity and affirmative action; specific affirmative action/educational equity issues; strategic plans and mission statements; and goals, outcomes, or both.

Thematic Motifs

The Influence of Mentors

Several interviewees cited the impact of mentors on their careers. Men and women mentors were equally important in the process. The president from Ravine indicated that she had two mentors, both males, which affected her positively for short periods as she began her career in administration. Another participant identified a mentor for almost every professional position she occupied and noted that the strong influence of mentors commenced in her undergraduate classes and continued in later graduate programs. This supports the Eberspacher and Sisler (1988) argument that mentors may be the single most important factor in the career development of administrators. The president of Wood University remembered rushing out of her own high school commencement to go to her mother's master's graduation. She stated that her mother was her first and most important mentor. Granite's president acknowledged that her mother was instrumental in encouraging her to seek her PhD, even locating funding through a foundation for minorities interested in earning doctoral degrees.

The president from Lake indicated that she had no acknowledged mentor. However, she studied leadership style and actions of the male president when she was vice president and provost; she noted that no professional guidance was offered. The absence of this guidance prompted her to be concerned about assisting faculty, staff, and students in their career development.

Several participants indicated that they are mentors to young women interested in academic careers and other professions, which is in agreement with Dreher and Ash (1990) that mentoring relationships may be critical to the advancement of women in organizations. The president from Ivy indicated that as an executive at an all-women's college, she automatically acts as mentor and role model to the women at her school. Similarly, the President at Wood maintains that because she is a minority woman in an executive position, she hopes that young women on her campus view her as a role model and mentor. As women in the highest executive position on a coeducational campus (with one exception) could they also be seen as mentors to their male students? Can women be considered a role model to men? Creating expectations for individuals regardless of race, gender, ethnicity, economic status, disability, or other special group differences is a portion of the definition of educational equity. However, another perspective would be that of the male student who has a woman as the leader of his university. Further investigation could add to a better understanding on how equity and affirmative action efforts affect the male student perspective on gender, race, and leadership.

Perceptions of Race and Gender

The belief that expectations were higher for women than for their male counterparts was a constant theme in the interviews and consistent with Kanter's (1993) theory on the nonofficial structures and norms within institutions. The participants, as they advanced through their careers, were entering a male-dominated environment where, Hacker (1992) postulates, the dominant group's desire to maintain power would be a basis for discrimination. The president from Wood University viewed the difference in expectations for women executives as a source of motivation. "I really don't think that I can be mediocre in the system at all; I don't have permission to be." The president from Ravine felt that gender does not assist in the pursuit of professional goals and suggested "women find a way that is helpful" in achieving these goals. An example might be having a sponsor or mentor to assist in navigating the organizational structure.

The president at Lake University asserted that she was criticized or questioned in a manner that a male president would not have been. She noted, "White males don't expect Black females to be knowledgeable or assertive." While attending a meeting with the chief executive officer of a Fortune 500 company, her male assistant was pulled aside and advised that his boss talked too much. She did not fit the stereotype that women should be seen and not heard, which concurs with North's (1991) findings on individual and group perceptions and norms that women who use language comparable to that of men are judged more harshly than men.

It is intriguing to note that the president from Plains University did not believe that gender-specific issues affected her at the executive level. In contrast, the president from Ravine stated that even at the executive level it takes women longer than men to "get into the inner circles and the power centers." This is due to the power and bureaucratic structures (Kanter, 1993; Hacker, 1992). The presidents from Plains and Ivy (both European-American women) declared that gender and race did not affect them negatively as they advanced through their careers. The president from Plains stated, "I don't think you're helped or hurt regardless of whether you are a man or a woman. I think there are some global things that are very helpful to be able to do in executive positions." She remarked that her scientific background helped to prepare her for an executive position. As a researcher she had infiltrated one male-dominated world and found it easier to enter another. The president from Ivy believes that gender and timing aided her career. She stated, "I came through the job market in the 1970s, 80s and 90s and so I think, if anything, timing has worked for me. . . . I think that those institutions were anxious to have qualified women on their faculty so they hired me." Gender was also in her favor in securing the presidency of an all-women's college. In this position she views herself as a role model and mentor to the students of her institution, which is in the tradition of Ivy leadership.

The presidents from Wood and Granite mentioned that affirmative action was instrumental in their careers. A 1970s program designed for minorities interested in completing a PhD funded their graduate educations, dissertation field research, or both. Timing was also a salient factor in their career paths. The president of Wood noted that when hired for her first job, her sponsor advised the dean of her department that "you have a woman, and a minority . . . you need to hire her and if you don't, it's going to look bad."

In essence, the three African-American women and one European-American president clearly experienced that gender and race matter (West, 1993; Glazer, 1997; Lindsay, 1999). Initially the president of Ivy did not concur; however, on closer reflection, gender did indeed make a difference in her career. For the lone president who is a scientist, perhaps she no longer reflects on the personal aspects of gender and race or on the presence of very few women in her male-dominated field enabled her acceptance.

On Leadership

In *Talking Leadership: Conversations with Powerful Women*, Ruth Simmons, then President of Smith College, stated, "I am not sure that leadership is anything more than achievement" (Hartman, 1999, p. 238). The participants in this study have achieved a great deal professionally. They shared the qualities that assisted them in accomplishing their professional goals in becoming educational leaders. The president from Plains declared that being a good listener and considering all sides of an issue is key to her role as a leader. She noted that having trusted advisers when making administrative decisions was crucial. She also felt that it is important to be open and honest and to acknowledge mistakes. The president from Granite felt that confidence garnered from her extensive administrative experience helped her to be an effective leader. Many participants mentioned communication ability as instrumental in dealing with faculty disputes, union issues, student concerns, and budgetary issues.

DeFleur (1992) described the president's role as that of chief disseminator of knowledge. Indicating that presidents, in their role as leader, must monitor ideas, trends, and research, and participate in the development and support of faculty. Added to this list could be the design of strategic plans and mission statements. Utilizing their leadership, participants in this study have found innovative and effective ways of designing and implementing missions and goals for their institutions. The President of Lake University stated, "Public higher education institutions are under the mandate to serve the people of the region and of the states that support them." In designing her strategic plan, she focused her efforts on meeting the needs of an urban institution where city council people and local state legislators often raised queries. She emphasized the need to raise academic standards and increase the number of European-Americans on her campus. The president of Plains University designed her strategic plan using the state Board of Regents strategic plan as a guide. Her leadership skills enabled her to clearly communicate to the strategic plan committee the salience of designing a strategic plan that focused on the goals of the State Board of Regents.

The president from Ivy College was, at the time of this article, designing a participatory strategic plan using a process that features town meetings on campus, electronic responses to specific questions on the school's web site, and meetings with faculty, students, alumnae, and community leaders. She has collected information from all stakeholders. This information will be used to create what she believes will be a collaborative strategic plan addressing the needs of academic, alumni, and community constituents.

Both Lake and Plains Universities are comprehensive public institutions that must consider how their strategic plans will be viewed on campus and, simultaneously, the impact and response of the public and political structures of communities and state. The president from Ivy, however, was able to use more creativity in designing her strategic plan and had less pressure from any political structure. Hence she has more autonomy in her leadership role in strategic planning. Using their skills as leaders and their knowledge of the institutional climate at their respective universities, each president worked within her system appropriately and effectively to design and create strategic plans and mission statements. These documents reflect input garnered from the university community and from outside of the university community.

Table 10.1 depicts thematic areas that emerged from the interviews with the six women. Executive support for educational equity with a focus on affirmative action is central to the thinking and planning of these university leaders. Hence Table 10.2 evinces their conceptions, the specific issues influencing their campuses, components of strategic plans and mission statements to establish an institutional framework for equality, and actual or envisioned outcomes to achieve equity.

Educational Equity and Affirmative Action

In 1997 the American Educational Research Association (AERA) and the Center for the Comparative Study of Race and Ethnicity at Stanford University launched a project designed to inform public policy by a broad array of the social science literature that addresses the intersection of race and higher education. One of the conclusions from this work stated that racially diversified environments, when properly utilized, lead to gains in educational outcomes for all parties (AERA, 1999). The women executives in this study are creating policies that will diversify their campuses and lead not only to enhanced educational outcomes, but also to lasting effects on society at large.

Each participant, in this study, has the responsibility of contributing to and impacting on the future of her institution. As the guiding member of the administration, each envisions the ideals of the organization and develops the necessary procedures and operations to achieve goals. All participants stressed the salience of equal access for everyone and noted the importance of demonstrating sensitivity to the various university populations. In agreement with Cox (1993), they all felt that properly managed diversity leads to higher retention rates. They believe in ascertaining ways to ensure success for all elements of the institution. The president from Wood University defined

TABLE 10.1
Presidential Statements and Initiatives

Institution	Educational Equity/Affirmative Action Definitions and Concepts	Specific Affirmative Action or Educational Equity Issues
Wood	"The employment and identification of procedures and strategies that may be avant-garde, or may be certainly nontraditional that will enable people who are nonmainstream to have equal opportunities."	"Equal opportunity and access is having a sensitivity to the population with whom you are involved and finding ways to make them all successful."
Granite	"Affirmative action is a way of leveling the playing field . . . educational equity and affirmative action are both means to an end. I'd like to provide an environment in which every student, regardless of who he or she was could achieve the success they want to achieve."	When dealing with affirmative action and educational equity "you have to find a kind of common conversation that people are interested in. As stakeholders you have to show them what it is they have at stake . . . then I think you can begin to engage people who don't see how this has anything to do with them and their lives."
Plains	"I support affirmative action [by] increasing student body and staff/ faculty positions with a qualified and representative pool . . . a national pool is needed for states with few minorities."	"It is important from an educational perspective for us to diversify our population, because our population of under-represented minorities in-state is lower than 3 percent."
Ravine	"I'm interested in action to achieve a more harmonious working environment and more harmonious learning environment, so I look at the actions."	"Indigenous residents of the state and the number of residents living in rural areas create a unique situation for the university."
Ivy	"The playing field is not equal and never has been equal . . . until we get there, which is a very long way off, we have to continue to speak. A lot of the concept of educating those who otherwise might not have the opportunities to be educated has a kind of logic that moves other kinds of diversity as well."	"[We] need to increase minority faculty . . . [the] difficulty is due to a shortage of minority candidates in certain fields."
Lake	"Affirmative action is giving people an equal chance . . . in order to remove some of the inequities of the past."	"Equity and diversity on my campus is reversed. Our student population is 75 percent African-American, 10 percent Hispanic, and 15 percent European-American."

TABLE 10.2
Presidents' Current Plans and Envisioned Outcomes

Institution	Strategic Plans/Mission Statements	Desired Outcomes
Wood	• Address the diverse educational needs of students. • Guide students to become critical thinkers . . . globally aware, and engaged by the diverse challenges facing the region. • Attract and retain a high-quality and diverse student population from within and beyond the region.	• Identity the learning needs of both traditional and reentry students and respond to identified needs. • Incorporate global and multi-cultural perspectives into the curriculum and link faculty and students to global education opportunities. • Use comprehensive long-term and annual enrollment management targets. • Develop a plan for recruiting and retaining a high-quality and diverse student body.
Granite	• Prepare students to live, work, and thrive in the global village. • Appreciate and embrace diversity, and build bridges, as the world becomes smaller. All aspects of our society are informed by the need to broaden our perspectives.	• In the next 2 years increase community activities on campus. • Creating a positive diverse image of the institution to the larger community and the state. • Increase enrollment by 5 percent for each of the next 2 years.
Plains	• Maintain a culturally diverse and inclusive university community. • Support strong ties between the university and external constituencies. • Maintain a high quality academic and working environment.	• Enrich student population with minorities from out of state. • Thirty-six percent of under-graduate enrollment is from out of state.
Ravine	• Demonstrate consistently how gender, racial, and cultural diversity strengthen a university and society. • Provide high-quality undergraduate education for traditional and nontraditional students. • Continue to be a leading partner with communities, industry, and govern-ment to solve specific state and national needs.	• Increase indigenous population on campus by hiring faculty, administrators and increasing student population. • Strong effort in distance education so that all students are reached.

(continued)

TABLE 10.2
Presidents' Current Plans and Envisioned Outcomes

Institution	Strategic Plans/Mission Statements	Desired Outcomes
Ivy	• Provide a rigorous education and encourage the pursuit of knowledge as preparation for life and work. • Strive to create a living and working community based on mutual respect and personal integrity. • Maintain institutional character as a small residential community, which fosters close working relationships between faculty and students.	• Each faculty search committee is briefed regarding the college's affirmative action policy and procedures, and regarding possible approaches to creating an inclusive pool of applicants. • Developing a strategic plan that will include components to foster diversity.
Lake	• Continue to recruit and retain a dedicated, caring, and culturally diverse faculty. • Improve recruitment, retention, and graduation rates of a culturally and economically diverse student body. • Foster a collaborative and intellectually stimulating community that promotes academic freedom, mutual respect, integrity, and high expectations of academic and professional achievement.	• During the next 3 to 5 years, I would like to see the European-American population increase to 25 percent of the student body. • Funds garnered from corporations and private foundations assist in maintaining a diverse population.

educational equity, as "the employment and identification of procedures and strategies that may be avant-garde or non-traditional, yet will enable people who are non-mainstream to have equal opportunities." She clearly stated that the country could not attain equity by using the standards that have been used in the past; hence proactive nontraditional behavior is required. She further stated, "equal opportunity and access is having a sensitivity to the population with whom you are involved and finding ways to make them all successful."

One of the goals of Wood University is to attract and retain a high-quality and diverse student population from within and beyond the region. Other strategic goals of Wood University reveal the president's commitment to educational equity. These include: addressing the diverse educational needs of students by offering flexible program options in responsive ways; guiding students to become critical thinkers who are globally aware; and engaging students in the diverse challenges facing the region.

The president of Wood University is dedicated to sustaining a learning environment that encourages all members of the campus community to expand their intellectual, creative, and social horizons. To address these goals,

Wood University has created objectives to address specific strategic goals. In order to attract and retain a high-quality and diverse student population, Wood will use comprehensive long-term and annual enrollment management targets to guide and assess outreach and other recruitment efforts. It will also develop a plan for recruiting and retaining a high-quality and diverse student body and for improving student retention and graduation rates. To address the diverse educational needs of students, Wood will identify the learning needs of both traditional and reentry students and provide full-time undergraduate students with access to courses that will enable them to complete degree requirements in a maximum of four years.

In addition to documenting strategic goals and objectives for her university, the president of Wood University discussed her appointment of a qualified and energetic European-American male as Equal Opportunity Executive Director. She was proud to share that this is one of the most powerful positions on campus, which reports directly to her. What is noteworthy is that a European-American male, while assisting in the guarantee of equity, is still in a powerful position where he can influence structural norms, as Kanter (1993) posits. Many recent appointees to similar positions have been minorities or women, and one wonders whether the same level of power is present, particularly since they are often administrators without faculty tenure. Appointments without academic tenure usually have limited power.

The president from Plains University portrayed her support for affirmative action and educational equity by focusing on increasing the student body and staff/faculty positions from a qualified and representative pool. She suggested that a national pool was needed, especially in states with few minorities, stating "it is important from an educational perspective for us to diversity our population, because our population of underrepresented minorities in-state is lower than 3 percent." To address this issue she has focused energy on a specific strategic goal: to maintain a culturally diverse and inclusive university community.

In order to enrich the student population at Plains University, minorities are recruited from out of state. Thirty-six percent of undergraduate and 30 percent of graduate students are out-of-state residents. The campus has witnessed a modest increase in the minority student population from 9.2 percent in 1995 to 9.5 percent in 1997 and is hoping to reach 12 percent by 2001. The president at Plains is also interested in increasing the number of women faculty and the number of women in administrative and managerial positions. Targets outlined in the Plains strategic plan are to increase the number of women faculty from 22.3 percent to 25 percent between 1998 and 2001, and to increase the number of women in administrative positions from 27.9 percent to 32 percent during the same period of time. The president of Plains stated that affirmative action is crucial and needed to maintain a diverse population.

The president from Lake University indicated that affirmative action "gives people an equal chance" to succeed. On a campus were the student population is 75 percent African-American, 10 percent Hispanic, and 15 percent European-American she views affirmative action and equity as somewhat reversed in light of the demographic profiles of the larger society. Equity is clearly revealed in some of her strategic goals. One goal is to continue to recruit and retain a dedicated, caring, culturally diverse faculty. A second is to improve recruitment, retention, and graduation rates of a culturally and economically diverse student body. For example, Lake University's president envisions the European-American population increasing from 15 to 25 percent within the next decade. Third, in an attempt to link external powers to the university, she invited critical local, state, and federal government officials to her inauguration and other events. Hence, the door is opened for recognition and dialogue enabling the university to have a voice at the city, state, and national levels.

Ravine's president opined that action was more important than classifying or defining terms. She stated actions are needed "to achieve a more harmonious working environment and more harmonious learning environment." Equity on Ravine's campus is faced with what she described as a unique situation. Her state has a large indigenous population and a large number of residents living in rural areas. The strategic plan at Ravine has incorporated both of these populations. One strategic goal focuses on demonstrating consistently how gender, racial, and cultural diversity strengthen an institution; a second strategic goal is providing high quality undergraduate education for traditional and nontraditional students. To accomplish these strategic goals, Ravine plans to hire more full-time administrators, staff and tenure-track faculty from the indigenous population, including a liaison person to serve as special adviser to the president. To become more responsive to the needs of its students and their communities, a third goal is to create collaborative programs and outreach units for rural areas, including national leadership in distance education.

As an urban institution, Granite University's strategic goals include retention and preparing students to live, work, and thrive in the global village. The president of Granite declared that she would "like to provide an environment in which every student, regardless of who he or she was could achieve the success they want to achieve." Her projected outcomes for the 2 years following the interview are to increase community activities on campus, create a positive diverse image of the institution to the larger metropolitan community and the state, and increase enrollment by 5 percent for each of the 2 years.

This examination of the mission statements and strategic plans of five institutions indicate that equity via affirmative action acts as an underpinning of programs and plans. Ivy's strategic plans and revised missions are still underway. Such missions and plans emphasize recruitment of student and faculty, professional retention, and career preparation in diverse areas. The individual perspectives of the women executives reveal how such mission statements and strategic plans are developed. For instance, the president of Granite University states, "You have to find a kind of common conversation that people are interested [in]. As stakeholders you have to show them what it is they have at stake." In essence, finding common ground is a tool in the justification of providing equal opportunity, access, and retention to various populations and demographic groups.

The philosophical or working premises for equity, articulated in strategic plans and mission statements, are borne in the outcomes. Specific equity outcomes include reaching a graduate enrollment with 36 percent derived from out-of-state populations as desired at Plains. Simultaneously, financial resources must be obtained from state legislators, philanthropic bodies, and other external sources. A women's college or a university that is predominantly African-American, Hispanic, or both produce different equity outcomes. Equity in these institutions means ensuring that student bodies include various male students and European-Americans.

In essence, a holistic approach to educational equity, strategic plans, and educational outcomes portends a nexus among plans, policies, and programs within the universities. Simultaneously, the presidents at public institutions maintain constant communications with civic and political leaders in their respective cities and states. This allows for networking and strategizing to create opportunities that will broaden the scope of the individual institution in their thrust toward equity.

Forging University Initiatives and Policies

The commitment and dedication of these women executives contribute to their continuing quest for educational equity via focused and proactive strategic plans and mission statements. Institutional policies initiated under these women presidents have been designed to offset some of the measures implemented at the state and national levels to eliminate or lessen affirmative action. The initiatives of these women executives stem from their critical awareness and continuing examination of the lingering effects of inequities that have an adverse impact on minority and female students, faculty, and administrators. Addressing these discrepancies guides their commitment to change and results in policy and programmatic initiatives to improve the climates at their universities. The women executives are forging new university initiatives for equity in the twenty-first century. As the president of Wood University stated, "Institutions have to change to be successful with achieving the kind of equity that we want, the kind of affluence that we want, the kind of [cultural] valuing of cultural diversity that we want."

Lake University, for example, has initiated policies to raise the academic standards for incoming students. It is anticipated that this new policy will increase retention rates for a university with a relatively open-door admissions procedures. Raising the entry standards should enable matriculants to participate fully in a more rigorous academic curriculum. The equity result: students graduate with skills and expertise to enter the competitive labor market, which means they are not handicapped by negative stereotypes as they enter or change professional careers, as Biernet and Kobrynowicz (1997) would explicate. At Lake, such policies are designed also to increase the percentages of European-American matriculants at this de facto minority university which, in turn, means enhancing cultural diversity for the student population and curriculum. It may be asserted that such measures are forms of affirmative action in so far as they are positive actions to increase the European-American populace yet not decrease options for African-Americans and Latinos.

Another example of initiating equity through policy alternatives is that of Ravine's president in providing recruitment outreach and a high-quality resident education for the large indigenous resident population. Commitment is to increasing the percentages of students, faculty, and administrators from the native demographic. This policy is expected to make indigenous students comfortable in the university community and offer role models and mentors of the same race. Attempting to achieve this same type of equity result is witnessed via a different policy format at Granite University, where historically European immigrants entered this public urban university along with contemporary American minority groups. At Granite, despite efforts of the city council and state legislators to tighten funding for academic development options for students requiring assistance, the president continually advocates open admission policies and appropriate funding for students with diverse academic abilities. The demographic, political, and civic realities of the state and urban milieu, in essence, impact university executive policy initiatives to achieve and maintain equity.

Plains University, interested in maintaining a culturally diverse and inclusive university community, is taking proactive steps to increase the number of minority students. In a state with a low minority population (3 percent), the president of Plains has established a strong recruiting effort to attract minority students from out of state. The recruiting efforts affect both the undergraduate and graduate populations and allow Plains to maintain a quality academic environment. Minorities and women are being sought for faculty and administrative positions. Seeking only the most qualified applicants, Plains has implemented an aggressive search procedure that will ensure that everyone qualified will be considered during faculty and administrative selection process.

As we approach the new millennium, it is the role of university presidents to recognize that they are intellectual stewards and proactive leaders for the rapidly evolving university and broader community. The presidents in this study continually articulated that equity and diversity issues are critical to this role. Recognizing the benefits of diversity for all members of the university community and of the society, these women presidents are maximizing and integrating various dimensions of diversity affecting student, faculty and administrative composition. They are creating more inclusive curriculums and structuring and continuing dialogue across racial and ethnic lines. The respondents continue to advance concrete plans and programs at their respective institutions to ensure educational equity.

Despite resistant social and political climates, continued discourse and action will be a primary means to ensure educational equity in the academies of American higher education. Based on their own professional experiences in higher education, the six women presidents interviewed for this study clearly believe that affirmative action is a legitimate and effective means of achieving equity, as exemplified by the plans, policies and initiatives that they have undertaken at their respective institutions.

In conclusion—to paraphrase Connerly's queries cited at the beginning of this chapter—absent affirmative action as a form of equity, minorities, and women students and faculty would not be integral parts of the university scene.

Note

1. An analysis of protocol questions 1–7 appeared in a 1999 article by Beverly Lindsay, "Women Chief Executives and Their Approaches Towards Equity in American Universities," in the British journal, *Comparative Education*.

References

American Association of University Professors. (1999). Diversity & affirmative action in higher education. Retrieved July 1999 from the World Wide Web: http://www.aaup.org/aaintro.htm.

American Council on Education. (1998). *Status report on minorities in higher education.* Washington, DC: American Council on Education.

American Council on Education. (1999). *Making the case for affirmative action in higher education.* Washington, DC: American Council on Education.

American Educational Research Association. (1999). *Compelling interest: Examining the evidence on racial dynamics in higher education. A report of the AERA panel on racial dynamics in colleges and universities.* The American Educational Research Association: Washington, D.C.

Bellas, Marcia L. (1994). Comparable worth in academia: The effects on faculty salaries of the sex composition and labor-market conditions of academic disciplines. *American Sociological Review, 59,* 807–821.

Benjamin, Lois (1997). (Ed.). *Black women and the academy: Promises and perils.* Gainesville, FL: University Press of Florida.

Bentley, Richard J., & Blackburn, Robert T. (1992, Summer). Two decades of gains for female faculty? *Teachers College Record, 93*(14), 697–709.

Biernet, Monica, & Kobrynowicz, Diane (1997). Gender and race-based standards of competence: Lower minimum standards but higher ability standards for devalued groups. *Journal of Personality and Social Psychology, 72,* 544–557.

Chilwniak, Luba. (1997). Higher education leadership: Analyzing the gender gap, *ASHE-ERIC Higher Education Report, 25*(4), Washington DC: The George Washington University Graduate School of Education and Human Development.

Chrisler, Jean C., Herr, Linda, & Murstein, Nelly K. (1998). Women as faculty leaders. In Lynn H. Collins, Jean C. Chrisler, & Kathryn Quina, (Eds.), *Career strategies for women in academe: Arming Athena* (pp. 189–245). Thousand Oaks, CA: Sage Publications.

Christiansen, Martha D., Macagno-Shang, Laura, Staley, Kathleen H., Stamler, Virginia L., & Johnson, Mary. (1989). Perceptions of the work environment and implications for women's career choice: A survey of university faculty women. *Career Development Quarterly, 38,* 57–64.

Collins, Lynn H., Chrisler, Jean C., & Quina, Kathryn (Eds.). (1998). *Career strategies for women in academe: Arming Athena.* Thousand Oaks, CA: Sage Publications.

Connerly, Ward. (1998, April). Speech given to The Young Americans for Freedom, The Pennsylvania State University.

Cox, Taylor H. (1993). *Cultural diversity in organizations: Theory, research & practice.* San Francisco: Berrett-Koehler.

Daniel, Elnora. (1997). African-American nursing administrators in the academy: Breaking the glass ceiling. In Lois Benjamin (Ed.), *Black women and the academy: Promises and perils* (pp. 3–22). Gainesville, FL: University Press of Florida.

DeFleur, Lois B. (1992, Winter). Intellectual leadership: A president's perspective. *Educational Record,* 46–49.

Dresher, George F., & Ash, Ronald A. (1990). A comparative study of mentoring among men and women in managerial, professional and technical positions. *Journal of Applied Psychology, 75,* 539–546.

Eberspacher, Jinger, & Sisler, Grovalynn. (1988). Mentor relationships in academic administration. *Initiatives, 51*(4), 27–32.

Flawn Peter. (1990). *A primer for university presidents: Managing the modern university.* Austin: University of Texas Press.

Fletcher, Michael A. (1998, September 19). President accepts report on race. *The Washington Post*, p. A8.

Glazer, Judith S. (1997) *Affirmative action in higher education: Critical national and regional perspectives.* Panel conducted at the annual meeting of the American Educational Research Association, Chicago, Illinois.

Gorena, Minerva. (1996). *Hispanic women in higher education administration: Factors that positively influence or hinder advancement to leadership positions.* Paper presented at the Annual Meeting of the American Educational Research Association, New York, 8–12, April 1996.

Hacker, Andrew. (1992). *Two nations: Black and white, separate, hostile, unequal.* New York: Charles Scribner's Sons.

Hanna, Charlotte. (1988, July/August). The organizational context for affirmative action for women faculty. *Journal of Higher Education, 59*(4).

Hartman, Mary S. (Ed.). (1999). *Talking leadership: Conversations with powerful women.* New Brunswick, NJ: Rutgers University Press.

Kanter, Rosabeth M. (1993). *Men and women in the corporation* (2nd ed.). New York: Basic Books.

King, D. K. (1990). Multiple jeopardy, multiple consciousness the context of black feminist ideology. In Micheline Malson, E. Boyi, J. F. O'Barr, & M. Wyer (Eds.), *Black women in America: Social science perspectives* (pp. 77–92). Chicago: University of Chicago Press.

Kram, Kathy E. (1988). *Mentoring at work: Developmental relationships in organizational life.* Lanham, MD: University Press of America.

Lindsay, Beverly. (1980). *Comparative perspectives of third world women: The impact of race, sex, and class.* New York: Praeger.

Lindsay, Beverly. (1997). Surviving the middle passage: the absent legacy of African American women education deans? In Louis A. Castenell & Jill M. Tarule (Eds.), *The minority voice in educational reform: An analysis by minority and women college of education deans* (pp. 3–37). Greenwich: Ablex.

Lindsay, Beverly. (1999). Women chief executives and their approaches towards equity in American universities. *Comparative Education, 35*(2) 187–199.

National Center for Education Statistics. (1992). *Digest of education statistics: 1992* (GPO No065-000-00532-8). Washington, DC: U.S. Government Printing Office.

National Center for Education Statistics (NCES). (1996). Degrees and other awards conferred by institutions of higher education: 1993–1994. Retrieved July 1999 from the World Wide Web: gopher://gopher.ed.gov: 10000/00/publications/postsec/ipeds/completions/94edtabc.

North, Joan D. (1991). Strangers in a strange land: Women in higher education administration. *Initiatives, 54,* 43–53.

Quina, Kathryn, Cotter, Maureen, & Romenesko, Kim. (1998). In Lynn H. Collins, Jean C. Chrisler, & Kathryn Quina (Eds.), *Career strategies for women in academe: Arming Athena* (pp. 215–245). Thousand Oaks, CA: Sage Publications.

Sandler, Bernice R. (1986). The campus climate revisited: Chilly for women faculty, administrators, and graduate students. In Judith S. Glazer, Estela M. Bensimon & Barbara K. Townsend (Eds.), *Women in Higher Education: A Feminist Perspective* (pp. 175–199). Needham Heights, MA: Ginn Press.

Scandura, Terri, A. (1992). Mentorship and career mobility: An empirical investigation. *Journal of Organizational Behavior, 12,* 1–6.

Sosik, John J., & Godshalk, Veronica M. (in press). Women mentors may be better role models, but men are vital to career advancement. *Journal of Vocational Behavior.*

Sosik, John J., & Godshalk, Veronica M. (2000). The role of gender in mentoring: Implications for diversified and homogenous mentoring relationships. *Journal of Vocational Behavior, 57*(1), 102–122. Retrieved August, 2000 from the World Wide Web: http://www.apnet.com/www/journal/vb.htm.

Turner, Caroline, & Myers, Samuel L. (1999). *Faculty of color in academe: Bittersweet success.* Boston: Allyn and Bacon.

Twale, Darla J., & Shannon, David M. (1996). Gender differences among faculty in campus governance: Nature of involvement, satisfaction, and power. *Initiatives, 57*(4), 11–19.

U.S. Bureau of Census. (1996). *Census briefs* (GPO No. 0146-F-04; SuDocs No. C3.205/10). Washington, DC: U.S. Government Printing Office.

U.S. Department of Labor. (1998). *Bulletin 2307: Employment situation summary* (GPO No. 0768-T; SuDocs No. L2.53/2). Washington, DC: U.S. Government Printing Office.

Welch, Lynne B. (Ed.). (1992). *Perspectives on minority women in higher education.* New York: Praeger.

West, Cornel. (1993). *Race matters.* Boston: Beacon Press.

Wilson, John K. (1996). The myth of reverse discrimination in higher education. *Journal of Blacks in Higher Education, 10,* 88–93.

Civil Society's Cross-National Response to Affirmative Action

MAXINE THOMAS

Many of the world's nations and their institutions are confronting the issue of how to incorporate diversity into their societies while maintaining overall equity. In the process, governments must be proactive in the steps they take to ensure that changes in population demographics do not unduly injure minority members. Recognizing that there are benefits to be derived from the richness that diverse people bring to a society, few nations can escape facing such issues, and higher education has often been the battleground for conflicts surrounding these issues. While nations seek to resolve these issues by a variety of means, many have developed steps to move affirmatively toward resolving the differences between minorities and nonminorities.

Affirmative action in higher education continues to be a hotly debated issue in any nation that allows such debate. While this volume looks at affirmative action in higher education mainly in a national American context, this particular chapter compares four cross-national examples of affirmative action programs that seek to deal with the interaction between minorities and nonminorities or to redress gender inequality in higher education. One section of this chapter will consider programs that provide support preferences, aid, and other mechanisms to address the needs of minorities and women in society. These programs will be grouped under the general umbrella of affirmative action, although such programs are called by various other names outside the United States. Another section will look at the constitutional and legislative bases for such programs, the contents of the programs, and the results of the implementation of these programs.

The common questions and issues that colleges and universities face in these programs and the issues they raise in each culture will also be considered. The culture of a nation plays a much more important role in the success or failure of affirmative action than one might imagine. This factor will also be considered. The last section will consider thoughts on the implications these programs have for the future of the nations, higher education, and our global civil society.

Affirmative action as defined in this chapter is any program that seeks to take steps aimed at enhancing opportunities for a protected group. The benefits of affirmative action have traditionally been attributed to the belief that preferences are a way of compensating for losses or burdens suffered by people who fit within the definition of the class (Thomas, 1998; Anderson, 1999).

Affirmative Action: The United States Experiment

The term *affirmative action* first appeared in the United States, in an executive order signed by President John F. Kennedy. Kennedy's Executive Order 10925 forbade federal government contractors from discriminating on the basis of race, creed, color, or national origin and required all government contractors and subcontractors to take affirmative action to expand opportunities for minorities. But it was President Lyndon Johnson's implementation of affirmative action and President Richard Nixon's requirement of goals and timetables in affirmative action plans that are seen by most Americans as the beginning of America's affirmative action experiment (Executive Orders 11256 and 11375).

This experiment grew out of the Civil Rights Act of 1964. After a particularly fractious decade in the United States where the nation grappled with the different treatment suffered by minority members and women, the United States Congress passed a package of legislation that focused on reparation for losses suffered by minorities and women. While these laws sought to require equal treatment regardless of race or gender, it was soon realized that simply not discriminating in the future would not change the relative position of those who had been discriminated against in the past.

The affirmative action that grew out of the Civil Rights movement of the early 1960s was, like the relevant executive orders and laws themselves, controversial from the start. It required federal contractors to take affirmative steps to ensure that applicants were employed without regard to race, ethnicity, or sex. These orders encompassed upgrading, demoting, transferring, laying off, terminating, and changing rates of pay for employees. Other forms of compensation, selection criteria, training, and apprenticeships also came under scrutiny. Affirmative action in the United States also required the establishment of goals for compliance with the executive orders. In effect, the orders sought to level the employment playing field for people from protected classes. As a means of redressing discrimination complaints, the agencies given authority to review claims against government contractors (the Equal Employment Opportunity Commission, the Department of Labor, and other agencies) often expanded the scope of complaint-based investigations. These agencies sometimes required employers to develop and implement affirmative action plans as a means of eliminating discrimination.

Public and some private colleges and universities came within the executive orders' purview because of federal grants for university research and government support of financial aid to students who attended these institutions. Later legislation, including Title IX of the Education Amendments of 1972, specifically focused on gender inequality. By the beginning of the 1970s, the courts became the venue for testing the limits of what affirmative action meant in both employment and education in the United States. Here, too, there was controversy.

A major blow to affirmative action in university admissions was dealt by the court in *Regents of University of California v. Bakke*. Allan Bakke applied to the University of California Medical School and was denied admission. He charged that the school was using an unconstitutional race-based admissions criterion and argued that had he been a member of a minority group, he would have been admitted. The *Bakke* court held that the university's policy of setting aside a fixed number of slots for minority applicants to the University of California Medical School was unconstitutional. While the case did not prohibit affirmative action programs and clearly endorsed the practice of using race as one of a number of factors in choosing among equally qualified applicants, the court allowed affirmative action only to remedy discrimination in the school's own past practices. The court did not allow a more societal remediation program. The University of California did not admit to nor did it prove that it had a pattern or history of discrimination against minority applicants who applied to their program. Without such a demonstration, the court concluded that the program adopted by the University of California was unlawful. But the decision itself was less clear. The Supreme Court split into two groups in its decision, with Justice Powell casting the swing vote, striking down the admissions program.

The Fourteenth Amendment of the United States Constitution was in contradiction to the legislative and executive order base of affirmative action in the United States. The Equal Protection Clause of that amendment guarantees equal protection of the law. This provision has been used both in support of and in opposition to affirmative action plans (U.S. Constitution Amendment XIV). To protect this guarantee while recognizing the need for special measures in certain circumstances, the U.S. Supreme Court developed different levels of analysis based on the category of the classification. Racial classifications were subject to the highest level of analysis—that is, strict scrutiny that require programs to be narrowly tailored to achieve a compelling state interest. But U.S. courts and, in fact, the U.S. Supreme Court itself, have split on the appropriate analysis for affirmative action plans. While it was Justice Powell's decision that generally guided development of affirmative action plans, after *Bakke* there was much confusion over the appropriate test to use in evaluating the constitutionality of an affirmative action plan.

By the late 1970s many Americans were confused about the status of affirmative action. While the courts focused on whether colleges and universities had engaged in a pattern or practice of past discrimination against minorities, schools were unwilling to admit that they had in fact been a part of such patterns of past discrimination. Many affirmative action plans included goals and timetables with numbers for defining how many minority students, professors, and other staff the college projected it would add to its rolls in the future. Some minority groups pointed to the failure to reach these goals as evidence that the school was not making appropriate progress toward equality. Other groups pointed to the goals as hard and fast number requirements that resulted in hiring or admitting unqualified minority group members. This sparked a larger debate on goals and quotas and further chipped away at the level of support for affirmative action.

The effectiveness of affirmative action waned in the 1980s. A number of other courts raised questions about what was and was not permissible in an affirmative action program. The courts struck down plans that were implemented to provide minority role models for minority students in *Wygant v. Jackson Board of Education*. The resultant layoff of more senior white employees was at issue. The court could find nothing in such an action that corrected past wrongdoing on the part of the school board and, therefore, held the purpose unconstitutional. Here again the *Bakke* court's notion of correcting past patterns and practices was the impediment to affirmative action, as the court sought a connection between past wrongdoing and the program implemented to eliminate the past wrongdoing. In the 1990s, the *Hopwood* decision in the state of Texas found a law school affirmative action plan unlawful (*Hopwood v. Texas*, 1996). The plan benefited African-American and Mexican applicants but was detrimental to white students. The court concluded the stated purpose was too broad and, therefore, unconstitutional. At this point the court seemed to have dealt the final blow to affirmative action.

Ultimately, it was Americans themselves who had begun to tire of what many deemed to be preferences. While many Americans saw affirmative action as a necessity for correcting the enduring effects of past harms, there were, at the outset, many questions. Some Americans wondered how long the preferences were to last. Others were concerned about whether some who had not suffered, even though a member of the defined class, should still benefit from the preferences allowed by the executive orders. Nagging concerns centered on the true beneficiaries of affirmative action programs. Many complained that wealthy Blacks and women were major beneficiaries and that this was not fair. Others questioned the inherent discriminatory effect of affirmative action plans. Even the confusion found in the courts was evidence to some that affirmative action was a candidate for dismantling.

In the end it was the American culture that inhibited affirmative action's success. Some Americans saw affirmative action as a zero-sum game. In conversations with Americans, it was clear that Blacks and whites often saw the matter differently (*USA Today*, 1995). Even within racial groups, there were differing opinions. With no way to resolve the confusion and the unfairness, many resorted to the ballot box, and popular state initiatives rolled back affirmative action. California was the first to get such a rollback measure on the ballot; after a bitter and divisive battle, the state of California passed Proposition 209 in 1996. This provision prohibited affirmative action in state employment, education, and contracting. The state of Washington took similar action in 1998, when it passed Initiative 200 banning affirmative action in that state. Through these various means, Texas, California, Washington state and others began to chip away at what many saw as the stranglehold of affirmative action on education and employment benefits in the United States. By the turn of the century, Americans were ambivalent about affirmative action. Polls showed that Americans supported it in principle but were divided on how and whether current mechanisms were effective or in need of change. There were also considerable differences among Americans on how to define affirmative action.

Responses to charges of reverse discrimination resulted in a legal policy of nondiscrimination with many remaining questions about the actuality and prevalence of continuing practices of discrimination. States like California and Washington made affirmative action unlawful; but there are continuing concerns about what effect this will have, not only on applicants to colleges and universities, but also on society as a whole. In both states, minority admissions to public universities dropped dramatically after passage of the nondiscrimination provisions.

Given the state of the U.S. experiment with affirmative action, it is instructive to observe how other countries have addressed similar issues. A number of countries have struggled with affirmative action in higher education. Some enacted statutes, regulations, or constitutional provisions that mandate or allowed affirmative action–like treatment for defined classes of people (e.g., South Africa). These provisions require nondiscrimination; some go further and allow positive or compensatory action in favor of people who are members of a protected class. Positive action works toward the goal of creating equal opportunities in the workplace. It might include funding for child care, flexible hours for working women, and stronger protection against sexual harassment. Positive action, like affirmative action, attempts to provide special treatment to ameliorate past discrimination. Like affirmative action, positive action is often challenged as reverse discrimination (e.g., Sweden). Many nations use positive action to implement true gender-neutral legislation. Others use it to address ethnic conflicts. The next section of this chapter will look at the international context of affirmative or positive action in three additional nations. It will consider various responses to ethnic, racial, and gender differences in higher education in these nations.

Postapartheid South Africa Addresses Diversity

Perhaps nowhere is affirmative action more central to the future of a nation than it is in South Africa. Defined as additional steps to allow those who have been historically disadvantaged to derive the full benefit from an equitable environment, affirmative action in South Africa attempts to speed up the creation of a democratic society. Here, too, the goal is parity. The beneficiaries of affirmative action in South Africa include Blacks, Africans, colored people, Asians, women, and the disabled.

During apartheid, Blacks were not permitted to attend certain universities. While there were universities Blacks could attend, these institutions were generally inferior. With the end of apartheid, the deficiencies in education for Blacks became apparent. South Africa then embarked on its own version of affirmative action. As in the United States, however, the use of race-conscious affirmative action measures to achieve equality has been controversial. The South African constitution differs from that of the United States in that it expressly permits the use of "measures designed to protect or advance persons or categories of persons, disadvantaged by unfair discrimination" (South Africa Constitution, 1996, Ch. 2, 9(2)). In South Africa the need to establish a past practice of discrimination is unnecessary. South Africans admit that under the apartheid system, many groups were deliberately and systematically excluded from meaningful participation in the country's economy. It is the need to heal this traditional rift that supports affirmative action as a means to eliminate the effects of past discrimination. The government's task, then, is to reincorporate people from previously disadvantaged groups. Affirmative action is a step toward accomplishing that.

The South African constitution expressly reserves to the government the power to limit rights (South Africa Constitution, 1996, Ch. 2, 36). While acknowledging that discrimination based on race is a breach of the principle of equality, the constitutional court will nonetheless uphold such discrimination if it is designed to protect or advance persons, or categories of persons, disadvantaged by unfair discrimination. The court has construed unfair discrimination to mean unreasonable discrimination. Affirmative action programs can be seen as constituting reasonable discrimination, but it is up to the courts to determine this.

While South Africa's constitution supports the use of affirmative action programs, this is not without difficulties. Affirmative action in South Africa has little to do with equal opportunity as espoused in the United States. It is concerned with transforming an economy that once barred 75 percent of its population from a meaningful role (Ford, 1996). South Africa seeks to achieve equality, and equality means the full and equal enjoyment of all rights and freedoms. Measures to protect or advance persons disadvantaged by unfair discrimination may be taken to that end; "the framers of the Constitution did not envisage affirmative action as a derogation from the right to equality, but as part and parcel of the right to equality" (Madala, 1999).

The South African constitution provides that "Everyone shall enjoy all universally accepted fundamental rights, freedoms, and civil liberties which shall be provided for and protected by entrenched and justifiable provisions in the Constitution." The constitution also ensures "equality of all before the law as an equitable legal process." But while the government wants to ensure equality of all citizens, it will not do so at the expense of measures designed to alleviate the effects of past discrimination. Legal analysis, then, often turns on a definition of "effects of past discrimination."

Equality before the law includes laws, programs, or activities that have as their objective the amelioration of the conditions of the disadvantaged, including those disadvantaged on the grounds of race, color, or gender. In 1995, the Labor Relations Act began to take a serious look at inequality in the South African workplace. The act imposed a 4 percent tax on company payrolls to finance training programs for Black workers. The Department of Home Affairs also implemented programs focused on the transition from apartheid. In higher education, these programs included set-aside programs that assisted Blacks, Africans, coloreds, and Asians. New constitutional provisions also resulted in the creation of several commissions focused on efforts to protect fundamental rights for all of South Africa's citizens.

As in the United States, affirmative action programs in South Africa are being met with resistance by many who believe that these programs are simply "neoapartheid." South African courts are also in the fray, with cases like *Motola and Another v. University of Natal*, where the South African Supreme Court upheld an affirmative action program that set aside a specific number of seats in the medical school based on race.

Certainly no one would say that affirmative action has ended discrimination in South Africa, and some have argued that moving to affirmative action is a step backward. Professor Ronald Griffin of Washburn University suggests that affirmative action ignores the fact that globally, whites are the minorities (Griffin, 1998). Economics will continue to skew this, Griffin suggests, due to control issues. Griffin asks whether Anglo-immigrant minority whites in South Africa will impose on themselves a cost to help others approach equality with them. He says the answer is yes if political equality is involved, but it is less clear in economic and social equality. Here the culture and the economy carry great weight.

South Africans worry aloud about the influence of affirmative action on the business culture, suggesting that affirmative action is the single most important issue facing business in South Africa and that the success of affirmative action depends on a change in the culture of the business community. Some suggest that in this context, most South African women accept subordination and do not feel a sense of oppression, even though in reality they might very well be oppressed. There are also concerns among African women that African men need jobs more than the women do (Meer, 1992).

Jan Visagie of Potchelstroom University in South Africa says changes in South Africa's business culture will be even more difficult due to the dynamic relationship between the many different cultures that make up South Africa. When you add in employee and employer behaviors and lack of clarity in definitions within the legislation (e.g., there is no definition of "effects of past discrimination"), the changes are often at odds with the very entrepreneurial culture itself.

In higher education the fear is of slipping standards and loss of status on the international stage. Medical school deans were outraged at suggestions that the government might cut their subsidies if the schools did not meet racial admission quotas. The familiar cry is that those admitted under such programs are less capable (Bisseker, 1998).

South Africa need only look to the United States to realize that waiting on the interpretations of the courts will not ensure cultural change. Other examples, however, suggest that even in societies where governments are most explicit about what affirmative action is and means, cultural change is still not easy. For that inquiry China offers a good example.

China's Consideration of Preference

Article 5 of Chapter I in the "General Provisions" of the Republic of China's Constitution provides that "There shall be complete equality among the various ethnic groups in the Republic of China." Chapter II, "Rights and Duties of the People," goes on to provide in Article 7 that "All citizens of the Republic of China, irrespective of sex, religion, ethnic origin, class, or party affiliation, shall be equal before the law." Article 10 of the "Additional Articles" of the Constitution of the Republic of China provides that "The State shall protect the dignity of women, safeguard their personal safety, and further substantive gender equality." Further,

> The State shall, in accordance with the will of the ethnic groups, safeguard the status and political participation of the aborigines. The State shall also guarantee and provide assistance and encouragement for aboriginal education, culture, transportation, water conservation, health and medical care, economic activity, land and social welfare, measures for which shall be established by law.

Coincident with the Fourth World Conference on Women in 1995, the State Council of the People's Republic of China set out a program of development for women for the period of 1995–2000. Following the Conference, there were additional activities similarly aimed. But the question in all of this is—What is the result?

Based on this writer's direct observations and participation in various endeavors within China, the Chinese government continues to profess the national importance of development and progress toward equality for women. The government publicizes its many activities toward that end through working groups on women and children and national campaigns. As is the case in most other countries, however, little has changed in the lives of most Chinese women.

While even less is known about the actual policies toward minorities in China, my interviews with Chinese scholars revealed the existence of a program closely analogous to affirmative action in the United States. Responsive to the sensitive cultural and political problems involved in asserting control over Tibet in 1951, the People's Republic of China maintains control of Tibet while providing for Tibetan cultural and sociopolitical autonomy (Coye, Livingston, & Highland, 1983; Chu, 1983). An affirmative action–like plan was created whereby top Chinese universities would be open to Tibetan students on preferred terms, in spite of Tibetans' insistence that they did not want "help" from the students of the Cultural Revolution, preferring to receive whatever help they needed from their own communities. Under the plan, quotas are set at Chinese universities for Tibetans and for those from other provinces along China's borders and in developing areas. Students from these areas are admitted into universities despite receiving lower test scores than other nonminority applicants, though there is often a requirement that such affirmative action admittees return home to serve in their communities for some period of time. There is also affirmative action in government employment for minorities and other benefits, such as exclusion from China's one-child policy.

While the Chinese seem to see such programs as necessary, in individual conversations people clearly acknowledged that the effect of the preference was that they themselves may be excluded from admission to some of the more prestigious universities or might miss out on preferred employment. Beneficiaries of the program, as in the United States, are also aware of the potential stigma that attaches to being known to be a part of a quota. Notions of second-class professionals and being thought of as underachievers are also prevalent.

China is now benefiting from and suffering under the fastest economic growth rate on earth. The benefits, however, are not equally distributed. As the economic disparities widen, it is not clear whether there will be continued support for affirmative action–like programs.

A glimpse into how this might affect Mainland China can perhaps be seen through Hong Kong. New legislation aimed at curbing sex discrimination modified somewhat employers' ability to operate in a laissez-faire environment in Hong Kong. While the government still purports to maintain a basically free-enterprise market system with minimal government intervention, employment discrimination legislation is seen as an impediment to effective operation of the market economy. Following a campaign that exposed the particularly blatant nature of sex discrimination in Hong Kong, 1995's first antidiscrimination laws were passed over the vigorous objection of business interests. While the legislation also applies to education, housing, and the provision of goods and services, the real impact is expected to be on employment. Credit for the new law, if there is any, should be given to the institutions of civil society in Hong Kong that uncovered the previous behaviors. But actual change in and acceptance by the business culture is less clear. Grudging acceptance of affirmative action by Hong Kong's business community does not bode well for the Mainland in its gender or minority programs. Business is a strong driver of Chinese society in these times of economic boom. Perhaps there is something of a lesson in a nation that prides itself in gender equality.

Sweden and Gender Equality

Sweden is often touted as one of the forward-thinking nations when it comes to gender equity. Like the United States, Sweden attempts to mandate equal treatment based on gender. The Swedish policy seeks to protect the ability of both men and women to achieve economic and educational independence. It does not require that people participate in all aspects of society, but it does mandate that any who wish to participate must be allowed to do so based on their capabilities and not on their gender (Swedish Institute, 1997).

Article 16 of Chapter 1 of the "Basic Principles" provides that "No Act of law or other statutory instrument may entail the discrimination of any citizen on grounds of sex, unless the relevant provision forms part of efforts to bring about equality between men and women or relates to compulsory military service or any corresponding compulsory national service."

As in the United States, the greatest strides in achieving this equality were made in the 1960s and 1970s. In both countries, although due to different reasons, these decades brought economic expansion. Because of that expansion, there was a need for more women in the workforce. In Sweden this economic expansion was based largely on reforms enacted in social, family and economic policy and in the activities of the women's reform movement. The Minister for Equality was given the major responsibility for such policies, but other ministers also have responsibility within their own ministries for equality-related issues. Legislative regulation of equality is found in "The Act on Equality between Men and Women at Work." The act promotes equal rights for men and women with respect to employment, working conditions, and opportunities for personal development at work. While stopping short of affirmative action requirements, the act does obligate an employer to take active steps to promote equality at the workplace.

Unlike the affirmative action policy in the United States, the focus of the Swedish statute is on equality with no requirement that the employer try to compensate for effects of past discrimination. But Sweden has set for itself a higher goal than simple nondiscrimination. It seeks to achieve an even distribution of power and influence between men and women. In effect, then, it seeks a result of true equality as opposed to just nondiscrimination. It hopes for equal power and influence between the genders. But while it has broadened representation by women in levels of government, that breadth is mainly in positions of relatively less power and influence.

The Swedish example suggests that radical change in the distribution of work and family responsibilities alone is insufficient to change discriminatory work patterns. Even a strong governmental commitment to individual responsibility and gender equality is not enough. Despite a generous array of family support policies and public policy that favors gender neutrality, Sweden still has a high degree of gender segregation in the workforce.

Sweden is also grappling with the effects of gender inequality in education. One of the initiatives taken in this area has been the creation of professorships and fellowships for women. This more closely parallels affirmative action in the United States and, unfortunately, with the same poor results. Higher education has clearly not been the bridge to broader equality in Swedish society. In effect, Sweden has engaged in a concerted effort toward equality for the last 30 years. While their focus has been equality, their result, like that in the United States, South Africa, and China, has largely been that women are still employed in occupations that are less well paid than those of men. While pay differentials between the sexes for the same work in Sweden are smaller, they still exist. Sweden has one of the world's most equal distributions of income, but wage levels of women still lag behind those for men. Some have suggested that gender-specific affirmative action is not really what is needed in Sweden, concluding that the needs of mothers and fathers are distinctly different. Here again, cultural norms die hard.

Toward a More Global View: Affirmative Action as a Civil Society Issue

Despite constitutional provisions and government orders, the United States, South Africa, Sweden, and China all still have serious minority issues, gender issues, or both to be addressed. Each now hears concerns about reverse discrimination. While there are similarities across the four cultures, there are very real differences in what gave rise to the need for affirmative action in each case and in what amounts to appropriate cultural responses. In the final analysis, if there is anything that might be universal in addressing affirmative action, it is the fact that it must be addressed by the very people who make up the host culture. By encouraging dialogue between and among the citizens who must, ultimately, endorse any resolution, civil society provides a way of doing this.

Civil society is the space in communities where people come together to do public work. It is the larger conversation where people in a community make key decisions about what the community is to be or how it is to operate. It acknowledges and incorporates changing cultural norms. In civil society, individuals are engaged in what is going on in the community and take the responsibility to act (Thomas, 1998).

By engaging in dialogue on deeply held issues, members of civil society guide democracy's reinvention of itself. While engaged in such discussion, they may observe the complexities embedded in issues like race and affirmative action. And as people engage in dialogue, they share their fears and consider others' views.

Civil society can be a forum for responding to the developing global concern about equality. Ultimately, it is civil society itself that holds the greatest promise for eliminating discrimination. The patchwork of diverse people in numerous associations, government-to-public efforts, and citizen-to-citizen initiatives must be quilted into civil society. The advantage of civil society over legislated affirmative action is the immediacy of its response to cultural norms: the law is simply an unwieldy mechanism for changing institutionally based conventions. Discrimination inheres throughout institutions, and it is the institutions themselves, not just the practices, that must be changed. Civil society allows for change within institutions by the public that makes up those institutions. While the response may be slightly different in each country, the policies will be reflective of the citizens within the countries that created the policies. And while it may or may not be universal, it will be culturally based within the particular country.

At the end of the 1990s, the W. K. Kellogg Foundation funded a study that considered the status of African-American males in the United States (Young, 1996). This study ended by seeking to rebuild civil society in America's communities. Among the conclusions of the study was that there is a need for civic dialogue between Blacks and whites and within the Black community, that affirmative action is not the ultimate answer. The National Issues Forums and the Study Circles Resource Centers have each produced materials on race and affirmative action that have encouraged dialogue within communities on affirmative action and other racially charged issues. President Clinton created an advisory board on race in 1997, calling on all Americans to "begin a national conversation on race." The Center for Living Democracy tracked the many conversations that were already going on pertaining to race (DuBois, 1997). In a report by the National Issues Forums (NIF) on the future of affirmative action, NIF found that when engaged in discussions about the issue, Americans see the complexities involved (John Doble Research Associates, 1997). But the difficulties they perceive turn, to some extent, on a fear that their own well-being might ultimately be harmed by any actions that follow the dialogues. Affirmative action, like the issue of race itself, is so personal that people ultimately focus on the things they value and the potential impact any change might have on those things (Doble, 1997). What we glean from civil society is that dialogue is central to any effort to address equality.

Civil society is not simply an American fix. It holds promise wherever citizens come together to deliberate about their concerns, even their concerns about affirmative action. Such dialogues can take place in China, in South Africa, or even in Sweden, where much of this early deliberative civil society work began.

Conclusion

In the final analysis, the question about the utility of affirmative action in any society turns on a common concern about persons who have been excluded from the mainstream of the larger society in education and employment. It is often the subject of controversy. The United States is certainly not alone in its effort to address inequality through affirmative action, but legal constructions and the juxtaposition of the concept with constitutional safeguards of equal treatment make affirmative action confusing for Americans. This has led many Americans to fight against affirmative action at the ballot box. While South Africa's historical base may provide a firmer foundation for affirmative action, it is not yet fully tested, and it too is finding a reality that falls short of its goal of reincorporating the previously disadvantaged groups.

The lack of details and the very differences in the nature of the role of government in China make it unclear whether the Chinese experience is indeed similar to that of other nations, but Hong Kong's experience suggests that legislation alone will not be enough. Sweden's experiment seems a much higher contest. Equality in distribution of power and influence seems difficult to accomplish through gender neutrality with only minimal affirmative steps to assist the disadvantaged gender.

Civil Society may offer a culturally based alternative to legislative action in dealing with the affirmative action issue. It is not without risk, however, nor is it a quick fix. Civil society, by its very nature, takes time.

The examples of each of the countries and the approaches advanced herein suggest just how complex this issue is. In the end, our nations continue to become more global, as does civil society. The way one nation addresses inclusion of diverse groups is relevant to others. And while there are no easy answers, perhaps a common civil society will finally engage citizens in the building of equality throughout the global society.

References

Abdelrahman, A. (1999). Affirmative action in the United States and South Africa: Why South Africa should not follow in our footsteps. *New York Law School Journal of International and Comparative Law, 19*, 21.

Anderson, C. (1999). A current perspective: The erosion of affirmative action in university admissions. *Akron Law Review, 32*, 181.

Ashmore, Harry. (1994). *Civil rights and wrongs: A memoir of race and politics 1944–1994*. New York: Pantheon Books.

Bell, Derrick. (1992). *Faces at the bottom of the well: The permanence of racism*. New York: Basic Books.

Bisseker, C. (1998). Times Media Limited (p. 34).

California Proposition 209, codified as Cal. Const. Art. 1, 31.

Canadian Constitution. (Constitution Act, 1982), pt. 1. Canadian Charter of Rights and Freedoms.

Chu, Godwin C., & Hsu, Francis. (Eds.). (1983). *China's new social fabric*. London: Kegan Paul International.

Civil Rights Act of 1964 (42 USCA 2000(e).

Coye, Molly J., Livingston, J., & Highland, J. (1983) *China yesterday and today* (3rd ed.). New York: Bantam.

Dowd, N. (1997). Taxing women: thoughts on a gendered economy: Symposium: A look at equality: Women's, mens, and children's equalities: Some reflections and uncertainties. *Southern California Review of Law and Women's Studies, 6*, 587

DuBois, P. M., & Hutson, J. (1997). *Bridging the racial divide: A report on international dialogue in America*. Hadley, MA: Commonwealth Printing.

Erickson, M., & Byrnes, A. (1999). Hong Kong and the Convention on the Elimination of All Forms of Discrimination Against Women. *Hong Kong Law Journal, 29*, 350–367

Executive Order No. 10925, 3 C.F.R. 448, 450 (1959–63).

Executive Order No. 11246, 3 C.F.R. 339 (1964–65).

Executive Order No. 11375, 3 C.F.R. 684 (1966–70).

Federal Employment Equity Act, S.C. (1995), c. 44.

42 USC Sec. (2000)(e).

Fields, R. (1996). In search of democracy: reconciling majority rule, minority rights, and group rights in South Africa and the United States. *Boston College Third World Law Journal, 16,* 65.

Fisher, G. (1998). Policy, governance and the reconstruction of higher education in South Africa. *Higher Education Policy, 11,* 121–140.

Ford, C. (1996). Challenges and dilemmas of racial and ethnic identity in American and post-Apartheid South African affirmative action. *UCLA Law Review, 43,* 1953.

Franks v. Bowman Transportation Co. S. Ct. 1976.

Fullilove v. Klutznick, 448 U.S. 448 (1980).

Gheorgha, N., & Tanaka, J. (1998). Public policies concerning Roma and Sinti in the OSCE region. Retrieved from the World Wide Web: www.Romaback.htm.

Ginsburg, R. B., & Merritt, D. J. (1999) Lecture: Fifty-first Cardozo Memorial Lecture affirmative action: An international human rights dialogue. *Cardozo Law Review, 21,* 253.

Griffin, Ronald C. (1998). Equality: A comparison of three countries. *Dayton Law Review, 21,* 559.

Hopwood v. Texas, 78 F. 3d, 932, 944 (5th Cir.). cert. Denied, 518 U.S. 1033 (1996).

International Convention on the Elimination of All Forms of Discrimination Against Women, G.A. Res. 34/180, U.N. GAOR, 34th Sess., Supp. No. 46, at, 193, U.N. Doc. A/34/46 (1979).

International Convention on the Elimination of All Forms of Racial Doc. A/ 6014 (1965).

John Doble Research Associates. (1997). *NIF report on the issues 1997: How can we be fair? The future of affirmative action.* Dayton: National Issues Forums Research.

Kay, H. H. (1988). *Text, cases and materials on sex-based discrimination* (3rd ed.). St. Paul, MN: West Publishing.

Johnson, Lyndon B. (1996). To fulfill these rights. In George E. Curry (Ed.), *The affirmative action debate* (pp. 16–24). Reading, MA: Addison-Wesley.

Langston, L. (1997). Affirmative action, a look at South Africa and the United States: A question of pigmentation or leveling the playing field. *American University International Law Review, 13,* 333.

Madala, T. (1999). Affirmative action—A South African perspective. *Southern Methodist University Law Review, 52,* 1539.

Martin, J. (1997). Bound for the promised land: The gendered character of higher education. *Duke Journal of Gender Law and Policy, 4,* 3.

Meer, F. (1992, February). The future for women. *UNESCO Courie,* 30–32.

Meisner, Maurice. (1977). *Mao's China: A history of the People's Republic.* London: Free Press.

Motala and Another v. University of Natal, (1995) (3) BCLR 374 (D).

Petersen C. (1997). Hong Kong's first anti-discrimination laws and their potential impact on the employment market. *Hong Kong Law Journal*, *27*, 324–355.

Regents of the University of California v. Bakke, 438 U.S. 265 (1978).

Sheppard, C. (1998). Equality rights and institutional change: Insights from Canada and the United States. *Arizona Journal of International and Comparative. Law, 15,* 143.

South Africa Constitution, draft (adopted 1996).

Swedish Institute. (1997). Equality between women and men. Retrieved from the World Wide Web: www.equality.htm.

Title IX of the Education Amendments of 1972, as amended.

Thomas, Claire. (1991). *Sex discrimination in a nutshell* (2nd ed.). St. Paul, MN: West Publishing.

Thomas, M. (1998). *Community leadership:1998 annual progress report* (monograph). Indianapolois, IN: National Association for Community Leadership.

Universal Declaration of Human Rights, pmpl. G.A. Res. 217A, U.N. Gaor, 3d Sess., pt. 1 at 71, U.N. Doc. A/810 (1948).

University of California Regents v. Bakke, 438 U.S. 265 (1978).

*USA Today/CNN/*Gallup Poll. (1995, February, March).

U.S. Constitution Amendment XIV, 1, cl. 2.

Visagie, Jan (1999). The influence of affirmative action on SMME culture in South Africa, *Participation & Empowerment: An International Journal*, *7*(6), 148–162.

West, Cornel. (1994). *Race matters.* New York: Vintage Books.

Wygant v. Jackson Board of Education, 476 U.S. 267 (1986).

Young, A., & Austin, B. (1996). Repairing the breach: Report of the National Task Force on African-American men and boys. Dillon, CO: Alpine Guild.

PART V

Toward the Evolution of
Dynamic Policies for Equity

CHAPTER 12

Toward the Evolution of Dynamic Policies for Equity: Emerging Paradigms for Policy Change

BEVERLY LINDSAY, MANUEL J. JUSTIZ,
AND MARILYN C. KAMEEN

Just as the first presidential primary races in the new century were eliminating peripheral candidates, the *Sacramento Bee*'s education columnist, Peter Schrag, analyzed candidate positions and concluded that despite highly publicized issues—school reform and college access—more attention must ultimately be paid to the broader needs of American children (2000). He cited findings from the Up in Poverty Project at University of California, Berkeley, and Yale University, which showed negative effects on children's social growth and school readiness—outcomes forced on them, Schrag added, by totally inappropriate day-care solutions stemming from mothers' departures from welfare programs.

His historical sketch also bears on this chapter's summary analysis:

> It's hard to recall any recent presidential election before 1992, or perhaps even 1996, when every candidate, certainly every Democrat, was expected to have a program to fix the schools. But today that's where the center is. Give the credit, ironically, to Ronald Reagan, George Bush (George I, that is) and other Reagan-era conservatives—Bill Bennett, Chester Finn, Lamar Alexander. With the help of business leaders like IBM chairman Lou Gerstner, they gradually managed to convert not only the issue of economic equity but a whole range of liberally oriented children's issues—health care, welfare, nutrition, preschools, daycare, decent housing, recreational opportunities, inner-city youth and job programs— into a debate focused almost exclusively on education and tougher standards of school reform, emphasizing not resources but outcomes. (Schrag, 2000)

Beginning in 1983 with the publication of *A Nation at Risk*, the report of the National Commission on Excellence in Education, which warned that "we have, in effect, been committing an act of unthinking unilateral educational

275

disarmament," and continuing through the early nineties, when President Bush and a number of business leaders proclaimed a set of national goals to pull the nation's schools out of the swamp of failure and waste in which they were supposedly stuck, we have been subjected to an ongoing barrage about failing schools, inadequate standards and a global economy that rewards only well-educated economic competitors. If we do not shape them up, somebody— Germany and Japan in 1983; Singapore and Taiwan now—will beat our economic brains out.

Such references express similar concerns about how the public university—particularly in key states such as Texas and California—will increase access to an increasingly diverse population (where minorities will shortly become the "majority"), contribute to economic competitiveness in a relentless global economy, and finally, resolve leadership dilemmas about their collective future. Whether stated explicitly or not, eminent sources express unease about the unknown path of twenty-first-century higher education, suggesting that massive change is accelerating, even though most campuses today remain blissfully unprepared for the new challenges. Indeed, we write with a corresponding sense of unease about the powerful forces—social, political, economic, and technological—that will compel not just one, but many responses. With respect, we suggest that too many post-*Hopwood* campuses have simply reacted to legal and social events, without choosing a coherent strategy for the next two decades, let alone 2050.

In a democratic society, according to Duderstadt (1995), "plurality, equal opportunity, and freedom from discrimination should be the foundations on which the University is built. It is more than what we do; it is what we must *be* if we are to call ourselves a truly public university" (1995). He adds that Michigan was the first large campus to admit women in 1869, just one year after the quiet Reconstruction debut of African-Americans. However, moral arguments about diversity have been eclipsed by more pragmatic academic studies, like Dionne and Kean's provocative analysis about a two-tier workforce of massive disparity arriving in less than 15 years. Stating flatly that their work is not a prediction but a "simple extrapolation" of U.S. earning patterns, they emphasize that higher education is more significant than ever in the face of the following "grave danger(s)" (Dionne & Kean, 1996, emphasis added):

- A much larger proportion of the population will fall below the standard of living considered average today.
- The real hourly wages of the average male worker will decline by about 25 percent in comparison to 1970s earnings. For those at the bottom of the wage distribution, hourly earnings will slip by about 44 percent.
- While family incomes in the highest earning bracket will increase by 50 percent, the earnings of the poorest families will decline by about 36 percent from the levels of comparable families in 1976, creating an unprecedented income gap between the nation's rich and poor.

- The proportion of immigrants in the population will increase to 12 percent of the labor force by 2015. Unless immigration policy changes, most of the new immigrants will come from Mexico and Central America, a group with historically low levels of education.
- *College education will not be equally distributed among ethnic/racial groups, creating little chance for underrepresented groups to improve their standard of living. As a result, the educational and economic fault lines in the United States will be drawn increasingly in terms of ethnicity and race.*

Based on this reality, Dr. Orlando Taylor, Dean of the Graduate School at Howard University, advised that inclusiveness is a "major issue of higher education" (2001). He explains that through inclusiveness, institutions of higher education fulfill the ideals of social justice, meet workforce needs, and benefit the national interest while providing a quality learning environment. Within the backdrop of such contemporary socioeconomic and political factors, we return to the several conceptual premises of our volume: legal and economic, interrogation of public and education policies, and university executive initiatives and international perspectives. Examining overall premises of the sections provides frameworks for new paradigms to address the central issue of fairness and equity within the walls of academe and its relationship to national and international spheres.

Legal and Economic Perspectives

The "Legal and Economic Perspectives" section of this volume explores an era filled with recent litigation struggles—not the least of which involve successful assaults on race-based admissions in Texas, California, Washington, Florida, and Michigan. In the first four jurisdictions, a combination of lawsuits, executive orders, and ballot initiatives dismantled the formal affirmative action system that had existed for more than three decades, forcing both legislatures and university administrators to redefine the increasingly competitive college admissions process. And while these painful institutional journeys were taking place, the Washington, D.C.–based Center for Individual Rights filed two class action lawsuits against the University of Michigan's process.

Ida Elizabeth Wilson surveys various relevant cases, building, for example, on Bowen and Bok's landmark "race-sensitive" admissions defense, *The Shape of the River*. However, conflict over how the impending Baby Boom II will include the nation's equally large diversity populations continues unabated. Amid constant media attention about how many African-Americans or Hispanics had been accepted at, say, the University of Texas Law School in the wake of the infamous *Hopwood* case, little scrutiny was given to the bigger picture.

Wilson's penetrating insight of judicial and legal perspectives focuses on student issues vis-à-vis financial aid packages, in particular, while looking extensively at various legal cases which are also highlighted in other chapters, such as those by James Stewart, Reginald Wilson, and Manuel Justiz and Marilyn Kameen. Her perspective is unique in two ways. First, as an attorney, she delves into the legal precedents and a discussion of how various justices of the U.S. Supreme Court have addressed affirmative action issues pertaining to students and financial aid. Second, her chapter focuses on the flexibility of private institutions, such as Duke University, Harvard University, and Columbia University. As an attorney and associate provost at Columbia University, she was constantly exposed to the interplay between federal court decisions and how they play out in select private institutions such as Columbia. Ultimately, her policy and programmatic implications are that select private schools such as Harvard and Columbia will continue to have more flexibility than public institutions. She contends that, after all, how many state or federal agencies really want to do battle with Harvard or Columbia? Yet, these select private institutions are, in fact, able to provide models for other select private and comprehensive public institutions. In this regard, her assertions are buttressed by works by Bowen and Bok, as she herself articulates. Hence, the overall policy issue is the ability of select private institutions to help set an egalitarian tone and be change agents for other institutions. The central policy matter is whether they will actually do so.

In Texas, for example, the legislature adopted a ten percent admissions rule, offering all students in the top 10 percent of their respective Texas high school classes admission to the state's selective public universities. Reginald Wilson cites Bowen's and Bok's doubt that this initiative would provide an effective substitute for race-sensitive admissions policies, but as in all complex public policy debates, there was much more. Texas has more than a thousand school districts generating potential college students, even though the state has suffered from a college graduation rate that does not even begin to meet its twenty-first-century competitive needs. Moreover, little attention was paid to the blunt reality that not all school districts are created equal; even though students may graduate with an "A" average, it does not mean that they are ready to tackle competitive university-level work. Regrettably, many low-performing high schools strongly influence the destinies of the state's burgeoning minority population, even though Texas enjoys a national leadership reputation for its tough accountability standards, including a rigorous standardized testing program.

Equally striking was the general assumption among many that affirmative action was gone, despite Ida Elizabeth Wilson's and Reginald Wilson's lengthy histories of case law that has accrued since passage of the 1964 Civil Rights Act. Indeed, amid larger questions about how to fix the pre-K to K–12 educational pipeline, public campuses in Texas had clearly entered a new era. But Ida Elizabeth Wilson argues that special admissions measures should remain intact "until urban schools do better by Black and brown students, who currently have little chance of first-rate preparation for college." Ultimately, they find hope in broad public support nationwide for diversity in an increasingly multicultural society.

Still, searing questions about race will not depart the academy, as Myers and Turner explain in their new work about how affirmative action has affected faculty of color in what they see as an era of "retrenchment." Particularly in the decade between 1980 and 1990, affirmative action helped to raise the numbers of both minority faculty and students, charting an unprecedented 14.2 percent increase in the representation of African-Americans, Hispanics, American Indians, and Asian-Americans joining tenure-track faculties. They posit without question that young faculty of color confront subtle forms of discrimination in higher-education institutions, adding that many face a "retrenchment" backlash in the post-*Hopwood* era.

Fresh from a 1999 book project, *Faculty of Color in Academe: Bittersweet Success*, the two scholars probe what has been historically a white male bastion "of privilege." For example, white males account for 70 percent of all faculty over 60, but only 39 percent under 30. Applying both quantitative and qualitative data, they attack the now-dated mythology of "unqualified" minority PhDs, arguing that "retrenchment occurs where the threat to white male dominance is greatest." They also confront the perception, expressed by many Latino and African-American professors, that their faculty colleagues believe they were hired because of affirmative action, instead of their own scholarly merit.

Popular belief regarding hostile climates at today's public research universities is examined by Myers and Turner's research. Sometimes minority faculty leave, expressing dissatisfaction. Campus administrators, according to Myers and Turner, respond: "I think we did everything humanly possible." To the vast majority of puzzled parents, students, and general public, the arcane politics of departments are invisible. Yes, students enter programs at the undergraduate and graduate levels to obtain degrees, but they all too often lack any understanding of the subterranean conflicts that mar the surface collegiality of campus faculties—whether a professor applies a quantitative or qualitative methodology, whether newly minted minority PhDs receive realistic mentoring in a specific department's institutionalized pathologies, and more important, whether those same minority scholars receive accurate information about which forms of publishing will receive credit from that department's oversight tenure committee.

James Stewart takes a careful examination of equity vis-à-vis dual systems of higher education with special emphasis on Pennsylvania and select southern states such as Mississippi. What he clearly articulates is that the career and economic life chances of graduates from Historically Black Colleges and universities (HBCUs) are comparable, in many ways, to those from other institutions. What this indicates is that some of the myths pertaining to differential economic outcomes of graduates of Historically Black colleges are not borne out by the facts. In essence, equal funding and resources for HBCUs not only provide economic benefits for African-American graduates, but also enable such graduates to participate more fully in the economic well-being of the state, the region, and indeed the nation. This certainly suggests that desegregation and enhancement policies directed at HBCUs in Pennsylvania and elsewhere should continue.

Interrogation of Public and Education Policies

Education, from the organized clamor of prekindergarten classes to the college diploma, faces a host of major problems—all engaging the public policy structure of our states and the nation. Justiz and Kameen focus on how the reform movement has strengthened accountability in the K–12 pipeline, but that effort has only drawn attention to the massive improvements needed at all levels. However, most elected officials and policy makers now confront the dilemma from common ground: economic prosperity results directly from a rigorous educational system, which is bracing for the largest influx of new students since the fabled post–World War II population explosion more than 50 years ago. At the same time, about 2.5 million new teachers will be needed to staff classrooms. At least a dozen major U.S. cities are competing with one another for scarce school superintendent talent, and the average tenure is down to just over 2 years.

Still, the situation—admittedly fraught with peril—is better than it was a decade ago, before affirmative action became synonymous with attenuated litigation. "Failure is not an option" has already become permanent rhetoric in the public policy discourse; predictably, the alternative is a two-tiered society—characterized by high-wage professions at one end versus a growing base of low-paying, unskilled jobs at the other. Ironically, both California and Texas—the world's 7th- and 11th-largest economies—carry the potential of becoming either wealthy or poor states in America, thanks to the equity dynamic.

Justiz and Kameen also point out that recently filed lawsuits over the accessibility of Advanced Placement courses—generally regarded as a more rigorous gateway to selective college admissions—are but one more variation on legal warfare in the post-*Hopwood* era. Inequity in the K–12 pipeline presage problems for higher education, including underprepared college applicants, a need for remedial education at the postsecondary level, and underrepresentation of minorities on those same college campuses. It will fall to both private and public university leadership to help solve these conflicts, before corresponding leadership cadres in state legislatures or business begin to recommend substantive changes that may alter the faculty-centered structure of today's campus forever.

Because a two-tiered society basically undermines the projected knowledge society of our immediate future in which wealth constantly gravitates to new forms of knowledge and citizens will constantly upgrade their abilities, Justiz and Kameen's chapter carries strong implications for policy makers. No longer will universities be held to one geographical location—technology has empowered the campus to become truly global at a time when lifetime learning will extend in a seamless web for all citizens. Access, therefore, for all social, racial, or ethnic groups can be offered by campuses that have truly become models of service for their different constituencies.

This vision, which is already on the desks of planners nationwide, contrasts vividly with case-specific portraits of affirmative action issues for women in Hawaii. A focus on equity issues at the end of the K–12 pipeline is evocative of the need to increase partnerships—in order to create a more egalitarian approach. Cooper, Kane, and Gisselquist offer a more gender-specific explanation of how women negotiate between several cultures to value community and service, even though they are trapped within the institutional norms of tenure on budget-cutting research campuses. Their chapter highlights the need for state legislators and higher education executives to ensure that universities maintain their commitment to equity and diversity despite economic downturns and budget retrenchments. University policies cannot be dictated by budget shortfalls directed at newly created programs (in contrast to long-established ones), when such emerging structures are designed to include new groups.

Garibaldi, Dawson, and English turn their attention to the continuing and expanding role of HBCUs. Howard University administrators clearly articulate the salient role that HBCUs have provided in terms of access, retention, and graduation for African-Americans, and indeed, other groups within the society. From their inception in the late 1800s to the present, HBCUs have included Native Americans, international students, and European-Americans. In short, their mission, while focusing on African-Americans, has been inclusive, in contrast to the historical origins of the vast majority of European-American universities. The demographics of Howard University, the only Historically Black University that is a Research I university, portrays a student body where nearly 20 percent of the overall population is non-African-American.

While HBCUs have been inclusive, an emerging concern is to provide a comprehensive curriculum that addresses both current society needs and emerging trends. Noteworthy is the fact that the majority of HBCUs have always focused on service and outreach to the community and the nation to address and alleviate problems encountered by African-Americans and other minority groups (Garibaldi, 1984; Stent, 1984). In this regard, HBCUs have consistently been at the forefront in what the National Association of State Universities and Land-Grant Colleges (NASULGC) refer to as "engagement" (NASULGC, 1999).

To accomplish "engagement" in the contemporary era, curriculum covering international issues and critical policy analysis is increasingly a feature of HBCUs. Such engagement is one mode to maintain access and equity in the university environment and also in subsequent career opportunities. Particularly during the last decade, HBCUs have formed partnerships with European-American universities. In one sense, this provides an equitable basis of interaction between minority and majority students; simultaneously it enables faculty and professionals at the respective institutions to interact on cooperative projects in a fair and equal fashion. In these arrangements, the traditional mission of the HBCU continues to be addressed, while engaging in equal partnerships lessens negative stereotypes and provides opportunities for students to see professionals interacting in a fair manner (Hacker, 1992; Kanter, 1993).

In some ways, the two comparisons of Cooper and Garibaldi offer strong parallels to what sociologist Max Weber once called "the iron cage," referring to lifeless bureaucracy stifling creative human endeavor. And considerations of race, gender, and culture load the equation with even more challenges. Ironically, the strong fiscal pragmatism of Hawaii's institutions of higher education helps to dismantle women's academic advances, because the most severe cuts have occurred precisely in new areas of research such as women's studies. Concomitantly, HBCUs, which were once outgrowths of a racially segregated society, must forge new roles to expand their future in a world of conflicting policies.

Executive Initiatives and International Perspectives

The brave new world of the public research university is changing radically, even as these sentences appear in print. Understandably, many scholars of color react unfavorably to what they perceive as a white male power structure, and even more remark on the always puzzling collections of slights and interpersonal hurts that can derail any new scholar, let alone a first-generation PhD, either male or female, of color. It will remain to be seen whether Baby Boom II's college students will fully understand the complexity of racial and ethnic breakdowns on the nation's campuses, let alone penetrate the political factions and stereotypes that rob individuals of their unique human worth after long apprenticeships in a PhD graduate program. Clearly, in the decade following the year 2000, there is little understanding at any level in an academy marked by affirmative action litigation and much ill feeling. Still, there is also opportunity for exemplary leadership to help improve the situation—for the sake of higher education.

Perspectives and initiatives of university executives provide clarification and analysis of critical issues of equity. In their key roles as intellectual leaders, fiscal stewards, and community liaisons, these executives concentrate on equity issues not only within their respective universities, but also in their relationships with local, regional, state, national, and international audiences. An examination of these chapters reveals generic motifs that provide evidence of current and emerging trends—trends that embody new themes and paradigms with which to address equity, diversity, and affirmative action in higher education.

An initial area addressed in the several chapters is the demographic profile present within higher education and within their particular universities. The guiding premise of a comprehensive land-grant university is to provide higher education for state residents, which draws on the demographic pool of the state for undergraduates. In Pennsylvania, for example, minority populations are concentrated in the eastern part of the state in the Philadelphia metropolitan area. To the west, the Pittsburgh metropolitan area contains concentrations of minorities and identifiable European-American ethnic groups. The remainder of the state contains relatively few minority communities. Since the Pennsylvania State University has 24 campuses, including the flagship one centrally located at University Park, the question of minority enrollment arises in terms of minority presence at the flagship site versus other sites. Interestingly enough, the greater concentration of minority students is at the flagship campus, in contrast to the urban campuses where the entry standards are not as high. Perhaps this phenomenon is due, in part, to the presence of several other comprehensive state and private universities in the Philadelphia and Pittsburgh areas.

The demographic profiles of the several universities headed by women presidents differ considerably. At one northeastern university, there are recent immigrant and first-generation European-American, African-American, Puerto Rican, and Asian-American students. The demographic profile of Granite University (name fictitious) more closely mirrors that of its urban setting and that of the nation. In the area surrounding one northwestern university, there are large concentrations of original indigenous Americans, but their numbers are not mirrored in the university matriculants. And at Plains University (name fictitious), situated in the Midwest, the profile is overwhelmingly European-American.

Equity, in light of such demographic profiles, is analyzed via three key areas, namely access, retention, and successful completion of a program or graduation. Access, according to Spanier and Crowe, means that universities are to be inclusive while maintaining fairness and appropriate standards of admission. Equity encompasses policies to accommodate flexible criteria wherein admissions qualifications are examined via the requirements of a particular major, and in the case of athletes, guidelines from the National Collegiate Athletic Association (NCAA). For example, equity and access should ensure equal opportunities for various demographic groups to matriculate, while simultaneously considering students who need requisite basic skills to succeed in the university environment. These demographic groups are expanding to include the physically disabled, mentally challenged, and other groups often not historically included in traditional definitions of disadvantaged. However, once matriculation occurs, key support services and a welcoming institutional climate must be present to ensure retention and program completion.

An interesting thesis articulated by Spanier and Crowe addresses the concept of comparing the standards in a public university (designed to accommodate appropriate state, metropolitan, or local populations) and those of very select private institutions. Similarly, the flexible policies of private universities such as Duke were addressed previously in Ida Elizabeth Wilson's chapter. In essence, new frameworks for higher merit standards, as observed in select liberal arts colleges such as Ivy College (name fictitious), where women executives' initiatives were examined in Lindsay's chapter, portend different perspectives and policies for equity in admission standards. Hence minimum standards differ among institutions, thus meaning equity in one site is inequity at another. Fostering *positive* or *affirmative opportunities* (Wilson, 1999; Lindsay, 2000) is the policy challenge for university administration in diverse settings.

A second critical thesis is retention vis-à-vis the institutional climate. Key university executives at Penn State, Howard University, and the several women university presidents (represented in Part IV) maintain that an institutional climate is critical to student and faculty success. *Institutional climate should provide a welcoming and enriching environment for identifiable demographic groups and for older students, nontraditional students, gays, students with physical disabilities, and those with learning or emotional disabilities— groups that are often overlooked in the equity equation.* The institutional climate dictates that there be appropriate support services and modes for students and faculty to interact across demographic groups and various disciplines.

For minority and women students, faculty, and administrators, a critical issue is ensuring that diverse curricular and intellectual perspectives and leadership styles are handled in a legitimate fashion. Intellectual and academic endeavors are often polarized along racial and gender lines. Of critical importance is the constant articulation and dissemination of plans for equity and fairness by the president, provost, and deans. The challenge of recognizing diverse intellectual and curricular perspectives is sometimes manifested where there are sizable numbers of "minority" groups at a university; for example, at Granite University (name fictitious) there are large numbers of African-Americans, Hispanic, Jewish, and various European-American ethnic groups. A university situated in a large urban area is influenced by the politics within the urban milieu, which is translated into curricular and research matters. A challenge for the president of such a university is ensuring that the institutional climate is conducive to a fair and open exchange of perspectives. In this regard, the institutional climate promotes equity in quality experiences, to include minority and women faculty and administrators on critical decision-making, promotion, and strategic planning and budget committees. Otherwise, overt and subtle measures subvert equity.

Institutional climate, as articulated by several executives, is tempered by budget allocations from state legislatures or city councils. In the case of private universities, it is crucial to provide appropriate tuition, external sources, or both to make available substantive academic programs, support services, cocurricular activities, and the like. The salience of adequate financial resources to universities is extremely important in terms of equity. As witnessed in the discussion by the president of Granite University, the state and city government initiated policies and plans to decrease funding for developmental assistance to minority and other groups who needed assistance for academic success. Even at large comprehensive research universities, fiscal resources, as allocated by the state legislature (or by Congress, in the case of Howard University), are needed to ensure that quality programs are available to address diverse student needs. Such resources must also be sufficient to maintain the infrastructure, including laboratories, equipment, and space for teaching and research. Absent adequate fiscal resources, the institutional climate is not conducive to learning and scholarship.

Transnational lessons may assist in the examination of the domestic policies and programs regarding equity and civil societies. Maxine Thomas, a senior executive with the Kettering Foundation, surveys affirmative action-like policies and programs from a difficult international perspective, beginning with the U.S. experiment and then transiting to postapartheid South Africa, the Peoples' Republic of China, and Sweden, with a final analysis of equity as a civil society issue. She believes that civil society may ultimately offer a culture-based alternative to legislative actions such as affirmative action. Dialogue between different racial and ethnic groups will remain central to any resolution of conflict, regardless of whether the civil discussion takes place within U.S. boundaries or globally. She also argues that the enormous complexity of confronting social groups who have been excluded from the mainstream of a larger society remains extraordinarily complex—in short, there is no easy "quick-fix" in the United States or in any other country, whether it be South Africa, China, or Sweden.

Future Policy Implications

It is striking that several university executives articulated the relationship of higher education to both subsequent career opportunities for students and the socioeconomic and political welfare of the nation, with international implications as well. This realization is related to successful graduation by students and successful tenure and promotion for faculty and professionals. These outcomes contribute to success in the world of work for graduates and at respective universities for faculty and professionals. The viable sociopolitical and economic welfare of the state and the nation are ensured, in part, by the policies and programs taken by university leaders. In other words, there is a dynamic interactional relationship between the policies and programs of the university and those of the larger society. Whatever happens within the university in terms of programs for equity, for instance, diverse student and professional bodies and affirmative action programs become part of the equation in relationship to success in the greater society.

Students and faculty must be prepared for a diverse workplace within which to build individual careers. Preparing students for the workplace also means that executives are cognizant of new and emerging trends and how equity in the university setting affects emerging career options. A very prominent example of this is in the area of technology—what former Senator and presidential hopeful Bill Bradley refers to as the "digital divide" (2000) and what Robert Slavin discusses as the inequitable access to computers and other forms of technology by minority and disadvantaged students (1983). Precollegiate experience has ramifications for the university setting. If minorities and other disadvantaged have not been adequately prepared in precollege experience to use technology, it is unlikely that they may consider careers in emerging areas, which in turn means that there are still inequitable university curriculum options for disadvantaged groups.

On NPR's (National Public Radio) *Weekend Edition*, Margo Adler (Sunday, March 5, 2000) reported on the digital divide as highlighted in a Harvard University study. Research indicates that the digital divide is greatest between Blacks and whites in the income group making less than $30,000 a year. For upper-income Blacks and whites the digital divide is barely noticeable. Many lower income minorities also attend schools, where if they are connected to the Internet, there may be very few computers for use by students and faculty. There is also a difference among colleges; many Research I universities are now requiring freshman to enter with computers. In contrast, many smaller state and private universities have insufficient facilities, so computer laboratories are shared by hundreds of students, hence current and subsequent inequities abound.

Another future trend is the proliferation of distance education, supported strongly by one of the women presidents whose student population is dispersed over a large rural area. Offering courses and degrees is seen as a way to offer quality education to those with access to e-mail, web sites, or satellite. With technological advances many institutions are offering web-based courses, certificates, and degrees to students regardless of their locale. Simultaneously, a university and public policy challenge is ensuring that disadvantaged groups, despite locale, have access to appropriate technological transmissions. The use of new digital-television technologies between public television and universities can extend the outreach and extension mission of academe thereby reaching even broader groups (NASULGC *Newsline*, 2000). Certainly, the broader groups include those in international venues, as observed when the leaders of the G-8 governments formed the Digital Opportunities Task Force in July 2000 (Weiner, 2000). A chief concern of the Task Force is to address opportunities for developing nations so that various people throughout the world can participate equally in technological advances.

We emphasize that our public universities enjoy almost monopoly status, yet clearly, they are no longer bound by geography. Technology has already liberated campuses from the constraint of location. They have truly become global citizens, regardless of whether it is Harvard University, the University of Texas at Austin, or University of Southern California with interactive Web linkages with university partners in Africa, Asia, Australia, Europe, and South America. Stukel posits that the Internet followed two earlier revolutions: "The first was the land-grant movement of the nineteenth century, which gave the lower and middle classes access to college educations. Next came the community college development of the twentieth century, which gave us universal access to a higher education at the district level. The third, the technology revolution of the twenty-first century, will give us access beyond the bounds of time and place" (Stukel, 1998).

In an insightful piece, McGinn (1996, p. 357) declares "the great experiment . . . is to learn how to use all kind of education to build a society that honors all people and where all work together in the pursuit of the good of all." This "good of all" can encompass what Wilson (1999, 2000) and Lindsay (2000) refer to as *affirmative opportunities* for everyone to participate in all educational levels. Whether it be contemporary forms of technology or historical methods of inequity that curtail fairness and equity in education—especially colleges and universities, which prepare professional and leadership cadres—the overarching policy challenge is for the academy to devise and revise programs, and for university professionals to interact with public policy makers to ensure student, faculty, and administrative success.

Note

The authors gratefully acknowledge the assistance of Chuck Halloran, Maria Poindexter, and Janet Haner in writing this chapter.

References

Adler, Margo (2000, March 5). Report on the digital divide. National Public Radio *Weekend Edition.*

Atkinson, Richard C. (1999, Winter). The future arrives first in California. *Issues in Science and Technology.*

Bowen, William G., & Bok, Derek C. (1998). *The shape of the river: Long-term consequences of considering race in college and univertsity admissions.* Princeton, NJ: Princeton University Press.

Bradley, William (2000). Speech at the Harlem Democratic Debate, Apollo Theater, New York.

Commission on National Investment in Higher Education. (1996). Breaking the social contract: The fiscal crisis in higher education. Retrieved from the World Wide Web February 11, 2000: http://www.rand.org/publications/CAE/CAE100/#overview.

Dionne, Joseph L., & Kean, Thomas. (1996). Breaking the social contract— The fiscal crisis in higher education. Commission on National Investment in Higher Education, Council for Aid to Education. Retrieved February 11, 2000 from the World Wide Web: http://www.rand.org/publication/CAE/CAE100/#overview.

Duderstadt, James J. (1995, Fall). Diversity at the University of Michigan. Retrieved January 4, 2000 from the World Wide Web: http://milproj.ummu.edu/version2/papers//legacy/diversity/.

Duderstadt, James J. (1999, September 1). Back to the future: The changing social contract between the university and the nation. Retrieved January 5, 2000 from the World Wide Web: http://milproj.ummu.edu/version 2/papers/presentations/contract.

Duderstadt, James J. (1999, Winter). New roles for the twenty-first century university. *Issues in Science and Technology.*

Duderstadt, James J. (2000, January 5). Fire, ready, aim! University-decision making during an era of rapid change. Retrieved January 6, 2000 from the World Wide Web: http://milproj.ummu.edu/papers/presentations.

Etzkowitz, Henry. (1994, August 14). The triple helix: A North American innovation environment. Retrieved from the World Wide Web December 4, 1999: http://edie.cprost.sfu.ca/summer/papers/etzkowitz.draft1.html.

Finneran, Kevin. (1999, Winter). Wider education. *Issues in Science and Technology.*

Garibaldi, Antoine M. (Ed.). (1984). *Black colleges and universities: Challenges for the future.* New York: Praeger.

Hacker, Andrew. (1992). *Two nations: Black and white, separate, hostile, unequal.* New York: Charles Scribner's Sons.

Kanter, Rosabeth M. (1993). *Men and women in the corporation* (2nd ed.). New York: Basic Books.

Klor de Alva, Jorge. (1999, Winter). Remaking the academy in the age of information. *Issues in Science and Technology.*

Lindsay, Beverly. (2000, April). The people who could fly: A new millennium research agenda on Black education. A critique focusing on international policy and educational matters. Presented at the American Educational Research Association Annual Conference, New Orleans, LA.

McGinn, Noel F. (1996). Education, democratization, and globalization: A challenge for comparative education. *Comparative Education Review, 40*(4), 341–357.

National Association of State Universities and Land-Grant Colleges. (1999). *Returning to our roots: the engaged institution.* Washington, DC: National Association of State Universities and Land-Grant Colleges.

National Association of State Universities and Land-Grant Colleges. (2000). *Expanding the international scope of universities: A strategic vision statement for learning, scholarship and engagement in the new century.* Washington, DC: National Association of State Universities and Land Grant Colleges.

National Association of State Universities and Land-Grant Colleges. (2000, January) Volume 9, Number 1, A monthly update of news and analysis from the National Association of State Universities and Land-Grant Colleges (NASULGC).

Rosenzweig, Robert M. (1999, Winter). Universities change, core values should not. *Issues in Science and Technology.*

Schrag, Peter. (2000, March 6). Education and the election. *Nation Magazine.* Retrieved from the World Wide Web February 2000: http://www.thenation.com/issue/000306/0306schrag.sh.

Slavin, Robert (1983). *Cooperative learning.* New York: Longman.

Stent, Madelon D. (1984). Black college involvement in international and cross cultural affairs. In Antoine M. Garibaldi (Ed.) *Black colleges and universities: Challenges for the future* (pp. 93–115). New York: Praeger.

Stukel, James J. (1998, February 19). The future of land grant universities. Presented at the National Association of State Universities and Land-Grant Colleges Extension Directors Meeting. Retrieved from the World Wide Web January 26, 2000: http://www.adec.edu/clemson/papers/stukel.html.

Taylor, Orlando L. (2001, January). Inclusiveness in graduate education in the post-affirmative action environment: Challenges and opportunities. Speech given at the Pennsylvania State University.

University of California. (1997, October 21). Approaching the twenty-first century. Prepared for California Citizen's Commission on Higher Education. Retrieved from the World Wide Web January 15, 2000: http://www.ucop.edu/ucophome/pres/WhitePaper/21stwp/html.

University of Southern California. (1999, January 29). President Sample charts course for university. Retrieved from the World Wide Web February 11, 2000: http://www.usc.edu/hsc/info/pr/1vol5/503/sample.html.

Weiner, Eric. (2000, July 23). Report on the G-8 Summit. National Public Radio *Weekend Edition.*

Wilson, William Julius. (1999) *The bridge over the racial divide: Rising inequality and coalition politics.* University of California Press.

Wilson, William Julius. (2000, March 5) *Lead story* BET (Black Entertainment Television), Washington, D.C.

Biographical Statements

Beverly Lindsay

Beverly Lindsay is dean of the University Office of International Programs and professor of higher education and policy studies at the Pennsylvania State University, where she addresses academic, research, and public service international matters for the University System. She is the immediate former Dean of International Education and Policy Studies and Executive Director of Strategic Planning at Hampton University. Over 70 of Dr. Lindsay's articles, chapters, and essays appear in academic publications, as well as in her three books: *The Political Dimension in Teacher Education* (with Mark B. Ginsburg), *African Migration and National Development,* and *Comparative Perspectives of Third World Women.* She holds a PhD in administration and management from the American University (Washington, D.C.), and an EdD in comparative sociology of education and policy studies from the University of Massachusetts, Amherst.

Manuel J. Justiz

Manuel J. Justiz is dean of education and A. M. Aikin Regents Chair in Education Leadership at the University of Texas at Austin. He oversees the administration and coordination of education programs and support units; provides leadership in program development and evaluation; and represents the college in the local, state, and national educational communities. He has held numerous positions in higher education and government. Recent journal publications include "Collaborating for Success: Case History of a School-College Partnership," in the *Educational Record*; and "Factions, Human Diversity, and Education," in the *Community College Journal*. He edited *Minorities in Higher Education* in 1994 with Reginald Wilson and Lars G. Bjork. Dr. Justiz wrote two chapters for the book, *Minorities in Higher Education*, "Demographic Trends and the Challenges to American Higher Education;" and "Assessment in Higher Education and the Preparation of Minority Teachers" (with Marilyn C. Kameen).

Joanne E. Cooper

Joanne E. Cooper, PhD, is an associate professor in the Department of Educational Administration and coordinator of the Higher Education Program at the University of Hawaii at Manoa. Dr. Cooper's research focuses on the study of women and minorities in education, the study of organizational and curricular change and the study of narrative, as both phenomenon and method. She has published numerous articles in *The Review of Higher Education*; *The International Journal of Intercultural Relations, Initiatives, Qualitative Inquiry*; and *The International Journal of Qualitative Research in Education.* Her latest books include, *Let My Spirit Soar: Narratives of Diverse Women in School Leadership*; *Indigenous Educational Models for Contemporary Practice: In Our Mother's Voice* (with Maenette Benham); and *Tenure in the Sacred Grove: Issues and Strategies for Women and Minority Faculty* (with Dannelle Stevens, in press).

Mary Beth Crowe

Mary Beth Crowe is director of special projects in the Office of the President at Penn State where she writes on many issues of relevance to higher education and works with the University Board of Trustees. She received her PhD in educational psychology from Northwestern University.

Horace G. Dawson Jr.

Horace G. Dawson, Jr., is director of the Patricia Roberts Harris Public Affairs Program and the Ralph J. Bunche International Affairs Center at Howard University. A retired diplomat in the U.S. Foreign Service, his last overseas posting was Ambassador to Botswana, following service in Uganda, Nigeria, Liberia, the Philippines, and Washington, D.C., where, among other domestic assignments, he was cultural adviser (worldwide) in the U.S. Information Agency (USIA) and director (Africa) of USIA. Ambassador Dawson has published extensively in the fields of communications and foreign affairs, including a chapter, "Race as a Factor in Cultural Exchange: A Practitioner's View," in *Exporting America: Essays on American Studies Abroad*, Richard P. Horwitz, editor. Dawson earned his bachelor's degree at Lincoln University (Pennsylvania), master's at Columbia University, and PhD at the University of Iowa.

Richard A. English

Richard A. English is dean and professor at the Howard University School of Social Work. His career of teaching, research and service in higher education spans more than 30 years. He has held faculty and administrative positions at the University of Michigan, and was the Robert L. Sutherland Chair in Mental Health and Social Policy at the University of Texas at Austin, Visiting Scholar at the Paul Baerwald School of Social Work at Hebrew University in Jerusalem, Israel, and the Whitney Young, Jr., Scholar at Western Michigan University. Dr. English's numerous publications and research have covered a wide range of subjects, including human service organizations, African-American families, refugees and immigrants, the homeless, child welfare, social welfare policy and reform. He recently completed a research study (with Fariyal Ross Sheriff) on homeless families, and a monograph (with Michael Austin and Fred Ahearn), *The Professional School Dean: Meeting the Leadership Challenges*, published by Jossey-Bass. Dr. English has a PhD degree in social work and sociology, master of social work and master of arts (in history) from the University of Michigan, and an AB degree (with honors) from Talladega College. He is a past president of the Council on Social Work Education, the national accreditation body for social-work degree programs in the United States.

Antoine M. Garibaldi

Antoine Garibaldi is senior fellow at the Educational Testing Service in the Office of the Corporate Secretary, where his work focuses on higher education issues. Between 1996 and 2000, he was the first provost and chief academic officer at Howard University in Washington, D.C., where he was also a tenured professor in the School of Education's Department of Human Development and Psychoeducational Studies. He has had more than 25 years of teaching and administrative experience in higher education, the federal government, and elementary and secondary education. He is chair-elect of the American Association for Higher Education's board of directors, and will serve as chair in 2001–2002. From 1982 to 1996, he was professor of education at Xavier University of Louisiana and also served as vice president for academic affairs, dean of Arts and Sciences, and chairman of the Education Department. Garibaldi is a fellow of the American Psychological Association, and author of 10 books and monographs, and more than 70 research articles and chapters in scholarly journals and books. Some of his books are: *Black Colleges and Universities: Challenges for the Future* (1984); *Educating Black*

Male Youth: A Moral and Civic Imperative (1988); *The Education of African-Americans* (coedited with Charles V. Willie and Wornie L. Reed, 1991); *Teacher Recruitment and Retention* (1989); and *The Revitalization of Teacher Education Programs at Historically Black Colleges* (1989).

He received his undergraduate degree magna cum laude from Howard University in 1973 and his PhD in educational psychology from the University of Minnesota in 1976.

Marilyn C. Kameen

Besides serving as associate dean of Academic Affairs and Research, Dr. Marilyn C. Kameen also holds the title of associate professor in the Department of Educational Administration. From 1992 to 1998, she was associate dean for Teacher Education and Student Affairs. During the academic year 1997–1998, Dr. Kameen was acting associate chair of the Department of Curriculum and Instruction.

From 1974 to 1990, Dr. Kameen was at the University of South Carolina where she served as director of the Office of Accreditation, director of Field Experiences and coordinator of the Higher Education Administration Program in the Department of Educational Leadership and Policies. She has published on topics relating to college student development, minorities in education, effective college teaching, and comprehensive assessment programs in higher education.

Kathleen O. Kane

Kathleen O. Kane, PhD, is a faculty specialist at the Center for Teaching Excellence and an Affiliate Faculty in the Women's Studies Program and Lecturer in the Department of Political Science at the University of Hawaii at Manoa, where she teaches courses on theory and pedagogy, film, media, and politics. Her professional and research interests in pedagogy and culture bridges the work she does in political science, women's studies and faculty development. She is coeditor of *Women in Hawai'i: Sites, Identities, Voices*, a special edition of *Social Process in Hawai'i*, and most recently contributed an article to *Teaching Introduction to Women's Studies: Expectations and Strategies* (Bergin & Garvey).

Samuel L. Myers Jr.

Samuel L. Myers, Jr., is the Roy Wilkins Professor of Human Relations and Social Justice at the Hubert H. Humphrey Institute of Public Affairs,

University of Minnesota, where he conducts research on racial economic inequality. He received his undergraduate training in economics at Morgan State University and his doctorate in economics at MIT. Recent publications include: *Faculty of Color in Academe: Bittersweet Success* (with Caroline S. Turner) 1999; "Exploring Underrepresentation: The Case of Faculty of Color in the Midwest" (with Caroline S. Turner and John W. Creswell), *The Journal of Higher Education*, January/February 1999; " 'If It Shall Seem Just and Proper:' The Effect of Race and Morals on Alimony and Child Support Appeals in the District of Columbia, 1950–1980" (with Sheila D. Ards and William A. Darity), *Journal of Family History*, October 1998; "Racial Earnings Disparities and Family Structure" (with William A. Darity, Jr., and Chanjin Chung), *Southern Economic Journal*, July 1998; and "The Effects of Sample Selection on Racial Differences in Child Abuse Reporting" (with Sheila Ards and Chanjin Chung), *Child Abuse and Neglect: The International Journal*, February 1998.

Graham B. Spanier

Graham B. Spanier is President of the Pennsylvania State University and Professor of Human Development and Family Studies, Sociology, Demography, and Family and Community Medicine. He has been the guiding force behind several academic initiatives at Penn State, including the creation of The Schreyer Honors College, the Penn State World Campus, and the School of Information Sciences and Technology. He oversaw the merger with the Dickinson School of Law, and promoted a new general education curriculum, including increased internationalization of the University. A distinguished researcher and scholar, he has more than 100 scholarly publications, including 10 books. He has served as chair of the NCAA Division I Board of Directors and the Kellogg Commission on the Future of State and Land-Grant Universities, and is chair-elect of the National Association of State Universities and Land-Grant Colleges. He earned his PhD in sociology from Northwestern University, where he was a Woodrow Wilson Fellow, and his bachelor's and master's degrees from Iowa State University.

James Stewart

James Stewart is a professor of labor studies and industrial relations and African and African American studies at the Pennsylvania State University. He previously served as vice provost for educational equity. In that capacity he was responsible for formulating the university's diversity strategic plan and overall coordination of diversity initiatives. In addition to being the author, coauthor, editor, or coeditor of six monographs, Dr. Stewart has published over 50 articles in economics and Black studies professional journals, and over 20 chapters in edited volumes. He is currently president of the National Council for Black Studies. He holds a PhD in economics from the University of Notre Dame.

Maxine Thomas

Maxine Thomas is secretary and general counsel for the Kettering Foundation and, with the president and two vice-presidents, serves on the operations group, which runs the affairs of the foundation. As a program officer, Thomas directs a number of Kettering projects in the areas of higher education, community leadership, and the relationship between citizens and officeholders. She has been a member of the Kettering Foundation task force on China since 1993.

Before coming to the Kettering Foundation, Thomas was associate dean of the University of Georgia School of Law where she had also served as associate and assistant professor. She was previously on the faculty of the University of Oregon School of Law. From 1973 to 1976, Thomas was assistant attorney general for the State of Washington.

Thomas is a member of the Ohio State Bar Association, the Ohio Women's Bar Association, and the American Bar Association. She was a Fulbright lecturer at Tohoku University in Sendai, Japan (1988–1989) and has served on the Fulbright Association Board since 1991. Thomas was made a Kellogg Foundation National Fellow in 1985. She received her BA degree in English from the University of Washington, and her JD degree from the University of Washington School of Law.

Caroline S. Turner

Caroline S. Turner is professor in the Division of Educational Leadership and Policy Studies at Arizona State University, Main Campus. Access and equity in higher education are her major research interests. Recently, she served as research coordinator, Faculty Development Programs, Office of the Associate Vice President for Multicultural and Academic Affairs at the University of Minnesota. In this capacity, Professor Turner provided research and scholarly support for an initiative related to the recruitment, retention, and development of faculty of color. Her most recent publication is a book (with S. L. Myers, Jr.), entitled *Faculty of Color in Academe: Bittersweet Success*. She holds a PhD in administration and policy analysis from Stanford University.

Ida Elizabeth (Beth) Wilson

Until recently, Beth Wilson was associate provost at Columbia University in New York City. She is an internationally known administrator, professor, attorney, consultant, and civic activist in the areas of affirmative action, diversity, and sexual harassment. As an administrator Dr. Wilson has more than 20 years experience in developing and implementing affirmative action plans and programs. She has held leadership positions in professional organizations that promote affirmative action at the city, state and national levels. Currently, she is president of the American Association for Affirmative Action, and just completed tenure on the Board of the National Bar Association. Dr. Wilson was a panelist with Ward Connerly on a television show devoted to affirmative action. She has appeared on *The Cutting Edge* and many other television and radio programs to discuss affirmative action and diversity, and is a strong and able proponent for both. She was also a panelist on the sexual harassment teleconference sponsored by Black Issues in Higher Education that included Professor Anita Hill, and Michael Grieve of the Center for Individual Rights. Since 1987, Beth Wilson has been adjunct associate professor of human relations at the University of Oklahoma.

Reginald Wilson

Dr. Reginald Wilson is the Senior Scholar Emeritus of the American Council on Education. He was appointed senior scholar in October 1988. Prior to joining the Council, Dr. Wilson was president of Wayne County Community College in Detroit for 10 years. Other positions he has held include dean, director of test development and research, director of Black studies, and director of Upward Bound. Dr. Wilson has authored numerous books, articles, and research studies. He is a coauthor of the American Council on Education's *Annual Status Report on Minorities in Higher Education,* which he began in 1982. He is an editor of *Minorities in Higher Education and Race and Equity in Higher Education,* an author of *Civil Liberties and the U.S.,* and a coauthor of *Human Development in the Urban Community.* Dr. Wilson is on the editorial board of the *American Journal of Education, The Urban Review,* and *About Campus.* Dr. Wilson received his PhD in clinical and educational psychology from Wayne State University and is a licensed psychologist in Michigan and Washington, DC. He received the Harold Delaney Exemplary Leadership Award from the American Association of Higher Education.

Author Index

Subject Index

SUNY series, Frontiers in Education
Philip G. Altbach, Editor

317

Critical Perspectives on Early Childhood Education—Lois Weis, Philip G. Altbach, Gail P. Kelly, and Hugh G. Petrie (eds.)

Textbooks in American Society: Politics, Policy, and Pedagogy—Philip G. Altbach, Gail P. Kelly, Hugh G. Petrie, and Lois Weis (eds.)

Black Resistance in High School: Forging a Separatist Culture—R. Patrick Solomon

Emergent Issues in Education: Comparative Perspectives—Robert F. Arnove, Philip G. Altbach, and Gail P. Kelly (eds.)

Creating Community on College Campuses—Irving J. Spitzberg, Jr. and Virginia V. Thorndike

Teacher Education Policy: Narratives, Stories, and Cases—Hendrik D. Gideonse (ed.)

Beyond Silenced Voices: Class, Race, and Gender in United States Schools—Lois Weis and Michelle Fine (eds.)

The Cold War and Academic Governance: The Lattimore Case at Johns Hopkins—Lionel S. Lewis

Troubled Times for American Higher Education: The 1990s and Beyond—Clark Kerr

Higher Education Cannot Escape History: Issues for the Twenty-first Century—Clark Kerr

Multiculturalism and Education: Diversity and Its Impact on Schools and Society—Thomas J. LaBelle and Christopher R. Ward

The Contradictory College: The Conflicting Origins, Impacts, and Futures of the Community College—Kevin J. Dougherty

Race and Educational Reform in the American Metropolis: A Study of School Decentralization—Dan A. Lewis and Kathryn Nakagawa

Professionalization, Partnership, and Power: Building Professional Development Schools—Hugh G. Petrie (ed.)

Ethnic Studies and Multiculturalism—Thomas J. LaBelle and Christopher R. Ward

Promotion and Tenure: Community and Socialization in Academe—William G. Tierney and Estela Mara Bensimon

Sailing Against the Wind: African Americans and Women in U.S. Education—Kofi Lomotey (ed.)

The Challenge of Eastern Asian Education: Implications for America—William K. Cummings and Philip G. Altbach (eds.)

Conversations with Educational Leaders: Contemporary Viewpoints on Education in America—Anne Turnbaugh Lockwood

Managed Professionals: Unionized Faculty and Restructuring Academic Labor—Gary Rhoades

The Curriculum (Second Edition): Problems, Politics, and Possibilities—Landon E. Beyer and Michael W. Apple (eds.)

Education/Technology/Power: Educational Computing as a Social Practice—Hank Bromley and Michael W. Apple (eds.)

Capitalizing Knowledge: New Intersections of Industry and Academia—Henry Etzkowitz, Andrew Webster, and Peter Healey (eds.)

The Academic Kitchen: A Social History of Gender Stratification at the University of California, Berkeley—Maresi Nerad

Grass Roots and Glass Ceilings: African American Administrators in Predominantly White Colleges and Universities—William B. Harvey (ed.)

Community Colleges as Cultural Texts: Qualitative Explorations of Organizational and Student Culture—Kathleen M. Shaw, James R. Valadez, and Robert A. Rhoads (eds.)

Educational Knowledge: Changing Relationships between the State, Civil Society, and the Educational Community—Thomas S. Popkewitz (ed.)

Transnational Competence: Rethinking the U.S.-Japan Educational Relationship—John N. Hawkins and William K. Cummings (eds.)

Women Administrators in Higher Education: Historical and Contemporary Perspectives—Jana Nidiffer and Carolyn Terry Bashaw (eds.)

Faculty Work in Schools of Education: Rethinking Roles and Rewards for the Twenty-first Century—William G. Tierney (ed.)